THE CHURCH MILITANT

THE CHURCH MILITANT

Spiritual Warfare in the Anglican Charismatic Renewal

Graham R. Smith

FOREWORD BY
Mark J. Cartledge

◆PICKWICK *Publications* • Eugene, Oregon

THE CHURCH MILITANT
Spiritual Warfare in the Anglican Charismatic Renewal

Copyright © 2016 Graham R. Smith. All rights reserved. Except for brief quotations in critical publications or reviews, no part of this book may be reproduced in any manner without prior written permission from the publisher. Write: Permissions, Wipf and Stock Publishers, 199 W. 8th Ave., Suite 3, Eugene, OR 97401.

Pickwick Publications
An Imprint of Wipf and Stock Publishers
199 W. 8th Ave., Suite 3
Eugene, OR 97401

www.wipfandstock.com

PAPERBACK ISBN: 978-1-4982-2943-2
HARDCOVER ISBN: 978-1-4982-2945-6
EBOOK ISBN: 978-1-4982-2944-9

Cataloguing-in-Publication data:

Names: Smith, Graham R. | foreword by Cartledge, Mark J.

Title: The church militant : spiritual warfare in the Anglican charismatic renewal / Graham R. Smith.

Description: Eugene, OR: Pickwick Publications, 2016 | Includes bibliographical references.

Identifiers: ISBN 978-1-4982-2943-2 (paperback) | ISBN 978-1-4982-2945-6 (hardcover) | ISBN 978-1-4982-2944-9 (ebook)

Subjects: LSCH: Spiritual warfare | Pentecostalism—Church of England | Church renewal—Church of England |

Classification: BX5125.5 S64 2016 (print) | BX5125.5 (ebook)

Manufactured in the U.S.A.   10/19/16

Unless otherwise indicated, Scripture quotations are from the Holy Bible, New International Version® Anglicized, NIV® Copyright © 1979, 1984, 2011 by Biblica, Inc.® Used by permission. All rights reserved worldwide.

Contents

Foreword by Mark J. Cartledge | vii
Acknowledgments | xi

1. Introduction | 1
2. Anglican Charismatic Spiritual Warfare in Historical Perspective | 24
3. The Origins and Development of Charismatic Spiritual Warfare: A Study of Some Anglican Pioneers | 49
4. Spiritual Warfare in the Charismatic Anglican Context: A Case Study | 81
5. Nigel Wright: The Ontology of Evil | 124
6. Amos Yong: A Triadic Metaphysics of the Demonic | 146
7. Gregory Boyd: A Spiritual Warfare Worldview | 165
8. Constructing a Charismatic Theology of Spiritual Warfare | 183
9. Conclusion and Recommendations for Praxis | 240

Appendix 1: Interview Questions for Pioneer Leaders | 247
Appendix 2: Analysis of Pioneers' Warfare Theology and Praxis | 251
Appendix 3: Case Study Protocol | 254
Appendix 4: Case Study Category Analysis | 258

Bibliography | 265

Foreword

Mark J. Cartledge[1]
Regent University School of Divinity

It is a very great honor to be invited by one of my successful doctoral students to write either an endorsement or a foreword to their published thesis and this invitation is no different. During my time working with Dr. Smith at the University of Birmingham, UK, I got to know him personally, as well as his family, and it was a pleasure to do so. I understand how a project such as this one sits at the interface of a personal faith journey, public ministry, and academic interests. For many of us working in the field of theology, it is not merely an objective academic pursuit, as if that were actually possible, but genuinely *fides quaerens intellectum* ("faith seeking understanding"). Dr. Smith, as a Church of England priest in the charismatic tradition, has explored an aspect of his own tradition, as well as placing it within broader theological and philosophical discourse, while adopting a practical-theological framework. The subject of spiritual warfare is an important one, yet it has received very little academic treatment. With the publication of this book we have a significant contribution that will serve church leaders, students, and scholars. As such, it serves multiple and diverse audiences.

The research addresses those interested in understanding the history of the Charismatic Renewal Movement in the United Kingdom. Without doubt, this movement, which emerged in the early 1960s, has had an incredible influence on the Church of England and the wider Anglican Communion around the world. Of course, it is related to the diverse Pentecostal movement associated with the twentieth century and its leaders have interacted with and drawn from the much broader movement, which is now a global phenomenon that is having huge impact on the worldwide church.

---

1. Mark J. Cartledge, PhD, FRSA, is Professor of Practical Theology at Regent University Divinity School and Director of the Center for Renewal Studies at Regent University.

The discussion of figures such as Michael Harper, David Watson, and Michael Green on the hot topic of spiritual warfare offers insight and wisdom from important figures in the history of the Charismatic Renewal Movement in the Church of England.

This study provides much needed empirical work. Very often contemporary theology discusses what people think, say, and do, without actually paying actual attention to what people actually think, say, and do. Not so with this particular study, which is placed within a practical-theological research framework that includes an empirical case study. Empirical research is vital to the church's ministry and the church increasingly needs to listen to ordinary voices from among its members in order to understand their beliefs, attitudes and practices on the ground. This study, therefore, also contributes to advancement of empirically orientated practical theology and it is the first study that I am aware has attempted a sustained, rigorous approach to the subject of spiritual warfare.[2]

This work is deeply theological and philosophical in a way that transcends boundaries of specific theological traditions, be they Anglican, Pentecostal, or Charismatic. Dr. Smith has not been afraid of jumping in at the deep end of the discussions concerning evil and the demonic. By engaging with three very different writers such as Nigel Wright, Amos Yong, and Gregory Boyd he has brought into dialogue not just three writers, but the broader Christian tradition, in addition to addressing philosophical concerns. It is rare that a practical-theological project has engaged as deeply and as seriously with such issues, but Dr. Smith has done it with skill and rigor.

This project addresses constructive Pentecostal and Charismatic theology, or what we might call Renewal theological scholarship. This type of theology takes seriously the contributions that are emerging from the most recent Pentecostal and Charismatic theology and seeks to evaluate them critically in the light of both Scripture and Christian tradition. Dr. Smith engages in an original reading of the key biblical texts in order to appreciate for himself what might be said concerning the topic of spiritual warfare. His understanding is brought into conversation with Renewal scholarship and, I believe, he has made an original contribution to knowledge in this field. He has done so from the perspective of a realist ontology with regard to the nature of evil. Academically, this is now a minority position, but it is one that deserves careful attention and respect because of its place within the history of Christianity.

2. My own study of John Wimber's theology and practice of deliverance using a practical-theological approach did not engage with empirical research but was based on literature. See: Cartledge, "Demonology and Deliverance."

While we might characterize theology as *fides quaerens intellectum*, it should never be understood as a solitary exercise, "my faith seeking my understanding," but rather "our faith seeking a shared understanding." At times it surely does feel solitary, but when one's work is shared and discussed then it becomes a corporate endeavor that benefits far more people. It was during Dr. Smith's work that two other doctoral students joined him in the pursuit of knowledge in this field and I was delighted to work with them at the same time. They were Dr. Stephen Torr and Dr. Janet Warren. We had a number of discussions together and it was extremely useful for a mini-research cluster to develop, in addition to being part of the regular research seminar in the Centre for Pentecostal and Charismatic Studies at the University of Birmingham, UK. Of course, they did not agree with each other, which made life both fun and interesting as a supervisor! Dr. Warren and Dr. Torr have both now published their PhD theses,[3] and, with the publication of Dr. Smith's research in this book, it feels as though the work of this mini-research cluster has now been made complete.

Finally, in true practical-theological fashion, Dr. Smith returns at the end his study to praxis, that is, the theological value-laden practices of the contemporary church. Throughout his research Dr. Smith maintained a passion for the work and ministry of the church in contemporary society. May his book inspire and challenge the thinking of church leaders, students and scholars, as well as ordinary church members around the world for the sake of God's glory and the extension of his kingdom.

---

3. Stephen C. Torr, *A Dramatic Pentecostal/Charismatic Anti-Theodicy*; and E. Janet Warren, *Cleansing the Cosmos*.

Acknowledgments

FIRST OF ALL, I wish to thank my family, my wife Kiew for her care and support over the long journey of completing this project, and my daughters Lydia and Zoe who have also had to be very patient at times when Dad seemed to be far too unavailable.

Thanks too to my clergy colleagues in Bushbury parish, Philip Dobson and Ian Poole, for generously supporting me in taking the time amidst church duties to complete this several years, and to Ian for his stimulating theological discussions on this and other topics. Thanks also to the members of the Church of the Good Shepherd in Low Hill for their gracious forbearance, especially in the closing stages of writing.

Thanks are also due to diocesan leaders in Birmingham and Lichfield for their personal, financial, and moral support; firstly to the then Bishop of Birmingham, John Sentamu, for enabling me to begin this project whilst in training for ordination at Queen's College and through curacy in Yardley in Birmingham, and then Bob Jackson whilst he was Archdeacon of Walsall, together with Bishops Jonathan Gledhill and Clive Gregory, for enabling me to complete it whilst in parish ministry in Wolverhampton.

Special thanks are due to Professor Allan Anderson, my first supervisor, for his support and encouragement, especially in the early stages, and to Mark Cartledge, for his perceptive supervision and many constructive suggestions that has helped to draw out the best of my abilities in shaping this thesis, as well as his friendship and support. Thanks also to fellow students at the Birmingham Research Seminar over the years for their stimulating discussions and presentations, including specific help given by Andy Lord, Connie Au, Janet Warren, and Stephen Torr.

A number of people also helped specifically along the journey with access to their private libraries or lending books—notably Gordon Mursell, but also Richard Massey, Hugh Scriven, Bob Dunnett, and Brian Miller. Paula Gooder has been a great inspiration in relation to biblical studies, and George Kovoor was the first person to clearly challenge me to think of doing a PhD. Thanks to Wendy Bright who generously gave much of her time in typing up the interview transcripts, to Amos Yong for his input and correspondence in relation to chapter 6, and finally to Dan Yarnell for kindly proof reading the near final draft, and for his helpful and constructive suggestions. And finally, thank you to the leaders and members of "St. George's" church for their kind hospitality during my research visits.

1

Introduction

1.1 The spread of Pentecostal and charismatic Christianity

THE UNPARALLELED GROWTH AND spread of Pentecostalism has been described as "the most dramatic development of Christianity in the [twentieth] century";[1] not just in terms of the Pentecostal churches that arose from the Azusa Street revival of 1906 (as well as other independent but parallel origins in other countries[2]), but also charismatic movements such as the one which widely penetrated the traditional historical churches from the 1960s, both Protestant and Catholic, in what has been termed the charismatic renewal. The total number of Pentecostals and charismatics worldwide numbers at least a quarter of a billion.[3] There is thus now a highly significant proportion of Christians and churches that can be termed "charismatic," i.e., those that have an emphasis on a dynamic experience of the Holy Spirit[4] and the operation of gifts of the Holy Spirit.[5]

A number of observers have attempted to account for this rapid growth of Pentecostalism worldwide.[6] From a sociological perspective, the

---

1. Martin, *Pentecostalism: The World Their Parish*, 1.

2. See Anderson, *Origin & Development of Global Pentecostalism*, 170–71; Pomerville, *The Third Force in Mission*, 52.

3. Martin, *Pentecostalism: The World Their Parish*, 1. Including newer independent charismatic, and local indigenous churches would bring it nearer to half a billion. See Anderson, *Origin & Development of Global Pentecostalism*, 1.

4. Different terms are used for the initial experience. Being "filled with the Spirit" is more prevalent in charismatic renewal, playing down the potentially divisive emphasis of "baptism in the Spirit," and enabling openness to a number of significant "infillings"—see Steven, *Worship in the Spirit*.

5. Especially the gifts mentioned in 1 Cor 12–14, often with an emphasis on tongues (cf. Acts 2:1–4).

6. I consistently use "charismatic" as a descriptive term as defined above (regularly with "renewal" or "Anglicans"), and "Pentecostal" to more clearly link with classical or denominational Pentecostal churches. I use "Pentecostalism" as an all-embracing

initial tendency was to emphasize external social factors to account for this growth, with its origins predominantly among the Black American and working-class population in America, and its phenomenal growth amongst the poorer sections of Latin American society.[7] More recently, the ability of Pentecostalism to leap across class and cultural divisions has led sociologists to emphasize its exploitation of the globalization of a market culture.[8] Some sociologists have described this global spread in terms of a confident expansion into an "unbounded" global space.[9]

Anderson, however, points out that it is reductionist to consider only such external factors; to fully account for the process it is also necessary to consider internal religious and cultural factors;[10] and sociologists Martin and Droogers recognize this too.[11] Droogers identifies three broad features of Pentecostal ideology that makes Pentecostals feel part of a global community, and one of these is a dualistic worldview that distinguishes between the "world" and the "church," the "devil" and the "divine," and between "sickness" and "health."[12] He points out that the simple war schema between God and Satan, and the combination of healing and/or exorcism that potentially offer a solution to almost any problem that may occur, are two of the few simple, "hard-selling" schemas that make up the basic repertoire that forms the Pentecostal identity. He also recognizes that the dimensions of "global space" that Pentecostals seek to conquer includes a sense of "spiritual space," where Pentecostals can combat the terror of the demons, through the Holy Spirit seeming to reduce their territory, using spiritual weapons such as prayer and healing.[13]

---

term, including the charismatic movement and newer Pentecostal or "neocharismatic" churches. Anderson, *Origin & Development of Global Pentecostalism*, 1.

7. For example, Lalive d"Epinay, *Haven to the Masses: A Study of the Pentecostal Movement in Chile.*

8. "Pentecostalism takes advantage of that global culture and exports itself around the globe for mass consumption." Dempster, *The Globalisation of Pentecostalism.*

9. André Droogers (Lecture, Birmingham University, Oct 2003); and Coleman comments: "Pentecostal Christians create a global culture with a sense of reaching out into an unbounded realm of action and identity." Coleman, *The Globalisation of Charismatic Christianity*, 6, 66–69.

10. Anderson, *Origin & Development of Global Pentecostalism*, 238–39.

11. Martin recognizes the importance of understanding their repertoire of religious images in order to understand their story. Martin, *Pentecostalism: The World Their Parish*, 168.

12. Droogers, "Globalisation and Pentecostal Success," 44–6.

13. Lecture, Birmingham University, Oct 2003. See also Droogers and Versteeg, "A Schema Repertoire Approach to Exorcism: Two Case Studies of Spiritual Warfare," 105–24.

Spiritual warfare has also begun to figure in theological analyses of the spread of Pentecostalism. Anderson observes that "the main attraction of Pentecostalism in the Majority World is still the emphasis on healing and deliverance from evil"; others have identified deliverance from evil spirits as one of the main factors in Pentecostal growth.[14] This emphasis globally on spiritual warfare may have increased alongside evangelistic initiatives around the millennium.[15] In this way the concept of "spiritual warfare," which often encompasses healing and deliverance ministry on the individual level with more large-scale strategies for mission,[16] has become a key element in the theology and spirituality of the Pentecostal and charismatic worldview. As such it is the main focus of this thesis, as manifested primarily in the Anglican charismatic renewal.[17] Focusing here specifically on the Church of England illuminates how the charismatic approach to spiritual warfare (or the spiritual battle, a term used similarly by many Anglicans) operates contextually in a particular Christian tradition. As a practical theological study, it also engages with wider theological discussions in pneumatology, particularly concerning the ontology of evil, and offers a model for the renewal of praxis in the charismatic Anglican context.

1.2 Theological study of charismatic spiritual warfare

The increased attention on prayer and spiritual warfare in Pentecostal and charismatic churches worldwide has only recently been strongly reflected in more serious theological study. Pentecostalism, formerly reliant on oral theology and suspicious of academic theology, it has begun to produce its

---

14. Allan Anderson, *An Introduction to Pentecostalism*, 234. Pomerville lists "encounters with demonic spirits" among 5 factors that church growth specialists have identified—Pomerville, *The Third Force in Mission*, 100. Donald McGavran's five causes include Pentecostal acceptance that "most men and women today believe that demons/evil spirits exist and can threaten them—and offer a solution, as well as healing, through the name of Jesus"; and Peter Wagner includes the "power" ministries of healing and deliverance from evil spirits in his four factors—see McClung, *Azusa Street and Beyond*, 122, 29.

15. Peter Hocken lists "Prayer Movements and Spiritual Warfare" as one of the ten major global trends in the worldwide Charismatic Movement. Burgess, *New International Pentecostal Dictionary*, 500–505.

16. Ibid., 502. Peter Wagner has popularized "spiritual mapping" and other methods of "prayer warfare"; although not highly significant in the contexts studied for this thesis. See Wagner, *Warfare Prayer*.

17. This has not only influenced churches in Britain, the main focus of this study, but also in areas where the worldwide Anglican church has grown rapidly, e.g., Africa (particularly Nigeria) and South East Asia.

own Pentecostal academics,[18] such as Cecil Robeck and Amos Yong.[19] In addition, the growth of charismatics since the 1960s within traditional denominations, with their long history of academic enquiry, has contributed to a growing body of serious study engaging with charismatic phenomena and their theology and spirituality.

There have been a few attempts at providing an overview of Pentecostal or charismatic theology, but until recently coverage of the spiritual warfare dimension in these was brief.[20] For example, in his classic study of Pentecostal history and theology, Hollenweger only has a brief chapter on demonology;[21] and Land's theological study of Pentecostalism spirituality, whilst recognizing the final victory over death and Satan as a key element in the concept of the coming of the kingdom in the Pentecostal apocalyptic vision, has little discussion of the spirituality of spiritual warfare.[22] However, Warrington's study of Pentecostal theology began to correct this imbalance, with a significant section on exorcism and spiritual warfare.[23]

Serious study of specific elements of Pentecostal and charismatic theology and spirituality has mainly concentrated on issues such as baptism in the Spirit,[24] speaking in tongues,[25] or the nature of charismatic worship and ritual.[26] Studies at academic level focusing on issues relating to spiritual warfare have until recently been relatively few. Thomas has written a careful biblical study of the Pentecostal approach to healing and deliverance generally, including the role of the Devil and the demonic in sickness and healing;[27] and there are a number of more popular but serious treatments, such as the influential work of the Catholic charismatic Francis MacNutt on healing and deliverance,[28] or the accumulated wisdom of a number of

---

18. Hollenweger, *Pentecostalism: Origins and Developments Worldwide*, 196–97.

19. Yong's many publications relating to his metaphysics of evil will be referenced in chapter 6—e.g., Yong, *Discerning the Spirits*.

20. For a rare early example, see chapter 9 "Demonology and Exorcism" in Mather, "Theology of the Charismatic Movement," 265–98.

21. Hollenweger, *The Pentecostals*.

22. Only brief comments, such as "Spirit baptism equipped the believer to do spiritual battle in tearing down strongholds of the enemy and reaching the lost." Land, *Pentecostal Spirituality*, 70–71, 91.

23. Warrington, *Pentecostal Theology: A Theology of Encounter*, 293–302.

24. Dunn, *Baptism in the Spirit*; Turner, *The Holy Spirit and Spiritual Gifts*.

25. For example, Williams, *Tongues of the Spirit*; Cartledge, "Tongues of the Spirit."

26. See Steven, *Worship in the Spirit*; Albrecht, *Rites in the Spirit*.

27. Thomas, *The Devil, Disease and Deliverance*.

28. MacNutt, *Healing*; MacNutt, *Deliverance from Evil Spirits*.

Anglican practitioners in healing and deliverance ministry.[29] On the international scene, two studies in Ghana, Opuku Onyinah's thesis and Meyer's anthropological *Translating the Devil*, are highly significant;[30] and Ferdinando's thesis brings African traditional and charismatic worldviews into dialogue with the biblical worldview.[31] Two collections of theological papers reflecting on angels, demons and the heavenly realm include charismatic and Pentecostal perspectives, and offer a major contribution to the debate, particularly concerning the ontology of evil;[32] another collection, and two British doctoral theses, relate to a fall of the angels and the origin of evil spirits.[33] Similarly, the recent book *Exorcism and Deliverance* looks at this key practical aspect of spiritual warfare from a multi-disciplinary perspective.[34]

The influence of the so-called "Third Wave"[35] on Britain from across the Atlantic brought new areas of interest and debate concerning spiritual warfare. John Wimber's ministry influenced Anglican churches significantly in the 1980s and 1990s, including a strong emphasis on "power encounter" as "the clashing of the kingdom of God with the kingdom of Satan."[36] This has led to both popular and scholarly debate, notably Martyn Percy's analyses, and discussion in journals.[37] This was also a catalyst for an increase in charismatic deliverance ministries with some associated controversy.[38] Then in the late 1980s and 1990s, a focus arose on a new arena of spiritual warfare, particularly following the high profile given by Peter Wagner to his ideas concerning "territorial spirits," the suggestion that the biblical "principalities and powers" include evil spirits assigned to particular pieces of territory that can be engaged through "strategic level spiritual warfare." The books

29. Perry, *Deliverance*. See also Woolmer, *Healing and Deliverance*; Richards, *But Deliver Us from Evil*.

30. Meyer, *Translating the Devil*; Onyinah, "Akan Witchcraft." See also a more recent collection of anthropological case studies—van Doorn-Harder and Minnema, *Coping with Evil in Religion and Culture*.

31. Ferdinando, "Biblical Concepts of Redemption."

32. Riddell and Riddell, *Angels and Demons*; Lane, *The Unseen World*.

33. Wright, *The Origin of Evil Spirits*; Auffarth and Stuckenbruck, *Fall of Angels*; Lloyd, "The Cosmic Fall."

34. Kay and Parry, *Exorcism and Deliverance*.

35. Mainline evangelicals who "do not teach a crisis experience of baptism in the Holy Spirit subsequent to conversion, and . . . see tongues as only one of the many gifts of the Spirit." Synan, *The Holiness-Pentecostal Tradition*, 271–74, 285.

36. Wimber and Springer, *Power Evangelism*, 29.

37. Percy, *Words, Wonders and Power*; Hunt, "The Anglican Wimberites," 105–18; Ma, "A First Waver Looks at the Third Wave," 189–206.

38. See Hunt, "Deliverance: The Evolution of a Doctrine," 10–16. Also the critical appraisal of Parsons, *Ungodly Fear*.

he edited on the subject[39] were controversial, and prompted some serious academic attempts to refute these ideas.[40] A further significant development considers the potential for community transformation primarily through prayer which takes seriously the spiritual warfare dimension, popularized particularly through a series of videos entitled *Transformations*.[41] These developments also gained the attention of British Anglicans, as evidenced by three contributions in the Grove series on strategic level spiritual warfare and community transformation.[42] Meanwhile, looking more widely, there has been considerable renewed theological interest in "principalities and powers" prompted by Walter Wink's innovative analysis in his "powers" trilogy, espousing the practice of non-violence as a spirituality of resistance to the powers of the Domination System affecting our societies.[43] Wink discusses charismatic spiritual warfare,[44] and this study will in turn engage seriously with his radical re-visioning of Satan, demons and "the Powers." A former Oneness Pentecostal, Gregory Boyd, has also produced a two-volume theological and philosophical presentation of "a spiritual warfare worldview"; Boyd has engaged the attention of some Anglican charismatics, and will be examined in this book.[45]

Focusing on the British charismatic renewal, there have been some historical studies, particularly Peter Hocken's excellent detailed analysis of its origins and early development,[46] as well as accounts of Anglican charismatic renewal;[47] and a number of reflective and self-critical studies of the charismatic movement in Great Britain, some of which have included sections assessing critically the approach to spiritual warfare.[48] The most

---

39. Wagner, *Territorial Spirits*; Wagner and Pennoyer, *Wrestling with Dark Angels*.

40. For example, Lowe, *Territorial Spirits and World Evangelisation*; Reid, *Strategic Level Spiritual Warfare: A Modern Mythology?*

41. Otis Jr, "Transformations." Alistair Petrie, a Scottish Anglican based in Canada, contributed to the research for this—Petrie, *Releasing Heaven on Earth*; Otis Jr, *Informed Intercession*.

42. Bowsher, *Demolishing Strongholds*; Leach, *Community Transformation*; Beckley, *Mission in a Conspiracy Culture*.

43. See Wink, *The Powers That Be*. See bibliography for details of the 3 volumes of which this is a summary.

44. Ibid., 197.

45. Boyd, *God at War*; Boyd, *Satan and the Problem of Evil*.

46. Hocken, *Streams of Renewal*.

47. Notably Buchanan et al., "The Charismatic Movement in the Church of England."

48. McBain includes a critique of Wimber's approach—McBain, *Fire over the Waters*, 98–107. See also the chapter on "The Spiritual Battle" in Scotland, *Charismatics and the New Millenium*, 129–51.

theologically reflective of these is the work by Smail, Walker, and Wright;[49] Andrew Walker's chapter on demonology and the charismatic movement, significantly critiques the "paranoid universe" which may be fostered by the approach of practitioners and teachers such as Derek Prince and Bill Subritsky (both influential in Britain);[50] and Nigel Wright takes issue with the "heightened dualism" of the signs and wonders movement associated with John Wimber, where "a high profile is given to the ideas of Satan and spiritual warfare," developing in a separate book his own theology of the ontology and nature of evil, which we will study in chapter 5.[51]

Within the Anglican context, a number of books have been written on Anglican spirituality; but discussion of charismatic spirituality, or of spiritual warfare, is very limited.[52] In terms of theological developments, Bishop John V. Taylor's theology of the Holy Spirit (partly influenced by his involvement with African Anglicanism, but largely preceding charismatic renewal) has been highly influential;[53] and the Church of England also responded to charismatic renewal by not only producing its assessment of the movement in 1981,[54] but a decade later issuing a guide to the doctrine of the Holy Spirit, including a brief section on good and evil power in relation to signs and wonders.[55]

Overall, therefore, little has been written in secondary literature concerning the Anglican charismatic renewal's approach to spiritual warfare. This study, drawing together information from primary sources written by Anglican charismatics and interviews with pioneer leaders and practitioners, together with detailed case study fieldwork in a charismatic Anglican congregation, thus aims to make a significant contribution to the theological

---

49. Smail, Walker, and Wright, *Charismatic Renewal*.

50. Ibid., 86–105, chapter 6. See also his book on the subject—Walker, *Enemy Territory*. Guelich and Theron also debate the "paranoid universe"—Guelich, "Spiritual Warfare: Jesus, Paul, and Peretti"; Theron, "A Critical Overview."

51. Smail, Walker, and Wright, *Charismatic Renewal*, 71–85; Wright, *Theology of the Dark Side*.

52. For example, Purcell identifies David Watson's spirituality as typical of Anglican evangelicalism with no recognition of the distinctives of charismatic renewal; Purcell, *Anglican Spirituality*, 85. Gordon Mursell's comprehensive spirituality study only observes the significance of tongues and praise in spiritual warfare, in relation to the Black Pentecostal churches in England. Mursell, *English Spirituality*, 407.

53. Taylor, *The Go-between God*.

54. Buchanan et al., "The Charismatic Movement in the Church of England."

55. Church of England Doctrine Commission, "We Believe in the Holy Spirit." A subsequent practical report on healing ministry includes a section on deliverance—Perry, Gunstone, and others, "A Time to Heal."

understanding and assessment of this important area of charismatic experience and practice in an Anglican context.

1.3 Main research questions

In seeking to discover the significance of the "spiritual warfare" motif in this renewal movement, my two initial research questions had a backward-looking, and a current, forward-looking emphasis. Firstly, what was the significance of a theology and spirituality of spiritual warfare in the growth and development of the Anglican charismatic renewal? And secondly, what significant contribution does this theology and spirituality offer to the Anglican church today?

These general questions gave rise to a number of questions of more specific interest. Soon after charismatic renewal began in Britain, the concept of "spiritual warfare" was highlighted.[56] In view of the undoubted interest in spiritual warfare among early Anglican charismatics,[57] what were the origins of this, and the original influences upon its theological formulation (and any significant subsequent influences)? What are the key elements of its theology and spirituality, in relation to the broader framework of charismatic theology and spirituality? And how do spiritual warfare concepts affect the thinking and practice of charismatic Anglican churches in England today, particularly in relation to mission?[58]

In this regard, my primary initial emphasis was both a historical investigation and theological description of charismatic Anglican spiritual warfare. However, as time developed this shifted to a practical theological methodology, in which the advantages of an in-depth sociological study of one congregation rather than a wider sampling became clear. The historical and descriptive aims thus became subsidiary to engaging with fundamental questions that came to the fore from this research—notably the whole question of the ontology and nature of the evil powers that the charismatic

---

56. Harper, *Spiritual Warfare*. According to Ediger (p. 267), this was the first published use of the term—Ediger, "Proto-Genesis of March for Jesus," 247–75. However, it was already in use in renewal circles, as used by Harper in an early headline (1966) in *Renewal*—Harper, "Ministry in Spiritual Warfare."

57. Harper was soon followed by Watson, who published *God's Freedom Fighters* in 1972—reissued as *Hidden Warfare* in 1980. Green's more theological analysis followed a few years later—Green, *I Believe in Satan's Downfall*.

58. A key challenge facing contemporary Anglican congregations is re-orienting from the inherited maintenance-minded "pastoral mode" of the Anglican parish system, to an outward-looking "mission mode" seeking growth and community transformation. See Warren, *Building Missionary Congregations*.

Anglicans studied were envisaging. This therefore became the main focus of the critical evaluation of the main dialogue chapters with key theologians (chapters 5 to 7), increasingly bringing such questions to the biblical material that forms the primary source of charismatic spiritual warfare theology, before attempting to construct a theological praxis model for charismatic spiritual warfare.

1.4 Methodology

Practical theological methodology and the structure of this book

My primary locus for this research is one of contextual theology. It has been observed that "all forms of Christian expression are tied up with the cultural context from which they originate."[59] Just as social sciences have realized that there are many cultures throughout the world, each with its own set of meanings and values, so there is not just one overarching theology, but theology is the way religion makes sense in a particular culture.[60] Schreiter suggests that theological tradition is made up of a series of local (i.e., contextual) theologies growing up in response to needs in certain contexts.[61] Each local theology can be formed from a number of factors, such as other theologies already in place, and events within the community or external theological developments that present themselves and call for a response.[62] The Anglican charismatic renewal is itself a complex religious culture, not as discrete and closed as some Pentecostal churches, but nevertheless having its own distinctive characteristics and tendencies arising from common experiences and elements of a shared cultural and religious background. Theology often develops alongside the spirituality of a community, such that they properly belong together.[63] Thus, in this study I aim to describe the theology and spirituality of spiritual warfare in its Anglican charismatic context (both in relation to the pioneers studied, and the specific context of the case study church). I also hope to illuminate some of the antecedent theological influences, and events within the experience of the Anglican charismatic community, that have formed this theology.[64]

59. Ukpong, "What Is Contextualisation?" 179.
60. Bevans, *Models of Contextual Theology*, 7.
61. Schreiter, *Constructing Local Theologies*, 32.
62. Ibid., 25–26.
63. Ibid., 24.
64. See in particular chapters 2 and 3.

Within this general contextual approach, I have adopted a practical-theological methodology, taking my primary starting point as the present, concrete situation, in dialogue with the theological disciplines (including philosophical theology) and a degree of inter-disciplinary interaction with social science methodology.[65] It can be helpful to distinguish between methodology, methods, and models. Thus, my overall theoretical approach (*methodology*) is fundamentally theological, although I use some sociological *methods* with their own methodological basis;[66] but the framework for my theological reflection and inquiry is the praxis *model*, as appropriated in pastoral theology as "the pastoral cycle," which typically has four phases, experience, exploration, reflection, and response or action.[67]

However, a simplified version of Cartledge's "Dialectics in the Spirit" provides the most helpful framework for the approach I have adopted, particularly in relation to two significant features.[68] Firstly, Cartledge parallels the common spirituality process of search-encounter-transformation with the process of practical theology, noting that for the charismatic practical theologian there is a dialectic between his academic enquiry and his charismatic spirituality.[69] This causes him to ask what the Holy Spirit is doing in a particular context, to relate this to the Holy Spirit's revelation in Scripture, and then to discern what the Spirit is saying to the church. A theologian thus seeks to encounter God and enable people to understand and speak of the encounter.[70] Secondly, whilst recognizing the cyclical (or spiral) nature of the theological process, he also notes that in reality this encounter oscillates dialectically between two poles: encounter with the "lifeworld" of concrete reality (here, that of the Anglican charismatic pioneers, and the case study church), and that of the theological "system" (centered on the love of God revealed in Jesus Christ and the normative role of Scripture) and its metanarrative and critical theory.[71] Interdisciplinary engagement is both at

---

65. Ballard and Pritchard, *Practical Theology in Action*, 62, 66; Cameron et al., *Studying Local Churches*, 18.

66. For example, in using a qualitative method it is interpretivist rather than positivist in its epistemological orientation—see Bryman, *Sociological Research Methods*, 20.

67. See Green, *Let's Do Theology*, 24–30; Ballard and Pritchard, *Practical Theology in Action*, 66, 77; Cameron et al., *Studying Local Churches*, 23–24.

68. Cartledge, *Practical Theology*, 27–30. Cartledge describes taking two turns around the cycle, following van der Ven—see van der Ven and Schweitzer, *Practical Theology—International Perspectives*, 323–39. However, I have simplified it to apply to my single cycle of investigation and reflection.

69. Osmer, *Practical Theology*, 12–14; Cartledge, *Practical Theology*, 27–30.

70. *Practical Theology*, 27; McIntosh, *Mystical Theology*, 5–6.

71. The language of "lifeworld" and "system" is borrowed from Jürgen Habermas via the hermeneutics of Anthony Thiselton. Thiselton argues for the critique of a

the level of the social sciences in the methodology of encounter with the lifeworld, and in the subsidiary engagement with other disciplines (mainly philosophy) in the critical dialogue with the "system." Out of this encounter emerges the recommendations for renewed ecclesial belief and practice that potentially brings "transformation."[72]

This dialectic thus provides the methodological framework for this thesis:

1. *The initial search phase (chapter 1)*. Having observed situations in the lifeworld that raised questions in relation to charismatic spiritual warfare, I initially explored literature relevant to the area (see 1.2 above), articulated some key issues, and decided to set up two main exploratory research projects.

2. *Encounter with the "lifeworld" (chapters 2 to 4)*. Here I undertake the descriptive-empirical task of describing what is going on when charismatic Anglicans talk about, or engage in, spiritual warfare. My first project was historical-theological, investigating the historical origins and outline of the Anglican charismatic renewal and its theology and practice of spiritual warfare, primarily through key pioneer leaders in this area (through interviews and bibliographical research). The historical background and context are described in chapter 2; chapter 3 concentrates on theological developments, initially focusing on the three pioneers who published books concerning spiritual warfare, and then analyzing them as a group. Secondly, I used case study qualitative research method to investigate empirically how spiritual warfare is conceived and practiced in a charismatic Anglican congregation, through an extensive in-depth congregational case study (following an initial pilot study), described in chapter 4.

3. *Encounter with the "system" (chapters 5 to 8)*. The dialectic here moves (in anthropological terms) from the "emic" categories and expressions of the everyday discourse of charismatic Christians to the "etic" concepts of academic discourse, as I engage with critical theory from the "system" of theological scholarship.[73] The primary question that arose

---

"transcontextual system"; for him, this is primarily the love of God expressed in the cross and resurrection of Christ. Cartledge, *Practical Theology*, 23, 29; Thiselton, *New Horizons*, 388, 614–15.

72. Cartledge, *Practical Theology*, 28–29.

73. Thus moving from Cartledge's levels 1 and 2 to level 3 discourse. In practical theology this level 3 academic theology offers a mediating discourse between confessional theology and the wider Christian tradition and the social sciences. Cartledge, *Testimony in the Spirit*, 18–20.

from the case studies was the fundamental theological one concerning the reality and nature of evil forces; so I concentrated on systematic and biblical theology as the potentially most illuminating arena for dialogue, with some interaction with philosophy. I chose to do this by engaging in chapters 5 to 7 with the theoretical models of three main dialogue partners (Nigel Wright, Amos Yong, and Gregory Boyd),[74] as well as their key sources (most notably Karl Barth and Walter Wink).

In Cartledge's model, "theological normativity is located in Scripture and can challenge and modify the values embedded in theological praxis."[75] Chapter 8 thus particularly focuses on the contribution of Scripture in seeking to construct a charismatic theology of spiritual warfare. I therefore begin with a discussion of the charismatic approach to hermeneutics that I have adopted. In a process of "triangulation," the chapter seeks to combine biblical scholarship with insights from both in-depth studies in the lifeworld (pioneer leaders and case study congregation) and the academic discourse and analysis emerging from chapters 5 to 7. I thus proceed to examine specifically the nature of evil (with some insights from psychology), its origin, the extent of evil and how evil is defeated, particularly in relation to the most relevant biblical material highlighted in the encounter phase and the ensuing theological dialogue. I then present a simple Trinitarian theological model as a recommended basis for renewal of theology and praxis. This is essentially a rescripting exercise; having engaged with the norms of the Christian script of Scripture and the interpretative tradition, concepts used in the case study church are rescripted in a way that is both in continuity but also some discontinuity with their existing script.[76] It also takes into account some of the theological and pastoral criticisms from both inside and outside the charismatic renewal, enhancing the normative value of the Anglican charismatic model of spiritual warfare presented.[77]

4. *Transformation phase (chapter 9)*. Having summarized the conclusions of the study and given suggestions for further research, specific

---

74. All three of these theologians have been positively influenced by experience in charismatic and Pentecostal contexts, but in developing their theoretical positions have engaged with wider Christian tradition. See also the introduction to chapter 5.

75. Cartledge, *Practical Theology*, 29.

76. See Cartledge, *Testimony in the Spirit*, 16–20, 179.

77. See Schreiter, *Constructing Local Theologies*, 117–21.

recommendations are given for the renewal of praxis in the main case study church.[78]

This practical theological model thus begins and ends in practice, hopefully leading to better practice that more faithfully participates in the Trinitarian actions of God in the world.[79]

Within this broad contextual and practical theological approach, I shall in addition be using three subsidiary methodologies: church historiographical, biblical-critical theological, and sociological qualitative research. Firstly, particularly in examining the origins and history of the spiritual warfare approach in the Anglican charismatic renewal in Britain, I used a church historiographical investigative method. Thus, I examined not only the secondary sources listed above,[80] but also primary sources from participants in the Anglican charismatic renewal. I used a number of the published writings of leaders and pioneers in this renewal—both books describing the new charismatic theological approach in popular or practical terms;[81] and more autobiographical accounts of key figures[82] or the stories of the renewal in churches in which they were involved.[83] Secondly, I conducted some archive research into magazine and newsletter publications of charismatic renewal, notably *Renewal* and *Anglicans for Renewal*,[84] as well as examining some tapes and notes from charismatic conferences. In addition, some biographical information was obtained from biographies written by friends or associates of key figures.[85] Much specific information, regarding some of the pioneer leaders and the origins and influences upon them in the area

---

78. At the end of chapter 8, recommendations are also given as to how the proposed model might be applied generally in charismatic congregational praxis (8.6.3), and in the context of Anglican tradition (8.7).

79. See Swinton and Mowat, *Practical Theology and Qualitative Research*, 24–25.

80. See chapter 1.2, particularly Hocken, *Streams of Renewal*.

81. Such as those by Harper, Watson, and Green—see footnote 57.

82. For example, Watson, *You Are My God*; Harper, *None Can Guess*; Green, *Adventure of Faith*; Pytches, *Living at the Edge*.

83. E.g., Warren, *In the Crucible*, for St. Thomas Crooke's, Sheffield, and Tom Walker, *Open to God*, for St. John's, Harborne.

84. *Renewal* was the newsletter of the Fountain Trust, initially published under Michael Harper in 1966, continuing until it eventually merged with *Christianity* magazine in 2001. *Anglicans for Renewal* began as the newsletter of the London Committee for Renewal in 1979, when it announced the launching of Anglican Renewal Ministries under John Gunstone, it became its newsletter—see Buchanan et al., "The Charismatic Movement in the Church of England," 1. I also looked for relevant articles in the more theologically reflective *Theological Renewal*, published under Tom Smail's editorship from 1975 to 1983.

85. Notably Saunders and Sansom, *David Watson*.

of spiritual warfare, was obtained through semi-structured interviews (see fieldwork methodology below) with these pioneers.[86]

In my theological construction (in chapter 8), I shall be using some of the tools of biblical criticism and hermeneutics to consider some of the texts particularly favored by Anglican charismatics in building a theology of spiritual warfare. This will assist in coming to some tentative pneumatological conclusions concerning the nature, origin and defeat of evil powers, and then in constructing a charismatic model for a theological praxis of "spiritual warfare." However, in earlier chapters (2 to 4) I will be presenting much qualitative research material based on fieldwork, whose methodology draws insights from the social sciences, to which I now turn.

Social science methodology

Participant observation

In sociological terms my methodology for fieldwork is essentially qualitative research from an approach of participant observation. This approach accords with one of my primary aims, to describe the "native" Anglican charismatic insider's understanding of spiritual warfare issues.[87] Steven used this methodology in a similar context to my own, in observing and describing charismatic worship in the Church of England. This relied both on participation in the worship at case study churches, and on informal interviews with co-participants in the acts of worship.[88] In my main and pilot congregational case studies (see chapter 4), I operated on similar principles, in that I was primarily an "observer-as-participant," "whose contact with informants is brief, formal and openly classified as observation."[89] And particularly in the main case study, I was also for a time an ordinary participant in the worship and meetings of the conferences and services at the church

---

86. With the obvious exception of David Watson who died in 1984. I interviewed his worship leader and colleague at St. Cuthbert's, York, Andrew Maries, although this did not yield much specific information concerning Watson's approach to spiritual warfare.

87. In anthropological terms, this compares with the goal of ethnography, which is "to grasp the native's point of view, his relation to life, to realize *his* vision of *his* world." Malinowski, B, *Argonauts of the Western Pacific* (London: Routledge, 1922), quoted in Spradley, *Participant Observation*, v, 3.

88. Steven, *Worship in the Spirit*, 37–47. Unlike Steven, however, I concentrated on only one study (rather than several) after the pilot.

89. The participant observer also enters into conversation with participants to discover their interpretations of events. Ibid., 42, 45; Burgess, *In the Field*, 79. See also Osmer, *Practical Theology*, 61.

over a number of weeks, and participated in the form of prayer ministry they were recommending both as recipient and on a few occasions as part of the prayer teams.

Reflexivity and epistemology

Reflexivity, being my critical self-reflection as the researcher in monitoring my contribution to the proceedings, plays an integral part in qualitative research, and thus also in practical theology.[90] I shall here consider it on three levels: methodological, personal, and epistemological.

Adopting a methodological role as "participant observer" highlights the observer's simultaneous experience as both an insider and outsider.[91] In general terms, I am an insider in that I have been an "ordinary participant"[92] in various activities of Anglican churches and conferences relating to charismatic renewal continually (apart from long absences overseas in Sudan [1983–86] and China [1991–2000] with short breaks in the UK) from 1980 until the present.[93] This assisted me in reflecting critically and seeking to understand the experience from within; and my position as one sympathetic to renewal also enabled me to be received with a high degree of trust and openness by respondents in interviews, hopefully sufficient to be able to depend on the information gleaned.[94] This genuine rapport with the respondents is essential to enable them to become genuine "co-researchers"[95]—as they themselves reflected critically in interpreting their experience as we worked together in a process of phenomenological investigation and reflection. On the other hand, during this research I needed to overcome the relatively high degree of selective inattention typical of an ordinary participant, to observe a broader spectrum of information and possible interpretations of an event, and to become more of a detached observer.[96]

Personal reflexivity takes seriously that all research is, to an extent, autobiography, being carried out in the context of my own experiences

---

90. Swinton and Mowat, *Practical Theology and Qualitative Research*, 59–61.

91. Spradley, *Participant Observation*, 56–57.

92. Ibid., 53.

93. I also briefly participated in some of the experiences referred to by Michael Green whilst attending St. Aldate's, Oxford in 1980–82.

94. See Jorgensen, *Participant Observation: A Methodology*, 69–71.

95. Reason, *Participation in Human Enquiry*, 10; Moustakas, *Phenomenological Research Methods*.

96. Spradley, *Participant Observation*, 55–57.

and beliefs.[97] Thus, my key research question (what can be learnt from the renewal's understanding and practice of spiritual warfare?) is personally relevant as an Anglican vicar engaging in local mission, but also in reflecting on my mission experience here in the 1980s (in Anglican charismatic context), and for many years overseas in Sudan and China. Answering this question took into account my precommitments, as I critically reflected on how and why an issue such as spiritual warfare affects the life of the church practically—hence my choice of a practical (rather than systematic) theological approach.[98] Undertaking the main field research in late 2007, when essentially between clerical posts, enabled me to better immerse myself in the context of the main case study church.

Epistemological reflexivity recognizes how my presuppositions, beliefs and values may have influenced how the research questions are framed and investigated, and how conclusions are drawn. For example, whilst the interview questions were drawn up after reading and considering issues raised in the literature, they were also the questions I considered to be of particular interest, as a charismatic theologian and pastor faced with the challenges of mission in Britain today. Nevertheless, in the end it was a key issue raised in the research process (the ontological question) that became dominant rather than my own interests (more concerning the role of prayer in evangelism and social transformation).

Discovering the strong influence of the researcher's metatheoretical perspective has led to a certain crisis concerning the scientific representation and legitimization of the adequacy of much empirical research, prompting the need for greater epistemological reflexivity.[99] The use of qualitative research methods in a practical theological methodology also presents particular epistemological difficulties, for many social scientists have very different presuppositions from theologians concerning the nature of reality and truth.[100] On the other hand, the praxis model in theology has become popular partly due to the cultural shift towards postmodernity, where experience as the prime mediator of truth and reality is preferred. As

---

97. Swinton and Mowat, *Practical Theology and Qualitative Research*, 60.

98. See Frances Ward, in Cameron et al., *Studying Local Churches*, 18.

99. Osmer, *Practical Theology*, 57–58. The classical criteria of validity, reliability, and generalizability are only partially appropriate in relation to legitimating qualitative research; for example, a few in-depth case studies can rarely be generalized to a broader population. However, a researcher may choose to "generalize to theory" as in this study.

100. For example, some constructivist social scientists propose that it is never possible to agree on a version of reality, which is a social construction; truth is always subjective. Swinton and Mowat, *Practical Theology and Qualitative Research*, 36, 167–69; Denzin, *Interpretive Ethnography*, 265–66.

a charismatic practical theologian, I do not fully subscribe to the postmodern approach, since I retain a strong commitment to truth as orthodoxy as well as orthopraxy (championed by liberationists), and a charismatic commitment to orthopathy (right affections).[101] I do however concur with aspects of pragmatic truth theory that truth claims are partial and fallible, such that a *critical realist* epistemology is appropriate; our knowledge may need to be revised in the light of external reality—for example, whether in practice it really makes a difference.[102] But I also hold to the possibility of apprehending truth concerning reality through revelation (whilst recognizing the inevitable interpretative dimension in relation to Scripture and tradition).[103] Cartledge thus argues that "in practical theology, there should be no doubt as to which is the dominant discourse, however sympathetically and critically other discourses are used."[104] An attitude of *critical faithfulness* to revelation through Scripture and tradition can thus help to integrate the discourse of qualitative research into the praxis model above.[105] This also accords with my own personal convictions, including a high regard for the inspiration of Scripture, but also recognizes that particular interpretations should always be open to re-examination, and tested against our experience and those of others in the Christian community, both now and in the tradition.[106]

Case study approach

The scope of my field research is relatively modest, adopting something of a case study approach, on two levels. Firstly, in my historical assessment I

---

101. See Cartledge, *Practical Theology*, 17, 40.

102. Much academic theology prescribes what should work; practical theology, like Astley's "ordinary theology," begins with the working—"to look and see what works in practice, and then to reflect theologically on that;" as long as it is also coherent. Astley, *Ordinary Theology*, 73–74. See also Pattison's "mutual critical conversation"—Pattison, "Some Straw for the Bricks," 2–9.

103. I concur with Wright's critical realist epistemology, which sees knowledge of particulars as taking place within the larger framework of the observer's "metanarrative" and its associated worldview (which Christians believe to be revealed in Scripture). Wright, *The New Testament and the People of God*, 37.

104. Cartledge, *Practical Theology*, 16, and 33–34 (footnote 29).

105. Faithful to "the givenness of Scripture and the genuine working of the Holy Spirit in its interpretation"; but, aware of the interpretive dimension, open to a critical dialogue between situations, Christian tradition, and knowledge from qualitative research methods. See Swinton and Mowat, *Practical Theology and Qualitative Research*, 93–97.

106. See chapter 8.1 for specific discussion on hermeneutics.

have chosen to study and interview the key leaders who first wrote books on spiritual warfare, as well as other influential Anglican charismatic pioneers. These were often associated with influential early centers of Anglican charismatic renewal in England.[107] I also interviewed leaders and a few Anglican pioneer practitioners who became involved in particular areas of spiritual warfare,[108] and three leaders who had not to my knowledge been openly or explicitly so involved.[109] I used content analysis on their interview scripts to tabulate key issues that came to the fore concerning their theology and spirituality of spiritual warfare, and some influences upon it.

Secondly, as the main part of my fieldwork concerning the practice of charismatic spiritual warfare in the Church of England today, I conducted a pilot study and then an in-depth congregational case study. Both had a strong charismatic identity, with a focus on mission rather than pastoral maintenance.[110] In theoretical terms, both studies were primarily descriptive and inductive, but were chosen because they had the potential to be revelatory, in terms of Robert Yin's categories.[111]

The use of semi-structured interviews

For my fieldwork, I have relied heavily on the methodology of qualitative research, especially the use of semi-structured interviews. Qualitative research is appropriate for studying theology in context, having "an unrivalled capacity to constitute compelling arguments about how things work in particular contexts"; while on the other hand, it has the potential for facilitating inferences of wider general application, since "the qualitative

---

107. The leaders and centers were: Michael Harper (Fountain Trust); David Watson (St. Michael-le-Belfrey, York); John Collins (St. Mark's, Gillingham/Holy Trinity, Brompton); Tom Walker (St. John's, Harborne, Birmingham); Michael Green (St. Aldate's, Oxford—also John Woolmer, Jane Holloway); Robert Warren (St. Thomas Crookes, Sheffield); and David Pytches (St. Andrew's, Chorleywood/New Wine). David MacInnes was also associated with 3 of these centers (Gillingham, Birmingham, and St. Aldate's, Oxford).

108. David Pytches, John Woolmer, Jane Holloway.

109. Bishop Simon Barrington-Ward, John Collins, and Canon Robert Warren. See chapter 3.

110. For a description of "maintenance" and "mission" focused churches, see Warren, *Building Missionary Congregations*.

111. A *revelatory* case study is one of a kind that had not previously been academically documented, so it is justified on the grounds that the descriptive information alone could be revelatory—Yin, *Case Study Research*, 42–44. See chapter 4.2.

habit of intimately connecting context with explanation means that qualitative research is capable of producing very well-founded cross-contextual generalities."[112]

Semi-structured interviews seemed the best way to gather information not available in any other form;[113] and to encourage interviewees to express their views openly, rather than in a questionnaire or fully standardized interview.[114] Most of my interviews, were "expert interviews,"[115] being fairly extended (typically one and a half hours), using a standard set of questions to keep the conversation focused and to steer it onto relevant areas. I occasionally added more confrontational questions, such as hypothesis-directed questions that raised issues oriented to the theological literature on the topic.[116] I generally used Spradley's question types for ethnographic interviews, beginning from "grand-tour" overview questions down to "native-language" questions for clarifications of terms or concepts used by insiders.[117]

Research ethics

The strong element of field research here requires a consideration of research ethics. The ESRC Framework for Research Ethics (FRE) helps identify possible areas of risk to research respondents.[118] Whilst nearly all were deemed minimal for this study, it was however necessary to gain access and seek approval for research at the main case study church through its "gatekeepers";[119] and so alongside the case study protocol, a review of research ethics was prepared and submitted. This sought to address the key principles of ethical research, which are identified in the FRE.[120]

The main "gatekeeper" was the vicar of the case study church; after explaining my request to conduct the research, he was given time to consult

---

112. Mason, *Qualitative Researching*, 1. This helps explain how this study "generalizes to theory"—from insights from the case studies, through dialogue with theoretical models (chapters 5 to 7), to constructing my conclusions (chapter 8).

113. Ibid., 66.

114. Flick, *An Introduction to Qualitative Research*, 74.

115. Ibid., 89–90.

116. Ibid., 81.

117. As presented in Jorgensen, *Participant Observation: A Methodology*, 85.

118. For example, as in the FRE checklist in Appendix A, pages 33–34. My references are to the 2010 version (FRE)—ESRC, *Framework for Research Ethics*.

119. Research is normally considered more than minimal risk when it involves groups where permission of a gatekeeper (such as a community leader) is required for initial access to members. ESRC, *Framework for Research Ethics* 9.

120. ESRC, *Framework for Research Ethics* 3.

with his leadership team before agreeing to the case study. The relationship with the gatekeeper was obviously an important one, as he may have concerns over the impact of the research.[121] In the event the research benefitted from a high degree of trust—for example, the gatekeeper helped select some suitable interviewees, but gave permission for me to freely select others from the congregation.

Interviewees participated on the principle of informed consent, using a statement of intent (explaining the purpose of the research, the value placed on their views but without value judgments, their freedom to stop at any time), and signed consent form.[122] The risk of any detrimental effects on interviewees was deemed very low.[123] Confidentiality was stressed, on the basis that pseudonyms would be used for them and the name of the church, and personal material otherwise kept confidential. All main interviewees were given the opportunity to read through and suggest corrections to their interview transcript, as were the church leaders in relation to the chapter draft.

1.5 Definitions, scope, and limitations

As indicated, the main arena of my research is within the charismatic renewal of the Church of England. I have found "**charismatic renewal**" to be the most helpful term—"**charismatic**," as describing any form or experience of Christianity that emphasizes the charismata or spiritual gifts (such as tongues, prophecy, discernment, etc.) listed in 1 Corinthians 12 and elsewhere, as well as a dynamic experience of being "baptized" or filled with the Holy Spirit; "**renewal**" describing the expression of this new form of spiritual life (often called "Pentecostalism"[124]) within previously existing historic main-line churches or denominations, such as the Church of England (C of E), Methodist, Baptist or URC churches, or the Roman Catholic Church. The term "**charismatic movement**" has often been used almost

---

121. For example, whilst Oliver suggests that the relationship can be fully symbiotic, but the gatekeeper potentially has more to lose as he may have to reduce the impact of insensitive research practice after the researcher has left. Oliver, *The Student's Guide to Research Ethics*, 39–40.

122. An attempt was made to inform participants of anything they might need to know in order to make a decision as to whether or not to participate. See ibid., 28–31.

123. This was assessed as a possible psychological risk in inviting participants to discuss personal beliefs and relating experiences. There might be embarrassment in sharing personal views, or some emotional discomfort in relating experiences that may have been traumatic. See ibid., 31–32.

124. See Anderson, *Origin & Development of Global Pentecostalism*, 1.

interchangeably with "charismatic renewal," but suggests something hard to define and transcending denominational boundaries. Not only charismatic experience but also some individuals involved moved fairly readily between denominations,[125] and teaching and sharing of experiences was even less confined, such that I consider a wider range of material than purely that emanating from Anglicans; however, my focus on the charismatic elements that have penetrated into the C of E (especially in chapters 2 and 3) makes renewal a more appropriate term.[126] Some consolidation of the intra-denominational networking of charismatics within the C of E facilitated making Anglican renewal the main locus of this study.[127]

Within the charismatic renewal, spiritual warfare (SW[128]) is the topic of study—how it is described and understood at the level of ordinary as well as academic theology;[129] and also its **spirituality**, which I take as referring to both "the individual prayer and communion with God . . . and with the outer life that supports and flows from this devotion";[130] with particular emphasis on the latter outward dimension, that is, the practice of spiritual warfare. In charismatic circles theology and practical spirituality are often closely interlinked;[131] **praxis** (or "theological praxis") is thus also an appropriate term, in denoting actions, habits and practices that are value-laden

---

125. Some key leaders, for example, changed denominational allegiances (e.g., Michael Harper and Andrew Walker left the C of E and joined the Orthodox Church; Colin Urquhart became independent).

126. It is also perhaps the most widely recognized term. However, by the twenty-first century, the breadth of charismatic penetration across the churches, especially in its influence on songs and forms of worship, is such that "charismatic tradition" is becoming more appropriate, alongside other contemporary spiritual traditions in Anglicanism (such as evangelicalism, Anglo-Catholicism, liberalism, etc.).

127. Notably through the New Wine Networks, started by David Pytches; and the looser network associated with the Alpha Course. *Resource* was also founded in 2004 by Martin Cavendish and others (following the closure of Anglican Renewal Ministries) partly to connect with charismatics in local churches that might not naturally link with networks such as New Wine.

128. I have kept this shorthand abbreviation in some of the analysis arising from interview transcripts.

129. Whilst much of my own reflections here relates to academic theology, my practical theology approach draws on the "ordinary theology" of members of the case study churches—theology which is grounded in the challenges and fulfillments of ordinary life, often by those who have received little or no theological education of a scholarly or academic kind. See Astley, *Ordinary Theology*, 54–57.

130. Jones, Wainwright, and Yarnold, *The Study of Spirituality*, xxii.

131. For example, O'Sullivan notes that most of the songs written by Graham Kendrick for "March for Jesus" in the 1980s "provided a vehicle for combining theological instruction with spiritual activity, particularly in the area of prophetic ministry and spiritual warfare." O'Sullivan, "Roger Forster and the Ichthus Fellowship," 62.

theologically, linked to a person's worldview, beliefs and values.[132] The term **"spiritual warfare"** is not specifically mentioned in the Bible, but the concept would appear to be supported by a number of references in both Old and New Testaments. Within the concept there are a wide range of views as to its content and significance; for example, a good number of theologians would take references to evil spiritual forces such as demons, sometimes including Satan, as mythological and not describing ontological realities. I have nevertheless already defined this in a way appropriate to its charismatic context, as the theological belief in the existence of demons or evil spirits and of Christians' involvement in a warfare between God and Satan;[133] and the practical outworking of this belief in their spirituality of prayer, intercession, and healing and deliverance ministry.[134] The term **"spiritual battle"** is also used almost interchangeably by many charismatics.[135] For many, spiritual warfare immediately brings to mind **exorcism**, which can be defined as "a specific act of binding and releasing, performed on a person who is believed to be possessed by a non-human malevolent spirit," or sometimes "the spiritual cleansing of a place believed to be infected with the demonic";[136] however, detailed study of this specific phenomenon and the methods involved (also requiring expertise in psychology as well as theology) is beyond the scope of this study. I will be referring to exorcism in the broader context of **deliverance ministry** (defined as freeing people from the bondage of Satan as a result of folly, unbelief, sin or the works of the devil, but not necessarily implying "possession" by an evil spirit[137]). The belief in the ubiquitousness of oppressive evil (particularly in the case study

---

132. Cartledge, *Practical Theology*, 17; Wright, *The New Testament and the People of God*, 32–46.

133. Keith Warrington summarizes the main tenets of current belief as: 1) the devil and his demons are antagonistic foes of the church, 2) they have been eternally overcome by Christ, 3) they still affect individuals malevolently, 4) they can be resisted and overcome by and through Christ. Warrington, *Pentecostal Perspectives*.

134. I am using it in its broadest terms—whereas some used it to refer to the "spiritual warfare movement" particularly associated with Peter Wagner's emphasis on the battle against "territorial spirits." See Theron, "A Critical Overview," 89–90.

135. For example, see chapter 6, "Spiritual Battle," in Scotland, *Charismatics and the New Millennium*, 129–51. It can be perceived as having less dramatic overtones, and more taken as metaphorical for struggling or wrestling as in the key Pauline biblical text of Eph 6:12—"our struggle is not against flesh and blood, but against the rulers, against the authorities, against the powers of this dark world and against the spiritual forces of evil in the heavenly realms."

136. Perry, *Deliverance*, 2.

137. Ibid. Although pastoral deliverance ministry relating to individuals was not my primary focus, it become a significant area of investigation in the main case study church.

church) was a factor leading to subsequent reflection in the interpretive task being focused on the question of the **ontology** of evil forces. Ontology means "being," the being of something in itself; I use this both in the narrower philosophical sense of the description of the metaphysical substance of evil, but also relating to the place of evil forces in the created order (cosmology), and at times more broadly as "the nature of the thing under discussion,"[138] which in a theological context often includes description of its characteristics, e.g., in moral terms. **Evil** itself is a difficult word to define; I use it primarily in its common moral usage, where evil is usually defined as a negative concept, understood as the opposite of that which we hold to be good;[139] but being in a theological context where I subscribe to the basic belief that "God is good," evil can also be defined as that which is opposed to God, which helps to remove it from the subjective realm of what I perceive to be "bad" or evil. Evil as what is morally opposed to good is similar to "sin" in the religious context—but is often widened to consider so-called "natural evils" particularly in relation to theodicy. The latter is an area I will touch on but is largely beyond the scope of this thesis.

The term "**Anglican**" actually encompasses the worldwide Anglican Communion; and the majority of Anglicans are in fact now in the two-thirds world.[140] In recognition of this increasingly significant global dimension, I started some preliminary research and interviews in relation to West Africa and South East Asia (both strongly influenced by charismatic renewal), but this proved too ambitious for the scope of this study. Therefore, here I use the term "Anglican" here to mean "relating to the Church of England," unless otherwise specified or obvious from the context.

---

138. Cf. Cartledge, *Practical Theology*, 259.

139. See Schwarz, *Evil: A Historical and Theological Perspective*, 1–2.

140. For example, the Church of Nigeria alone may have around ten times as many members (seventeen million) as attend the Church of England regularly. See Ward, *A History of Global Anglicanism*, 1.

— 2 —

Anglican Charismatic Spiritual Warfare in Historical Perspective

2.1 The historical Anglican tradition in relation to spiritual warfare

WE CANNOT SPEAK DIRECTLY of "spiritual warfare" in the British Anglican context prior to the 1960s, since it was not a recognizable term in theological or pastoral language. However, certain historical strands of theology and spirituality reveal that it is not entirely foreign to the Anglican context.

Christianity first came to the British Isles through various Roman merchants. Christianization of the Celts was relatively quick, bringing also literacy, such that much of the oral tradition of the Celts pre-Christian culture was soon preserved through the writings of Christian scribes, scholars and bards; this also meant that some of the pre-Christian thought and belief was maintained and absorbed. It is very difficult historically to ascertain the genuine contours of Celtic Christianity, much of which was Graeco-Romanized over several centuries; thus sympathetic writings from within the fringe communities of Wales, Scotland and Ireland still influenced by their Celtic roots may shed more light on the worldview of the Celts and the Christianity that blossomed in the British Isles before the Romans took control.[1]

Such writers highlight aspects of the Celtic outlook that predisposed Celtic Christians to take on a strong conception of the struggle between spiritual forces. Mackey agrees with O'Donoghue (one of his contributors) that "no one who does not come to grips with the nearness of the spirit world will ever understand Celtic Christianity," maintaining that "the nearness, the ubiquitous *presence* of the spiritual in all things and at all times . . . is indeed a powerful, permanent, and characteristic Celtic conviction,

---

1. Mackey, *An Introduction to Celtic Christianity*, 3–8. Most of Mackey's contributors qualify in this respect, as does Bradley, *Celtic Christianity*.

[which] may prove to be the most important contribution which the Celtic mind can still offer to the modern world."[2] This presence is ultimately the presence of the divine, even if many spiritual powers are depicted as persons and meant to be thought of as persons, for example in the form of choirs of angels "as real as the sun and moon";[3] Celts also had a full and uninhibited acceptance of the natural world in full continuity with the spiritual, with God's gracious power everywhere within it, with no real dichotomy between spirits and materials things and the modes of God's presence in both for the Celtic Christian, who invokes spirits to protect or to praise.[4] However, whilst for the pre-Augustinian Celts the natural world and human nature are good through and through as Genesis insists (and the newborn child is innocent), "this good world is in bondage, in the manner of a good land under occupation by malevolent forces."[5] The traditional Celtic Christ, however, comes not to confront the corruption of nature, but "to release a beautiful and holy world from its bondage; not to replace the revelatory light of nature with a new and different light, but to scatter the dark forces so that the original light (the light which the prologue to the Fourth Gospel says enlightens everyone who comes into the world) could shine for us again, and guide our footsteps home."[6]

Thus in relation to "spiritual warfare," the Celts displayed an awareness of God's ubiquitous presence by his Spirit; a theology that integrates spiritual forces into the natural order without dichotomy; and an awareness that malevolent dark forces have occupied the land, but can be scattered by Christ's light.[7] Although since then many other layers of spirituality have influenced Anglican Christians, the Celtic roots have never been entirely

---

2. Mackey, *An Introduction to Celtic Christianity*, 10–11. Mackey contrasts this with the reductionist argument of many scientists that "mind" is *nothing* other than a sequence of thoughts and feelings set off by the brain in its interaction with our physical world.

3. Quoting O'Donoghue—ibid., 12, 52.

4. Mackey laments how in Western theology Augustinian "created grace" (produced within God's creatures) has overshadowed the uncreated grace of God's creative, life-giving, beneficent presence to and within all, characteristic of Celtic Christianity. Ibid., 13.

5. Mackey continues: "However much contemporary minds may feel like resisting the traditional Celtic personification of such forces, there can be no doubt that malevolent forces operate in our world and through our own spirits, and that we need saving from them." Ibid., 16.

6. Ibid.

7. One Anglican charismatic found strong parallels between this Celtic spirituality and a balanced approach to "spiritual warfare" in the charismatic renewal. See Mitton, *Restoring the Woven Cord*.

lost, as evidenced in a recent resurgence of interest in Celtic spirituality amongst Anglicans.[8]

Medieval times and the Reformation

Much study on the spirituality of medieval devotion has focused on individuals or groups who left influential writings, such as the fourteenth-century mystics Rolle, Hilton, the writer of the "Cloud of Unknowing," and Julian of Norwich. However, this emphasis is often out of all proportion to their actual impact on the religion of most ordinary people at the time.[9] This "popular" or "traditional" religion, whilst undoubtedly influenced by paganism and superstition, was probably equally formed by the liturgy and sermons in church, the visual portrayals on walls, screens and windows, the enacted miracle plays, and orally in rhyming verse treatises and saints' lives.[10] In such traditional religion, we find certain Scriptures regularly used in exorcism or defense against evil.[11] A particular focus of cleansing the land from evil were the Rogation Day processions "beating the bounds" of the parish. Late medieval Rogationtide processions, with handbells, banners, and the parish cross, were designed to drive out of the community the evil spirits who created division between neighbors and sickness in man and beast.[12]

This traditional religion of late medieval Catholicism had a strong hold and imagination over the loyalty of the people right up to the Reformation; and even after the purges of early Protestantism, the preservation of the prayer-book pattern of the old rites of passage helped keep enough of the old imagery and resonances in the churches to complicate the new teachings.[13] For the Church of England, the new as well as much of the

---

8. For example, centering on the communities in Northumbria, particularly the writings and liturgy of David Adam, e.g., Adam, *The Rhythm of Life: Celtic Daily Prayer*.

9. Duffy, *The Stripping of the Altars*, 1.

10. "Traditional religion," as deriving from a flexible repertoire of inherited beliefs and symbols shared between the literate and illiterate, is a better term than "popular." Ibid., 2–3.

11. The prologue to St. John's gospel was one of four passages in the popular primers seen to have protective power. It was read at the baptismal service, with Mark's description of the exorcism of a demoniac boy, and was used in exorcism ceremonies; and was widely used as a charm against all evils, frequently worn on parchment round the neck to cure disease. Ibid., 215–16.

12. The gospel was proclaimed at the boundary, especially at landmark stational points with a stone or wooden cross. These were important occasions, and the gospel promises of power over evil (e.g., Mark 16:17–18) read from the primers were significant. Ibid., 136, 139, 214–15.

13. Ibid., 4.

old became enshrined in the liturgy of the prayer book. Here the strongest representation of such prayers against evil is in the Litany, which was said on specific occasions but most notably during Lent on Wednesdays and Fridays.[14] The Litany includes prayers of penitence, but also deprecations which are essentially expansions of the clause "deliver us from evil" in the Lord's prayer.[15] They include prayers for deliverance from spiritual evil, temptation, moral evils, physical evils, evils afflicted by man or affecting Church or State (such as heresy or rebellion), blindness of heart, pride, hypocrisy, deadly sin, and deceits of the world, the flesh and the devil. There is a recognition that prayer is answered "by thine Agony, by thy Cross and Passion . . . precious death . . . and glorious Resurrection and Ascension"; and it ends with prayers for strength in spiritual conflict, and "to beat down Satan under our feet" (Rom 16:20).[16] Such prayers, slightly modified, remain in the Book of Common Prayer used in traditional church services today.[17] Thus, although the phrase "the church militant" (used as the title for this book) in the prayer book does not of itself signify an aggressive stance towards spiritual enemies, there are signs elsewhere within it of the oppression of sin, evil, and deception from the world, the flesh, and the devil, that caused Anglicans to pray for protection, and deliverance.[18]

2.2 Revd. Alexander Boddy: the first Pentecostal Anglican

Whilst we might investigate other strands of spirituality outside the Church of England, such as the Puritans who had a strong sense of the spiritual battle, or in the Wesleyan revivals, it is not until the twentieth century that the theme becomes prominent in an Anglican context, beginning with the forerunner to the Anglican charismatic renewal, the Pentecostal pioneer, Revd. Alexander Boddy. Following a Pentecostal revival in his own Sunderland congregation in 1907, Boddy became a focus for an annual Pentecostal

---

14. Litanies originated very early in the British Church, used in times of calamity. Specific invocations to angels and saints added later were removed in Cranmer's prayer book. Daniel, *The Prayer-Book*, 190–91.

15. As explained in the Catechism—"from all sin and wickedness, and from our ghostly enemy, and from everlasting death." Ibid., 194–95.

16. Ibid., 197–99, 204–10.

17. England, *The Shorter Prayer Book*, 24–30.

18. The phrase "militant here in earth" was added after "let us pray for the whole state of Christ's Church" before the general intercessions, to clearly limit the prayer to those living, and to exclude prayer for the dead. Daniel, *The Prayer-Book*, 358–59.

convention in Sunderland, and the editor of the Pentecostal periodical *Confidence* from 1908 to 1926.[19]

Despite his "Pentecostal" experiences, Boddy remained very much an Anglican clergyman, subscribing to the Thirty-Nine Articles, practicing infant baptism and keeping his regular pattern of services and prayers, following the *1662 Book of Common Prayer*.[20] His freedom to continue within the church was no doubt due in part to his relatively sympathetic bishop, Handley Moule, who shared his background in evangelicalism and the Keswick Holiness Movement.[21] His first experience of being overwhelmed by the power of the Holy Spirit in 1892 in fact came during a regular communion service, as he read 2 Cor 4:6.[22] After visiting the Welsh Revival in 1904 and initiating "prayer for revival" meetings, subsequent experiences followed—of "holy laughter" during a visit to Thomas Barratt's meetings in Oslo in 1907 (which he later described as his baptism in the Spirit), and eventually speaking in tongues after Barratt's meetings initiated the Pentecostal outpouring in Sunderland in 1907.[23]

The fact that this outpouring was, according to Barratt, accompanied by "many exorcisms of a dramatic nature" will have heightened Boddy's awareness of the supernatural spiritual conflict accompanying the work of the Spirit.[24] He similarly saw signs of the enemy's activity in those who came to the meetings seeking to oppose and cause division.[25] Whilst conflict with evil was not a major theme in Boddy's writings, it is always in the background, particularly in relation to Christ's victory over Satan, and various aspects are mentioned which are paralleled later in the charismatic renewal

---

19. Steven, *Worship in the Spirit*, 11; Wakefield, *The First Pentecostal Anglican*. Harper described him as a "precursor to the Charismatic Movement"—Harper, *As at the Beginning*, 39. Robinson's dissertation includes a helpful comparison between Boddy and Harper—Robinson, "The Charismatic Anglican."

20. Even after his Pentecostal experiences he tended to add extra services (such as evening Pentecostal prayer meetings), rather than change the existing pattern. He saw the Pentecostal outpouring as a renewal movement, "to bless individuals where they are." Wakefield, *The First Pentecostal Anglican*, 30, 181–2; Boddy, *Confidence* 4 no 3, 60.

21. Wakefield, *The First Pentecostal Anglican*, 182.

22. Ibid., 69–70, 185–86.

23. Ibid., 76–89.

24. Barratt describes this as one of the signs marking out this Sunderland revival as extraordinary even in Barratt's own ministry. "*My visit to England*", T. B. Barratt's Diary (unpublished), 5–8, quoted in Robinson, "The Charismatic Anglican," 53–54.

25. "Many came out of curiosity, some deliberately to oppose and cause division. . . . But the enemy made these times for us very trying, 'cranks' and mischief makers . . . came to meetings and caused the writer much pain and anxiety." "The Pentecostal Movement," Boddy, *Confidence* 3 no 8, 195.

in the 1960s. In the very first article in the first issue of *Confidence*, Mary Boddy sets out key beliefs in the power of "His Own Blood" to give "Perfect Victory over sin, disease, and all the powers of darkness."[26] And in the next edition she records "verses given by the Spirit," including:

> But fears will often come; dear Lord,
>
> Lest Satan should deceive;
>
> "Fear not, my child, for thou art safe,
>
> My Blood doth shelter thee."[27]

This theme of the cunning deceit of the devil through doubts and fears, and the right response in magnifying Jesus, is taken up by Boddy himself in the subsequent article:

> But worst of all is the Devil's cunning, using God's children to inject fears and doubts as to our heavenly Father's love . . . shall we yield to man-made doubts and fears, and open the door thus to Satan's emissaries? . . . The pleading of the Blood in the power of the Holy Spirit will put to flight all the powers of darkness. Best of all, let us magnify Jesus until he is so great as to completely shut out the Devil from our thoughts. A great Christ means a very small devil.[28]

The awareness of the Devil's ability to deceive and counterfeit are always in the background for Boddy. This is not surprising, as the Welsh Revival, the Sunderland outpouring and speaking in tongues were at times criticized as being "of the devil"—not only publicly by Jessie Penn-Lewis, who convinced Evan Roberts that much of the Welsh Revival had been demonically inspired and leveled similar charges at Boddy's writings; but such doubts also more painfully affected his own brother-in-law, Pollock, after his dramatic experience of baptism in the Spirit.[29]

The other specific context showing awareness of conflict with Satan is in healing. Boddy considered the victory of the cross to include victory

---

26. Mary Boddy, *Confidence* 1 no 1, 4.

27. Mary Boddy, *Confidence* 1 no. 2, 3.

28. Boddy, *Confidence* 1 no 2, 3–4. Wakefield observes that similar thoughts occur consistently in virtually every edition of *Confidence*. Wakefield, *The First Pentecostal Anglican*, 159.

29. Penn-Lewis describes how she believed Christians can be deceived by Satan in their experiences in Penn-Lewis and Roberts, *War on the Saints*. Pollock had been influenced by the opposition of Reader Harris from the Pentecostal League. Robinson, "The Charismatic Anglican," 61–63; Wakefield, *The First Pentecostal Anglican*, 83, 89.

over disease, and he explicitly states that "sickness is *generally* from Satan or his emissaries."[30] Thus, in his standard procedure for anointing with oil following James 5, he would first "rebuke the sickness, the pain, and all the evil powers behind the disease" (following Luke 4:39), and place the sufferer under the Precious Blood for cleansing and also "for protection from all evil powers, and for victory (Rev 12:11)."[31]

Despite Boddy's role in the early days of Pentecostalism, the latter's influence in the Church of England was to be minimal until charismatic renewal began in the 1960s, and to this we now turn.

2.3 The history of charismatic renewal in the Church of England

There have been some excellent historical studies of the advent of charismatic renewal to the Anglican and other traditional churches in the 1960s and 1970s—most notably Peter Hocken's detailed study *Streams of Renewal*, and also a summary chapter by James Steven.[32] Rather than duplicate such accounts, I shall here summarize the history, but include more detail in relation to many of the pioneers that I studied, in order to give a clearer historical context to their entry into charismatic experience; and where relevant also in relation to the issue of spiritual warfare.[33]

Harper and All Souls

Whilst some of those who initially experienced a baptism in the Spirit through contact with Pentecostals left the Church of England,[34] Pentecostal stirrings especially amongst some of the curates at All Souls, Langham Place from 1962 to 1964 were soon channeled into the emergence of the charismatics as a movement within the mainline churches—particularly through Michael Harper, who resigned from All Souls in July 1964 and founded the Fountain Trust to encourage leadership in the emerging movement.[35]

---

30. Boddy's own italics. Boddy, "Faith Healing in Scripture and Experience," 233; Wakefield, *The First Pentecostal Anglican*, 176.

31. Boddy, *Confidence no 129*, 22; Wakefield, *The First Pentecostal Anglican*, 172.

32. Hocken, *Streams of Renewal*, 67; Steven, *Worship in the Spirit*, 11–37.

33. See chapter 3 for an introduction to these pioneer interviewees, and the history of more theological issues.

34. Notably Richard Bolt, and John Forester of St. Paul's, Beckenham. Hocken, *Streams of Renewal*, 58–65.

35. For a study of the early dynamic of charismatic unity at the Fountain Trust see Au, "Grassroots Unity."

Hocken sees the fervent prayers of some lay parishioners at All Souls as significant in this.[36] Thus, the events that happened around Michael Harper and the other All Souls curates,[37] despite the eventual repudiation of a concept of a post-conversion Spirit baptism by John Stott himself early in 1964, ensured that through these Oxbridge men who were "Anglican to their bones" the charismatic movement became anchored firmly within the national Church of England.[38]

Harper had remained resistant to personal renewal until in September 1962 he was asked to lead a conference at Farnham, Surrey speaking on the book of Ephesians. As he prepared for this, he seemed to experience fresh "supernatural" knowledge coming in "waves of wisdom and understanding," as he prayed for "the power to comprehend" (Eph 3:21).[39] For several months, he frequently preached on the power of the Spirit, and commended the experience of "being filled with the Spirit"; it was only later, through meeting with Philip Smith (from St. John's, Burslem) and his wife in Cambridge in August 1963, and through the visit 3 weeks later of Larry Christenson, that he first began to speak and be released in the gift of tongues.[40]

Burslem and Gillingham

Two Anglican parishes were of particular historical significance in the early stages of renewal—Burslem having the first Anglican priest (Philip Smith) since Alexander Boddy's time to hold "charismatic" prayer meetings in his parish; and St. Mark's, Gillingham as the first parish to be corporately influenced by this move of the Spirit.[41]

In 1962, Philip Hughes had written an influential article in the evangelical journal *The Churchman* describing the wonder of a new movement of

---

36. George Ingram and others began the "Anglican Prayer Fellowship for Revival" in 1959, seeking Pentecostal fullness, and praying for their clergy, especially Michael Harper. Hocken, *Streams of Renewal*, 73–75.

37. The other two were John Lefroy and Martin Peppiatt—Hocken, *Streams of Renewal* 75, 78, 241–42.

38. Hocken, *Streams of Renewal*, 78.

39. Ibid., 75; Harper, *None Can Guess*, 21–22.

40. Hocken, *Streams of Renewal*, 77–78; Harper, *None Can Guess*, 54–55. The sequence of events is detailed in Robinson, "The Charismatic Anglican," 141–44. Whilst later influenced by Philip Smith and others, Hocken notes that Harper was one of a few at this time who came into the initial experience of the Holy Spirit without prior contacts with Pentecostals or early charismatics (and Collins, Watson, and MacInnes only had minimal contact). Hocken, *Streams of Renewal*, 106, 65.

41. *Streams of Renewal*, 91.

the Spirit including speaking in tongues, most surprisingly amongst "high church" American Episcopalians, including Dennis Bennett.[42] Hocken has demonstrated in detail that although the beginnings of renewal in America mostly predated those in Britain, the latter were parallel beginnings rather than a direct transfer across the Atlantic; no American participants visited before summer 1963. However, Hughes' article helped to convey the news of an emerging movement transcending national boundaries yet compatible with existing denominational loyalties.[43] It also particularly encouraged new beginnings amongst evangelicals. For example, this article from a respectable evangelical helped melt the resistance of Philip Smith in the potteries to happenings amongst some of his parishioners, some of whom then prayed with him to receive the baptism of the Holy Spirit, with speaking in tongues and much joyful praise, on 28 September 1962. News of this spread to a prayer group at Gillingham, where Michael Harper happened to be speaking and heard the news in January 1963.[44]

Others were also touched by Smith's ministry, for example Bob Dunnett, later associated with the Birmingham Bible Institute and "Prayer for Revival." Dunnett, after training at Oak Hill College, found himself after his first curacy in a parish in the potteries (Bucknall and Bagnall) from 1960 to 1973. He describes his initiation into "things charismatic" in interview:

> The more I read the book of Acts, I saw that my ministry was not matching up to what I saw there, and realized that the missing factor was the presence of the Holy Spirit; I'd heard about the Pentecostalists, but had thought they were an aberration; but then began to hear about things charismatic, and I and my curate became interested. First my curate got filled with the Holy Spirit, then he prayed for me, and I got filled with the Holy Spirit, though it was not so dramatic, a more gradual affair; and then I got in touch with St. John's, Burslem, and I went along to one of the early Fountain Trust conferences, which blew me out of my mind—but I realized I'd found what I was looking for, and my ministry began to change quite radically . . . it all worked itself out in me in terms of the revelation of spiritual warfare, a deeper understanding of the word, all sorts of aspects as well as particularly the gifts of the Spirit, in church life on that particular estate for about seven years.[45]

---

42. Hughes, in *The Churchman*, 131–35. See Steven, *Worship in the Spirit*, 13; Hocken, *Streams of Renewal*, 110–12.

43. *Streams of Renewal*, 108–14, 128.

44. Ibid., 65–67.

45. According to Hocken, Dunnett was "a recipient [of the baptism] through

At St. Mark's, Gillingham, a move of prayer was the most noticeable factor that led to the outbreak of renewal. An associate of George Ingram in Gillingham, Arthur Harris, persuaded Collins to support the idea of a Night of Prayer in Gillingham;[46] but the Collinses also sensed that people's prayers opened the way for this, such as their curate David MacInnes, who took days off monthly to earnestly pray for a new dimension.[47] Michael Harper fortuitously stood in for a cancelled speaker at the preliminary meeting on 26 January 1963; and the actual night vigil during which the Holy Spirit fell was on Friday, February 1st, attended by over thirty, despite heavy snow.[48] For three weeks to a month "many felt they were walking on air," and Collins also recalls an immediate fresh awareness of spiritual warfare subsequently:

> It was very interesting, shortly after I went up to London, I noticed a reaction of people who'd come up in a sort of spiritual warfare that seemed to react to my presence, would shake their fists in my face, quite obviously demonic . . . and dogs fawned on me . . . .[49]

All this reinforced for John and Diana Collins the importance of prayer in the spiritual battle.[50] St. Mark's, Gillingham was also significant for further opening up the reality of "spiritual warfare" for Harper, when (at Collins' invitation) leading a holiday houseparty for young people from St. Mark's in Sussex in Aug/Sep 64.[51] A talk on spiritual warfare exacerbated the rebelliousness of the youngsters, but after praying for some to be filled with the Holy Spirit, more followed; and there was a dramatic transformation in

---

Smith's ministry around 1965." Dunnett (Interview 11.7.07) clarified that this was when he received the gift of tongues—he and his curate had prayed for each other earlier and received the baptism of the Spirit independently. Ibid., 65–67, 68.

46. He was ashamed that a lay working man was more willing to pray through the night than his vicar—Collins Interview 30.4.04.

47. Diana Collins (interviewed with John) believed that his days of prayer "paved the way for the woman who asked if we would have a night of prayer." Collins Interview 30.4.04

48. Different clergymen spoke an hour each, one on repentance, one on the cross, then Collins gave a talk on Luke 11:13, and at about 2.20am the Spirit fell on the whole meeting. Some had never felt such a sense of the presence of God, and still rejoicing at 7am did not wish to leave. Collins Interview 30.4.04; also Hocken, *Streams of Renewal*, 92.

49. Collins Interview, 30.4.04.

50. "Nothing grows without the spiritual battle in prayer being given top priority." Diana in Collins Interview 30.4.04.

51. Hocken, *Streams of Renewal*, 249, footnote 15.

the young people, which encouraged Harper in this new ministry involving "spiritual warfare."[52]

David Watson, after ordination at Cambridge in 1957, had like MacInnes chosen to become curate in St. Mark's, Gillingham under John Collins, whom he knew would provide excellent training in parish evangelism.[53] However, in September 1962, before these nights of prayer, Watson had moved back to Cambridge, to the Round Church for his second curacy. Here a spiritual hunger grew, until after some long personal studies in the Beatitudes with much prayer during that same winter of 1962/3, "I had a quiet but overwhelming sense of being embraced by the love of God," but with no other startling manifestations.[54] Even though he came to understand this not as a "second blessing" but a filling with the Spirit,[55] his entering into charismatic experience gradually painfully forced him to go his own way in championing charismatic renewal amongst Anglicans; he was excluded from CICCU[56] when it was heard he spoke in tongues, and was eventually cold-shouldered at his beloved "Bash Camps."[57] He then became the second charismatic Anglican, after Michael Harper, to publish a book on "spiritual warfare."[58]

The renewal spreads

Initially, around 1963, Hocken identifies three clusters of charismatic experience, partly geographical and partly theological-denominational—the "independents" (such as Lillie and Arthur Wallis, focused on the South West),

---

52. Harper, *None Can Guess*, 89–91. See also chapter 3.2.

53. *Towards the Conversion of England*, London: Church Assembly, 1945—as quoted by Saunders and Sansom, *David Watson*, 44–45.

54. Watson knew significant had happened at the nights of prayer after he left Gillingham, contributing to his own expectation that God would meet with him. Watson, *You Are My God*, 53–54; Saunders and Sansom, *David Watson*, 61.

55. "It was a major step forward for him, certainly, but not a step upward into a different category. It could only be classed as a "second blessing" in that it came between the first and the third in a long series." *David Watson*, 67.

56. The strongly evangelical Cambridge Inter-Collegiate Christian Union.

57. Saunders and Sansom, *David Watson*, 84–85. Watson first went in 1955 to help on this evangelical camp for public schoolboys at Iwerne, Dorset, founded in 1932 by Scripture Union worker Rev Eric Nash, nicknamed "Bash"; he eventually attended 35 Bash Camps. Ibid., 28–30. Other evangelical Anglicans who became prominent renewal leaders, including my interviewees Collins, MacInnes (who had encouraged Watson to attend), and Green, had also developed a love for the Scriptures and evangelism through these camps.

58. First published as Watson, *God's Freedom Fighters*.

those around Philip Smith in the potteries and the Midlands, and the cluster of Anglican evangelicals around Harper and Collins in the South East. The networking between these around the visits of Larry Christensen and David Du Plessis[59] helped give birth to the Fountain Trust under Harper in 1964.[60]

Right from the beginning, some Anglican sacramentalists and Anglo-Catholics were touched by the renewal of the Spirit, notably William Wood.[61] Two who became more prominent were Michael Meakin and John Gunstone.[62] Colin Urquhart was another prominent high church Anglican, and the story of renewal at his catholic parish of St. Hugh's, Lewsey became well known.[63] He became a popular speaker at Fountain Trust Conferences.[64] However, after leaving St. Hugh's in 1975 to minister more widely, he became increasingly independent of Anglican structures.[65] Michael Harper in setting up the Fountain Trust specifically sought "to serve every section of the Church, without fear or favor," and his contacts who had attended conferences came from a number of backgrounds; nevertheless, amongst the larger group of Anglicans, the evangelicals were clearly in the majority.[66] Although the first Anglo-Catholics to attend found the evangelical bias something of a culture shock, they were encouraged by the experience of High Churches in the renewal in the American Episcopal Church and beginnings in the Roman Catholic Church, and were able to adapt the Pentecostal emphases to their theology, also organizing annual pilgrimages to Walsingham from 1974 which grew into the annual Anglo-Catholic

---

59. For example, Simon Barrington-Ward after his return from Nigeria to Cambridge got to know David Watson in 1964, and was taken by him to hear David du Plessis in Westminster Chapel where he was filled with the Spirit. Barrington-Ward Interview 20.4.04. Barrington-Ward thus became a regular at the Fountain Trust meetings, and like Watson, Walker, MacInnes, and Collins, also spoke at them (see Fountain Trust tape archives in St. John's College Library, Nottingham).

60. Hocken, *Streams of Renewal*, 115–19, 129.

61. From the London Healing Mission. Wood's contact with Pentecostals such as Agnes Sanford, Donald Gee and David du Plessis led him to promote "baptism in the Spirit" probably before any other Anglicans, although he never became a prominent figure in the emerging movement. See chapter 9 in ibid., 50–55.

62. Gunstone became the most articulate spokesman for the renewal amongst Anglo-Catholics—see ibid., 102–3; Steven, *Worship in the Spirit*, 18; Gunstone, *A People for His Praise*.

63. See Urquhart, *When the Spirit Comes*.

64. Steven, *Worship in the Spirit*, 18.

65. See Urquhart, *Faith for the Future*, 9–20, 101–2.

66. See Hocken, *Streams of Renewal*, 105–6, 118. Similarly, charismatic Christianity is less prominent now amongst Anglo-Catholics but has permeated much of mainstream evangelical Anglicanism.

Charismatic Convention at High Leigh.⁶⁷ The moving of the Episcopalian Graham Pulkingham and "the Fisherfolk" to Britain greatly influenced the introduction of charismatic worship styles into a wide range of Anglican churches, including David Watson's St. Cuthbert's in York, and St. John's, Harborne, Birmingham through Tom Walker.⁶⁸

Three events were particularly significant for charismatic Anglicans in the late 1970s. Firstly, *Gospel and Spirit,* the report of dialogue between charismatic and non-charismatic evangelicals, was published in 1977, leading to greater reconciliation (and charismatic style worship) at the NEAC conference later that year.⁶⁹ Secondly, the first international conference of charismatic Anglicans was held before the 1978 Lambeth Conference, climaxing in an extended Eucharist in Canterbury Cathedral with Bill Burnett (Archbishop of Cape Town) leading the bishops in a liturgical dance at the altar.⁷⁰ And thirdly, Colin Buchanan (principal of St. John's, Nottingham, heavily influenced by renewal) asked the 1978 General Synod to prepare a report on charismatic renewal, which he and John Gunstone and others then published.⁷¹ This report highlights spiritual warfare as one of seven distinctive facets of the "sub-culture" of the Anglican charismatic renewal. The report notes that this is not new (though the demonic may largely have been overlooked for a century and a half⁷²), but there is a new mood with a renewed awareness of the demonic, a sense across the movement that "we wrestle . . . against principalities and powers," often with a desire to discern the invasion of the devil and be committed to this battle. With the increase in the practice of exorcism, some "stupendous deliverances" had

---

67. The Anglo-Catholic Bishop of Pontefract, Richard Hare becoming publicly charismatic also increased their confidence and influence. Steven, *Worship in the Spirit,* 18–19.

68. Ibid., 19–20.

69. Ibid., 20.

70. This led to the founding of S.O.M.A. (Sharing of Ministries Abroad) in 1979, which still sends ministry teams and networks charismatic renewal across the Anglican Communion.

71. Buchanan et al., "The Charismatic Movement in the Church of England." John Gunstone played a key role in this, and in editing the later report commissioned by Archbishop Carey on healing, Perry, Gunstone, and others, "A Time to Heal."

72. A footnote asserts: "Indeed some would go so far as to argue that this aspect ought not to be dealt with under the heading of 'sub-culture' at all, but that the movement's involvement in this marks the recovery of a 'holistic' gospel thrust that rehabilitates the classical trio of preaching, healing, and deliverance from unclean spirits [Matt 10:5–8]." Buchanan et al., "The Charismatic Movement in the Church of England," 51n18.

New centers for renewal

Historically 1980 was a significant year marked by the "humanly astonishing decision" to close the Fountain Trust, which sensed that renewal was well enough established in the parishes and churches for its role to come to an end.[74] Whilst the independent Restorationist networks grew and developed at this time,[75] various Anglican centers of renewal continued, some becoming even more significant in the 1980s and 1990s. The Church of England report had included several of these; apart from those already mentioned (e.g., St. Hugh's, Lewsey, and St. Michael-le-Belfrey, York), the authors particularly highlighted St. John's, Harborne in Birmingham, under Tom Walker.[76] I shall also use Birmingham here as an example of how renewal, and the "spiritual warfare" associated with it, developed in such centers (particularly in relation to three interviewees, Walker, MacInnes, and Dunnett).

Walker's move into charismatic experience was also mediated through St. Mark's, Gillingham. For some time he had been in "the middle of the battle area" in the early 1960s around the phrase "baptism in the Spirit"; his own dramatic conversion in his student room at Keble College, Oxford in 1954 during a mission with John Stott had been for him truly a baptism in the Spirit empowering him in various ways.[77] However, whilst a little wary of it, he appreciated not only the excitement and enthusiasm of friends for their new life in the Spirit, but also their graciousness, humility, and depth of insight, and a new power in their evangelistic ministry (including stories of healing and deliverance from evil powers). One of these friends was David

---

73. Ibid., 37–38.

74. The Trust had remained predominantly Anglican (also its three directors, Michael Harper, Tom Smail, and John Richards); charismatic Anglicans still valued such a service agency, as seen from the founding of Anglican Renewal Ministries, with regular Swanwick conferences, and magazine *Anglicans for Renewal*, from 1980. Steven, *Worship in the Spirit*, 23–24.

75. See Walker, *Restoring the Kingdom*.

76. They also included St. John's College, Nottingham, which had become known as being more open to charismatic renewal; by the mid-1970s more than half of its ordinands were charismatic. Buchanan et al., "The Charismatic Movement in the Church of England," 15–21.

77. The Spirit since conversion had brought the Bible alive, gave him a great desire to pray, called him into full-time ministry, guided him, and in evangelism even spoke biblical words through him before he had even read them. Walker, *Renew Us by Your Spirit*, 62–63.

Watson, with whom he shared university mission work.[78] Watson invited Walker to a young people's weekend at St. Mark's, Gillingham to minister, "but found that I was the one who was being ministered to." The spirit of love and willing service amongst the youth impressed him, as well as their quality of worship, both in quiet reverence and glad praise. His eyes alighted on 1 Cor 14:4,[79] and he suddenly saw that the gift of tongues was significant for building him up, and during worship his opposition to receiving tongues broke. As InterVarsity Fellowship secretary driving to visit a Christian Union the day afterwards, as he prayed through Paul's prayer in Ephesians 1, he was released into praying and praising in tongues.[80] Three years later in 1967, Walker joined the staff of Birmingham Cathedral working alongside David MacInnes, already more experienced in charismatic renewal.[81] Whilst MacInnes stayed on at the Cathedral as Diocesan Missioner,[82] Walker in 1970 took on the evangelical parish of St. John's, Harborne, which he was to see transformed into a key center for charismatic renewal in the Midlands.

When Tom Walker began at St. John's, it was a "successful" but inward-looking middle class evangelical church that had stopped growing, and he sought to develop a strategy to transform and widen its impact, principally through changes in prayer, worship, evangelism, and strengthening the dynamic of fellowship and lay ministry in the church as the living body of Christ.[83] However, he saw all this against the backdrop of specific spiritual warfare, which he gave as a key factor in the conversion growth of the church.[84] Concerning prayer, he started the weekly "Open to God" prayer

78. Ibid., 10–12, 24–26.

79. "He who speaks in a tongue edifies himself." Walker realized he "had been fighting God" over the issue of tongues, scared of being labeled as a Pentecostal freak. Ibid., 34.

80. As the same thing was happening to his wife Mollie praying at home, unknown to him. Walker immediately found it to be a fruitful aid in his prayer life, and ministry among students. Ibid., 39–43.

81. "I was sent to Birmingham Cathedral . . . , and working with David MacInnes, who was much more advanced and aware than I was in this whole area [of spiritual warfare]." Walker Interview 28.3.04.

82. MacInnes was on the staff there for twenty years, from 1967–87.

83. His strategy is described in Walker, *Open to God*.

84. Asked how much the church grew at St. John's, Walker responded: "When I arrived they were talking at St. John's of scrapping the evening service because the numbers were down below sixty and . . . my predecessor said to me, 'it's amazing that here we are in an evangelical church with Jim Packer who was one of my curates, and we haven't seen any conversions for nine years.' I later discovered that that was due to specific spiritual warfare that would never have been overcome apart from charismatic insights, the awareness of God's power, the ability to minister in difficulty." Later the evening service grew to over 500. Walker Interview 28.3.04. He also writes: "I could no

and worship meetings focused on listening to God for inspiration—"it took us years [here] to learn how to worship the Lord." It was here, having discovered that some who seemed to hear the opposite of what he preached were attending a spiritualist meeting at a local school, that such places and events were brought in specific prayer.[85] In evangelism, despite his previous success in youth ministry, Walker found here a fear that prevented young people (even from church families) from coming; "having discernment . . . we had a lot of Christian adults whose children had all fled the nest without faith . . . God showed us that we had to pray," and gradually a thriving youth ministry developed. As his ministry grew, Walker also depended on the prayer of others for evangelism and mission.[86] Although Walker had resisted the temptation to write much on spiritual warfare as he did not want to be the devil's publicity agent, he eventually saw the value of "prevention is better than cure," and wrote a booklet focusing on how people get drawn into magic, superstition and witchcraft, to help young people "make a hasty retreat before it is too late."[87]

Birmingham became a place where Walker, McInnes, and others helped spiritual warfare gradually develop at citywide and even diocesan level. Walker quotes John Wesley with approval:

> [Wesley] recorded in his journal in January 1750: "I rode to Birmingham. This had been a dry uncomfortable place; so I expected little good here: but happily I was disappointed." We could say the same over the years, mainly because of the praying people . . . who have provided that primary prayer backing which is essential for supporting such ministry against a powerful enemy . . . as we looked for more of God, so we did indeed find more of him.[88]

---

longer play games at ministry, nor could we as a church order our life according to the pattern of a social club, irrelevant to the spiritual battle raging in the 'heavenly places.' We had rather to become God's commando corps, contending against 'the world rulers of this present darkness.' (Ephesians 6:12)." *Renew Us by Your Spirit*, 70.

85. Another specific instance brought to the group for prayer was when a witch from Wimbledon Common came up and daubed insignia on the church; it then felt inexplicably cold near this wall. Walker Interview 28.3.04.

86. "Because I had two parishes, was on twenty-four diocesan committees, had 16 parishes in the Deanery that I was responsible for and a world-wide ministry of evangelism. I could never do what Bob Dunnett did in making that a thrust of prayer. I could only rely on being part of my local home base to resource me and everyone else in all our ministry. But yes prayer is fundamental [in evangelism and mission]." Walker Interview 28.3.04.

87. Walker, *The Occult Web*.

88. Walker, *Renew Us by Your Spirit*, 76.

MacInnes also often sensed being in a battleground; for him this was a positive sign, that when the Spirit was working intensely on the offensive in major spiritual advance, the conflict is accentuated; and at times the Spirit may lead us into the wilderness. He mentions one period when his wife was helping someone who had been partly involved in the occult when "for a few weeks the whole spiritual dimension was acutely apparent to both of us . . . I could see demonic entities in the street, it was most exhausting. I learnt how God protects us from that for a very long time. But also the power of God was just overwhelming too . . . if you stepped outside of that you were immediately vulnerable."[89] MacInnes and Walker started a small group praying for renewal in Birmingham, where they were often aware of being in a battle;[90] and this grew and developed in different ways in the future—not least through "Prayer for Birmingham," led for a while by Bob Dunnett.[91]

There was also encouragement in ministry and mission in Birmingham, and growth in understanding, as others came to minister and teach. Firstly, John Richards worshiped at St. John's whilst teaching courses at Queen's College in 1971–72 on deliverance and exorcism, bringing in several experts.[92] Secondly, practitioners such as Pentecostal pastor Jean Darnell and David Smith (formerly lay reader at St. Mark's, Gillingham) came and did four-day missions at the Cathedral, and regularly taught the clergy of Birmingham, all of which helped Walker to learn "by apprenticeship,"[93] and to spread understanding of these issues across the diocese. Walker also learned from those from other backgrounds, such as Archdeacon Perry who edited the official Anglican report on the subject,[94] and later Dominic

---

89. MacInnes Interview 6.4.06. In the same way he sensed heightened conflict in seasons when the Spirit was moving with great power and intensity—in the 1960s, when Wimber came, and in the 1990s the Toronto and associated waves—for him at St. Aldate's, Oxford coming more as a wave of repentance.

90. "In fact, the clearest evidence of the power of God working in those times of prayer for Birmingham was the exceedingly great reluctance with which some of us attended them. It was as though the enemy tried hard week after week to prevent us attending, and time and again God turned [this] reluctance into a time of superabundant blessing." Walker, *Renew Us by Your Spirit*, 88–89.

91. See chapter 3.6. The development of united prayer breakfasts in Birmingham, "asking God to break through in our unbelieving city" encouraged Walker, who lamented how easily the church had been "preoccupied with problems and divisions, rather than uniting with those who know the life-changing reality of God to batter the citadels of Satan and the massed defenses of modern materialism." Ibid., 57.

92. Whilst writing his classic study of deliverance ministry, *But Deliver Us from Evil*.

93. Walker Interview 28.3.04.

94. Perry, *Deliverance*.

Walker[95] from a more Catholic background, appreciating his ordered mind and insight on what was psychological and what was spiritual.

The Church of England report on charismatic renewal recognized that the increase in the number of exorcisms had produced some "stupendous deliverances," as well as raising some doubts and anxieties; resulting in the Bishop of Exeter commissioning a report on exorcism.[96] In places study and training for leaders became more formalized, and groups formed in a number of dioceses. MacInnes had approached Bishop Brown in 1973 about setting up such a study group, but it was laughed at initially until a couple of years later the film *The Exorcist* came out, and Archbishop Ramsey asked all bishops to make some preparation for pastoral dealing with people affected by the film. MacInnes and Walker both belonged to the exorcism group in the Birmingham Diocese. There was thus a much wider sharing, ministry in cinemas, and (especially after the tragic Barnsley case in 1975,[97] which aroused a greater desire to understand this spiritual dimension), seeing some Christians (such as a vicar who was a completely skeptical scientist, and a New Testament academic from Selly Oak) totally revise their theologies as a result of attending deliverance prayer sessions.[98] MacInnes saw all this as very significant—"rather like tongues it was challenging rationalism. I can't say it would change the face of the Church of England but it would make the Church of England aware of the spiritual dimension." Eventually Walker became the resource person for this, or "diocesan exorcist." Following the Church of England's report highlighting the "renewed awareness of the demonic" that the charismatic renewal had brought, by the mid-1990s the Church of England had appointed at least one official exorcist in each diocese, and bishops liked to be kept informed about exorcism matters.[99]

---

95. Later on, when Walker was Archdeacon in Southwell, and helped organize speaker meetings with people like Dominic Walker. Walker Interview 28.3.04.

96. Petitpierre, *Exorcism*; Buchanan, Craston, and others, "The Charismatic Movement in the Church of England," 37–38.

97. A man, having been the subject of an all night exorcism, savagely murdered his wife; this was reported with much sensationalism in the secular press, such as *The Sun* on 26.3.75. See Robinson, "The Charismatic Anglican," 209.

98. "[This academic] was very liberal, a very good man but he said, 'I've always interpreted the demonic in terms of psychology and yet I've seen something here which I have to say I see as being much more in keeping with Biblical interpretation.' So he revised his New Testament lectures. It was having a real impact in that way." MacInnes Interview 6.4.06.

99. Buchanan et al., "The Charismatic Movement in the Church of England," 37–38; Scotland, *Charismatics and the New Millennium*, 149–50.

Wimber and signs and wonders

Like St. John's, Harborne in Birmingham, some centers took on local or regional significance in the late 1970s and 1980s, such as St. Michael-le-Belfrey in York, or St. Aldate's, Oxford under Michael Green.[100] But two centers in or near London became associated with new waves of renewal in the 1980s and 1990s. The first was St. Andrew's, Chorleywood, which initially came into renewal under John Perry catalyzed by visits from Michael Harper in 1964.[101] St. Andrew's had also hosted missions from John Collins and David Watson, and visits from other leading charismatics, such as Dennis Bennett. After Perry moved to be warden at Lee Abbey (another renewal center), missionary Bishop David Pytches was appointed vicar there in 1977 when he returned to England from Chile. He had recently come into personal renewal and overseen significant growth through charismatic renewal in the Anglican church in Valparaiso,[102] also having his first dramatic experiences alongside others of praying for people to be delivered from evil spirits.[103]

In Chorleywood, Pytches found himself searching for a model to help equip the laity to use their charismatic gifts in the work of the ministry—and when John Wimber first came across at Pentecost, 1981, he was impressed with Wimber's humility and the common ground he shared with evangelical charismatic Anglicans.[104] After getting over the unorthodox and controversial approach of Wimber and his team,[105] he began a fruitful cooperation over a number of years with Wimber, whose visit to an Anglican Evangelical convention at St. Andrew's in 1982 proved to be a turning point towards the church becoming one of the leading centers of renewal in Britain.[106]

---

100. Green's *I Believe in Satan's Downfall*, published in 1980, was the third book by an Anglican charismatic concerning evil and spiritual warfare—the most theological, and also the most controversial. See chapter 3 for Oxford as a center, also involving two more interviewees, John Woolmer and Jane Holloway.

101. Harper, *None Can Guess*, 87; Hocken, *Streams of Renewal*, 101–2.

102. Pytches, *Living at the Edge*, 141–44, 222.

103. Pytches Interview 1.4.04.

104. Wimber was influenced by Anglicans such as Jim Packer, John Stott, and Michael Green in his evangelical theology, and charismatics such as Harper, Watson, and Tom Smail. Pytches, *Living at the Edge*, 255–56. However, whilst Hunt recognizes Wimber's ministry as a natural step forward for many charismatic Anglicans such as David Watson, what Hunt sees as a profound theological dualism in spiritual warfare, and the Fuller Seminary emphasis on signs and wonders, seem less obviously compatible with Anglicanism. Hunt, "The Anglican Wimberites," 108, 111–12.

105. Pytches, *Living at the Edge*, 256–58.

106. Hunt, "The Anglican Wimberites," 111; Pytches, *Does God Speak Today*, 5. Wimber later encouraged Pytches to write a practical handbook for charismatic ministry which became influential—*Come, Holy Spirit*; *Living at the Edge*, 266.

His friendship with David Watson also helped Wimber to gain wide acceptance with the charismatic movement, particularly Anglicans, following Watson's death in 1984.[107] At his meetings and conferences, undramatic teaching was followed by often dramatic "ministry times" preceded by the invitation "Come, Holy Spirit."[108] As Percy puts it, "for Wimber the kingdom of God is a kingdom of power—announced, then practiced, which overthrows the controlling power of Satan."[109] One regional leader deeply touched at Wimber's first big 1984 conference in Westminster Central Hall was Robert Warren, vicar of St. Thomas Crookes in Sheffield, who then organized a number of such conferences in the late 1980s in the North of England. He commented that their experience of renewal had been "running out of steam," but these conferences became a turning point; not only did growth return to St. Thomas's after a plateau in 1984 to 1985, but through local leaders' training weekends hundreds of people had been trained in this style of ministry by 1987.[110] Other regional centers also emerged, for example in Manchester.[111] There is little doubt that Wimber's emphasis on church growth and evangelism did result in many churches enjoying significant growth, even on some rare occasions in inner city areas.[112]

In the South St. Andrew's, Chorleywood remained a key center, also holding leadership days sending out "Faith Sharing Teams" to other parishes; and soon many charismatic parishes had set up "ministry teams."[113] Although many Anglicans influenced by Wimber's ministry eventually left

---

107. See chapter 21 in Saunders and Sansom, *David Watson*. Michael Mitton described Wimber as "one of [Watson's] parting gifts to the church." Mitton, "Editorial."

108. The main teaching themes were moving out of a Western rationalistic worldview, the kingdom of God invading this present age particularly through "signs and wonders" of healing and casting out demons, and Jesus's emphasis on training his disciples to continue this ministry. See Steven, *Worship in the Spirit*, 27–28; Wimber and Springer, *Power Evangelism*.

109. Percy, *Words, Wonders and Power*, 18.

110. Warren, *In the Crucible*, 191, 203–8. I also interviewed Warren, see chapter 3.

111. Hunt notes that Anglican structures allowed the freedom for networks of "special subject groups" to emerge especially within dioceses in geographical clusters, such as around a dozen in Manchester, where David Hughes annually organized Vineyard conferences. Hunt, "The Anglican Wimberites," 115.

112. St. Michael-le-Belfrey in York grew to over a thousand, St. Barnabas's in north London under John Coles from forty to 360 (Hunt); but Gunstone highlights Holy Trinity, Parr Mount, a deprived Merseyside neighborhood, growing to over two hundred and sending faith-sharing teams to more affluent areas, as being "a wonder in the biblical sense of the word." Gunstone, *Signs and Wonders*, 82–88; Hunt, "The Anglican Wimberites," 107, 116.

113. Springer, *Riding the Third Wave*, 173–75; Steven, *Worship in the Spirit*, 29–30; Springer, *Riding the Third Wave*.

and joined the new Vineyard Christian Fellowships that younger Anglican clergy persuaded Wimber to sanction in the late 1980s, nevertheless the New Wine summer camps that Pytches started at Shepton Mallet in 1989, and the associated New Wine Network of leaders, remain a focus for large numbers of Anglican charismatics.[114] New Wine also gave rise to Soul Survivor, an equally successful conference for young people that, under the leadership of Mike Pilavachi (former St. Andrew's youth leader), mobilized Christian youth to help communities in Urban Priority Areas in Manchester, Watford, and elsewhere.[115]

Post-Wimber, the Toronto Blessing, and Alpha

The other center which was to become even more significant in the 1990s and beyond was Holy Trinity, Brompton. John Collins became vicar there where he ministered from 1980 to 1989, joined by Nicky Gumbel as curate in 1986. Collins and his successor, Sandy Millar, also welcomed Wimber's ministry, such that "HTB" became a base during Wimber's conference visits, and a big channel of influence for Wimber into the Anglican churches;[116] and was to become even more well known as a key center of the next wave of charismatic phenomena, which became known as "the Toronto Blessing."

Wimber's original "signs and wonders" theology was in itself controversial;[117] but as the Wimber phenomenon developed in the late 1980s, certain emphases emerged which became even more so. Whilst Pytches and others remained supportive of Wimber's association with Paul Cain and the Kansas city prophets,[118] which took the emphasis on "words of knowledge" and the prophetic to a new level and heightened revivalist ex-

114. Pytches, *Living at the Edge*, 322–26, 358. Out of eight hundred churches represented at New Wine camp in 1994, a "sizeable majority" were Anglican; an estimated twelve hundred Anglican clerics were on the Vineyard's regular mailing list. Hunt, "The Anglican Wimberites," 107. In the late 1990s Pytches handed over the leadership of the New Wine Network to John Coles, still overall leader in 2015.

115. Pytches, *Living at the Edge*, 327–31.

116. Sandy Millar is credited as saying "Wimber has had a greater impact on the Church of England than anyone since John Wesley." Hunt, "The Anglican Wimberites," 106, 16. This extended to some Anglo-Catholic leaders such as John Gunstone, who reconciled Wimber's healing ministry with the stress on the sacraments. Gunstone writes positively concerning Wimber's ministry, though cautioning that "it is dangerous to try and minister deliverance in a public meeting" as often happened in Wimber's conferences. Gunstone, *Signs and Wonders*, 110.

117. For example, see Pratt, "A Review of the Debate," 7–32.

118. He wrote a book based on his experience supporting their ministry. Pytches, *And Some Said It Thundered*.

pectations, other charismatic leaders became more critical, such as Michael Mitton, who saw this revivalism as distancing him from many in Anglican charismatic renewal, perhaps the beginning of a post-Wimber Britain.[119] Wimber also initially lent support to the phenomena associated with the "Toronto Blessing" that spread to Britain primarily (but not exclusively) from the Airport Vineyard in Toronto. A number of observers gave positive assessments of the fruit of this experience (including leading Anglican charismatics such as Mitton and Green).[120] However, this "fourth wave" of renewal was probably the most divisive; Scotland in his careful analysis generalized that since Toronto two distinct strands of charismatic Christianity seem to have emerged, "revival charismatics" who talked up such phenomena who supported Toronto, and others with roots in the earlier Fountain Trust emphasis often standing more aloof.[121]

Even though within its first year as many as three thousand churches were experiencing the "Toronto Blessing," one criticism was that it rarely seemed to cause much church growth; however, Holy Trinity, Brompton was a notable exception to this.[122] And then in the wake of the Toronto Blessing, the Alpha course that began there in the early 1990s took off beyond all expectation. According to statistics from Christian Research, in 2007 more than one and a half million people completed Alpha around the world (15 percent more than in 2006), and ten million had completed it worldwide since 1993. Whilst Pytches saw this as perhaps the fulfillment of Paul Cain's prophecy of revival spreading from London in 1990, in John and Diana Collins' view the worldwide expansion of the Alpha course is largely due to the leadership of Jeremy Jennings, whom God had given a special gift of leading big prayer meetings.[123] The spread of Alpha has no doubt been a factor in ensuring that a basic understanding of spiritual warfare remains part of the charismatic tradition, as one course session examines the question "How do

---

119. Mitton, "Editorial," *Anglicans for Renewal*, 45 (Summer 1991). Steven also cites criticism from Andrew Walker who noted Cain's earlier association with the even more controversial William Branham. Steven, *Worship in the Spirit*, 33.

120. See ibid., 33–36; Scotland, *Charismatics and the New Millennium*, 220–50. Both refer to the positive assessment of a well-known physician—Dixon, *Signs of Revival*, chapter 5.

121. Scotland, *Charismatics and the New Millennium*, 247.

122. Ibid.

123. Pytches Interview 1.4.04; John and Diana Collins Interview 30.4.04. The latter defined "spiritual warfare" broadly as "prayer," so for them the spread of Alpha was a consequence of those at "HTB" having learned to take the spiritual battle in prayer seriously.

we resist evil?," arguing for taking the existence of a personal devil seriously, quoting Michael Green's *I Believe in Satan's Downfall* in support.[124]

Charismatic controversies over spiritual warfare

Alongside these developments, occasional controversies surfaced in relation to particular practices and theologies of spiritual warfare. At the end of the 1980s, the term "territorial spirits" began to be used and publicized, particularly by former South American missionary and Fuller Theological Seminary lecturer C. Peter Wagner, in relation to what he called "strategic-level spiritual warfare."[125] Even though John Wimber often worked together with Wagner at Fuller and in conferences, he himself distanced himself from the emerging emphasis that the key to evangelization was to identify and pray against the particular ruling spirits over neighborhoods, cities and nations, concerned over the lack of biblical references and specific teaching on how to handle "principalities."[126] Some charismatics argued against the concepts, seeing them perhaps forming a modern mythology uncritically taking on pre-modern, non-Western worldviews of evil spiritual beings and gods.[127]

Around the same time, the "March for Jesus" movement arose out of the growing popularity of the songs of one charismatic songwriter, Graham Kendrick, and his ability to combine this new style of worship with a witness to the gospel, prayer for the nation and a demonstration of Christian unity, beginning with the "Make Way" open-air musical processions in 1987.[128] Whilst this was often highly effective in mobilizing Christians from different backgrounds to come together, some remained critical of its underlying

---

124. See Gumbel, *Questions of Life*, 150–52. It is not surprising that this has a prominent role in the course, as the prototype for Alpha was in fact Michael Green's "Beginners Course" used at St. Aldate's, Oxford, which Gumbel experienced whilst training at Wycliffe Hall. Green, *Adventure of Faith*, 40.

125. See Wagner's edited collection (including an excerpt from Michael Green's *I Believe in Satan's Downfall*)—Wagner, *Territorial Spirits*.

126. Ibid., 39. Pytches recalled this also in interview—"I remember when we were in London, the first conference, some of [Wagner's] people were casting out the demonic spirit over London and I was quite impressed with this, you know. And John shook his head and said 'you don't do it that way.'" Pytches Interview 1.4.04.

127. See Reid, *Strategic Level Spiritual Warfare: A Modern Mythology*; Lowe, *Territorial Spirits and World Evangelisation?*.

128. Steven, *Worship in the Spirit*, 31; "Praise Marches." See also Ediger, "Proto-Genesis of March for Jesus."

theology, with its emphasis on "reclaiming the ground" by taking authority over territorial spirits.[129]

Certain "deliverance ministries" also attracted some controversy. The conferences and writings of Bill Subritsky from New Zealand emphasized casting out demons and identifying and naming demons, and his approach was very influential on the setting up of a center specializing in deliverance ministry at Ellel Grange under Peter Horrobin.[130] Whilst some clearly benefitted from such ministry, some of their methods and theology has been called into question by a number of observers.[131]

A perhaps healthier development was that some individual Anglican ministers seemed to develop special gifting and emphasis on this area, whilst nevertheless primarily operating out of a local church, for example the ministry of the often eccentric Peter Lawrence in the outer estates of Birmingham.[132] Occasionally there were accounts of where crime and poverty seemed to have been affected in deprived estates through Anglican ministry with an awareness of the power of prayer in spiritual warfare in bringing some social transformation, though examples are hard to find.[133]

Reactions to some of the excesses of the deliverance ministry in the 1970s and 1980s meant that its popularity decreased in the 1990s, although it was still practiced in some charismatic circles. Collins notes that there is much evidence to suggest it frequently became routinized; an example of this was the popular ministry of Neil Anderson, emerging out of the Third Wave and popularized in Britain through "Freedom in Christ" courses; this "represents a wider return to more orthodox and thoughtful Evangelical

---

129. Most of Kendrick's "March for Jesus" songs "provided a vehicle for combining theological instruction with spiritual activity, particularly in the area of prophetic ministry and spiritual warfare." O'Sullivan, "Roger Forster and the Ichthus Fellowship." Kendrick himself states in his Song Book introduction: "Satan has the real estate of villages, towns, and cities overshadowed by ruling spirits which work untiringly at his command to bring about his malevolent will . . . ," quoted in Scotland, *Charismatics and the New Millennium*, 136.

130. Horrobin and Subritsky hosted *The Battle Belongs to the Lord* conferences in Brighton and elsewhere in the 1980s, following which Ellel Grange was purchased as a center.

131. See for example Parsons's case studies, some of which were "casualties" from ministry at Ellel Grange—Parsons, *Ungodly Fear*. David Pytches found that some would return from Ellel Grange and say they had had large numbers of demons cast out and six months later be back in the same position—such that he preferred such ministry being based in the local church. David Pytches Interview 1.4.04.

132. Vicar of Christ Church, Burney Lane, Birmingham from 1979 to 1993. See Lawrence, *The Hot Line*, 6.

133. See Brown, *Angels on the Walls*.

forms of confronting demonic oppression."[134] A newer form of such "routinized" deliverance ministry we shall find surfacing in the main case study church in chapter 4.

---

134. James Collins, "Deliverance Ministry in the Twentieth Century."

3

The Origins and Development of Charismatic Spiritual Warfare

A Study of Some Anglican Pioneers

HAVING DESCRIBED THE "LIFEWORLD" of the historical context in which spiritual warfare concepts arose in the Anglican charismatic renewal, we now focus on "spiritual warfare" itself as seen through the eyes of key leaders and practitioners. The church has always had its theological positions concerning evil, and traditionally this invariably included a theology that recognizes the existence of evil spiritual forces, in the form of Satan and demonic forces of various kinds. However, especially since the Enlightenment, active theological debate in Western theological circles in this area was often almost entirely relegated to philosophical deliberations concerning the problem of the existence of evil, with little discussion of how such a belief might affect the Christian's worldview and practical spirituality. In Protestant theology, this was particularly true as a result of the Reformation and its Enlightenment thinking, when the power of reason called into question the whole basis of demonic activity and tended to dismiss much popular spirituality (venerating of images, healing shrines, holy places, etc.) as scornful superstition. This rationalistic thinking still largely prevailed in the Universities and seminaries where Anglican priests, such as Michael Harper and David Watson, received their theological training.[1]

However, for those who became associated with charismatic renewal in the mid-1960s, a change was soon noticeable. Within a decade, two of the most prominent Anglican renewal leaders had published books of a practical nature on "spiritual warfare." Indeed, the first published use of the term appears to be *Spiritual Warfare*, Michael Harper's book published in 1970;[2]

---

1. Harper noted this effect of the Enlightenment in his own discussion of the history of "spiritual warfare"—Harper, *Spiritual Warfare*, 39–40. Harper feels that in almost entirely dismissing evil spirits the Reformation "poured out the baby with the bath water." *Jesus the Healer*, 35.

2. The other book was Watson's *God's Freedom Fighters* (1972), reissued in 1980

although it had already appeared in 1966 in *Renewal* under his editorship.[3] In the Fountain Trust conferences which influenced many early charismatics in Britain, the topic was highlighted by speakers such as Arthur Wallis,[4] and the Anglican David MacInnes.[5] In view of the considerable influence of some of these early Anglican charismatic pioneer leaders such as Michael Harper, David Watson, David MacInnes and Tom Walker, as well as Michael Green (who wrote the third book on the subject) and David Pytches in the 1980s and 1990s, both the origins and main features of the theology and spirituality of "spiritual warfare" of these (six) leaders are an important subject for investigation, and the main focus of this chapter. I also included three Anglican charismatics who became practically involved in spiritual warfare in a quieter way behind the scenes, and have remained significant and influential in the practice of spiritual warfare both in and beyond Anglican circles in this country (John Woolmer, Bob Dunnett, and Jane Holloway); and three others who were "spiritual fathers" who helped encourage the growth of Anglican renewal, but had not written anything publicly on the subject (John Collins, Robert Warren, and Simon Barrington-Ward).[6]

These are the twelve I selected to study, for the reasons given as well as ease of access, where there might have been many more.[7] It thus does not claim to be a comprehensive historical analysis of the development of spiritual warfare thinking, but rather a series of interlinked descriptive "case studies" of key pioneers in various aspects of Anglican charismatic spiritual warfare in the latter half of the twentieth century. In so doing, I drew on transcripts of interviews with each one of them,[8] and also their written works and some secondary sources. Here I shall first describe the historical development of spiritual warfare theology for three key writers (Harper,

---

as *Hidden Warfare*.

3. Notably in a 1966 main article headline in *Renewal* 3—Harper, "Ministry in Spiritual Warfare."

4. "Knowing Our Enemy and Knowing Our Position in Christ: The War of Possession," and "Prayer Warfare: Binding and Loosing" were talks given in 1977 (St. John's Nottingham Library: Fountain Trust Tapes F139).

5. MacInnes, *Conflict with the Devil*.

6. As noted in sections 1.4 and 2.3, nearly all were also active in some of the key centers of charismatic renewal in England.

7. Others I considered, and in some cases spoke to, were Graham Dow, John Richards, Mike Stibbe, Colin Gunstone, Tom Smail, Colin Urqhhart, Martin Cavendish, Sue Hope (for many years involved in Anglican Renewal Ministries), Wallace Brown (author of *Angels on the Walls*) and others.

8. With the obvious exception of David Watson, who died in 1984—though I interviewed his colleague and worship leader in York, Andrew Maries. I thus generally refer to the group as "pioneers" rather than "interviewees."

Watson, and Green); then summaries a comparative analysis of the theology and spirituality of all twelve, highlighting some similarities and differences; and in conclusion summarize how they developed and validated their concepts of spiritual warfare, and some of the influences upon them.

3.1 Introduction to Interviewees

Biographical information for Harper, Green, and Watson is included in chapter 2.3 and section 3.2 to 3.4 below. The majority of interviewees were interviewed between 2004 and 2006, except Robert Warren who was interviewed in 2008.[9]

John Woolmer, originally a Mathematics teacher at Winchester College (where he witnessed a mini-revival[10]), trained at Westcott House and then St. John's, Nottingham; he served his first curacy under Michael Green at St. Aldate's, Oxford, based at St. Matthew's in South Oxford, from 1975 to 1982, where he became unexpectedly involved in deliverance ministry. In his next parish in Shepton Mallet, Somerset, his experiences were more centered on places than people; and a number of trips ministering abroad with SOMA[11] brought him again into more direct contact with people affected by spiritual powers, especially in rural Zambia.[12] In Britain he has continued to teach and write on areas of prayer, healing and deliverance, and also angels,[13] as well as regularly assisting evangelist J. John in the prayer preparation for his citywide "just10" missions.[14]

John Collins was the son of a Church of England vicar, and after public school and a spell in the RAF studied for ordination at Cambridge, where he was one of the most outstanding presidents of the Christian Union (CICCU).[15] Like Harper, but before him, he spent several years (1951–57)

---

9. Appendix 1 shows the interview schedule I used in this last of my interviews. It is a slight simplification of the interview schedules used for the other interviewees, but which all covered essentially the same areas. In analysis (see Appendix 2), section C (*Origins and Influences*) together with E(1) is largely reflected in Table 4; otherwise I sought to highlight 10 main questions that came to the fore concerning the ontology and nature of evil, the nature and extent of spiritual conflict, and praxis; and these are summarized in Tables 1 to 3.

10. One of the pupils converted was Mark Stibbe, who later became a leading charismatic Anglican theologian.

11. See section 2.3, footnote 70.

12. Woolmer, *Healing and Deliverance*, 26–27.

13. Ibid.; *Angels*; *Thinking Clearly About Prayer*.

14. For example, during one I attended in Birmingham in 2005.

15. Saunders and Sansom, *David Watson*, 44.

as a curate at All Souls, Langham Place, and then became vicar of St. Mark's, Gillingham, a struggling dockers' parish which he was to utterly transform with the help of two curates, first David MacInnes, later joined by David Watson in 1959. He was also vicar of Holy Trinity, Brompton from 1980 to 1989 (where Nicky Gumbel, who founded the Alpha course, became curate in 1986), during the time John Wimber's ministry became prominent in London, and Holy Trinity became one of the main centers. His wife, Diana, was often his partner in prayer and ministry, and they were interviewed together.

David MacInnes trained for ordination at Ridley Hall, Cambridge (55–57) a year ahead of David Watson, whom he also preceded by a year as curate under John Collins at St. Mark's, Gillingham (57–61). His own experience of being filled with the Spirit came on his own shortly after leaving to join Dick Lewis at St. Helen's, Bishopsgate (61–67), and he was a regular attendee and speaker at Fountain Trust conferences. From here he moved to the staff of Birmingham Cathedral for twenty years (67–87), becoming Diocesan Missioner (79), and then took over from Michael Green as Rector of St. Aldate's, Oxford in 1987, until retirement in 2002.

Tom Walker (having been dramatically converted as an Oxford student in 1954), went to train for Anglican ordination at Oak Hill (1958–60). After his second curacy at St. Leonard's-on-Sea (1962–64), for three years he was travelling secretary for the InterVarsity Fellowship (during which a visit to St. Mark's, Gillingham helped release him in charismatic renewal). Walker moved to the staff of Birmingham Cathedral in 1967, joining David MacInnes. In 1970 he took on the evangelical parish of St. John's, Harborne, which he gradually transformed to be a key center for charismatic renewal in the Midlands, and stayed there until he became Archdeacon of Southwell, Nottingham in 1991 until retirement in 1997.

Bob Dunnett was baptized in the Spirit whilst ministering in the Potteries in the early 1960s. He has since been much appreciated both for his teaching ministry (especially during his time at Birmingham Bible Institute from 1972 to 1996, as Vice-Principal from 1984 onwards), and leadership and support behind the scenes in promoting prayer, both in the City of Birmingham and more widely in the country during his leadership of "Pray for Revival" from the late 1980s to beyond 2000.

Jane Holloway has been active since the late 1970s in the ministry of prayer, intercession, and evangelism (especially organizing and delivering training for city-wide missions in UK, North America, and New Zealand);[16]

---

16. Drawing on her "vast experience of setting up mission ventures" (Green, *Adventure of Faith* 132), she co-authored Green and Holloway, *Evangelism through the Local Church*. In interview she recalled organizing up to thirty city-wide missions in UK, America, Canada, and New Zealand.

working alongside Canon Michael Green firstly as his personal assistant for fourteen years both in Oxford and Canada (where he was Professor of Evangelism in Vancouver), and then around Britain with "Springboard" (the Archbishop of Canterbury's initiative for the decade of evangelism in the 1990s);[17] and more recently with various para-church organizations and prayer networks.[18] Having come to faith in the charismatic renewal in the 1970s, she brings her own insights into "spiritual warfare" issues from years of involvement in practical prayer and intercession. Like Bob Dunnett, she remains an Anglican attending an Anglican church, but has a much broader experience, as many of the prayer and mission networks increasingly work across denominational boundaries.

David Pytches was appointed as a missionary Bishop for Chile, Bolivia, and Peru, where he oversaw the growth of the Anglican Church there after renewal broke out in the 1970s. He returned to become vicar of St. Andrew's, Chorleywood in 1977, and was initially instrumental together with David Watson in hosting John Wimber and his Vineyard conferences in the UK from 1981. Out of this "Third Wave" Pytches started the New Wine summer camps at Shepton Mallet in 1989, and the associated New Wine Network of leaders, which is still a focus for large numbers of Anglican charismatics. He continued to speak out on areas of charismatic controversy such as the Kansas City Prophets,[19] and the "Toronto Blessing" in the 1990s; and continued to be a significant figure in supporting emerging charismatic leaders[20] and promoting creative Anglican church planting initiatives.[21]

Robert Warren was a curate under Michael Baughen in Manchester (65–68), and after second curacy in Wolverhampton took over St. Thomas, Crookes in Sheffield in 1971, remaining there until 1993. After a major rebuilding project, it became a center for charismatic renewal especially after hosting some of John Wimber's Vineyard conferences in the 1980s.[22] He was appointed by Archbishop Carey as a National Officer for Evangelism in 1993, writing also on leadership and to help churches move "from mainte-

---

17. See ibid. She has also written articles on prayer and intercession—e.g., Holloway, "Understanding Intercession."

18. Notably prayer secretary (also evangelism) with the Evangelical Alliance for nine years, then since 2005 with the World Prayer Centre based in Birmingham.

19. Pytches, *And Some Said It Thundered*. The classic *Come Holy Spirit* (1985) was on spiritual gifts generally; he later wrote on handling local prophetic ministry—*Prophecy in the Local Church*.

20. Such as mentoring Mike Pilavachi into leadership in the Soul Survivor church plant and camp, aimed at young people. See Pytches, *Leadership*.

21. See for example Pytches and Scotland, *Recovering the Ground*.

22. Most of the story is told in Warren, *In the Crucible*.

nance to mission."[23] In 2010, he continued to provide mission development consultancy to Anglican churches of all kinds.

Simon Barrington-Ward trained at Magdalen College, Cambridge where he stayed on as chaplain (56–60) before becoming a CMS[24] missionary in Nigeria (60–63). When he returned as a Fellow at Magdalen (63–69) he was invited by David Watson to attend a meeting with David du Plessis where he was deeply touched by the Spirit. He served CMS as Principal of Crowther Hall (69–74) and then General Secretary (75–85) before being appointed Bishop of Coventry from 1985 until retirement to Cambridge in 1997.

3.2 Michael Harper: pioneer origins

After evangelical conversion at Cambridge in 1951,[25] Michael Harper changed from law to theology, then studying for the Anglican priesthood in a thoroughly evangelical setting at Ridley Hall. Here he imbibed a traditional evangelical view of spiritual warfare, including a belief in Satan and the power of evil, that Christ has given us victory, and the idea of putting on the whole armor of God (Ephesians 6); but this was all in his mind, whereas the reality of it was very little.[26]

We have seen how Harper remained resistant to personal renewal until preparing to speak on the book of Ephesians at a conference in September 1962. In particular, through the prayers of Ephesians 1 and 3, he seemed to experience what Paul described as revelation knowledge (*epignosis*) coming to him as fresh "supernatural" knowledge in waves of wisdom and understanding, "the power to comprehend" (Eph 3:21), seeing this prayer as unashamedly one for power, a new kind of power that he found gradually (but not compulsively) taking over inwardly.[27] It was not till several months later that he first spoke in tongues.[28]

In interview, Harper commented that the whole thing about spiritual warfare came at a very early stage. He wrote in his first autobiography "we were . . . pitch-forked into this ministry";[29] as described earlier in *Spiritual*

23. *On the Anvil*; *Building Missionary Congregations*; *Being Human, Being Church*.
24. Church Missionary Society (now re-named as the Church Mission Society).
25. Described in Harper, *None Can Guess*, 13–14.
26. Interview 20.4.2004.
27. Hocken, *Streams of Renewal*, 73–75; Harper, *None Can Guess*, 21–22.
28. See 2.3 for details.
29. He gives two linked examples of a lady and a man in an Anglican church who expressed the desire to be filled with the Holy Spirit; but nothing happened initially as

Warfare, stumbling on it unexpectedly through personal experience and a vivid awareness of this reality that significantly changed his practice, for example in responding to a phone request he might otherwise have ignored.[30]

A significant early event was a holiday houseparty in Aug/Sep 1964,[31] for young people from St. Mark's, Gillingham (under his friend John Collins). The youngsters were disinterested and rebellious; after a talk on "spiritual warfare," "Satan overplayed his hand: for the next two days he gave us such blatant demonstrations of his nasty tactics that everyone recognized his attacks."[32] However, after Harper spoke on the need to be filled with the Spirit, a number of young people were filled, such that the leaders asked for further opportunities to receive until "there was hardly a young person not filled with the Spirit";[33] the boy with the broken arm was healed (later demonstrated by X-ray), as were others too, such that Harper concludes:

> As fast as young people were being taken sick, the Lord was healing them through the laying on of hands. If anyone had ever doubted before the reality of Satan's power, and the greater power of the name of Jesus, they would never doubt it again. It was truly spiritual warfare, and Jeanne and I were encouraged in this new ministry which was opening up to us.[34]

The vicar, John Collins, wrote in a letter afterwards concerning the extraordinary transformation of the young people, all full of joy and life.[35]

Clearly Harper sees this experience as something of a paradigm for him; he describes how many times "one has had the same kind of experience, with the most difficult time being in the middle of the conference, "winning through in prayer," and then the moment of victory, and the

---

"there seemed to be some blockage." The lady broke down, confessing she had become absorbed in witchcraft and begging for deliverance; she was filled with the Spirit after a prayer of confession. The other manifested with animal noises; "we bound the powers of darkness which were tormenting this man, and cast out evil spirits until he was completely freed." After prayer to be filled with the Holy Spirit, he was "quickly filled to overflowing and spoke fluently for many minutes in an unknown tongue." Harper, *None Can Guess*, 139–40.

30. See *Spiritual Warfare*, 56.

31. Hocken, *Streams of Renewal*, 249, footnote 15.

32. He lists sudden accidents such as a broken arm, strange illnesses, the young people feeling inexplicably miserable and homesick, and the youth leaders becoming rebellious. Harper, *None Can Guess*, 89.

33. There were almost fifty young people present—Hocken, *Streams of Renewal*, 94.

34. Harper, *None Can Guess*, 90.

35. Ibid., 91. Being impressed with these young people's spiritual life helped remove Walker's resistance to receiving the gift of tongues—see chapter 2.2, and Walker, *Renew Us by Your Spirit*, 33–34.

mopping up operation that follows."[36] In this instance, then, it would seem that the description of "spiritual warfare" was used by Harper primarily to describe the hindrances that seemed to occur as they were seeking to lead people into the baptism of the Holy Spirit, and the "victory" was effected mainly through those involved entering fully into this charismatic experience. His first experiences of a need for deliverance ministry also arose in the context of a desire to be filled with the Holy Spirit.[37]

Experiences such as these battles were so significant that even before he published *Spiritual Warfare* in 1970, in 1968 his short book on how to live life after being filled with the Spirit begins the main section with the words: "Many of the important stages in our lives as Christians are anticipated or followed by satanic attacks. It was strikingly true in the experience of Jesus Christ . . .",[38] and he makes direct references to Satan and our warfare with him throughout this chapter ("In the Wilderness"), and later in the book. For example, chapter 5, "The Gospel of the Kingdom" begins with likening our conflict with guerrilla warfare where enemy agents are everywhere and attack from every direction, seeing the message that Jesus preached centered on "the Kingdom" was primarily concerned with delivering people from the power of Satan.[39] Experience had not been his only teacher however—he first uses the term "spiritual warfare" in describing the influential visits of two Dutch evangelists in the early days of the Fountain Trust.[40]

Development of a charismatic theology of spiritual warfare

The way the context of his practical experience provoked Harper into a study of spiritual warfare is spelled out in the introductory chapter to his book, *Spiritual Warfare*. He begins with an example at a Fountain Trust conference in November 1965 of the surprisingly dramatic change in an ordained minister after Dennis Bennett prayed for his deliverance from evil

36. Harper, *None Can Guess*, 90.
37. Ibid., 139–40.
38. *Walk in the Spirit*, 25.
39. Ibid., 49–50.
40. Kees Noordzij, and de Graaf, early in 1966. Noordzij ministered "baptisms in the Spirit and deliverance from bondage to evil spirits, and healings" in nearly every place, and gave "practical instruction in personal ministry" in relation to "delivering others from bondage and sickness." Harper, "Ministry in Spiritual Warfare." Harper was already publicizing taped talks on "spiritual bondage and warfare" by Edgar Trout, Arthur Wallis, and Dennis Clark. *Renewal* 2 (Mar/Apr 66). Bob Dunnett, who attended early Fountain Trust conferences, commented that "those early charismatics, they were all acutely conscious of [spiritual warfare]." Bob Dunnett Interview 28.3.04.

powers.[41] This incident leads Harper to describe three main reasons for writing the book:

1. The reality of the spiritual battle raging, often "behind the façade of religious life."[42] The reality of this battle, and the need for the church to see this spiritual dimension so that it can engage in this battle effectively, was still a concern of Harper's in 2004.[43]

2. That he is concerned with "spiritual warfare in general" and not just "with discerning and expelling of evil spirits in particular, which is one part of the total conflict."[44]

3. He perceived that the world situation at the time of writing was one of "expanding supernaturalism, good and bad," with the charismatic revival on the one hand, and on the other "a resurgence of the power of evil supernaturalism on a truly daunting scale. This book is written to alert people to this spiritual warfare and the dangers of ignoring it."

In chapters 2 to 4, he summarizes his biblical and historical perspective on spiritual warfare; then in the "Devil's Pentecost"[45] (chapter 5), he describes some current phenomena such as witchcraft, divination, cults, spiritualism and moral decay as signs of a resurgence of such forbidden evil supernaturalism.[46]

---

41. *Spiritual Warfare*, 11–12.

42. "There seem to be many who are not fully aware of this warfare. From time to time there is a dramatic collision between the power of the Spirit and that of Satan. In that meeting that night Satan's grip on a young minister was first exposed and then loosed by the power of God. The battle will often not be as sharply defined as this; but it is no less real." Ibid., 12–13. Harper's language of "collision" is reminiscent of Wimber's later terminology of "power encounter."

43. "It does seem that as you've got enormously carnal powers in the world today, so at another level you have Satanic powers, and spiritual warfare at a spiritual level, which of course is why a lot of the church doesn't see it, because it doesn't see the spiritual dimension, the world doesn't see it, that's all the more important why we need to see it, we need to do battle against it." Interview 20.4.2004.

44. Quoting in support from Unger, *Biblical Demonology*, 1.

45. He links this with the visions in Revelation (notably 9:1–11, "locusts" released from the abyss, deceiving and destroying), where "the activities of evil spirits are foretold as part of the total conflict of the Church with the powers of darkness."

46. Harper here draws considerably from Merrill F. Unger. Harper, *Spiritual Warfare*, 13, 26, 29, 43; Unger, *Biblical Demonology*. Unger, an American evangelical Old Testament professor at Dallas Theological Seminary (1948–67), like Harper is critical of a church that denies the existence of the enemy, thus unable to warn against him or expose his craft. *Demons in the World Today*, 187; Harper, *Spiritual Warfare*, 13. Harper

In considering the nature and power of the enemy, Harper holds to the traditional and evangelical view that Satan & evil spirits are fallen angels;[47] and that just as there was a rebellion (by people) on earth against God's power, so there was in heaven. We are thus dealing with personalities, like God's angels, not impersonal influences.[48] Harper is careful to not only warn of the dangers of "denying the existence of evil spirits and Satan, and taking an unrealistic and benevolent view of the world and man in it," but also the dualistic error of "attributing most, sometimes even all, evil and sin to Satan and demonic activity."[49] Such dualism attributes everything that happens either to a divine or satanic cause, with no place for natural or human factors.[50] For him, one of the Achilles heels of charismatic renewal is its natural instinct to become dualistic, tending to over-spiritualize everything, not giving a real place for the human dimension, of man made in the image of God.[51]

Thus, Harper emphasizes that Satan and demons do not have unlimited power, only what we allow them to have; man has free will, and with God there is a strong emphasis on synergy with the church—God has chosen to exercise his omnipotence through the free will of man, thus developing the divine in the human along the same lines as the divine. Similarly, just as there needs to be a strong place for the human, he also sees the natural as a separate dimension—natural events like earthquakes, etc., are part of the world God has created, part of the fallen side of the world if you like; yet they can be an arena for spiritual warfare, for God uses these sort of occasions, and Satan uses them too—so it is worth seeking God's protection against Satan's desire to mess things up (so he and his wife always pray before they go out in the car).[52] And if our physical bodies are the temple of the Holy Spirit, they will also be a target of Satan; so spiritual causes of

---

also draws support from of Kurt Koch's detailed case studies on occultism, particularly in his denunciation of spiritualism. Koch, *Between Christ and Satan*; Harper, *Spiritual Warfare*, 48.

47. For example, based on the fall of the "day star" in Isa 14:12–14, whilst recognizing that the Bible says very little about the origin of evil—*Spiritual Warfare*, 19.

48. Interview 20.4.2004. Ibid., 32.

49. Ibid., 17.

50. Ibid., 93.

51. Robinson notes in 1976 that Harper's "acceptance of a degree of natural theology and the consequent avoidance of dualism has been of great value in maintaining stability," through *Spiritual Warfare*, Fountain Trust conferences, and through recommended reading. See also Harper's criticism in *Renewal* of Don Basham's over-dualistic approach—"Deliver Us from Gullibility," 128; Robinson, "The Charismatic Anglican," 209.

52. Interview 20.4.2004.

illness can be specifically demonic ones (requiring casting out of evil spirits as Jesus sometimes did), a more general Satanic attack, or caused by sin or the sin of others; he thus emphasizes the need for discernment in healing ministry, as well as a compassionate spirit.[53]

Harper often strikes a note of caution, noting the need to protect against the dangers of deception.[54] In *Spiritual Warfare*, he suggests that those engaging in deliverance ministry should do so under the general permission of the bishop (for Anglicans) and the control of the local church,[55] then describing our weapons (chapter 8) and our protection in the armor of God, the name of Jesus, and the angelic hosts (chapter 9).[56] Significantly, one of three safeguards he lists is "the mind of Man," the power of reason—not normally high on such a list for Pentecostals or charismatics.[57] This accords with his character, predating his charismatic experience;[58] it is also a key feature of Anglicanism, even in its charismatic manifestation, as in Hooker's "tripod" of Anglican foundations: Scripture, reason, and tradition; although by openly relying on his own experience in developing a charismatic theology of spiritual warfare, Harper equally follows Wesley, who departed from his Anglican roots by introducing "experience" as the fourth pillar of revelation.[59]

3.3 David Watson: evangelist and inspirational leader

Watson also came to charismatic experience from previous conversion into the evangelical tradition, strongly reinforced through the Bash Camps that produced many evangelical leaders.[60] However, his entering into charismatic experience gradually painfully forced him to go his own way in championing charismatic renewal amongst Anglicans.[61] He was the second to write a

---

53. Harper, *Spiritual Warfare*, 95–96.

54. After two deliverance accounts, Harper concludes: "In no area is there need for greater caution than in this one," warning of possible harm from inexperienced or over-zealous ministry. *None Can Guess*, 140.

55. *Spiritual Warfare*, 62.

56. Ibid., 72–92.

57. *As at the Beginning*, 120.

58. As noted by fellow students at Cambridge—Robinson, "The Charismatic Anglican," 130.

59. Unlike Wesley, Harper helped the renewal to stay within the Anglican and other denominational churches. Ibid., 208–9.

60. See chapter 2.3.

61. He was excluded from CICCU when it was heard he spoke in tongues, and eventually cold-shouldered at his beloved Bash Camps.

book on spiritual warfare, essentially the published text of Bible studies he had given at Filey;[62] he further elaborated its teaching in later works.

Watson never saw himself as a serious theologian; much influenced by Billy Graham, he saw his role in teaching primarily as to build faith. Watson's hermeneutical approach remains characteristically evangelical in style—he regularly begins his writing with a text and exposition of it. His introduction to his book on spiritual warfare begins with Eph 2:1–7, contrasting the ways of those who follow "the prince of the power of the air" with God who in the riches of his mercy has delivered us from the power of the world, the flesh and the devil[63]—but who has "set us *free to fight*," such that "every single Christian is a freedom-fighter engaged in Christian Warfare," quoting Eph 6:12.[64] However, like Harper, Watson highlighted spiritual warfare because of his own personal experiences in ministry, linked to the evil he saw in the society around him at that time—after citing Eph 6:12, he gives his three reasons for writing as *the intense reality of this warfare,* which for example he saw in preparing these studies, both in his family and to some extent in his church; *a marked increase of satanic activity* in Britain at that time (especially forms of spiritism and occult); and the *sad ignorance of Christians,* or forgetfulness, about this warfare, which often left him overwhelmed in ministry by its casualties, "depressed, defeated or oppressed by some dark powers, or suddenly filled with doubts." He thus prays that his Bible studies will help Christians to "fight the good fight of faith," believing that "there are few subjects which are more important for us to tackle seriously than this, . . . and few subjects which seem to be so little understood."[65]

Unlike Harper, however, as time went on his awareness of the spiritual battle was particularly heightened because of his continuing role as a prominent evangelist. We see clearly his own hermeneutical approach in a significant passage in *I Believe in Evangelism,* where he integrates his own experience and key Scriptures (in Ephesians, Corinthians) as a basis for a

---

62. Filey Bible Week was initially set up to teach converts from the Billy Graham crusades in the early 1950s.

63. This foundational approach continues in chapter 2, "Dying to be Free," concentrating on Romans 6, significant for both him and John Collins in entering into fullness of the Spirit (Collins Interview 30.4.04, Hocken, *Streams of Renewal* 96). Here he reveals the influence of evangelicals such as Lloyd Jones and Watchman Nee, and the lasting impact of meeting Corrie ten Boom at Gillingham. Watson, *God's Freedom Fighters,* 45.

64. Ibid., 11.

65. Ibid., 11–13.

passionate appeal to his hearers to be ready to battle in prayer (and fasting) for blindness to be removed as the gospel is preached.[66]

Out of some difficult years lived in community in York, came what he considered his most important and lasting book, *Discipleship*; a key book on the nature of the church, which devoted a twenty-five-page chapter to the church as the army of God.[67] What has clearly developed since the earlier days is a deeper understanding of the link between human vulnerability and the enemy's attacks.[68] Thus, he recognizes how important it is to be quick to put right wrong relationships,[69] the way the "roaring lion" will often bring or exploit mental afflictions such as depression amongst Christian workers,[70] and he recognizes with Bonhoeffer the deep cost of discipleship.[71] He also explores how "suffering, although evil, does not always mean tragedy";[72] as proved true later in his own battle with cancer, which led him to a deep,

---

66. "One of the most crucial lessons to grasp in evangelism is that we are engaged in a powerful spiritual warfare. Behind the apathy which Paul found so hard to overcome in his day (as most of us do today), there is the god of this world blinding the minds of unbelievers . . . [quotes 2 Cor 4:4]. Therefore whether we realize it or not, we are battling with unseen Satanic forces as we urge people to turn from darkness to light and from the power of Satan to God. Nowhere does Paul speak so clearly about this as in Ephesians, Chapter 6. . . . He particularly asks them to pray for him 'that utterance may be given me in opening my mouth boldly to proclaim the mystery of the gospel.' Paul knew the absolute folly of trying to proclaim the gospel without Spirit-inspired prayer. How can we expect to see miracles of new birth taking place without much prayer, and possibly fasting as well? How can we ever see men and women brought out of Satan's kingdom into God's Kingdom, unless we humbly acknowledge our own utter weakness and call upon God for his strength? [ref. 2 Cor 10:4–5]." *I Believe in Evangelism*, 181–82.

67. Having been a junior officer himself (1952–53), he naturally adapts Winston Churchill's "blood, toil, tears, and sweat" speech before the Battle of Britain as a closing exhortation to a disciplined life for the army that "God is preparing . . . to fight against the powers of darkness that rage in the world." *I Believe in the Church*, 140–64.

68. This book was the most difficult he had ever written, during testing times living in community, and "tense problems in the church in York." *Discipleship*, 13. See Saunders and Sansom, *David Watson*, 137–38, 152–60; Watson, *You Are My God*, 163–71.

69. "If there is any break in fellowship between two Christians, the devil will be quick to exploit it." *Discipleship*, 182–83.

70. As directly affected Spurgeon and Luther. Watson acknowledges the notorious difficulty in discerning root causes here, suggesting there may be an interplay of physical and psychological factors, the fallen nature, and demonic attack. Ibid., 173–74.

71. Discipleship can lead to the way of the cross from which the devil will attempt to dissuade us; and also the struggle in living in the world but not being of the world. Ibid., 235–7. "Obedience to the gospel in a world where Satan is still active means living in tension. This is part of the meaning of the Incarnation." Bonhoeffer, *Cost of Discipleship*, 89; Watson, *Discipleship*, 242.

72. He cites the example of Richard Wurmbrand, tortured in his prison cell yet dancing with praise. *Discipleship*, 254.

revolutionary experience of God's presence, and "a love that casts out all fear."[73] Despite special prayers for healing from John Wimber with whom he had forged a special relationship, David Watson died in February 1984.

3.4 Michael Green: evangelist theologian

Neither Harper nor Watson had the level of scholarship and academic theological attainment to be able to systematically propose a theology of spiritual warfare influenced by charismatic experience. Michael Green, however, who had before Watson attended the "Bash Camps" and also studied at Ridley Hall,[74] was already a Theological College Principal (St. John's, Nottingham, 1969 to 1975) when he entered into charismatic renewal.[75] He has written or co-authored more than fifty books since 1964,[76] and has had wide experience of charismatic renewal in the Anglican Communion, from its earliest days here to provinces such as Canada, South Africa and South East Asia. He has also had particular influence in Anglican theological development.[77] Even though he does not consider himself to be an expert on spiritual warfare,[78] his views on what he considers a vital topic[79] and reflections on his wide personal experience are thus of special value in this study.

73. Saunders and Sansom, *David Watson*, 232–33. His biographers here refer to his own struggles chronicled in his final book, Watson, *Fear No Evil*.

74. After evangelical conversion at Clifton College, Bristol in 1944, he soon joined the Iwerne "Bash Camp"; and later helped in its leadership, gaining basic teaching and pastoral skills and a heart for evangelism. He became president of the Christian Union (OICCU) at Oxford, and confirmed a sense of call to ordination. After two years National Service, in 1955 he embarked on a research degree at Ridley Hall, Cambridge during training. Green, *Adventure of Faith*, 7–13.

75. He has been described as a rare example of those who "combine profound learning with evangelistic zeal and vision" (Carsten Thiede); such are his "variety of gifts, and . . . range of experiences" that "he is able to evaluate first-hand many different ministries, movements, and controversies." (Dr John Stott). Ibid., ii,iii.

76. See list in ibid., 395–96.

77. On the Doctrine Commission of the Church of England in 1967, and consultant at the Lambeth Conference in 1968; and after Regent's College, Vancouver (1987–92), he returned to launch the Archbishop's Springboard initiative of the Decade of Evangelism. Ibid., 394.

78. Michael Green Interview 18.3.04. He only wrote *I Believe in Satan's Downfall* after failing as series editor to persuade David MacInnes (who considered himself not so proficient at theological writing) to write on the subject. David MacInnes Interview 6.4.06.

79. "I think it is enormously significant and one that . . . none of us take seriously enough except the lunatic fringe that can talk about nothing else," going on to underline that the existence of an anti-God force is plain in both Testaments, as well as in the

Like many other evangelicals, Michael Green believed there was a force of evil from which it was part of his spirituality to seek deliverance, and that "the New Testament has a lot to say about Satan," but beyond that had never really thought about spiritual warfare, certainly not the idea of "spending major time in company with others beseeching the Lord to break the power behind the presenting situation," which was now clearly part of his understanding and practice;[80] and he used to be "very dubious" about challenging evil forces in the name of Christ and driving them out.[81] But once he experienced renewal in the Holy Spirit early in the 1970s,[82] like others that he knew he found that there came "an acute awareness of the unholy spirit" almost "in a double pack."[83]

He then moved to the busy Oxford parish of St. Aldate's,[84] which (partly through the influence of David Watson, and a regular prayer meeting that spontaneously arose[85]) he soon led into a powerful experience of charismatic renewal.[86] He began to write briefly on spiritual warfare in *I Believe in the Holy Spirit*,[87] including an assessment of evangelistic preaching being a "titanic confrontation" with the principalities and powers of Eph 6:12 in

---

world both East and West. He later added, "I think it's an absolutely vital thing, this spiritual battle, I just wish that I was stronger in prayer myself, because I know it easily gets squeezed out." Michael Green Interview 18.3.04.

80. Michael Green Interview 18.3.04.

81. Green, *Adventure of Faith*, 265.

82. Firstly, when the pastor of St. Margaret's Church in Vancouver prayed and prophesied over him, "you're not going to get tongues at any rate now, you're going to get the wisdom to run your college," then in 1973 receiving tongues on a visit to Singapore through Bishop Chiu Ban It. Michael Green Interview 18.3.04, ibid., 259–60; *Asian Tigers for Christ*, 8.

83. Michael Green Interview 18.3.04; see also *Adventure of Faith*, 279.

84. He was Rector there for twelve years from 1975 to 1987. In the middle of this period, from 1980 to 1982, I attended St. Aldate's and had personal experience on his ministry teams.

85. "In those early days, David Watson and I were very close friends . . . he brought two if not three visits to St. Aldate's, and it was through those things really and through the experience that I'd gained in different parts of the world that the renewal spread." Michael Green Interview 18.3.04.

86. Green found himself "gifted to a greater or lesser extent in tongues, healing, and deliverance," and had to wrestle with how to introduce such gifts without dividing the congregation. Green, *Adventure of Faith*, 267.

87. In his assessment of the charismatic movement at that early stage, he notes that "increasing numbers of Christians are finding that they are called upon to perform exorcism these days . . . we in the West have too long pooh-poohed the idea of demon possession, and we are paying for our arrogance by a marked increase in demonic activity." (*I Believe in the Holy Spirit*, 201–2.)

a passage echoing that of Watson.[88] A few years later these were developed into a full-length book on the subject, *I believe in Satan's Downfall*.

The subject at this time grew significantly in importance for him:

> When I was brought face to face with the naked evil in someone in this most sophisticated city of Oxford who was deeply into the occult and deeply into the dark arts and was manifesting all over the place, it was as hairy as it could be. I realized then what I wouldn't have realized before, namely, that I can't minister in this effectively on my own and secondly, that I can't do it without a prayer backing behind.[89]

This was only one of a number of significant cases requiring deliverance ministry he was confronted with at Oxford.[90] Such cases still did not cause him to major on the issue of spiritual warfare, but it became significant when such cases arose;[91] and also as he became more aware of the spiritual battle involved in evangelism during special times of mission, as I also experienced during my two years at St. Aldate's (1980–82).[92]

Some development can be discerned in this area in his theological writing. One of his early and most scholarly works, *Evangelism in the Early Church* (1970), keeps a certain "academic distance" as Green makes

---

88. "The preacher is involved in a titanic confrontation, in which he is a tiny Lilliputian. He becomes aware that 'the god of this age (i.e., the devil) has blinded the minds of those who do not believe' . . . every effective preacher knows that proclamation involves not mere communication, but confrontation. 'For we are not contending against flesh and blood, but against principalities and powers, against the world rulers of this present darkness' (Eph 6:12) . . . a preacher can talk till he's blue in the face, but he can never bring anyone to faith in Christ. Yet the Holy Spirit can take his words home to the conscience of the hearer . . . ." Ibid., 70.

89. Michael Green Interview 18.3.04. John Woolmer shared this experience in 1975/76; it threw both of them into "deliverance ministry, which was a big surprise" (Woolmer Interview 16.3.06). He describes the case in Woolmer, *Healing and Deliverance*, 24–26. Green also refers to this "memorable initiation," and help from Watson's church—Green, *Adventure of Faith*, 265–66.

90. In his first five years at "supposedly sophisticated Oxford" he saw "more of it than in the previous eighteen years of my ministry." *I Believe in Satan's Downfall*, 114. Jane Holloway, then his PA, remembers writing these cases up in preparation for *I Believe in Satan's Downfall*. Holloway Interview 17.8.06.

91. Michael Green Interview 18.3.04.

92. During that time, I accompanied Michael Green and a large team on missions to Newport in Gwent, and Huddersfield (Yorkshire). In Newport, I recall how Green himself was shocked at the amount of occult activity he discovered people had been involved in, requiring deliverance prayer, and I was involved in backup prayer alongside him in two such incidents. One involved someone who had recently become a Christian, but had formerly been involved in 10 different forms of occult activity, such as fortune telling and astral travelling.

a detailed case for the power and effectiveness of Christian exorcisms in the New Testament;[93] and gives evidence that this continued into at least the second and third centuries.[94] By 1975, he is ready to argue for contemporary exorcism and encourage those gifted to practice it, recognizing that he had himself been used on occasions in this.[95] Then in *I believe in Satan's Downfall*, he presents a strong case for the existence of Satan as a personal Devil, arguing that it matters if we are to be consistent theists and to rightly discern the cause and cure of the world's ills.[96] And in recent reflections on the weaknesses and strengths of the charismatic renewal, he cites awareness of the spiritual battle "which rages all around us" (and awareness of "the unholy Spirit and his determination to wreck God's work at every turn") as the last of nine positive benefits, concluding:

> The New Testament leaves us in no doubt of this. . . . The Church, however, has long been silent about spiritual battle and its members have no idea that there is a war on and that they are combatants, not civilians. Until the Church in the West as a whole comes to see this, and until we are driven to prevailing prayer and fasting (a weapon of whose power the Third-World Christians are well aware), we shall not grow. I, for one, thank God for the awareness of the spiritual battle to which the charismatic movement has alerted us.[97]

In this autobiographical reflection, Green also tellingly admits that, despite all his former deep theological learning, this practical awareness of charismatic deliverance ministry was "something which I would never even have imagined to be real had it not been forced upon me by encounters like these"[98] (such as the case mentioned above with John Woolmer). Like Harper and Watson before him, it was primarily experience mediated

---

93. He comments that some theologians believe we are not bound by beliefs which Jesus shared in common with a very different age; yet "all agree that Jesus did believe in these forces, and that he sent forth his apostles not only to preach repentance but to cast out demons;" Green, *Evangelism in the Early Church*, 188–93. He cites specifically Mark 6:12–13.

94. Green quotes Justin Martyr (2 *Apology* 6), that Christians exorcising in the name of Jesus Christ succeeded in driving out demons "when all other exorcists and specialists in incantations and drugs have failed"; and Irenaeus, Tertullian, and Origen (*Contra Celsum*). Ibid., 190–92.

95. He bases his argument on philosophy, theology, world environment, experience of temptation, occult, Scripture and Jesus. *I Believe in the Holy Spirit*, 201–2.

96. *I Believe in Satan's Downfall*, 15–32.

97. *Adventure of Faith*, 279.

98. Ibid., 267.

through charismatic renewal that led him to a renewed theological praxis of spiritual warfare.

3.5 Integrated analysis of spiritual warfare theology and praxis

I shall here both give an overview of the main theological beliefs that emerged for all twelve charismatic Anglicans concerning evil forces and spiritual warfare, as well as attempting to analyze reasons for some of the differences in viewpoint that emerged.[99]

The ontology, nature, and origin of evil powers
(Appendix 2 table 1)

Regarding the ontology of evil, all interviewees agreed on the existence of Satan or the devil as a separate spiritual entity with some personal characteristics, though they varied in the language they used. Some used straightforward ontological and biblical language, describing "Beelzebub the prince of demons" as "a real, personal, spiritual being" (Walker), or corporately as "independent and intelligent powers/evil forces" (Collins, Holloway), the regular phrase "fallen angels" (e.g., Pytches, Dunnett), or "personalities like angels" (Harper), or even more specifically "disembodied spirits" (Watson). Some added rational justification, giving specific arguments (e.g., Green and Woolmer[100]) or a reflection on the evidential process of deciding this (MacInnes[101]). In relation to Wink's ontological proposals, some wished to

---

99. The initial analysis primarily drew on my interview material, but supplemented by written sources. A tabular summary can be found in Appendix 2.

100. Green, *I Believe in Satan's Downfall*, 18–28. Woolmer argued that this is an important part of Jesus's teaching and experience, the doctrine of God is unsatisfactory without obvious opposition, and experiences which lack psychological explanation, for example of spiritual powers physically leaving a place. He described an example from a Papua New Guinean missionary he interviewed, of demonic presence disturbing the missionary's family; after commanding spirits to leave, hearing a reaction in the village with all the animals and then children disturbed, then a reaction in the next village down the valley. Woolmer Interview 16.3.06. Another of his favorite personal experiences, of a spiritual presence leaving a stable and almost knocking over a staff member, is also relevant—see Woolmer, *Healing and Deliverance*, 344–45.

101. For example: "We're talking about a spiritual entity . . . so in that sense beyond the range of scientific observation; at the same time of course the effects can be identified and recognized. So the actual nature of the being has to come from revelation . . . *(then talking about "multiple personalities" etc.)*. . . . Is that really what it is rather than a special entity you're dealing with? Can you explain all the kind of

simply re-emphasize that evil spirits are not impersonal influences (Harper, Barrington-Ward, Dunnett—"wholly wrong to think evil is impersonal"); others were more sympathetic to Wink's analysis, but argued that they must be more than psychological or socio-spiritual forces (Woolmer, MacInnes, Warren—"forces often have socio-spiritual roots, but stand behind them . . ."). A few pointed to the traditional wider aspects of evil, not just the devil but evil operating through the world and the flesh (Watson, Green)— "carnal powers at another level" (Harper).

This leads us to the nature and character of such forces. Many listed some of the biblical images of Satan, some majored on his character, and some linked the two—thus, MacInnes used the two most popular images to highlight his intimidation ("roaring lion," 1 Pet 5:8), and deception ("angel of light," 2 Cor 11:14); others added "a subtle serpent" (Woolmer), "an enticing serpent/father of lies" (Watson), whose great design is to "deceive the nations" (Harper). Three other descriptions came particularly to the fore— firstly that Satan is our adversary because he is God's adversary (Watson/Walker), "the complete opposite of who God is, for example death not life" (Holloway), the god/prince of this world (Walker/Dunnett); secondly, that he seeks to devour and bring death (Pytches) as "the destroyer—fundamentally disintegration, alienation, dividing up, and breaking down" (Barrington-Ward); and thirdly, he "clearly possesses intelligence" (Harper)—e.g., "a malicious, secretive, hidden, personal intelligence" (Warren), possessing "powerful cognitive thinking" and able to find your weaknesses (Dunnett). Some took the chance to add more positive answers—that it is the cross which illuminates the nature of evil (MacInnes), and that Satan is a violent intelligent liar, but bound and fearful of the name of Jesus (Green).

Regarding his origin, most revealed a belief in a fall of the angels (e.g., "Satan fell with a third of the angels" [Pytches]; "a rebellion that parallels the human one" [Harper]); though some were more cautious than Harper, Watson, and Green, particularly concerning the OT texts alluding to the fall.[102] Some used Luther's phrase "he is still God's devil" (Green, MacInnes); Warren recalled Wink's discussion on Job that Satan is originally (and could still be?) one of God's agents—but also that some things are profoundly evil (e.g., genocide massacres); Woolmer quoting Cullmann as saying that the

---

things that are seen as opposition really in terms of human reactions? [But] if you deny the supernatural altogether then you will inevitably find some other explanation." MacInnes Interview 6.4.06.

102. "The Bible has very little on that" (Collins); "only hints in the Old Testament" (MacInnes); "Satan's origin and where he gets his power from are unclear" (Woolmer).

Devil can at times even loose himself from the line he is bound to. Barrington-Ward uniquely drew on Augustinian concepts of evil.[103]

After twenty years of experience, Woolmer remained overall cautious in drawing dogmatic pneumatological conclusions. Like Walker and MacInnes (and indeed all other Anglican charismatics interviewees), he on the one hand argues strongly against Wink's suggestion that evil powers could be essentially psychological forces;[104] yet, he accepts that there may be a "strange synthesis" with liberal theology in seeing the New Testament powers also as represented by corrupt governments,[105] recognizing that the Bible itself does not clearly identify what Paul's "principalities and powers" really represent. He is more cautious than others in his reluctance to attribute power over natural events to Satan.[106]

The nature and extent of spiritual warfare (Appendix 2 tables 2(a), 2(b))

The extent and focus of the spiritual battle between forces of good and evil was variously described, but could be separated into the general ways they saw Satan exerting his influence in the world as a whole, and specific areas they believed Christians experience attack.

Using military metaphors for the spiritual struggle came naturally to many of the early pioneers, some of them (e.g., Watson, Green, Walker, Woolmer, Pytches) having undergone military service. However, Green became a near-pacifist, and Watson warns strongly against using the cross as a banner for violent physical warfare.[107] Even though some were wary of the misuse of the term "spiritual warfare" (e.g., Holloway, Warren), seeing a lot of it as "projection not engagement" (Warren), they still saw the value of such metaphors.[108] Ward was keen on them for another reason, because

---

103. "I've had quite a dose of the Augustinian idea of evil as an absence of good as it were, or as something that is parasitical of good. That's how it seems to me that the demonic is ultimately vanquished when we are really in Christ. . . . He gets his power from a loss, our own loss of our true centre. A lie, a distortion. And the moment we begin to be enabled to discern where our true centre is to be, to be united with Christ, that's when suddenly this is shown up to be the sham that it is." Ward Interview 20.4.04.

104. Woolmer, *Healing and Deliverance*, 27–33.

105. Ibid., 38.

106. Woolmer Interview 16.3.06.

107. Not least because it distracts from our true conflict, which is not against flesh and blood but principalities and powers (Eph 6:12). Watson, *I Believe in the Church*, 159–60; *Discipleship*, 180.

108. Warren referred to Wink's comment that even for pacifists the only family of

they catch the popular imagination and point to the "reality of warfare."[109] MacInnes observes that you cannot escape the fact of conflict, the violent confrontation between two opposing forces; and several described the scope of conflict as "a total warfare between light and darkness" (Pytches, cf. Harper, Green), "a mighty conflict going on in the world" (Ward), "an intense reality" (Watson).

However, there was a recognition that a lot of the battle is hidden, because Satan's chief strategy is to deceive and blind the minds of people to the truth, both to the gospel, to Satan's existence, and more generally to the greatness of God who is on the throne.[110] Some also described the more active ways evil forces are at work in society—not only in the "Devil's Pentecost" that Harper, Watson, and Green wrote about in the rise of occultism and counterfeit religion in the 1960s and beyond, but also more contemporary concerns such as materialism, the culture of "my rights," and the breakdown of society (Woolmer), or more widely in cultures, groups, norms, and values—in oppressive regimes (e.g., in Zimbabwe), or drug and human trafficking, corruption or the credit crunch (Warren, speaking in 2008).

Concerning Christians, several commented that Satan was not interested in openly attacking those who are passive; but when Christians advance in the Spirit's power (particularly in evangelism, as a result of being filled with the Spirit, or ministering baptism in the Spirit[111]) the conflict is accentuated (which MacInnes saw as a positive sign). Then the enemy will "hammer any area of moral weakness" (Dunnett), hinder attendance at prayer (Walker), bring deceptions, division, and intimidation (MacInnes), or attack those on mission or their families with sickness and even death (Watson, Holloway, Collins).

---

metaphors that has the strength to describe defeating the powers are military ones; Holloway talks of the "huge battle" for the kingdom of God, where lives are at stake.

109. He saw not only Tolkien, but also Harry Potter and even "poor old Pullman" as catching the imagination and "pointing to Christ at the heart of this . . . it's crucial that we bring out the significance that the warfare's a reality, it's the truth, not just a wonderful story." Ward Interview 20.4.04.

110. Walker; but Dunnett, Green, Watson, and Pytches and others highlighted spiritual blindness or 2 Cor 4:4. Dunnett and Walker specifically mentioned experience of occult involvement confusing the mind, making it unable to see even the simple logic of statements concerning the gospel—e.g., see Walker, *The Occult Web*, chapter 1: "Inner Confusion," 5–9.

111. As described for Watson and Green, and Harper; also others, e.g., Dunnett and Collins for being filled with the Spirit and evangelism (Collins experiencing sudden fever or loss of voice just before preaching).

There was considerable hesitancy and some disagreement in terms of how much Satan could operate through affecting natural events. Whilst several had witnessed some "extraordinary physical effects (e.g., electrical ones)" (MacInnes) when dealing with the demonized, and Green interpreted the storm of Mark 4 as a demonic attack, Woolmer however did not believe that Satan had the power for example to have him struck with lightning before a mission.[112] The majority agreed that some sickness could be caused directly by evil spirits or Satanic attack (e.g., Harper), whilst recognizing the need for caution and discernment.[113] Whilst recognizing that demonic possession or oppression normally affected human beings, all pioneers agreed that evil powers could also attach to buildings; most accepted they could do so to larger territories, but often adding significant cautions;[114] and nearly all recognized evil powers at work through institutions.

Praxis in spiritual warfare: "weapons" and methods, dangers and outcomes (Appendix 2, table 3)

The "weapons" or charismatic gifts considered effective in spiritual warfare were too varied to adequately summarize, though table 3 is as comprehensive as possible. They range from general qualities such as holiness (Green), costly and humble service, overcoming by the "opposite spirit," standing fast (Warren), obedience (Pytches), the witness of divinely given love and a deep dependence on God (Barrington-Ward), and especially the power of the Holy Spirit (Harper, Watson, Green, Dunnett, Barrington-Ward); key activities such as praise and worshipping God, prayer (e.g., for protection, "putting on the armor"), and proclamation of the word of God (often linked to Ephesians 6); the power of theological truths, such as exalting Jesus and

---

112. As in fact happened, but he simply saw "accidents as part of the world we live in." Harper agreed that disasters are part of the fallen nature of the world, but maintained that Satan as well as God could use them—and cause things like car punctures, and other practical interferences, as Collins and Walker in particular maintained.

113. Walker suggested that when something could not be recognized medically, it was good to consider a spiritual source. Pytches and Woolmer implied an additional general, indirect demonic origin to sickness.

114. Possible in theory (Harper); probably, but not important to know (Warren); unbiblical territorial spirit language can generate fear (MacInnes, Walker); unhelpful to jargonize it as Wagner does (Dunnett); yes, but not the theology of different "levels" of spiritual warfare (Holloway). Woolmer was the most positive—"an important and dangerous subject . . . at a cursory reading Scripture gives little to support this view," but he feels that "a deeper study gives a very different impression," e.g., the underlying assumption of territorial gods in the Old Testament—Woolmer, *Healing and Deliverance*, 35–37.

his triumph on the cross (Pytches), and "knowing your enemy" (Watson); to more specific spiritual actions and spiritual gifts, authoritative prayer such as resisting/commanding in Jesus's name, discernment and words of knowledge, using tongues, and repentance/confession (MacInnes/Green) or "continuous repentance" (Barrington-Ward), and fasting (Green). The best summary phrase is Pytches' Johannine comment—"the answer to darkness is to switch on the light."

Harper summarizes the mood in relation to specific "methods" or "techniques" of spiritual warfare—he considered that systematic methods are generally too rationalistic to tune into *spiritual* warfare, which needs to be spiritually discerned; programs and methods can take our focus off God (Holloway). Similar cautions were applied to Wagner's techniques of "strategic-level" warfare[115] as to the language of "territorial spirits," with a particular dislike for casting out spirits over a city or nation (Pytches, MacInnes), or even more generally "praying against" (Warren). Nevertheless, several practitioners recognized the value of praying over the history of an area (Green, Walker, Dunnett, Woolmer—by God's leading[116]) or into a community's spiritual characteristics (MacInnes), and Holloway had found that "identificational repentance" could be very helpful.

All the pioneers saw dangers in the field of spiritual warfare to a greater or lesser extent, whether from a paranoid dualism (Green), supernatural deception, or inexperience (Harper). Interestingly more than one practitioner cautioned that those claiming to have an evil spirit most often did not (Walker, Pytches). Woolmer summarizes well some of the dangers. In particular, casting out non-existent demons can leave damaging feelings of guilt; some can wrongly minister with never-ending lists of demons; there can be a lack of clear spiritual authority in this ministry (though the Anglican system helps here considerably); and there can be a lack of common sense, or the use of strange practices lacking proportion and decency. However, the final danger he lists is that of refusing to act—"I freely admit that, before reluctantly getting involved in such prayer, that I too would have been fairly skeptical. [But] if the person really needs this sort of ministry, no other prayers, pills or psychiatric help will set them free. To refuse to countenance this possibility is to deny the ministry recorded of Jesus in the Gospels, and of the Apostles in the Acts."[117]

---

115. E.g., Wagner, *Warfare Prayer*.

116. Woolmer also believed challenging spirits in an area linked to local religions helps, particularly from his experience in Africa.

117. Woolmer, *Healing and Deliverance*, 35.

Positive outcomes of charismatic spiritual warfare were considered hard to measure. Warren, taking the narrow definition of spiritual warfare of engaging with manifestations of evil or a sense of strong opposition from principalities and powers, summarizes cautiously that it may be "5–10% of what matters in mission; yet at certain moments has the key to opening otherwise shut doors." Walker considered his experience at St. John's to be one such example—the astonishing lack of conversions for nine years there was, he later discovered "due to specific spiritual warfare that would never have been overcome apart from charismatic insights, the awareness of God's power, the ability to minister in difficulty."[118]

Those involved in evangelism widely across the country were also more conscious of the "titanic confrontation" (Green)[119] this involved them in, but noted the effectiveness of specific prayer to resist the devil in putting a stop to disturbances (Watson),[120] to "break through" or open doors in evangelism (Green, Woolmer), and also to release church growth and even bring some social transformation (Green, Holloway); though some referred to the profound cost that could be involved, even death, in seeing major breakthroughs against evil (MacInnes, Holloway).[121] Viewing the whole breadth of "spiritual warfare," Collins concluded that "nothing grows without [the spiritual battle in prayer] being given top priority"; Green is more aware of its continuing lack: "Until the Church in the West as a whole comes to see [that we are combatants, not civilians], and until we are driven to prevailing prayer and fasting . . . we shall not grow."[122] Holloway is more positive as she uses battle imagery to report increasing prayer, particular from growing internet 24/7 prayer campaigns—"today many Christians are rediscovering the power of intercessory prayer as God mobilizes his army . . . there are so many people praying [in worldwide prayer movements] it is impossible to keep records."[123]

---

118. Subsequently, the church grew from sixty to an official figure of 850 during his time at St. John's Harborne. Walker Interview 28.3.04.

119. Green, *I Believe in the Holy Spirit*, 70.

120. Watson, *I Believe in Evangelism*, 182.

121. MacInnes ponders the link between the death of Janani Luwum and the fall of Idi Amin; Holloway notes that "we lost three prayer co-ordinators who died untimely deaths in citywide missions."

122. Green, *Adventure of Faith*, 279.

123. Holloway, "Understanding Intercession," 9–10.

Similarities and differences in developing a theology of spiritual warfare

Some of table 4 (e.g., personal influences) will be summarized in the conclusion below. First, however, having seen how Harper, Watson, and Green developed similar but distinctive approaches to spiritual warfare, I will here comment on the development of spiritual warfare thinking for the other interviewees, attempting to account for some of the differences between them.

Collins most easily fits in behind Watson, in that they shared a passion for evangelism. After his church's renewal in the Spirit, Collins was to take lay teams around the country (and make visits to Africa), and thus he like Watson became most aware of an opposing force at times attacking family and health physically, that needed to be defeated by prayer. Furthermore, he was impressed with the solid commitment to prayer of people like Jeremy Jennings at "HTB" that in their eyes led to the worldwide success of the Alpha initiative, such that for John and Diana "prayer *is* spiritual warfare."

Walker and Dunnett also came from this strong evangelical tradition, and shared the same church for many years,[124] but their different characters, life experiences, and ministries produced different emphases. Walker's evangelical conversion experience seemed more like a baptism in the Spirit than most, so he was not initially impressed with the "tongues-speaking" movement until his own resistance was melted by the transformed young people of Gillingham. This led to the pragmatic discovery that tongues produced extraordinary results in deliverance ministry, such that for him "praying in the Spirit" (Eph 6:18) came to refer to tongues. He remained a curious mixture of a pragmatist, also willing to learn much accumulated wisdom from his deliverance ministry experience, in relation to such things as Hindu processions, freemasonry and accident blackspots as often being demonic entry points; and a biblicist, forthright in his warnings against teachings concerning "territorial spirits" (which mostly arose from Wagner's collecting information from pragmatic experience) as being unbiblical language likely to generate fear. He explained this as "allowing the Word of God to explain our experiences, but not our experiences to change our understanding of the Bible." Dunnett's charismatic experience essentially came in the midst of wilderness testing, battling alone in a council estate riddled with spiritualism in the Potteries, with little help except from his Bible, prayer and the newly received illumination of the Spirit; such that Old Testament experiences of the harassment of Sanballat and Tobiah in Nehe-

---

124. Bob Dunnett regularly attended St. John's, Harborne during and beyond his years as Vice-Principal of Birmingham Bible Institute. Both trained for ordination at Oak Hill.

miah resonated with his own experience and illustrated the "fact of spiritual warfare" of Eph 6:12. His experience thus reflects other early charismatics such as Harper, who similarly emphasized a sense of unfolding "revelation knowledge" through increased illumination from the Spirit on the word of God. Dunnett's attendance at early Fountain Trust meetings reinforced for him that an awareness of spiritual warfare was a normal part of the experience of a Spirit-filled life;[125] and this remained a constant backdrop for his leadership in the prayer movement, as well as in teaching and praying with churches seeking to overcome hindrances to growth.

MacInnes shared the evangelical background and formative student mission experience of Collins, Watson, Walker, and Green; but although his humility and inexperience in theological writing prevented him from writing *I Believe in Satan's Downfall*, he would have brought a different style to the subject. Whilst Green often allows the evangelist's passion to color his theological polemic, MacInnes tends to be more reflective and measured in his analysis (although they would agree on most matters). He is much more agnostic concerning whether Satan could affect storms or lightning, convinced that Satan could not move tectonic plates causing a tsunami, and more aware of the dangers of territorial spirit language in generating fear; and he particularly commends Wink (like Green) in balancing out charismatic insights in highlighting systemic evil in human institutions. Whilst finding scientific and psychological explanations for symptoms of demonic possession helpful, he carefully analyses his own journey in terms of experience from applying biblical methods in deliverance leading to a "paradigm shift" in understanding of the Scriptures; and concluding that evil spiritual entities do exist that are beyond scientific observation, but whose effects can be recognized; whilst admitting that those with other presuppositions will find other explanations.

Woolmer argues with similar logic and style to MacInnes. As a former mathematics teacher, the discovery of the reality of evil was a great surprise to his rational mind;[126] he was confronted with experiences that lacked psychological explanation, and discovered that if deliverance was needed, nothing else would set a person free.[127] But like Green, he could later analyze this

---

125. "I remember Michael Harper explaining how it came to him . . . those early charismatics, they were all acutely conscious of it." Dunnett suggested that the charismatic renewal's main contribution to an understanding of spiritual warfare was that it allowed people to be filled with the Spirit and so perceive the reality of spiritual warfare in their spirits, which they would not otherwise have understood. Dunnett Interview 28.3.04.

126. Woolmer, *Healing and Deliverance*, 27.

127. Woolmer Interview 16.3.06.

logically, setting out clearly his own list of factors that "helped to convince me of both the reality and necessity of this ministry."[128] Of these factors, one was biblical theology (its scriptural basis, especially in "huge chunks of the Gospels . . . especially Jesus" teaching to his disciples), and three arguments from praxis (the amazing power and efficacy of Jesus's name;[129] spiritual gifts—notably words of knowledge that have unlocked deliverance ministry situations; and the strange powers of the apparently demonized[130]). Woolmer's scientific mathematical background also helps explain his caution against attributing accidents such as lightning or punctures to Satan, seeing accidents as just a part of the world we live in.[131] Yet amongst interviewees he is most sympathetic to Wagner's analyses of spiritual warfare at higher levels—probably because his experiences both in Zambia and in his Somerset parish convinced him of the efficacy of challenging spirits linked to local religions, and using information from local history in prayer.[132]

Holloway was the most natural "ordinary theologian" of them all, having come to faith in the midst of vivid spiritual experience and straightforward practical prayer—"I read the book of Acts and I did it."[133] Her wide international experience in prayer for citywide missions led her to similar conclusions to Woolmer's, but more from intuitive reflection on praxis than logical reasoning. On one hand she appreciates the approach of South American evangelist Ed Silvoso and of Dutch Sheets, Peter Wagner's pastor, on intercession;[134] but from experience in many cities she favors encouraging united praise and Christ-focused worship leading to specific discernment how to pray (and who is given spiritual authority, not always being church leaders); rather than trying to systematically organize "spiritual

---

128. Woolmer, *Healing and Deliverance*, 27–31.

129. He gives two dramatic examples, the American Oxford student, with help from Green and Watson, finally set free from occult bondage when she herself called on the name of Jesus; and long healing lines in Zambia where simple authoritative prayers in Jesus's name brought calm amongst the pandemonium. Ibid., 28–29.

130. As when an apparently demonized woman said to him in remote rural Zambia "Go away, I'm not leaving this person!," astonishingly in a harsh, authoritative BBC Oxbridge English accent rather than the soft African one. Ibid., 32–33.

131. Woolmer Interview 16.3.06.

132. Nevertheless, he agrees with Dunnett and Holloway that local history information should only be used under the Spirit's leading.

133. She experienced this where she was living, with a mature older Anglican Christian as landlady—"I had my own personal healing, I prayed for healing, we had exorcisms, deliverance—I was used to it—I read the book of the Acts and I did it . . . short of actually raising the dead!" Holloway Interview 17.8.06.

134. See Silvoso, *That None Should Perish*; Sheets, *Intercessory Prayer*; Silvoso, *Prayer Evangelism*.

warfare" through programs inspired by Wagner's methodology. She believes she has seen firsthand the seriousness of the spiritual battle in mission and evangelism, such that one Scripture that has particularly influenced her is John 17;[135] the best "weapons" for her are thus to focus not on the enemy but on following Jesus and loving others, and worshipping God who will give needed discernment when asked.

Warren is even more eager to take attention off the devil and onto God. He carefully defines true spiritual warfare as engagement with principalities and powers and the manifestation of evil—for him much so-called spiritual warfare is projection and not engagement. He emphasizes the secretive and hidden intelligence of the enemy, such that "spiritual warfare itself is so open to spiritual warfare—and it gets distorted, and people develop fanciful doctrines, so once it becomes a theory, a technique, it is likely to go awry."[136] This may arise partly from his consultancy roles, giving wide-ranging contact with many different churches, exposing him both to many good things happening where there was little awareness of spiritual warfare, and to some who were over-focused on spiritual warfare;[137] but also out of his personal ministry experience. On the positive side, Warren was another early charismatic who found that experiencing renewal immediately brought with it a heightened sense of generally being in spiritual conflict, in that (like Collins) problems arose that drove them to prayer, without really being aware they were "doing spiritual warfare." And negatively, having overseen at Sheffield the origin of the earliest and initially most successful "fresh expression" in "The Nine O'Clock Service" at St. Thomas Crookes under Chris Brain, he also saw with hindsight how such dynamics as secrecy and personal power and charisma, deception, intimidation and control led to its spectacular downfall, the "enemy" thus working in hidden ways through a "successful" charismatic leader.[138] Not surprisingly therefore, experience influenced his

---

135. Jesus's prayer for unity, and protection for believers from the evil one. Believing that three separate premature deaths of prayer coordinators for citywide missions were linked to the spiritual battle, she thus describes it: "You're battling against the complete opposite of who God is, and the bottom line is, God is for life, the enemy is for death, for everything in every area. As I say, guys, he doesn't just loathe you, he hates you, in fact he wants you dead." Holloway Interview 17.8.06.

136. Warren Interview 23.7.08. Not surprisingly, he is opposed to Wagner's methodical approach—e.g., "Peter Wagner and his demonology and hierarchies I think is seriously unhealthy, not really Christian, more mystery religion."

137. He commented: "I think of one church I know where things were really going well, and they got into spiritual warfare, and basically the whole thing turned in on itself and became off-centre; they worshipped spiritual warfare instead of God really, and the whole church died." Warren Interview 23.7.08.

138. Warren's paradoxical assessment was very revealing: "I don't know really how

view of spiritual warfare being more on an intuitive, subconscious level; he is less keen on developing explicit "spiritual warfare theology." He always puts spiritual warfare in its broader context, such as the need to develop the opposites of evil to overcome it (e.g., costly, humble service; God-dependent prayer); and uniquely highlights Scriptures such as the stories of Joseph and David as influential in his understanding of spiritual warfare, in illustrating its wilderness and testing dimensions. This brings him closer to Dunnett in that he finds the OT stories of physical warfare useful as images and metaphors, although warning against taking them allegorically or literally. As we have seen, whilst he prefers keeping spiritual warfare in the margins of theological discussion, he agrees with Wink that the metaphors it supplies are the only ones strong enough to express its reality.

Bishop Simon Barrington-Ward, like Warren, is widely respected as a national leader in the Church of England (and also in the Anglican Communion). He is humble and open about his spiritual journey, which ranges much wider than his experience of charismatic renewal. It is perhaps surprising therefore that he not only agrees with Warren of the need for spiritual warfare metaphors to describe the "mighty conflict going on in the world," but goes further in asserting that the NT (centered on Christ himself) already gives a lead that we can follow in beginning to allegorize Old Testament physical conflicts in spiritual terms.[139] This is surely connected with his interest in literature, including Shakespeare and particularly C. S. Lewis (whom he knew at Cambridge), Charles Williams, Tolkien, and others (even Harry Potter), seeing how the great mythical tales and films of the conflict between light and darkness catch the popular imagination and can "point to what this is really illuminating about the Gospels."[140] However, whilst like others Barrington-Ward is clear that "the nature of the enemy (the "destroyer") is fundamentally disintegration, alienation, dividing up and breaking down . . . cunning and insidious," he seems reticent to use the personal name Satan, aware of the danger that "exact portrayal can become a caricature"; and also that it is only in the brilliant light of "the grace, love and power of the Spirit and what it can produce . . . that we can discern the

---

the enemy got involved, just that Chris Brain was an extravagant form of what all of us are, a mixture of light and darkness; and the 9 o'clock service was the finest expression of the Christian faith I have ever witnessed, and yet was totally contrary to the gospel at the same time, both things were true of it, with the control and abuse . . . ." Warren Interview 23.7.08.

139. Ward Interview 20.4.04. See section 8.1.

140. Ward Interview 20.4.04. For example as Bishop of Coventry he was a trustee of the Shakespeare Birthplace Trust—Barrington-Ward, "My Pilgrimage." And he spoke on C. S. Lewis at a centenary literary festival in Canada—see C. S. Lewis Centenary Group, "Centenary Programme Reports."

darkness." This surely flows out of his experience of the Spirit as immersing and outpouring love and victory received through the ministry of David du Plessis—explaining his reference to Johannine scriptures such as John 1:29, 33, 19:34 and 1 John 5:4; and how this revealed his own deep inner need. He reflects how coming to lead Crowther Hall after his time in Nigeria and then with this charismatic experience, "the charismatic and the East African Revival were fused. The Dove was released through the cross, wholeness through repeated brokenness."[141] For him, then, not just the Spirit's power but also "continuous repentance" became inseparable means of taking ground in the spiritual battle, as in his own personal experience through discovery of "the Jesus prayer." Experiences as a bishop trying to facilitate the sharing of resources from wealthier charismatic congregations to poorer churches, caused him to echo Warren in calling for charismatic churches to engage in the spiritual battle for reconciliation and justice.[142]

Before experiencing renewal in Britain, both Pytches and Barrington-Ward were strongly influenced by experiencing the value of going on the offensive against evil powers in Anglican Communion churches in the developing world, in South America and Nigeria respectively.[143] This gave them positive firsthand experience of Christ as conqueror;[144] but the Spirit's revealing of his own inner need for Barrington-Ward, and for Pytches his wider pastoral and renewal ministry, led them on the one hand to see that spiritual warfare is much wider than just deliverance from evil powers, and on the other the importance of focusing more on the positive. Thus Pytches became more aware of the broader spiritual battle since preaching more on the kingdom of God; and just as Barrington-Ward found the positive power of the Jesus prayer in engaging his spirit and changing him (more than praying in tongues), so Pytches recognized that those seeking deliverance ministry often were more in need of a deeper inner transformation and freedom from sin, best provided in integrated care in

---

141. Barrington-Ward, "My Pilgrimage," 5.

142. Highlighting a rare positive example of Graham Dow's church in Coventry helping poorer ones. Ward Interview 20.4.04.

143. This influence of experience from mission overseas was also present for other early charismatics, mediated more through writings such as those of Kurt Koch, J. O. Fraser (for Dunnett), frequent contact with returned USPG missionaries for Walker, and visits to Zambia for Woolmer, and Singapore and East Malaysia for Green (see Green, *Asian Tigers for Christ*.)

144. Barrington-Ward, in accompanying Nigerian students on mission, experienced this triumph over evil as integral to the gospel itself, for example ministering healing to people who had evil powers attacking them, and praying through their houses. Ward Interview 20.4.04.

the local church rather than travelling to "deliverance centers." Like Barrington-Ward and others, he emphasized focusing on Jesus rather than the enemy.[145]

3.7 Concluding summary: origins, influences, and core beliefs

Amongst these pioneers, the majority came into charismatic experience after a grounding in evangelical Anglican theology.[146] This included an intellectual belief that Satan existed primarily as the source of temptation, but with little or no experience of more direct encounter with personal evil. However, without exception once they experienced a baptism or filling with the Holy Spirit, they soon became "uncomfortably aware of the unholy spirit and his determination to wreck God's work at every turn,"[147] especially when engaged in evangelistic mission[148] or helping others to receive the baptism of the Holy Spirit, as well as in the new area of deliverance ministry;[149] awareness coming both through experiences but also in "the revelation of the fact of spiritual warfare" from reading the Scriptures.[150] This prompted them to discover the spiritual weapons available to them in this conflict, amongst which prayer in various forms was central,[151] with "praying in the Spirit" being interpreted by some as praying in tongues, which was found to be a powerful weapon in encounter with evil forces either in deliverance ministry[152] or in prayer and intercession;[153] as well as "the sword of the Spirit which is the Word of God" (Eph 6:17–18).[154]

Especially in the early days, pioneers often found little external help and guidance in understanding what was happening. Although there was some early contact with Pentecostals such as David du Plessis on his

145. For Pytches, as for Wimber, this became allied to a skepticism of Peter Wagner's focus on territorial spirits. Pytches Interview 1.4.04.

146. The main exception being Holloway, who came to faith straight into charismatic experience even before attending church.

147. Green, *Adventure of Faith*, 279.

148. Particularly Watson, Green, and MacInnes.

149. All became involved in this to some extent.

150. Dunnett Interview 28.3.04. Besides the obvious passages (e.g., Eph 6, 2 Cor 10:4–5), the practical ministry of Jesus in the gospels and his battle with Satan came alive for many of them (Harper, Green, Woolmer, Pytches). Holloway (and Woolmer) particularly mentioned Acts for praxis.

151. "Prayer is spiritual warfare" (Collins).

152. Walker, MacInnes, Woolmer, Green.

153. Dunnett, Holloway.

154. Watson and others.

travels,[155] people influenced by Pentecostals,[156] or independents such as Edgar Trout,[157] direct contact was infrequent, and they were often left to wrestle with their experiences on their own with the Scriptures,[158] or with support from one another.[159] Nevertheless some clear external influences are discernible—most notably Corrie ten Boom after her visit to Gillingham for both MacInnes and Watson, the case studies and writings of Kurt Koch[160] and other missionary experiences, C. S. Lewis,[161] early Fountain Trust members such as Arthur Wallis, and for Green theologians such as C. K. Barrett and R. A. Torrey. Nevertheless, even for well-trained theologians like Green, my interview data suggests it was primarily the experience of encounters and events that seemed inexplicable in terms of their previous rational theological reasoning which led to what MacInnes called a "paradigm shift" in understanding of spiritual warfare, following fresh experiences of the Holy Spirit in charismatic renewal. However, these Anglican pioneers did not develop a strong dualistic outlook, emphasizing God's omnipotence and overall sovereignty even over the devil and his forces;[162] often warning of the dangers of deception, or of attributing far too much to the power of evil spirits[163] by finding them under every bush or common cold.[164] Harper is eager to preserve the category of the natural, and Woolmer is very cautious in attributing any power to demonic forces in natural events (though others disagreed with him on this[165]). All would agree from experience and Scripture that evil powers can attach themselves to objects or places, and probably larger areas of territory; however, they are cautious in using non-biblical terms in warfare methodologies that can make spiritual warfare praxis too methodical and systematized, rather than depending on the leading and direction of the Spirit.

155. Particularly significant for Collins, Harper, and Walker.

156. Notably Philip Smith, himself an Anglican, who influenced Dunnett and Harper.

157. Mentioned by Collins; see also Hocken, *Streams of Renewal*, 31–38.

158. Especially Dunnett; thus he and Watson freely spiritualized Old Testament physical warfare.

159. Pioneers often identified one another as constructive influences, through friendship links (e.g., around St. Mark's, Gillingham), the Fountain Trust, and also through their writings (e.g., Harper for Warren, Green for Pytches/MacInnes).

160. E.g., Koch, *Between Christ and Satan*; *Occult Bondage and Deliverance*.

161. Lewis, *The Screwtape Letters*; *Four Broadcast Talks*.

162. MacInnes quotes Luther, that he was still "God's devil"—MacInnes, *Conflict with the Devil*.

163. E.g., Harper, *As at the Beginning*; *None Can Guess*.

164. Green, *I Believe in the Holy Spirit*, 202.

165. Certainly Harper, Watson, MacInnes, Walker, and Dunnett.

4

Spiritual Warfare in the Charismatic Anglican Context

A Case Study

4.1 Introduction and pilot study

THE MAIN CASE STUDY was preceded by a pilot study in June 2004 following similar principles for its selection,[1] and for its analysis.[2] Here I present a brief summary of the results as an introduction to the main study.[3]

St. Martin's (a pseudonym) is in an outer estate area of a large city. Its spirituality was very informal "low church," with a distinctively charismatic flavor.[4] Having over a hundred young people (many more than the

---

1. See 4.2. Specifically, it was known to have seen both considerable church growth and social change in the area, and had claimed that issues related to spiritual warfare were significant in these changes. At the time of the study, the vicar who had led the church through these dramatic changes had now left, so by interviewing several of those remaining there was already a degree of "critical distance" from those changes that assisted considered reflection upon them.

2. See sections 4.2 and 4.5. Unlike the main case study, rather than thirteen only four people were interviewed (two were lay leaders in the congregation), participant observation was much more limited (attending a main service, a prayer meeting and a children's "cell group"), but I also used twelve questionnaires to gather supplementary data. For analysis, a new "spider diagram" was drawn for each interview, and then I attempted a synthesis under the main categories that emerged from the data. The main categories were then used as a starting point for the category analysis of the main case study (see Appendix 4).

3. For brevity I focus here primarily on one church leader (pseudonym Nicholas), a lawyer involved in social regeneration projects; also because of his reflective self-awareness and the richness of his descriptive overview. The four interviewees were given the pseudonyms Nicholas, David, Jane (all in their forties or fifties), and Barbara (in her late sixties). They had been at the church for seventeen, eight, fifteen, and eighteen years respectively.

4. The service I attended was punctuated with laughter (even whistles and cat-calls!);

other outer estates churches in the city), the staff team also included several younger leaders. There was an emphasis on informal, participatory prayer meetings for all those involved in church life.

The church had seen considerable growth over the previous fifteen years. Nicholas described how the vicar and his wife (pseudonyms William and Marion), after arriving in about 1985, experienced many difficulties, but gradually changed the spirituality and outlook. They were tempted to leave within six months because of the gang of over thirty youths that used to gather round the vicarage, intimidating their children and rendering their ministry impotent. However, after some desperate prayer, Marion sensed that God directed her to the book of Nehemiah and for them to pray for angels to be posted around the vicarage, and within a few days the gang (that had been in the area for many years) gradually dispersed and never re-formed. This story clearly became something of a "paradigm" for spiritual warfare prayer in the congregation. After this, a group of up to twenty used to meet on a Tuesday night for charismatic "prayer and praise"; overt expressions of charismata gradually transposed into the Sunday worship, initiating a period of rapid growth over six or seven years, including some dramatic conversions, to about 120. During this time there were other apparent examples of change in the community through prayer. For example, where there had been a lot of "gang warfare," the church organized a Graham Kendrick "Make Way" praise and prayer march through the park. Despite threats beforehand from some youths, many who witnessed it went calm and were happy to listen to the marchers' songs and message; and afterwards the fighting greatly reduced.

Nicholas also described dramatic changes in the local area. The estate had moved out of the "severe" category in terms of indices of deprivation, unlike its neighboring estate where there was almost no spiritual witness. As an urban regeneration professional specializing in hard-pressed council areas, Nicholas observed that "we are almost an exact mirror image of the [neighboring estate across the valley] . . . so if you want a kind of pair of twins and seeing the difference one from the other, you can certainly make a case that the spiritual impact of this church has markedly changed the

---

the leaders all wore ordinary clothes, and there was a break for coffee in the middle of the service. Liturgical elements were scant, with no papers to hold—even though there were baptisms of adults and children (by immersion in a paddling pool) in the service, apart from the promises there was simply one liturgical prayer put up on the overheads for the congregation to join in. The music was mostly lively modern choruses using an instrumental band and singers.

area . . . the spiritual feel of the place, and economically, socially it's quite remarkable."[5]

Ontologically, Nicholas exemplifies the strong belief in evil spiritual forces, "principalities and powers" existing in "a parallel universe of spiritual forces which have an influence over powers and people in authority in the human universe." These beings have independence and volition; they act as "spiritual opposition to that which we're trying to do," and "whenever you are trying to change something spiritually or almost socially they don't like it, and things start happening" in what he would call a kind of "spiritual backlash." These forces were thus seen as being "reactive" to Christian initiatives; yet they could also be unpredictable, in that you may be "going about your business," when they suddenly emerge out of nowhere, like the giants throwing rocks in Lewis's *The Silver Chair* (and the slave-girl in Acts 16). This "spiritual opposition" could manifest itself through people, feelings of discouragement, illness, or "things going wrong."[6] Awareness of this battle was important; "if you expect the opposition" (which happens especially when you "try and wait on God and hear what he wants you to do"), then you are "that much more ready for it."[7] It was not intense all the time, but was most acute "at the beginning when we were pushing into the area." Nicholas nevertheless recognizes also a much broader dimension of the enemy's activity in the surrounding community, in terms of "vandalism, crime, fear of crime, poor self-image . . . untidiness, poor educational attainment, high death rate, more sick people, and so on."[8]

---

5. I was unable to access statistics for the late 1990s, but in the neighborhood around St. Martin's, in 2010 crime and antisocial behavior had reduced 1 percent (the regional average) to 1517 incidents, whereas in the opposite neighborhood it had increased 2 percent to 2098 incidents (from the neighborhood police website).

6. Jane listed almost the same categories—"he'll use other people to attack you, he'll use circumstances, . . . [and] making you feel not worthy [and] depressed; . . . depression among Christians is really a tool of Satan."

7. Having described a time where it seemed the enemy was determined to stop them gathering to pray and go out on evangelism, David observed how they actually found this encouraging: "it was still quite exciting; . . . if the devil bothers to try to upset us we must be doing something right." Jane described how they learned from such experiences to be more careful in prayer before an evangelistic initiative against what the enemy might do, and then things went better.

8. Jane showed a fairly strong dualistic approach, declaring that though it is God's creation, Satan rules on the earth, because it's been handed over to him since the fall— "Jesus's coming showed us what it should be like, that there shouldn't be sickness, and . . . people with demons, it should be good . . . ." She would nevertheless "not see demons under every bed." Barbara commented similarly: "We're fighting against the devil, because he is very powerful, I believe he rules the world in many instances [sic]."

Nicholas and the others took a broad view of the praxis of spiritual warfare, seeing "prayer" as "the main way" (rather than specific charismatic gifts such as tongues which had "never been a major feature");[9] for example, weekly as a leadership "trying to discern and spend a fair amount of time in prayer," or organizing "24-7 or 24-3 prayer" or a specific Tuesday prayer meeting before an evangelistic effort, or doing "some prayer walking in order to plough the ground spiritually." However, prayer was often linked to some social action.[10]

In summary, there is a belief in a "parallel universe of spiritual forces" which affect the natural. However, whilst this might appear as an over-dualistic model of angelic and demonic hordes, there was little evidence of such a "paranoid universe";[11] interestingly Nicholas used to believe in demons as "hobgoblins and mists," but his experience led him to believe that spiritual forces primarily influence "powers and people in authority," and operate especially through social problems of deprivation. His views then would seem to occupy a considered middle ground, not as skeptical as Walker in that he would believe that prayer walking and praise marching can indeed begin to "shift the demonic atmosphere"—but certainly not solve unemployment or racism merely by "a shout to the skies";[12] believing for example that congregation members will "make the area better as they live their lives out," seeing evil as combated primarily through "light driving out the darkness" across the area.[13]

---

9. Cf. the Collinses view that "prayer is spiritual warfare." See chapter 3.5.

10. Martin described practical actions to make the church "un-fortress-like" (removing barbed wire) and making the church gardens attractive and always tidy, also praying over it as well, such action and prayer being "a bit Nehemiah-like." Also, a new service in a school in a difficult estate had seemed to be a catalyst for new social initiatives in that area.

11. Walker, "The Devil You Think You Know," 88–101. This view was also popularized in Frank Peretti's novel, *This Present Darkness*. See also Guelich, "Spiritual Warfare: Jesus, Paul, and Peretti."

12. Walker, "The Devil You Think You Know," 103.

13. For Nicholas, this was both in general terms through "the presence of the church and the kind of worship [that exalts] Jesus's outworking on the community, as well as geographically as "little clusters of Christians" as pockets of light that "dispel the darkness throughout the parish." Two of the four (David and Barbara) did not commit themselves to a belief in "territorial spirits," but Jane was definite on this point ("certainly territorial [spirits], they are scriptural, in Daniel"); and Nicholas had reflected much on it: "I've been convinced over the last eighteen years that there are definitely spirits of areas, that's to say that there are certain characteristics of areas which relate to spirits with a small s and potentially a large S so to speak. The best one I can think of is [our city] as a whole; [our city] historically is an area of individualism, and getting the churches together is very difficult . . . ."

4.2 Case study selection and methods

St. George's, Oakhall (both pseudonyms) was similarly chosen because it was an Anglican church with a distinctively charismatic spirituality, with a focus on mission rather than pastoral maintenance. It was also chosen because of its "revelatory" value as a case study, in its potential to yield a rich qualitative description of a spirituality and theology of spiritual warfare.[14] It was thus also "instrumental" in the sense that it was chosen to investigate a particular phenomenon (spiritual warfare practice), rather than being an intrinsic study of the particular church.[15] It proved however to highlight rather different dimensions of spiritual warfare from St. Martin's.

The church was identified after two independent recommendations of suitability from charismatic leaders in the New Wine network.[16] Having discovered they were soon to host a conference which would touch on spiritual warfare issues, I then made initial contact with the vicar of the church as the main "gatekeeper."[17] After submitting my general proposal to the staff team, he agreed to give permission for the case study, and granted a high degree of access and intensive participant observation, as listed below. A case study protocol was then prepared.[18] The fieldwork was carried out for three-and-a-half weeks, during three visits from October to December 2007, as well as a follow-up visit during 2008. Five different sources of evidence were collected during this period, in order of significance: interviews, participant observation, teaching notes and other documentation (including the church website), sermon recordings, and archival records.

The method of Robert Yin was applied to this study. For *construct validity*, (1) multiple sources of evidence were used, (2) a chain of evidence was recorded,[19] (3) the interviewees were given the opportunity to check and comment on the interview transcript, and (4) a draft of this chapter was

---

14. A "revelatory" case study is one of a kind that had not previously been academically documented, justifying the case study on the grounds that the descriptive information alone could be revelatory. Yin, *Case Study Research*, 42–43.

15. Stake, *The Art of Case Study Research*, 3, as quoted in Cartledge, "Tongues of the Spirit," 75.

16. Michael Melluish, knowing St. George's had a well developed ministry in relation to spiritual warfare; and I then realized that David Pytches (at interview three years before) had recommended the vicar of St. George's as having a deeper understanding of spiritual warfare issues.

17. See chapter 1.4 relating to research ethics here.

18. See Appendix 3 for the interview schedule of the protocol. Pseudonyms are used for the church and all individuals involved.

19. Citing where evidence has come from, as for example in the summary of church history below. See Yin, *Case Study Research: Design and Methods*, 103.

sent to the two main leaders for comment. *Internal validity* is not so relevant to this as a primarily inductive and descriptive study, but some attempt was made to match the pattern with the pilot study, and to consider rival explanations.[20] For *external validity,* in its descriptive function this study was easily comparable with the pilot study, whilst exploring and developing new theoretical perspectives that could be further tested.[21] Several modifications were made to the interview schedule from the pilot study, including two elaborations (questions 20/21) seeking to probe a little deeper into ontological concepts; otherwise the questions remain open-ended and designed to generate theory inductively.[22] The study also aims to be *reliable,* in that all the interview scripts, sermon recordings and relevant field notes were gathered into a case study database, from which the analysis could be repeated.[23]

Interviews

Firstly I recorded a series of thirteen interviews with a cross section of leaders and members of the church using semi-standardized questions.[24] An additional interview was arranged with the vicar to ask more detailed questions arising during the study, and three shorter interviews were recorded with a relatively new Christian now attending the church, a visiting Bible College teacher from East Africa, and a vicar of a nearby church ("Tony" at "St. Thomas's"), who had begun to implement similar "Jesus Ministry" practices in his church.

Participant observation

This included:

- full participation in a week's conference hosted by St. George's (around 160 delegates, mostly from charismatic UK churches but also some from East Africa, Chile, South Africa, and India with mission links

---

20. Ibid., 36, 43, 109.

21. The main concern of this kind of case study is an analytical generalisation to theory (here, primarily concerning the ontology and nature of evil forces, discussed in subsequent chapters). See ibid., 37–38.

22. The questions used with pioneers (Appendix 1) influenced the original schedule of questions. Small modifications were made during the early interviewing stages, to improve usefulness and clarity.

23. Yin, *Case Study Research: Design and Methods*, 37–38.

24. See Appendix 3. Each interview lasted around an hour.

to the church), consisting of worship and teaching sessions and some prayer ministry sessions

- attendance at five services (three morning, two evening) over four Sundays
- attendance at two staff team mornings, for worship teaching and meetings
- participant observation of midweek ministry activities of the church, including home groups/central meeting, youth groups for teenagers, regular youth evening outreach meetings in a nearby hall, and walking the streets of the parish with the youth minister
- both receiving prayer, and listening on a prayer team for four two-hour sessions of "Freedom Prayer"[25] at the church, attending a regional evening for prayer team leaders from a network of local Anglican churches, and assisting in listening prayer for two one-hour sessions of Freedom Prayer at one of these ("St. Bartholomew's")
- Attending a Men's Day with several from St. George's at one nearby network church, and receiving Freedom Prayer afterwards.

A field journal was kept for observations and questions arising throughout the visit.

Documentation

The church did not have any vision statements, but their sense of identity and mission were described in a welcome booklet, and on the church website. During my visits I collected teaching notes (e.g., conference notes) given out at services or other meetings. I obtained copies of two informal papers written by Tony the vicar of St. Thomas's,[26] and of an M.A. dissertation surveying recipients of Freedom Prayer from the leader of another church in this network.

---

25. See description in 4.6 below.

26. Entitled *Re-discovering Jesus's ministry*, and *Repentance—Key to Freedom*, reflecting on his experience of receiving ministry on "Jesus ministry" principles and beginning to practice it with others.

Sermon recordings

All sermons in the church from the beginning of 2007 were available for download from the church website (sermons from St. Thomas's were likewise available, including talks for leaders from Mike Riches); and I was given CD recordings of significant seminar teaching for prayer ministry team leaders made in November between my visits, and a later series on healing.

Archives

I examined church records for attendance at services, baptism and weddings for the last eight years of the church's life. Some other figures were given as estimates from church staff team members.

4.3 Church context

Parish context

The church was in a backstreet of a busy suburban area with a number of other churches within a relatively short distance. The parish was thus quite small, but in two distinct parts—a group of around ten side roads around the church, consisting of expensive property mainly occupied by city professionals; and on the other side of a main road (with local shops and restaurants), a similar number of roads around a small park area that was part of a local council estate, where the social deprivation was most obviously manifested through the disenchanted youth.

Recent history, primary theological influences, and church relationships

By the 1950s and 1960s, the church was thriving as a local evangelical Anglican congregation, with active ministry for all ages (including home groups for the young people). In the late 1960s, the then vicar formed a group of elders to help lead the church, and through the early years of charismatic renewal. In the early 1980s the new vicar had a difficult time—as a conservative evangelical he was eager to avoid any overt influence from the charismatic renewal, although a number of members were still strongly sympathetic. In the first of two historical crises, a move to merge with the neighboring parish (because of the high concentration of Anglican churches in the area) was averted in 1984, and the vicar thus appointed led the church as a "balanced charismatic"—the church maintained a traditional style of worship and a broad evangelical congregation from very conservative to strongly charismatic.[27]

The second crisis was in the mid-1990s, when the archdeacon was determined to close down the church as there were too many evangelical churches in that area. Many in the congregation prayed, particularly a group of seven charismatics who had begun praying monthly "that the Holy Spirit should have free reign in the church" before the previous vicar left;[28] and members saw it as a miracle that the situation was turned around, mainly because of sudden change in senior leadership (bishop and archdeacon) in the diocese leading to Ian's unexpected appointment in 1997.[29]

When Ian came, there were around one hundred on the electoral roll (between fifty and seventy regular attendance). About 120 members came with Ian from the other church, there was fairly immediate overall growth bringing the roll to about 250.[30] Ian before ordination training had been an active member of Holy Trinity, Brompton,[31] and he led the church in "following a good Anglican charismatic renewal ministry,"[32] including an emphasis on counseling and healing. There was considerable fluidity initially (some from both groups left), and it was some time before it was clear who remained committed. This was not surprising, because Ian also brought a strong "commitment to relationships and to [biblical] truth," not to everyone's liking; he had "left the Wimber train tracks" some three years previously and begun to emphasize the importance of faith in the covenant promises of God.[33]

27. This early history was mainly provided by Jerry, who was a member of the church for the whole period. Jerry Interview 8.11.07.

28. Norna Interview 5.11.07.

29. There was a large turnout when the new archdeacon visited the church. The new bishop saw their faith that if Ian (from the clergy team of a thriving charismatic church nearby which was closing to divide and promote growth) was appointed the church would grow and contribute more to the diocese, and he overruled the pastoral committee and appointed Ian in 1997, after a two and a half year interregnum.

30. My calculation for regular Sunday attendance of the combined congregation in autumn 1997 similarly came out at exactly 250.

31. A center in the 1980s for the "Third Wave" of charismatic renewal, in the 1990s for the Toronto Blessing phenomenon, and for the initiation and growth worldwide of the Alpha course (see chapter 2).

32. Ian Interviews 9.11.07, 6.12.07.

33. He had been influenced by teachers such as Kenneth Hagin and Kenneth Copeland, seeing strength in the emphasis on taking hold of our inheritance in Christ by faith, although also seeing much "immaturity and abuses" in some Faith Movement

A major shift in the ministry practice and teaching of the church came as a result of Ian and Clare forging a link with Pastor Mike Riches and his church's ministry from Tacoma, USA in 2002, and beginning to implement "Jesus Ministry" principles starting with the leadership in 2004.[34] Whilst expressed in its own unique way at St. George's, this formed the foundation of the spiritual praxis and theology described below, particularly in spiritual warfare. It also gave a further impetus to church growth, in overall commitment of the membership as well as numbers; as the church and its ministry grew, they could employ several staff members, full or part-time;[35] and a rapid networking grew with other churches beginning to apply similar principles. Consequently, whilst there have never been strong links with non-charismatic churches in the immediate area,[36] there had developed a strong networking relationship with at least four charismatic Anglican churches in that sector of the city (and some other churches and ministries elsewhere in England). As with many suburban churches, regular members at St. George's often travelled in from nearby parishes; whilst the leaders simply asked that they should adopt a mission commitment to St. George's own parish area, at that time the focus was more on reaching out through equipping network churches in mission through "Jesus Ministry" principles.

Those interviewed were often attracted to the church because of the strong relational element and emotional support, and also the clear direction and emphasis on God's power rather than human works. Members were expected to be willing and active; it was "not a church where you can come and sit in a pew on a Sunday."

---

practices. Ian Interviews 9.11.07, 6.12.07. For example, I saw no evidence that commitment to strong relationships had moved into authoritarian "shepherding," nor any signs of a materialistic "prosperity gospel."

34. These principles are enshrined in the five-day Jesus Ministry Conference I attended during my first visit (including teaching from Mike Riches), and the similar "Living Free" evening course run regularly at the church. Riches's fast-growing, "safe" evangelical non-denominational church of over 1,500 was radically shaken by events during three months in 2000, including the shock of "dramatic demonic manifestations" and "two angelic visitations to explain what was transpiring" as many left the church. The story of how this gave rise to his "Jesus ministry" approach, based on a recovery of Luke 4:18–19, is summarized in Riches, "When God Invades His People," *Radiate*, July/Aug 2004, 14–16.

35. In 2007 the staff team consisted of an associate vicar; individual pastors for women, youth, children, and worship; a prayer coordinator and two administrators.

36. There were nevertheless friendly relations with the immediate neighbor on the same council estate—St. George's borrowed their old church hall, where the parishes meet, for weekly youth outreach.

Vision and values

The church leaders did not wish to be tied down by a specific vision statement, but looked to God for a continuous renewal of vision; and in my observation (and in welcome literature) four fundamental values were at the heart of church life:

1. A central place was given to preaching and teaching the Word of God; the Bible was clearly respected as the authority on all matters of faith and practice, and the main source of revealed truth.

2. A high value was placed on charismatic worship, corporately expressed primarily as a continuous block of singing, usually before teaching or other learning or interactive activities.[37] This consisted mainly of contemporary choruses which are God-focused,[38] but expected to release faith and expectancy.

3. There was a clear focus on the supernatural qualities of God, and an expectation that the church could reach out for more manifestations of this in its regular life and that of individual believers, aiming for a continuous personal and corporate transformation.[39] The ultimate goal was "to express the supernatural presence and power of God in the community and in our daily lives to bring personal salvations and community/national transformation."[40]

4. There was an emphasis on the church as a living and growing community of believers, a place to belong and make friends.[41] There was little obvious pressure to actively belong, but the Christian journey was presented as a "great and exciting adventure"; it was naturally expected that those who chose this church would wish to be committed to participate in its life practically and spiritually; and a high level of response from members was indeed evident.[42]

---

37. Worship is nevertheless seen as more than just singing—the emphasis is "lifting our adoration to Him and expecting Him to presence Himself with us, which makes all things possible." Ian, email communication, 19.12.07.

38. "Worship here is about God, to God, and for God." St. George's, *Welcome Booklet* (December 2007).

39. Newcomers are invited onto "a journey to know and experience the transforming love and truth that Jesus Christ offers." George's Church—Welcome," *Website* (17.12.2007).

40. Ian, email communication, 19.12.07.

41. Welcome letter by vicar, St. George's, *Welcome Booklet*.

42. Most obvious when hosting the conference—over 75 percent of the adult congregation were involved in praying on prayer teams, giving accommodation to

Leadership and structure

Although the vicar was clearly the main leader of the church, there was an ethos of mutual accountability in leadership which tended to preclude more autocratic styles of leadership. For overall vision and strategic decision making, the vicar submitted to a group of six elders, who also oversaw the different areas of ministry; and every now and then a much wider group of leaders in the church would meet for prayer and envisioning. Otherwise as in most Anglican churches business and financial matters were discussed at PCC (Parish Consultative Council); and the day to day running of the church program was coordinated through the staff team, who met weekly on Tuesday mornings for worship, teaching, planning, and prayer.

Pattern of church life

Beyond Sunday services, there were regular groups for different ages and midweek activities, with mentoring relationships available upon request. The church met on Tuesday evenings in a number of small "life groups," typically six to eight people in homes, where the program was largely under the direction of the leaders. However, these often combined centrally, sometimes for a series (e.g., for the month of February 2008). Adult training courses run from time to time, notably an eight-week "Living Free" course,[43] and a subsequent training course for prayer ministry. Teenagers met in two separate age groups (school years 6–8, 9+) on Friday evenings for "worship, transformation, energy, and friendship,"[44] and also in smaller "pastorate groups" for the older boys and girls on other weekdays. The youth "Sanctuary" on Thursday nights was a significant "fresh expression" of church and an outreach focus for youth on the church fringes.

Prayer was a vital part of church life. Small groups met to pray before the two main Sunday services; there was early morning prayer monthly for those supported in mission from the church, locally, nationally or overseas; and every couple of months an intercession evening on a Friday. Every Wednesday daytime, opportunity was given for individuals to book a two-hour ministry time with up to half a dozen prayer teams of three or four people, for "Freedom Prayer" (see *Praxis* below), to help them move

---

delegates, providing refreshments and meals, working on the site team, and running a program for children of delegates.

43. This course taught the basic spiritual principles of "Jesus ministry" similar to the "Jesus Ministry Conference."

44. St. George's, *Welcome Booklet*.

forward in their spiritual growth. These were popular and could be booked up several weeks in advance.

Sunday worship

There were two main Sunday services, at 10.30 am and 6 pm; church members tended to come to one or the other, and so the main sermon was repeated in the evening. The atmosphere was friendly and welcoming, with drinks available before and especially after the service. Generally families with children of all ages came to the morning service, with space at the back for tiny ones and separate groups (after initially worshipping together) for toddlers, pre-schoolers and primary children (years 1 to 5), and the older youth. On occasions the whole church stayed together for an all-age service; and communion was normally included twice a month, once in the morning and once in the evening.

Both services were long, the morning one lasting around two hours or more, and the evening one about half an hour shorter. The influence of the Vineyard worship culture, in the basic liturgical pattern of Worship-Word-Ministry, was evident in most of the services.[45] The climax of the service was the preaching, generally of around forty-five minutes, usually followed by a challenge and some kind of corporate prayer response, then a closing song. The first half of the service was dominated by worship songs led by the music group. This was partly seen as intercessory spiritual preparation for having open spirits to hear and receive the preached word; thus the leader occasionally asked for an additional song to help people to "break through" or "press in" to be hungry enough to receive—for example, encouraging singing in tongues at this point.

Formal liturgical elements were few.[46] Normally someone would read the text of the day before the sermon, and an individual or a family together might lead prayers, especially for the mission partners of the church; but sometimes the church would be asked to pray out loud all at once for the mission partners, with their pictures and information projected on the screen. Baptisms could be performed early in the service, with a simplified liturgy and a chance for the vicar to pray spontaneously and propheti-

---

45. Steven, *Worship in the Spirit*, 66–67. Despite their spontaneity in worship, Pentecostals and charismatics still have liturgical forms, for example as delineated in Albrecht, *Rites in the Spirit*.

46. For example, the normal Anglican prayer of confession was omitted from the service. The normal service outline and style was in fact remarkably similar to that followed by many other more independent charismatic churches, for example the one described by Cartledge, *Practical Theology*, 113.

cally over each child. As the children stayed in for the first half hour in the morning, after some initial worship songs there was usually a children's talk. Other elements in the first half might be notices and banns of marriage, and testimonies, particularly of healing. After the final song, there was often an invitation to receive prayer for healing, either coming to the front for prayer from ministry team members, or sometimes with a prayer team for a longer time of "Freedom Prayer."

4.4 Interviewees

All thirteen interviewees were given pseudonyms for this study. In describing them below I have combined two as a married couple (David and Kate), although they were interviewed separately. Just under half were on the church staff team, which helped to probe a little deeper theologically, although I found that most interviewees had a good awareness of the issues at the level of "ordinary theology."[47] All had been trained and now operated to different degrees in listening prayer teams ("Freedom Prayer").[48]

Staff members

Ian was the vicar of the church, in his forties, married to Clare, with four children mainly in their teens. Having become a Christian in his late teens, he has "never really known anything except an expectation of miracles and the life of the Spirit."[49] Coming from a business background, he was ordained in 1993 and served his curacy at a church linked to Holy Trinity, Brompton, coming from there to St. George's as his first vicar's post in 1997.

Clare became a Christian through her relationship with Ian, whom she subsequently married; she was the women's pastor, also sharing with Ian oversight of extended ministry beyond the church. Having been previously involved in counseling and healing ministry with Ian, this was still one of her key ministry areas.

---

47. Theology or "God-talk" grounded in the challenges and fulfillments of ordinary life, rather than controversies of the academy, by those who have received little or no academic theological education. Astley, *Ordinary Theology*, 54, 56.

48. This illustrates a leading characteristic of the church, the high degree of spiritual commitment and training in "every member ministry," often a feature of churches strongly influenced by charismatic renewal. See Scotland, *Charismatics and the New Millennium*, 32.

49. Ian Interviews 9.11.07, 6.12.07.

Peter was the associate vicar, married with three young children (one born during my study period). Having grown up in an Anglican church experiencing renewal he has "always been charismatic by persuasion," though in his teenage years had conservative evangelical input from school Christian Union mixed with attendance at a Pentecostal church.

Wills was the prayer coordinator, especially for prayer teams. He was in his forties, married with four young children, and also ran his own business. He became a Christian from a privileged background in the early 1990s, and moved to St. George's with Ian in 1997.

Gail was the worship pastor, in her thirties, who also came with the same group to St. George's in 1997. She became a Christian as a teenager, and as a student was invited to help lead worship on some courses that Ian and Clare were leading. She also helped with prayer team training, and mentoring.

Alexander was the youth pastor, in his thirties and married. He grew up through the youth groups of an Anglican church, and after sensing God's voice and presence rescuing him from near suicide at University, went on to become a youth worker and then a youth pastor in another Anglican church, before coming to St. George's five years previously.

Other church members

Norna was an older lady in her seventies, a widower who had been worshipping at St. George's for twenty-two years. She had always been an Anglican Christian, but was deeply impacted and brought into charismatic renewal by joining the Lydia women's intercession movement in the late 1970s. She was thus one of the key members of a group that prayed through the 1990s interregnum for a new openness to the Holy Spirit in the church. Now she is part of the wider leadership of the church, still involved in prayer and on the listening prayer teams.

Jerry was in his sixties approaching retirement; he grew up in the church and so had been attending for fifty-five years, the longest of all the interviewees. As a young man he had helped lead the youth group and youth home groups and joined PCC; he had joined the eldership when it was formed in the late 1960s, serving as church warden for a time; he became a reader in the late 1980s, remaining in leadership until two years previously when it was agreed he would step down. He was part of a small team who ran a social ministry of debt counseling.

Michael was in his early fifties, formerly working in computers, but currently unemployed; he spent much of his time helping with work on the church site, and recently also with listening prayer ministry. He started attending St. George's in the 1970s soon after becoming an evangelical Christian at boarding school, encountering charismatic renewal immediately afterwards.

David and **Kate** were a married couple in their thirties, with one three-year-old daughter. David began a living faith at boarding school, but this only fully came alive when he came to St. George's and did an Alpha course nine years previously. Kate came across the pastor Ian at school and so joined his church when she came to the same city. They often helped with the church youth groups.

Rachel was single, in her twenties, and also helped with the younger teenagers in church. She grew up in an Anglican church, tried various others at University (e.g., Baptist, Assemblies of God), but joined St. George's when she moved to the area. She was working in a Christian social project in the inner city, a drop-in center offering advice, counseling and prayer ministry, and as such was a mission associate supported by St. George's.

Eduardo was eighteen years old, completing his schooling in the city. At the time he lived some distance away in another suburb, but had moved location many times with his Argentine father who was in itinerant Christian ministry. Although he had a difficult period when he stopped coming, he was now well committed to the youth group and youth outreach at St. George's.

4.5 Analysis

This was carried out primarily by content analysis on the interview transcripts, building up a series of interlinked descriptive categories in relation to the interview schedule.[50] I was unable to reliably express weighting without computer analysis; and as the study is primarily descriptive a formal attempt at linking the data in causal or explanatory relationship was not attempted.[51]

---

50. In a similar way to that described in chapter 9 of Dey, *Qualitative Data Analysis*. The special delineations of Dey's system, for example of exclusive and inclusive categories, have not been attempted. See Appendix 4 for a diagram of the categories that emerged from the study.

51. Cf. Ibid., 152, 210–15. However, some significant explanatory links are implied in the category table (Appendix 4) and the analysis that follows here. As one example, the "spiritual weapon" of praise and worship, rather than being listed separately, is linked in as a subsection of the first primary weapon, truth ("the sword of the Spirit")— as one interviewee noted, praise also functions as "truth declared" (Gail).

Just as it is not easy to define what elements of worship are charismatic in a church,[52] it is difficult to isolate charismatic spiritual warfare elements from the wider charismatic praxis, and the principles behind these. Whilst many churches and individuals (including several interviewees in previous experience[53]) see spiritual warfare as something restricted to special circumstances, perhaps during evangelistic outreach, St. George's had come to see it as a mindset that permeated much of their spiritual lives. Thus in this analysis I have included all aspects of the spirituality of the church that relate in some way to spiritual warfare.

Spirituality and theology of course overlap, especially concerning narrative; in Wright's fourfold analysis of worldview, religious spirituality would focus mainly on symbols and praxis as well as narrative, and theology primarily on the key questions and the narrative ("controlling stories") that offers answers to many of them.[54] Here I describe "symbols" mainly from my participant observation, "praxis" primarily from the interview analysis, and "outcomes" from both. Having described above the local narrative of the church's story, I shall postpone analyzing the theological "meta-narrative" to the discussion section.

Symbols

Symbols can be both artifacts and events.[55] A number of symbols came to the fore, which gave a focus in three main areas of spirituality.

Firstly, within worship, there were the familiar charismatic symbols of freedom and lively leadership in praise and worship, the *overhead projector screens* and the contemporary *worship band* (of lead singer and keyboard, some instruments and usually two or three backing singers) in the center of the carpeted stage area, integrated from the mixing desk.[56] The high screens in particular not only convey the value-laden words of the charismatic songs, but do so on a varied photographic backdrop that often helped to reinforce the words and, in the bright blue skies and piercing sun, symbolize the reaching into the heavenly realms where the omnipotent God dwells and rules from his throne, a key belief in their theological worldview. At times, these worship symbols were reinforced with others—notably the spontane-

---

52. See Steven, *Worship in the Spirit*, 55.

53. E.g., "I always thought spiritual warfare was something you do out on the streets . . . and [that] its quite scary." (Kate).

54. Wright, *The New Testament and the People of God*, 124–25.

55. Ibid., 123.

56. Cf. Cartledge, *Practical Theology*, 116–17.

ous use of different colored *flags*, symbolizing also the dazzling rainbow colors of light shimmering before God's throne;[57] and, specifically in relation to spiritual warfare, symbols of celebration of victory—on one occasion towards the end of the conference the *"shofa"* was sounded;[58] and on another we were invited to give a *"festal shout"* of praise in unison together.

Secondly, there was united *proclamatory prayer* declaring truths into the heavenly realms—a symbol of moving in victory into greater spiritual freedom in the power of agreement. This was often used after a sermon or talk to declare and pray into the subject area of teaching and exhortation.[59] Sometimes other symbolic actions were linked with this—asking us to *stand on the chairs*, to symbolize that Satan was now under our feet; another, *stepping across an imaginary line* in front of us to represent walking free from an area of sin. A similar symbol linking with this power of agreement in prayer, was intercessory prayer out loud together, whether in English or in tongues—as once when praying for church link missionaries during Sunday intercessions.

Thirdly, a key symbol of receiving wholeness through repentance and deliverance, was the ministry event called *Freedom Prayer*, and its symbolic artifact, the *spiral notebook* (or "PukkaPad"). This is further described under "prayer ministry" praxis.

Praxis

Key weapons of warfare

Most interviewees listed three or four key weapons, and the top three favorites were clear—listed as *truth*, followed by *discernment* and *authority* by Ian, and supported by his flock with some variation in language: the truth of God's Word (seven interviewees), sometimes linked to the sword of the Spirit (Clare, Wills, Kate); prophetic recognition (Peter, Kate), insight and discernment (David), listening to God (Clare) or following the Lord's leading (Alexander); and authority (Michael, David, Rachel, Eduardo) to bind the enemy (Jeremy, Peter), to take territory (Norna), or to command

---

57. The vicar, Ian described this in a brief vision he believed he had received of heavenly worship.

58. The trumpet used in Joshua 3 around the walls of Jericho.

59. For example, after one Sunday sermon concerning breaking into a new level of expectancy of the supernatural, a need for many to break out of self-pity had been discerned, and so there was a corporate prayer of repentance and rebuke. Other examples I experienced were similar prayers against "insignificance" (conference session), and "inferiority" (after men's meeting at St. Bartholomew's).

a specific situation to change (David). Other surprising "weapons" were repentance (Clare, Wills) as a legal transaction (Peter, Rachel), forgiveness (Clare, Wills), and blessing (Wills); also prayer in general (Norna, Michael), worship and praise (Jeremy, Rachel, Gail), faith (Eduardo) or belief (Gail), the nature of people's identity (Peter), and loosing (Michael).

Asking about specific forms of prayer often yielded similar results, such that for later interviewees I did not always ask it as a separate question. When the further question (9)[60] of specifically charismatic gifts was added, the above list was further reinforced—prophecy (David), discernment (Norna, Michael, David, Eduardo—"asking the Lord what is going on") and word of knowledge (Jeremy) were again mentioned; and praise and worship (Gail, David, Kate) and repentance (Gail, Peter) also re-occurred—as well as authority (Michael), even as a charismatic gift in prayer (Norna, "recognizing authority"). This reveals that in a strongly charismatic church of this kind, the majority of prayer practices are considered charismatic, also in the general sense that there is "no set plan," seeking to follow the leading of the Lord (Alexander), in prayer "placing the whole lot under the Lord's leading" (Norna); and where there is a strong spiritual warfare mindset, virtually the whole range of spiritual activities can be seen as weapons in the spiritual battle.

However, some distinctions were retained. For example, (9) led many to mention the gift of tongues; but, with the exception of Alexander for whom it had a significant role as a form or warfare prayer in the past, the rest saw tongues as more important in its own right (Ian), more for edifying oneself (David, Kate), and building up one's spirit (Rachel). This was partly an issue of timing, and of teaching—because of the strong influence of the Tacoma team, who came from a non-charismatic evangelical background and did not speak in tongues or teach on it, St. George's had laid down some of its charismatic heritage for a while but was now picking it up again (Ian); thus Ian had recently been doing a lot of teaching on tongues.

Preaching and teaching

Similarly, though not obvious candidates as part of warfare praxis, preaching and teaching played a central role in two ways. Firstly, spiritual warfare was regularly the subject of sermons, whether in whole or mentioned in the sermon,[61] and around once or twice a month there was a corporate response

60. Question numbers refer to the questions listed in the interview schedule, Appendix 3.
61. For example, a series in September 2008, on "Living in and from Victory."

to the preaching through doing spiritual warfare prayer in the services.[62] It was also a key focus of the "Living Free" Course, which members were actively encouraged to attend, and the similar material of the Jesus Ministry conference.[63] Secondly, the truth or the Word was described as "the main weapon in warfare . . . [which is] fundamentally a truth encounter not a power encounter,"[64] because it is the truth that sets people free (Ian); "the truth of God's love and his Word" was also in the top three weapons for the other main preacher in the church (Peter).

Praise and worship

At St. George's, praise and worship play a central role in spiritual praxis, and are seen as significant in spiritual warfare. Gail (the worship pastor) explained that this is because praise incorporates truth, the primary weapon, as a declaration of God's character and nature. She also spoke from experience how exhorting a congregation who seemed to be in a spiritual stupor caused people to wake up and agree again in believing the truth, and come out of the confusion of not really knowing who God is. Clearly she believed this precipitated an experience of God's presence.[65] I indeed observed a strong focus in the songs on God and his goodness and greatness—two favorites were "How great is our God," and "He is greater still," another was "The good God." As worship leader and also songwriter, Gail hoped that in the songs she wrote "the people of God are singing the truth that God is now speaking to them about." In her songs therefore there are regularly themes of authority and victory, for example:

The regularity of this teaching to the whole congregation was in contrast to the pilot study church, St. Martin's, where teaching on spiritual warfare was generally given to a smaller group of leaders, being considered inappropriate for the main Sunday service which in that context were seen as the "shop window" of outreach to the community.

62. Kate's observation.

63. Of the ten main Conference sessions, the first introduces this world as a war-zone originating in the heavenly realms, the second ("Boldly facing the Enemy") introduces a series of five on how to fight, and the remaining four all have significant content relating to the battle Christians are in.

64. Ian acknowledged that he had picked up this phrase from Neil Anderson, without having particularly read his books—it is a key concept in his "Freedom in Christ" discipleship course, popular with many charismatics.

65. She added: "What better spiritual warfare can you have than the presence of God being present and his manifestation." Similarly Ian more than once exhorted the congregation to press through further in worship to be in the right place to receive the preaching of the word with faith.

> Where Satan has dominion
>
> The king comes in his power
>
> We are more than conquerors, crowned with his authority;
>
> Standing on His word, his power
>
> His blood has set us free
>
> The powers of darkness take their flight
>
> When we rise up in Jesus might
>
> The lion's roar defines our victory.[66]

Other themes are the power of God (e.g., "Your power is far beyond all measure, exalted king of light"), awe and wonder ("God of wonder, God of mystery"), and also the assurance that hope brings ("You are the only hope whose anchor never fails" etc.), which helps to express some of the yearning of the heart in times of spiritual dryness ("hope is rising in the darkness, hope is rising in the desert"). Although a large proportion of the songs sung were of vigorous high praise, nevertheless the block of worship tended to finish with more intimate devotional songs.[67] These again pick up local theological themes, such as living in the truth over against lies ("you were made to live in the truth, why do you listen to lies") that keep us in fear and feeling insignificant ("you were made for beauty displayed, why do you run and hide"). This is most notably in relation to the truth of God's original design for each person, yet not as a passive comfort but linked to an invitation and exhortation to stir our spirits and rise above the things that hold us back:

> "Creation longs and waits for you, child, to be revealed
>
> The one you were always meant to be . . .
>
> Hear his love song beckoning you
>
> Calling you to rise up higher

---

66. Not a throwback to one of the controversial phenomenon of the Toronto Blessing, people roaring like a lion—instead inspired by the roar Aslan gave to the white witch in C. S. Lewis's Narnia chronicles, when she audaciously asked him how she could know he would keep his word. (All the words quoted are from Gail's own songs, now copyrighted but here quoted with her permission).

67. As in much charismatic worship, especially where influenced by the Vineyard; as in one of Steven's case study churches, which had forty minutes of continuous singing "in the Wimber pattern of seamless music, finishing with devotional songs." Steven, *Worship in the Spirit*, 67.

Calling you to soar in freedom

Choose life 'cause I chose you."

Prophetic discernment

My question (5) was specifically how the need for spiritual warfare was discerned. However, asking God for discernment of what is going on, and expecting a reply, is central to the spirituality at St. George's.[68] Hence eight out of thirteen specifically highlighted "asking the question" from the Lord, what is going on, although some were more practiced at this than others—Rachel did so when she remembered, and David only slowly began to think he might need to consider something is spiritual if the situation didn't go away or respond to simple prayer. Ian and Gail emphasized this in pointing out the need to recognize first that there is actually a problem which could be spiritual, which comes first from understanding what our inheritance should be—"if you don't know what your inheritance is then you don't know you have been robbed." Gail's example was that the enemy wants to rob our relationship with the Lord—for example, if there is no joy, no peace, then there's a need to ask why not. Peter and Wills were both keen to realize it could be either natural or spiritual in its main causation, asking God "is there a spiritual component, or is it just a natural thing?"[69] Jeremy assumed every situation requires spiritual warfare—at least potentially—so was keen in asking God for protection.[70] Others found it got easier through experience, you might find you just sense certain things in your spirit, for example a sense of the occult (Clare). Other specific ways of discerning evil mentioned were headache, nausea, not being able to breathe properly (Eduardo), a "gut reaction"(Peter), "seeing" demons (Eduardo).

Motivating affections

The most mentioned motivation for spiritual warfare was anger, for both the men (Ian, David) and the women (Gail, Norna, Rachel—"sometimes getting mad"). Anger was directed at the enemy's nature as a thief and robber

---

68. Members are encouraged to continuously seek revelation by talking to God and asking questions, both positive (e.g., concerning God's gifts, qualities, and designs), and asking how the enemy is trying to block God's good purposes.

69. Peter gave an example in teaching of asking what was causing a headache, and the answer being the need to go and drink some more water!

70. Citing the influence of Dutch Sheets, *Intercessory Prayer*, in this regard.

stealing our inheritance (Ian, Gail, David); causing injustice, poverty, and suffering (David); and anger at the devil as a liar (David) with such a lying and deceitful manner, kicking people when they are down, and binding them up (Norna). In such a situation, once the Holy Spirit puts his finger on it, the anger rises up (David); Ian noted a corporate dimension to this, during a Bible study on David and Goliath in church a few years back. However, for these and others there were equally positive motivating emotions. Peter acknowledged that for some there was "an emphasis of getting into a fight with the enemy," but not for him—increasingly it was compassion for the person, a desire to see them set free (also Rachel); also wanting God's plan and vision for that person (Rachel). There was the longing to meet with God and engage with him (Gail), desire to walk closely with the Lord and be effective in seeing fruit (Michael); we are loved by the Father, and spiritual warfare is just part of what God wants us to be (Alexander). Thus there is the attraction of joy (Gail), the enjoyment of life and of discovering the power of the cross (Clare). Some mentioned the encouragement and hope from seeing their own and others' lives changed—for Michael this was the main motivation, for another seeing his marriage totally transformed (Wills); or just the reality of knowing that "if I don't do spiritual warfare, I'm going to stay miserable" and be unfruitful (Kate). On the larger scale, Clare displayed the ultimate soldier's determination and courage: "Ian and I have decided that we would rather fight and die fighting and not see it come about for people to be healed and set free, than not to have fought at all."

Strategy for spiritual warfare

Almost without exception, the interviewees saw the ideal strategy in spiritual warfare as going on the offensive to take back territory from the devil,[71] rather than defensive and reactive. Although some (e.g., Kate and David) recognized that in reality they still tended to react to problems arising, others sought to anticipate what would come up during the day and pray about that (Michael). Several thus said they had begun to ask God what the enemy might bring against them that day or in a particular venture (e.g., Ian, Rachel), and sensed that this avoided much unnecessary battling.[72] However,

---

71. This is not just an aggressive "warfare" stance; the wider context is a much more positive overall ambition, seeking to "restore that which was lost" (Luke 19:10 NKJV), including God's design for physical mental and relational health, before man first sinned; this is foundational to Mike Riches's "Jesus ministry" approach. Riches, "When God Invades His People," 16.

72. Learning to avoid battles by praying in advance was a similar insight in the pilot study church, St. Martin's—see section 4.1.

nearly all interviewees now prayed some kind of prayer against the enemy on a daily basis, and this was true too in the prayer life of the church. As Ian put it, "spiritual warfare is part of our strategy for whatever we are doing... if you have a worldview of two realms, then you have to live in that all of the time. You can't only switch that on for an evangelistic campaign." Thus, corporate prayer was integrated into all aspects of the church's life,[73] such as Tuesday staff meetings, mid-week "life groups," or before young people's group activities on Friday and Thursday. All such prayer includes now an element of listening for prophetic guidance, often after asking specific questions to God in prayer.

Concerning the bigger picture, Ian conveys the balance of priorities in the church's overall strategy at that particular time:

> I don't think right now our primary goal as a church is reaching this parish. I think our primary goal as a church is to help bring other churches and other pastors into restoration and freedom. Evangelism and social action for us as a church is not a side issue in that sense but it's a secondary. Because you only have so many people and only a certain amount of time and use a certain amount of energy. We have an awful lot of families with young children, it's not a good time to put more on them. . . . We're doing one or two things as well as we can and we'll wait for God to open up the others. That's more our strategy.

Prayer ministry

Prayer ministry was a very important part of spiritual praxis at St. George's. Often at the end of Sunday services, there might be a call to come to the front for healing prayer (sometimes in response to words of knowledge that were given), or for prayer ministry for a particular issue. Alternatively, team leaders were often called to form Freedom Prayer teams, sometimes pre-organized on a roster basis to ensure it was available. In addition, two-hour sessions of Freedom Prayer could be booked on a weekday morning or afternoon, and this kind of prayer was given regularly to prayer team leaders (especially on their regular monthly training days), at the end of the Living Free course and as part of the subsequent training course for prayer listening. In the church's extended ministry to other churches, Freedom Prayer was available after pastors' days for those visiting from the network, on the new Jesus Ministry introductory days, and shorter half-hour sessions were

---

73. See *Pattern of church life* in 4.3 above.

offered every evening during the Jesus Ministry conferences, then held once or twice a year. It is thus highly significant in the particular approach to spiritual growth and spiritual warfare at St. George's.

The prayer pastor (Wills)[74] was keen to point out that there was nothing magical or mystical about "Freedom Prayer," it is really just "prayer," in particular "listening prayer." Each prayer team generally consists of a team leader and two or three listeners. The team take a spiral notebook each, pray briefly together beforehand, in particular openly confessing anything that might hinder their ability to hear from God; for example if they had just had an argument with someone, or were feeling self-preoccupied or anxious about something, they would repent of anger or fear, and matter-of-factly rebuke the enemy in this area. The team leader would then "protect the time," usually binding the enemy and "binding the flesh" (shutting down the natural imagination as an act of faith that God would now speak through his Spirit). The leader would then listen, even for what questions to ask God concerning the person, and all the team would listen for his answers and write down on the notepads what they believed they received.[75] The person would then be led through a prayer process which was often summarized as "the four (or five) Rs."[76] From my own observations,[77] I would summaries the framework for this process as follows:

Recognition—of God's purposes for that person, in particular what He wanted to deal with (e.g., a particular area of enemy attack) during that particular session. If someone had not had Freedom Prayer before, they always first ask for positive revelation concerning God's original design for that person ("reading their spiritual DNA"), before going on to ask what enemy strongholds[78] might be in their lives—the enemy's strongholds were

---

74. This description is mainly from my own participant observation, and interview information from Wills.

75. A much higher value was placed on God's prophetic revelation, partly since the person's "presenting problem" (e.g., anger) might not be the root issue. For example, where I was listening on team, a root of *anger* discerned in the person was identified as being *"insignificance,"* resulting in feeling trapped and powerless (picture: standing at the edge of an incredibly busy road, unable to cross), and *fear* and *unbelief* stopping him stepping out (a zebra crossing was actually in front of his feet). The deeper roots were then discerned as having unmet love needs from his father, and feeling crushed in school, both of which he accepted.

76. It was not always easy to know which R's were referred to; as there had been development over time at Tacoma, and with Riches' permission each church had freely adapted them as flexible not rigid tools. Riches gives 4 pairs of R's in Riches, *Strongholds*, 82–83.

77. Helped by St. George's leaflet entitled "Living in Freedom," given to conference participants to help daily live out the four Rs.

78. A stronghold (see 2 Cor 10:3–5) was defined as "a fortressed base of

seen as part of his scheme to shut an individual down in areas where God had created him or her to be most fruitful.[79] Another question might be "What *core lies* has this person believed?" As always, anything heard by the listeners was shown or given to the leader, who would discern whether, when and how to pass them on to the prayer recipient. This was always done as an offering to be accepted or rejected, rather than as an authoritative word from God.

Repentance—if the revelation was recognized as correct, and the recipient was willing, the person would then be led through specific prayer of confession and repentance, perhaps also offering forgiveness to anyone who had offended him or her. They were then usually asked to imagine themselves *receiving* cleansing from Jesus, often through asking them to visualize themselves standing at the foot of the cross and allowing Jesus's blood to flow down over them and wash them clean; followed by a visualization of them being in a field, or on a beach, and seeing the risen Jesus there ready to welcome and perhaps embrace them as forgiven friends.

Rebuking—the person themselves is encouraged to exercise their own authority in Christ over the specific energizing work of the enemy they are dealing with; rebuking the powers of darkness (sometimes, addressed as "any spirits of . . . [fear, passivity, insignificance, etc.]") and putting them under Jesus authority (e.g., sending them under Jesus's feet)—or crushing them under the believer's feet.[80] They were frequently encouraged to *renounce* any lies they might have believed, and any sinful patterns of disobedience, and embrace the truth.

Replace—the old thoughts and behavior patterns with biblical truth and obedience. The team usually asked God for revelation as to how the person would look free of this stronghold; and for strategy as to how to stay free, often including some Scriptural verses to pray and meditate on. These pages of the Pukka Pads were usually given to the recipient to take away (with perhaps only the leader's summary notes of the earlier parts of the process, not wanting to over-focus on the negative).[81] The session would

---

operations"—cf. New American Standard Bible, "the weapons of our warfare are . . . divinely powerful for the destruction of *fortresses*."

79. For example, on one of my Freedom Prayer sessions, I noticed such a connection—in my "original DNA" I was seen as being a person of vitality, whereas one of the enemy's strategies was to sap my energy (e.g., through virus infection).

80. Cf. Ps 110:1, Rom 16:20.

81. In conference teaching, it was emphasized that 95 percent of the change comes as the person continues to work at the replacement of wrong attitudes in his or her own life.

end with the team standing and praying blessing upon the recipient, usually with laying on of hands.

Beyond this basic outline, particularly in longer Freedom Prayer sessions, prayer questions would be asked concerning the roots of highlighted strongholds, particularly from parents or previous generations—what Mike Riches calls "generational shadows" cast on subsequent generations, resulting in "generational strongholds" being passed on until the cycle is broken, through confession on behalf of their own sin and of previous generations.[82] In several of the sessions I was involved in, there would be an element of generational issues prayed through. Another area that might be prayed into would be curses—from God due to disobedience, from Satanic practices, or negative pronouncements from other people.[83]

Training

St George's is committed to training its own members in the principles of Jesus Ministry, especially in listening prayer. With the demand and effectiveness of this training, they were at that time no longer running Alpha courses so as to instead focus on running "Living Free" courses at least twice a year, as well as large Jesus Ministry conferences around twice a year, which apart from receiving Freedom Prayer included exercises and basic training in listening prayer. Prayer team leaders had regular seminar training sessions through the year, as their role is central.

Evangelism and social outreach

At the time, there were few explicit programs for either evangelism or social outreach.[84] Whilst clearly a current weakness, it was one recognized by the leadership, as being due to their focus on equipping Christians for a lifestyle of greater spiritual freedom.[85] However, they were nevertheless seeing an increased number of people coming to faith; and in the main area of social need in the parish, that of social deprivation and hopelessness amongst the youth, the youth pastor Alexander and his team were actively engaged. Al-

---

82. See Riches, *Strongholds*, 86–91. Lev 26:40–42 was one of the scriptural justifications for this kind of confession of generational sin.

83. Ibid., 119–20.

84. There was a group helping with debt counseling, and Rachel was a mission associate working in a Christian drop-in center in a nearby inner city suburb. The mothers and toddlers group had been suspended at present.

85. See quote from Ian under *Strategy* above.

exander and some of the Christian youth would regularly go onto the streets, praying as they go, and taking opportunities to talk with young people and sometimes pray for them, particularly in terms of asking God for revelation as to his "original design" for them. Many were touched by the very positive things they thus heard; and, helped by a Kick Week outreach (playing football together), for a season a large number of the youth wanted to come to the church. As they brought an element of disruption, sadly they had to be discouraged from coming at that point; but subsequently the Haven (a pseudonym) was launched on a Thursday night in a small hall belonging to a neighboring church, giving them their own space, with youth style worship, a message, and an opportunity to be prayed for. Whilst numbers were not large, when I attended the team were very encouraged with small but significant signs of gradual opening up, and some just beginning to receive listening prayer. Some had also joined the church youth on Friday nights, as well as smaller youth "cell groups" mid-week for food and fellowship.

Theology

Ontology

The cosmology and ontology of evil forces is obviously a key area; I shall therefore analyze this in the extended theological discussion below.[86]

Influences and validation

All those interviewed admitted to significant influences from all three main areas—the Bible, teachers and leaders, and their own (and others') experiences. However, most (eight) gave the Bible as the greatest influence, being the most reliable in validating their experience and what they heard taught or read. Jeremy, probably the slowest to embrace the teaching from Tacoma, emphasized the need to test everything; and Clare described Scripture as "the plumb-line," and experience as another. The teaching from St. George's leadership (Rachel), and specifically Mike and Cindy Riches and co-pastors from Tacoma, was considered to have "opened our eyes" (Clare)—and because it sat so squarely on the Scriptures and their books are full of Scripture, it often sent them back to the Scriptures "to compare and look through for myself" (Rachel), and to read them more and find them come

---

86. See also the "dynamic of conflict" table of categories in Appendix 4, summarizing demonic access points, areas of demonic activity and when the battle was considered most intense.

alive (Wills). Experience of being in a spiritual battle before connecting with Tacoma was varied; some had almost none, others had some more dramatic experiences—notably Alexander, of being protected in physical danger as a youth worker elsewhere; and Eduardo had many from his time in Argentina, where his father was a revivalist pastor,[87] or Peter when in Central Asia before ordination. For these, this new phase of teaching and experience was a re-confirmation of something they had seen before, giving additional validation.

Apart from Mike Riches and his books,[88] the only ones mentioned more than once were Bill Johnson (Clare, Gail), Dutch Sheets' *Intercessory Prayer* (Peter, Jeremy), and Rick Joyner's *Final Quest* (Gail, David). Other influential teachers and books were: John Wimber in the early days (Ian); Bill Subritsky[89] in the 1980s (Peter); Jack Deere, especially *The Prophetic Beginners* (Gail); Dick Lucas/David MacInnes/David Sheppard (Norna); Douglas MacBain *Discerning the Spirits,* Frank Peretti novels (Jeremy); Rees Howells *Intercessor* (David); Hatthaway *The Heavenly Man* (Eduardo); and Michael interestingly found himself going back to books he'd read years ago, such as Watchman Nee, especially *Sit, Walk, Stand*, and Roy Hession *Calvary Road*. During teaching, Ian and Peter also drew attention to two other more serious theological books.[90]

Apart from Ephesians 6 (especially 6:12), the most significant Scriptures mentioned by interviewees were from earlier Ephesians (e.g., 2:6, 4:27); taking thoughts captive (2 Cor 10:5); submitting to God and resisting the devil (1 Pet 5, Jas 4); and not having a spirit of timidity or fear, but of a sound mind (2 Tim 1:7).[91]

---

87. Specifically he remembers at age four being frightened seeing a demon in the kitchen (where he later heard someone had previously committed suicide), and being taught by his father there and then that he had seen it and so should take the authority to tell it to leave in the name of Jesus, which he did.

88. E.g., Riches, *Strongholds*; *One World—Two Realms*.

89. See Subritzky, *Demons Defeated*. However, Peter had distanced himself later from it as too experience-based; and Ian had reacted strongly against Subritzky's brash ministry style ("lack of humility and a deep arrogance . . . carpet-bombing approach . . . rather than listening to God . . . aggressive and controlling . . . not much space for restoration and healing"), and considered it badly thought through—although he recognized that knowing what he knew now, he surely wouldn't have such a strong reaction.

90. Foster and King, *Binding and Loosing*; Boyd, *God at War*.

91. For others see Appendix 4.

Outcomes

Interviews

There is not space here to recount the many stories told of the benefits of this kind of approach. However, when asked this specific question (29), and the importance of awareness of the spiritual battle for Christians (30), the following is a summary of the answers given.

The interviewees testified to personal spiritual transformation and healings, changes in relationships, and dramatic changes in others through Freedom Prayer ministry. For themselves, Peter felt lighter and more confident to be the person he was meant to be; and Michael described in similar terms a growth his friends had seen in him. Clare, Peter, and Rachel experienced loss of fears in their lives, Rachel being freed from a paralyzing fear of not being able to speak in group situations; and David experienced much greater freedom from low self-worth, being able now to embrace the truths of God's special love for him when he read them in Scripture. Clare was more focused on Christ, and now saw a lot more color in life, laughed more and played with kids more. David sensed a growth in faith for healing, and "had moved house on the basis of a spiritual warfare breakthrough." Healing reported included being healed from depression immediately after spiritual warfare prayer (David); and Norna's doctors were amazed at the speed of her recoveries after various operations such as leg artery replacement surgeries.

In relationships, one said his marriage was transformed, another that a difficult relationship she had struggled with in the church for years underwent extraordinary transformation. Peter noticed the dramatic difference with his children, being able to deal with abnormal behavior through intercession, spiritual warfare, and personal repentance as parents.

Some testified to growth in faith and expectancy (Gail, David) in praying for people, and most now had extensive experience in ministering in Freedom Prayer to others. Peter had "prayed for over a hundred people in Freedom Prayer in the last year, and on most of those occasions I have seen people go home happier than when they arrived," or "come back with testimony, and move on"; Rachel had "seen lots of people deal with heavy stuff . . . , and testify to walking free." Gail had seen many people "changed beyond belief," into "so much more who they are supposed to be"—people she had known for ten years and so could see the difference. And Wills described it as a "no-brainer"—he had seen how all the world had to offer at great expense from counseling or psychiatric help was often to no avail, whereas within a short time people could find a freedom that cost them nothing.[92] Also spiritual warfare prayer was seen as one factor that helped them in more effectively ministering God's love in social outreach—Jeremy saw debt counseling clients going away with heads held high; and Rachel in her coffee bar outreach told of a man regularly coming in and telling everyone "it's all not true about God," but after binding confusion next time he didn't say a word. In youth work, both Alexander and Kate saw how binding anger in a misbehaving child often quietened them, freeing them up to receive God's love; and Alexander had seen "rough kids from broken lives coming from nothing to be fully on fire for Jesus."

Asked how important it was for Christians to believe they are in a real spiritual battle, unsurprisingly all interviewees answered "very important," "essential" or "absolutely vital." Reasons given were that otherwise they would "be sleepwalking into losing their faith" (Michael), miss out on what God has for them (Peter); it was really important to know you can walk in the authority Jesus has for us (Rachel). It was seen as a very strong thread in Scripture, and being called a soldier in the baptism service means we should be prepared to go on the offensive for the kingdom of God which is a warring kingdom (Jeremy), and in this we need to ask for training from the Holy Spirit (Norna). Some however said it was not the most important thing—Alexander emphasized it was equally important "to believe they are loved by their Father," and David that it was not necessary for salvation—but important for seeing breakthroughs for you and others, bringing light into the darkness of people's lives—"a Christian embracing spiritual warfare is likely to be much more fruitful." Kate and Rachel also spoke of greater effectiveness in ministry.

Freedom Prayer

In addition, through participant observation of Freedom Prayer, I was able to observe for myself some outcomes.[93] After both two-hour sessions at St.

92. He mentioned one example of a girl who had been sexually abused when younger, who after two or three prayer sessions at the Conference I had attended was completely freed after ten years of struggle with nightmares and visions; also confirmed by the girl's sister some while after the conference.

93. A more extensive survey of outcomes from 115 sessions of Freedom Prayer (thirty-three recipients from nine churches), mainly by questionnaire, was carried out by May-Ward, "A Critical Examination of Freedom Prayer." Recipients stated that the prayer team had had accurate prophetic words for them (a straight "yes/no" question) in 84 percent of the "Freedom Prayer" sessions surveyed; also in their written responses a vast number commented on the power of the prophetic to reveal God's unconditional love for them or uncover hidden sins. This figure accorded well with the leaders' own estimate of 80 percent, from general feedback from hundreds of "freedom prayer" sessions.

George's where I listened on team, I followed up the two prayer recipients (again give pseudonyms) by email a few weeks afterwards.

Robert was a mature Christian with a young family, who had received and led Freedom Prayer sessions on a number of occasions. He had come for Freedom Prayer that day as he was aware of some hindrance blocking his spiritual growth. He was very familiar with this ministry approach and trusted the team leader, so she felt able to rely less on the revelation of the listeners and more on that of Robert himself, by leading him through some questions which helped him visualize his spiritual situation in imagery—also because she felt a need to get beyond his correct head understanding of truth to heart level, where some key lies were deceiving him.

His feedback was as follows:

> The revelation was spot on . . . all that was shared resonated.
>
> The imagery that we entered into, whether that was images of how I perceived God, Jesus or me, is so powerful. It puts things into pictures that you can't express in words, [although it] does come across "whacky" . . . my "experience" during that time is my testimony that it is real!
>
> Immediately after the prayer time I can't say that I felt physically different, but I knew spiritually something had happened. . . . In the days moving forward I have gained a great sense of God's love for me [and] my own self-worth—I am more internally solid than I have ever been. I know the power of some spiritual lies have been broken.
>
> But repentance is the walking out of all this, and as a result of the imagery, when I feel vulnerable or the lies are coming back in I have very effective imagery to return to help me take authority over the lies and get back on track again.

Sam was in his twenties; he had a church upbringing but had only been a Christian for a few years, but already quite committed to helping in the church where he could. This was only his second experience of a full session of Freedom Prayer, though he was well acquainted with the practices and principles, partly through his home group where they were often used in prayer for each other.

Sam responded:

> My session was dealing with generational issues rather than immediate and apparent problems, so analyzing the fruit from what happened is not an easy task. However, I believe that the revelation was accurate.

I can think of two apparent changes since the session. Firstly, that feeling of being "out of place," "exposed" and not where I was meant to be has vanished, totally. Secondly, I believe that I can hear the Lord's voice more clearly. . . . I think that the real fruit of the session will show itself further down the line, especially if I ever get married/have kids. I am confident that a break from the past was made and have renewed hope.

The blessing at the end meant a lot to me. The quote from Isaiah 61 was very moving to me as I have always felt a deep affinity with those verses.

Testimonies

In addition to my interviews, testimonies were occasionally given during services, one of which I subsequently obtained by email. Stories I have on record in outline are as follows:

A lady believed she was healed of a serious and painful growth in her thyroid, after persistent spiritual warfare prayer between the first examination by the doctors and her going for full diagnostic scan, at which point it had completely disappeared.

As the father began to move into spiritual warfare ministry, a five-month-old baby had five highly disruptive symptoms including eczema, struggling with breathing and vomiting every night, which did not respond to repeated medical treatment. After listening prayer on a Friday, which brought up four areas of generational sin and curses, with repentance and rebuking, over the weekend four of the five symptoms cleared up. After prayer based on a friend's ten-year-old daughter's "word of knowledge" about another area of generational sin, the vomiting also stopped.

A healing from infertility with conception within a week of receiving prayer that particularly brought up generational issues. (The children's pastor told me she knew of several couples who had conceived after Freedom Prayer.)

A healing from a long-term recurrent infection illness. The person was amazed that it could be instantly healed after one long session of Freedom Prayer that brought up several issues filling a sheet of A4 paper that she then prayed through.

After a young man's first freedom prayer session ("they did my spiritual DNA . . . it was absolutely spot on") and laying on of hands, "I was totally healed of the viral illness I had been off work with for three months. That was a year ago and I've never been sick since."

I heard various other stories—including a man who had battled in prayer for his wife over a brain tumor which had completely gone when she went for biopsy, and a pregnant mother whose cancer went into remission after prayer—but was unable to obtain written accounts.[94] There were of course some cases where healing had not come after serious prayer; I only personally came across two specific ones—a man (who had had previous extensive involvement in occult practices) who was still struggling with fibromyalgia; and the lady who had been healed of cancer when pregnant, sadly lost the child only days before it was due to be born.[95] However, I also spoke to a church leader who was less convinced of the benefits of the formulaic framework used, particularly for people with deeper psychological issues.[96]

Archival records and figures

Attendance—I calculated the "Usual Sunday Attendance" figure from averaging the October totals of morning and evening ordinary services in October biannually from when Ian became vicar in 1997:

Year	1997	1999	2001	2003	2005	2007
U.S.A.	250	215	192	210	225	266

These figures tend to confirm Ian's assertion that initially some left who didn't like the new focus, but since then there had been gradual growth. Three adult baptisms (over eighteen) in 2006 and one in 2007 (see below) after only one or two in the previous eight years could indicate some recent conversions.

Records of Marriages and Baptisms:

---

94. I understand the church later started keeping a record of testimonies.

95. However at my return visit a year later, one interviewee told me he had been impressed how this couple decided to "live in the opposite spirit" on the anniversary of their loss, choosing to bless another family by looking after their children that day.

96. He himself had benefitted from the prophetic insights of Freedom Prayer and affirmed its value in opening up deeper places to the Spirit's work; but having counseled some who had not had problems resolved "Jesus Ministry" approaches, he had reservations as to whether seeking to live out of a reclaimed spiritual identity, and rebuking "strongholds" as "Satanic" which were more aspects of human brokenness, might seek to "break off" parts of the ego that actually need to be integrated for long term spiritual and emotional health. (Personal phone conversation, 11.7.11). See another "negative outcome" in footnote 127 below.

Year	Marriages	Baptisms (total)	Baptisms (under three)
Average 1990–97		6	6
1998	6	6	6
1999	2	12	10
2000	3	5	3
2001	1	5	4
2002	1	6	2
2003	1	5	3
2004	*6*	*0*	*0*
2005	*2*	*3*	*3*
2006	*5*	*14*	*9*
2007	*2(+1)**	*9*	*7*

One marriage of a church leader to a member took place elsewhere.

There was a general perception of an increase in "fruitfulness," in terms of members becoming engaged, married and having children, since the congregation had begun to implement "Jesus Ministry" principles from 2004. Ian having said that after his first two or three years (1997–2000) "community" baptisms and marriages were rare, there is circumstantial evidence for such an increase after 2004 (in italics) in the figures above (though it may not be statistically significant).

4.6 Discussion

Many academic accounts of charismatic theology in relation to spiritual warfare have been broadly critical, even from commentators within the charismatic tradition. Clearly there was some justification for this, as alongside some benefits of the charismatic spiritual warfare approach, especially in the 1970s and 1980s there were some strong imbalances, immaturities (as noted by Ian and Peter) and some "casualties" from this approach.[97] As these Anglican churches revisit a strong spiritual warfare emphasis in the beginning of the twenty-first century, I here examine how this newer approach matches up to the former grounds of criticism, and will later continue and deepen this critical dialogue. Here I shall consider two main criticisms: a critique of the charismatic ontology of evil; and the charge that the "demon

---

97. Some were chronicled in Parsons, *Ungodly Fear*.

focus" of "a paranoid worldview" breeds fear, and is potentially manipulating or abusive.[98]

Ontology

The analysis reveals a strong and widely shared belief that not only are Satan and his demons the main focus of evil, but that as fallen angels these discrete independent spiritual beings have character and a degree of personality. Ian gives his views in some depth:

> *Ian:* My view is that they are fallen angels, they are spirit beings that fell with Satan, a third swept out of heaven. They are spiritual beings, they carry spiritual energy and spiritual capacity to influence humans in the way they think, act and feel at every level. [For example through] physical sickness. They are in total contrast and utterly opposed to God and his kingdom and his ways. The next best thing is to wound him through his children. They fundamentally want to wound God. They hate us because they are jealous of us because we are made in God's image. But I think they hate God more, so their main aim is to get at God through us; but they are very happy to get us as well because they just love tormenting and wounding and destroying. That's how I see them, I see them as entities who think, with personalities, they talk together, they discuss things. That's clearly revealed in the Scriptures.... They are rebellious, they are unruly, they want to control, they want to take over, they want to make people captive. And they are very sneaky and schemey [sic]. They are not often coming at Christians blatantly out and out. Looking through the Gospels how they talk to Jesus, "For we are many," they know who they are. "So what have you to do with us Jesus of Nazareth, have you come to destroy us?" ... There's obviously a corporate sense, what's happening, who is this man, is this our time.
>
> *Graham:* Are they personal or impersonal?
>
> *Ian:* As much as I think an angel has personality. They have names, [though] we don't tend to go after names very much. But sometimes we do. So I think for those reasons, as well as stories of people who have had heavenly realms experiences and seen

---

98. Another question is "can a Christian be demon-possessed (or demonized)?" However, this is relatively uncontroversial amongst British charismatics, who generally accept that Christians can at least be influenced by the demonic on various levels. See however Arnold, *Three Crucial Questions About Spiritual Warfare*, 73–141.

them talking to each other and seen them as having character. Because I'm not sure how you can have a living thing without character. I don't think its inanimate pockets of force. Because they talk and they think and they are frightened and they desire. They have feelings. They want to go into pigs, they don't want to be sent off. There's a desire, there's a want. They have all the characteristics of personality. Just utterly distorted and twisted.[99]

Of the different ontological views concerning evil, this is clearly enunciating the traditional view that evil was inherent in the fallen angels before the fall of man.[100] However, in more recent times this has been seriously questioned, and subtly different views proposed.

Firstly, in attempting to wrestle with the paradox of evil in God's good world, Karl Barth proposed the concept of *"Das Nichtige,"* usually translated "nothingness."[101] Barth denies that demons are fallen angels, seeing them as emerging from God's "no";[102] their apparent similarity arises from the falsehood of evil in their mimicking the good. "Thus Christians need not wrestle with dark angels and principalities, but should dismiss them with 'a quick, sharp glance.'"[103]

Whilst there is agreement at St. George's over the character of evil as lies and deception, for Ian they have all the personality of angels, for they have names, talk, think, and have feelings and desires. And concerning praxis, for Clare there was a sharp contrast between her previous strategy of ignoring evil for fifteen years or so, having been told after an experience with evil in her room that God was always bigger, so she shouldn't worry about it; and then "the beginning of a huge shift change watching people deal with stuff to do with the spiritual realms at a level we didn't really know

---

99. Ian Interviews 9.11.07, 6.12.07. Jeremy added: "They may not be complete personalities in that they are one trick ponies in many ways. There'll be a spirit of fear and presumably that spirit is locked into bringing fear.... Scripture also says... they knew who Christ was. I think they are personal beings and they do have intelligence and they do have group communication... borne out by seven spirits coming into the house if you don't fill it with something of God, so they work together."

100. There was no suggestion as to when an angelic fall might have happened, nor any commitment to a literalist seven days of creation: "I have no idea of the length of time between Creation and Adam and Eve and the fall;... I don't know how populated the earth was before they fell. The Scriptures don't address that. The only way I can understand it is that when Satan comes to Adam and Eve, he's already fallen.... So that must mean the spiritual precedes the natural...."

101. Or perhaps better "The Negative"; see chapter 5 for full discussion.

102. Noble, "The Spirit World," 206.

103. Noll, "Thinking about Angels," 1–27, esp. 23.

was there"[104]—requiring more than "a quick, sharp glance." Barth incorporated a clear asymmetry between good and evil to avoid a Manichaean dualism with Satan equal and opposite to God. Whilst the ascription of an independent existence of evil as fallen angels can present philosophical theological problems,[105] one strength of the approach at St. George's is that evil is seen as absolutely no match for the power of God:

> *Graham:* How much power do the forces of evil have?
>
> *Peter:* Compared to God, nothing. We do teach as well that spiritual warfare is a truth encounter not a power encounter. It's not about the power emphasis. The power comes from rebellion and it comes from Satan. Ultimately it comes from human free will and the choice of rebellion against God creates power. The only power they have is the power we give them by our sinful reaction to God. . . . The original source of energy and power they have, I don't know.

This brings us to the second alternative view, recently championed by Walter Wink, that supra-human evil is a projection and consequence of the fall of man.[106] Whilst Peter states that "the only power they have is the power we give them by our sinful reaction," he implies that there is a power that "comes from Satan" of unclear origin; and others agreed that the fundamental nature of the forces was rebellion, which did not square with their being just the by-product of human evil.[107] Ian agreed that neither Barth's nor Wink's view fit with their interpretation of their experience:

> *Graham:* Could they be a by-product of psychological and social forces?
>
> *Ian:* I don't understand that you can square that with the biblical revelation. If you look at the biblical revelation how can an inanimate force have a scheme. Paul gives them and the Old Testament gives them personality and character. They want attention and they want glory. For me it's a product of a western

---

104. This began when there was a clear manifestation of a spirit of death in her family, after prayer relating to her being nearly killed in a car accident when she was six.

105. These will be touched on in chapters 5 to 8.

106. In Cook's words: "Satan as the mythic personification of human society arising out of collective human evil . . ." Wink, *Unmasking the Powers*, 24-25; Cook, "Devils and Manticores," 165-84 (esp. 82). See also Noble, "The Spirit World," 207, 15.

107. E.g., Gail: "The fallen angels would be more my understanding obviously because of the nature of rebellion in sin, and the whole nature of Satan is rebellion."

mindset that puts before Scripture a tradition of man which is not a religious tradition but a "world" tradition.

The main stumbling block is seen as the purposeful intelligent "scheming" of the enemy, which seems to imply personality.[108] The only way round this, then, for the alternative explanations, is to either suggest that demonic beings only fulfill a minimalist definition of personhood ("a malevolent intelligence," "an agent able to think, to know, to will and to act," but being "inherently deception . . . it is impossible to give a structured meaningful account of it"[109]); or, to see this malevolent intelligence as merely on the level of machine intelligence, insufficient to warrant ascription of personality—as Wright begins to argue.[110] We return to this discussion in chapter 5.

However, there is common ground with Wink's approach in the recognition that on the personal, emotional and psychological level it is primarily our human choices that open the door for demonic influence; and secondly that it is not a priority to decide whether a person "has a demon" or not, but a recognition that human sin patterns, and the fallen world system, become "energized by the demonic" to various degrees, on which basis the devil is to be resisted.[111] This language of energizing was used at St. George's in describing the pervasive influence of the demonic in the wider community.[112]

---

108. Peter for example said: "I would say they were more intentional than 'Nothingness.'" Other interviewees also highlighted the enemy's intelligent scheming, also described as "very cunning and purposeful" (David), deliberately identifying our weaknesses and going for them (Norna, Michael, Kate, David, Rachel).

109. Noble, "The Spirit World," 63, 64.

110. "The devil possesses a much-reduced and essentially malevolent way of being, which to dignify as personhood would be vastly to overrate." Wright, *Theology of the Dark Side*, 73.

111. Mike Riches describes clearly their underlying approach: "We cannot separate the battle we face from the world system, our sinful nature, and demonic powers. All three are like individual strands tightly wound together making a formidable rope to keep us bound. Many followers of Jesus Christ in the Western culture get uneasy about directly addressing the demonic. Satan loves our trepidation! I believe that every effort of the world system to infiltrate my life, [and] when my flesh is tempted to rise up in violation of God's truth . . . is energized by demonic activity." He illustrates from Acts 5:3–4 (lying linked with Satan), and James 4 (resisting Satan). Riches, *Strongholds*, 72–74.

112. For example, David in his interview (my italics): "The wider society in your area, it's where the enemy would want to *energize* things that are not that great. So . . . the young people . . . haven't got anything to do and they get bored and they decide let's go and do a bit of joyriding or graffiti. I think the enemy can *energize* them because they're quite vulnerable in that place . . . just to bring destruction into a community, and you hear of where a community is bound by fear because of the young people doing all these things . . . they have their own choice, that's just an ideal opportunity for the enemy to bring hopelessness and destruction to people's lives." Kate and David Interview 13.10.07.

Demon focus: A paranoid worldview?

Walker's "paranoid universe" is one where a belief in being constantly under threat from demons, seeing God and Satan as warring over the most trivial issues in people's lives, leads to an insecurity that often demonizes others; from this it is a short step to persecution, and an atmosphere of fear and suspicion in churches. It can also lead to looking for "strong men" with "gnosis" and power to protect us, and to help turn us into "spiritual warriors."[113]

Some such dangers were indeed present, and leaders were aware of them; it was one reason why this style of ministry had been adopted very slowly over a number of years, beginning with the main leader and his family, and then the leadership team. A key phrase Walker uses is "but a short step" to paranoia and persecution, from a "demonized worldview."[114] A key question is how much this aspect of the cosmology of the worldview is at fault (the ontological question), and secondly how much the "safeguards" are lacking to prevent distortion. If there really is a war on, the solution is not to deny it but to be better trained and prepared, as taken very seriously at St. George's. Concerning cosmology, Ian made an interesting comment— "In one sense the two realms thinking . . . perhaps is more important than even the spiritual warfare practice."[115] In other words, even though "spiritual warfare is part of our strategy for whatever we are doing" (Ian), living in a worldview of two realms all the time was increasingly focused on being open to *God's* supernatural interaction with the natural realm, and less on what the enemy was doing.[116]

In relation to fear, the case study yielded surprising results. With the focus being first on God (particularly in worship) and Jesus's goal to restore what was lost,[117] one of the chief fruits of the Jesus ministry approach was actually freedom from fear rather than paranoia; partly because it gives practical, unsensational strategies for overcoming fear. For example, the emphasis on truth encounter rather than power encounter takes the focus

---

113. Walker, "The Devil You Think You Know," 88–96.

114. See also Kay, "A Demonised Worldview," 17–30.

115. Comment from Ian Interviews 9.11.07, 6.12.07. Thus in the "ontology" analysis table in Appendix 4, I have put the "two realms" cosmology first before that of evil spiritual forces.

116. Clearly there was a maturing here away from the danger of seeing all natural events as part of a dualistic battle between supernatural good and evil forces (see also Richard's comments in 4.7 above). The idea here of a ubiquitous interaction between the spiritual and natural realms, focusing first on God's presence and action, echoes Mackie's description of the Celtic worldview—see section 2.1.

117. See note 71 above for this foundational concept for Mike Riches in "Jesus Ministry."

off accessing the necessary power to expel a demon, and onto aligning a person's life with gospel truth which in itself has the power to set them free. Neil Anderson's "truth encounter" approach emphasizes this, and has come to the attention of biblical theologian Graham Twelftree, who maintains that the church may confront the demonic either in the form of an exorcism or in the form of truth.[118] The model here embodies a combination of both, but with greater emphasis on truth—the foundational truths of the greatness of God and his good created purpose for each person, that the ministry seeks to help discover and affirm; and the truth that it is our own sinful actions and reactions that can give a foothold to the devil and so should be the focus of attention under the Spirit's discernment, renouncing personal involvement not just in the occult but in negative thought patterns such as unbelief, anxiety and fear. Thus by seeing the world, the flesh, and the devil as interrelated, with the responsibility of repentance (and forgiving others) squarely on each person, the focus is more upon personal responsibility for sin and evil than on "blaming the devil."[119] These twin aspects, a focus on God and his goodness and a heightened sense of personal responsibility, together with the caring, unsensational, and open-handed way that ministry is offered, combined with careful training for prayer teams, seem to have not only provided safeguards against paranoia but actually led to greater freedom from the fear of evil, as victory is experienced regularly in individual's lives and through ministering to others. The egalitarian approach to prayer ministry, focusing more on listening to God and less on the charismatic leader, with encouragement to feed back any issues, also helped to dissipate any love of power and replace it with the power of love.[120] However, the formulaic framework might cause some who are wrestling with aspects of their own human emotional brokenness to keep going back and looking for "demonic strongholds" to dismantle that do not exist, which could increase anxiety.[121]

---

118. Twelftree, *In the Name of Jesus*, 293–94. See for example Anderson, "Finding Freedom in Christ," 126–59.

119. See note 111 above.

120. A danger analyzed by Smail, in Smail, Walker, and Wright, *Charismatic Renewal*, 133–52. This nevertheless required continual attentiveness; one freedom prayer recipient reported being put off by sensing frustration from a team member, when she did not seem to accept his listening prayer "revelation."

121. Such was the view of a local church leader who had counseled some people whose problems remained after receiving Freedom Prayer ministry. (Personal phone conversation, 11.7.11).

4.7 Concluding summary

St. George's shows a highly developed praxis of spiritual warfare undergirded with a strong awareness of its theological foundations. Their warfare worldview is one of cosmic dualism between God and Satan; whilst this is kept in sharp focus, it is a limited dualism, in that Satan's power is seen as minimal compared to God's and effectively neutralized through the cross of Christ, and by extension potentially for all believers who are in Christ.[122] The focus of their warfare theology is a positive one, of a creation restored to God's original design and purpose and a radical re-creation, with a strongly realized eschatology and a radical supernaturalism that sees believers equipped to become like Jesus in experiencing an abundant spiritual life (John 10:10) and doing even greater works than Jesus did (John 14:12), once believers learn to better hear the shepherd's voice (John 10:4) and thus do what they see the Father doing (John 5:19). The enemy only comes into the picture because he and his minions (believed to be fallen angels) are constantly at work trying to thwart God's purposes—to kill, steal, and destroy (John 10:10), based on his nature as the father of lies (John 8:44). This key characteristic of rebellion is seen as incompatible with ontological accounts of evil as "nothingness," because it is a willful and in that sense personal force—also in its ability to intelligently carry out malevolent schemes against God's purposes and God's people.

Their warfare spirituality is thus also well developed, and I would characterize it as one of *powerful humility* and *focused authority*. Powerful, in being seen as having great transformative potential ("the incomparably great power towards us who believe," Eph 1:19), particular in relation to restoring a sense of inner spiritual freedom, and physical and psychological healing. But the only way this power is legitimately accessed is through the gift of repentance, taking strong personal responsibility in *humbly* acknowledging one's own rebellion and sin in specific areas (often before others) and seeking cleansing at the cross of Jesus.[123] The leaders acknowledge that continuous repentance is an essential part of the holistic lifestyle they are recommending and modeling themselves, which also manifests *humility* in a strong awareness of the potential for abuse of power through controlling others. Thirdly, it is *authoritative*, in taking confidence in the truth of the biblical revelation, and in finding a firm basis in the theology of Christ's

---

122. This echoes Boddy's view of the power of the Blood in protecting believers: "A great Christ means a very small devil." See chapter 2.2, and Alexander Boddy, *Confidence* 1 no 2, 3–4.

123. Reminiscent of the East African revival in the mid twentieth century—*Calvary Road* by Roy Hession, which describes this, was on the Conference reading list.

substitution for the cancelling of any legal right of the enemy to occupy any *topos* (foothold, Eph 5:16) or strongholds, subsequent to genuine repentance and cleansing; and in exercising this authority, given directly by Christ (Luke 10:19), and based on the believer's exalted position seated in the heavenly realms in Christ (Eph 2:6) far above all other powers (Eph 1:21), to resist and rebuke the devil (1 Pet 5:9) where he has energized any areas of sin in the flesh, or lies from the world around. The restrained manner in which this authority is exercised, primarily by each individual believer but also in the gentle, unhurried and unpressurized way freedom prayer teams operate, increases self-esteem and helps eliminate fear, aided by the strong theological emphasis that Satan's power is as nothing compared to that of the believer in Christ. Finally, this authority is very *focused* through extensive use of prophetic listening prayer, especially seeking to hear God's specific positive purposes for individuals and the church, as well as to discern how the enemy has, or intends, to hinder those purposes—prompting the regular use of the metaphor that here God's power seems to be laser-guided, cutting to the root of people's problems with surgical precision.[124]

Within this scheme there is a proportionately high attention given to the work of the devil and associated evil spirits. Such an ontology should be viewed with an attitude of critical realism—it should not be ruled out *a priori*, but examined carefully both for its truth claims and with respect to its fruit, particularly the pastoral consequences. On the latter grounds, little evidence emerged here to justify calling it a "paranoid worldview." In fact, the strong undergirding of taking personal responsibility for personal failure, and confidence in the victory of the cross when resisting evil, tended to reduce fear of evil powers. Instead, many reoriented from a stance of fear of defeat before a mysterious foe, to one of confidence to move out on the offensive against all forms of evil influencing people around them, knowing that they had some tools to deal with it. However, there was clearly a need for training and close monitoring of those involved in ministry in Freedom Prayer teams, and care when teaching concerning the devil and demons, so that those with little exposure or previous negative experiences should not be unnecessarily exposed to fear.

---

124. This analogy was particularly appreciated by the Kenyan Bible College leader attending the first conference. She contrasted it with the over-dramatic "machine gun" approach of many Africans to prayer against evil powers, for example through long sessions of prayer or fasting, or loud prayers of exorcism.

— 5 —

Nigel Wright

The Ontology of Evil

5.1 Introduction

THE FOREGOING DESCRIPTIVE-EMPIRICAL RESEARCH of chapters 2 to 4 reveals a particular worldview in the "lifeworld" of Anglican charismatics, seeing the world as currently an arena of conflict between spiritual forces of good and evil. Whilst God is worshipped as wholly good, there are malevolent "personal" evil forces in rebellion against their creator, which have the "intelligence" to scheme and strategize to achieve their rebellious goals. God is thus deemed to be opposed to them; and, especially since the pivotal event of the crucifixion, is fighting against and destroying the evil effects of these forces, particularly through the struggle of spiritual warfare in which the church is called to engage through the power of the Spirit. These demonic forces have influence in the world for example at community level, through crime, poverty, hopelessness, and so on, and acting upon individuals, including Christians, particularly through sin patterns that give them access. The implications of this belief in strong and powerful evil forces for how God exercises his omnipotence varied—thus, some pioneers tended to emphasize that the devil was still "God's devil";[1] whereas in the main case study church, St. George's, there was a more heightened dualistic emphasis on God's implacable opposition to the devil and all his works.

We have also seen that this worldview is controversial, even amongst charismatics, with accusations of an exaggerated dualism that gives too high a status to Satan and encourages "demon-consciousness."[2] Others were

---

1. David MacInnes Interview 6.4.06. Tom Walker also took a Calvinist view of God's sovereignty over evil (Interview 28.3.04).

2. For example Subritzky, *Demons Defeated*; Hammond, *Pigs in the Parlour*. Scotland is particularly critical of such "expansive charismatics" and their "paranoid worldview." Scotland, "The Charismatic Devil," 88–96.

even more skeptical; when the rise of the charismatic worldview influenced the reintroduction of exorcistic practice into the Church of England, some Anglican theologians objected to resurrecting a belief in the existence of demons that is now culturally outmoded.[3] Whilst all may accept the reality of evil in some form, there are very different theories as to what evil actually is and how it should be dealt with.

And so before embarking on the normative task of constructing a charismatic theology of evil and spiritual warfare (chapter 8), we need to engage in the interpretive task, shifting focus from the "lifeworld" towards encountering the theological "system" and its academic discourse (chapters 5 to 7). What is really happening when charismatics claim to encounter and engage with evil forces? What is the ontology and nature of the evil powers that the charismatics we have studied claim to be encountering and struggling against? In considering different theories of the ontology of evil, I shall principally engage in dialogue with three theologians who have addressed this in some depth with particular focus on, or relevance for, a charismatic approach to evil. All three were positively influenced by experience in charismatic and Pentecostal contexts, but in developing their theoretical positions engage with wider Christian tradition. Thus here I examine Nigel Wright, then Amos Yong and Gregory Boyd in subsequent chapters.

5.2 The ontology of evil: a dialogue with Nigel Wright and his sources

We have already highlighted Andrew Walker's "paranoid universe" concept as one of the clearest theological critiques of the demon focus of some charismatics. He and others considered that Frank Peretti's highly popular works of Christian fiction reinforced the distortions of such a paranoid worldview.[4] Nigel Wright (who like Walker has been characterized as a "progressive charismatic"[5]) has gone further; countering what he sees as the "remythologizing" of even moderate charismatics, he proposes a "non-ontological realist" analysis of the devil and demons which highlights their deceptive and shadowy nature, seeking to deny them ontological substance

---

3. As implied by Cupitt, in a letter to *The Times* with G. W. Lampe objecting to the revival of exorcistic practice. See Cupitt, *Explorations in Theology 6*, 50–53.

4. See Walker, "The Devil You Think You Know," 88; Scotland, "The Charismatic Devil."; Guelich, "Spiritual Warfare: Jesus, Paul, and Peretti."

5. As opposed to "moderate charismatics" such as Michael Green, Clinton Arnold, and Graham Dow, or "expansive charismatics" such as Subritzky, Hammond, Derek Prince, and Don Basham. Scotland, "The Charismatic Devil," 88, 96, 100.

without reducing their reality.[6] He challenges traditional views of the devil as possessing personal existence, and of the fall of angels as the origin of demonic forces; he proposes that the powers are essentially non-relational and depersonalizing rather than personal, and chaotic rather than organized and purposeful.[7] Through dialogue with Karl Barth, Jürgen Moltmann, Walter Wink, and others, he seeks to define evil as a godless emptiness that nonetheless has complex ways of taking form in the experience of societies and individuals.

In this chapter, I shall examine and critique Wright's ontology, and use some of the results of the inductive studies of Anglican charismatic pioneers, and of the case study church of St. George's, to begin moving towards a charismatic ontology of evil that remains faithful both to their experience and to the biblical evidence.

5.3 Evil as nothingness

As the foundation of his non-ontological realist stance, Nigel Wright relies heavily on Karl Barth, particularly his concept of "nothingness" (*das Nichtige*) as a power in opposition to God; and so amongst his sources this requires our most detailed attention.[8] For Barth, although "nothingness" has nothing in common with God and his creature, "nothingness is not nothing," but exists in negativity, without any right to exist, or any value or positive strength. Barth's concept is different from Augustine's, who saw evil as a negative entity in his *privatio boni*; Barth makes a careful distinction for example between the negative, shadowy side of God's good creation, which is on the frontier of "nothingness" and always menaced by it but not to be identified with it.[9] It does however share with Augustine the same root in the meontic tradition of Plato, referring to "non-being" rather than "no-being."[10] It is revealed primarily in its contradistinction to Christ, as

---

6. Wright, "Charismatic Interpretations," 149–63; *Theology of the Dark Side*. He summarizes and extends his views in Wright, "Deliverance in Theological Perspective."

7. Wright, "Charismatic Interpretations," 158.

8. Barth's exposition is mainly in Barth, *CD*, III/3, 289–368, 519–31. There is also a helpful discussion in Hick, *Evil and the God of Love*, 132–204.

9. See Barth, *C D*, III/3, 295–302.

10. The ancient Greeks were the first to realize that "nothing" has two different meanings, and they were able to distinguish them in their language, as οὐκ ὄν and μή ὄν. Οὐκ ὄν connotes nothing in the absolute sense as the negation of everything; μή ὄν connotes that which negates a particular thing in a relative sense—or in Platonic thought, the not yet realized potentiality to be some specific thing. See Hendry, "Nothing," 274–89, esp. 76; Hick, *Evil and the God of Love*, 48.

the adversary whose hostility takes form as "real death, real devil" and real sin of human beings; yet it is an alien factor, not planned or willed, but only exists in negativity.[11] He thus sees no equality between angels and demons; for him angels are glorious beings who cannot deviate from God's will or fall, but demons exist in a "dreadful fifth or sixth dimension of existence" as an army never at rest, with falsehood as the manner of their being.[12] Barth's concept of nothingness subsumes all that is negated and opposed by God, and for him must include the devil and demons. He thus resolutely opposes regarding demons "as relatives and colleagues of the angels," or seeing any "final similarity" between the two kingdoms.[13] The apparent similarity of demons with angels is a manifestation of a mimicking of the good—without denying "the fact that the performance is real and constantly successful," nevertheless demons are simply "the powers of falsehood in a thousand different forms"; and so although he defends angels against demythologizing, demons are in his words "the myth of all mythologies."[14]

Barth's approach has much to commend it, and there are several emphases which would resonate with the charismatics I have studied. Most notably, in describing the otherness and alien nature of evil as clearly distinct from both God and his creation, and as negated and defeated by him, his desire is clearly to protect the goodness of God—a strong motivation shared by the charismatics at St. George's.

Secondly, Barth agrees with charismatics in seeing sin as the primary manifestation of the evil or nothingness, and that this can also bring sickness and suffering; and so Jesus's healing miracles are thus seen as manifestations of his victory over evil. "When seen in the light of Jesus Christ, the concrete form in which *das Nichtige* is active is the sin of man as his personal act and guilt."[15] Yet he also agrees that the evil effects of *das Nichtige* go beyond this—sin "also disturbs, injures and destroys the creature and its nature . . . attended and followed by . . . the suffering of evil and death."[16] Thus, for Barth Jesus's miracles of healing are "objective manifestations of His character as the Conqueror not only of sin but also of evil and death . . . he not only forgives the sins of men; He also removes the source of their suf-

11. Barth, *CD*, III/3, 305, 312, 349.
12. Ibid., III/3, 525, 527–28.
13. Ibid., III/3, 481, 524; Wright, *Theology of the Dark Side*, 64–65.
14. Barth, *CD*, III/3, 521, 525–27.
15. Ibid., III/3, 305–6.
16. Ibid., III/3, 310. Hick speculates that death (and presumably pain) might ideally be part of the innocently negative "shadow side" aspect of creaturely life, yet concretely within our sinful human experience they have become manifestations of *das Nichtige*. Hick, *Evil and the God of Love*, 138.

fering. He resists the whole assault. To its power He opposes his own power, the transcendent power of God. He shows himself to be the total Victor."[17]

Thirdly, he agrees that evil forces beyond sin are in some sense "real"; "nothingness is not exhausted in sin . . . even sin itself is described [in Scripture] as [man's] surrender to the alien power of an adversary." The infection of the shadow side of the world by *das Nichtige* produces "real evil and real death," and there are "a real devil with his legions, and a real hell . . . 'real' again means in opposition to the totality of God's creation."[18] He asserts that "*das Nichtige* is not nothing," and has "its own being, albeit malignant and perverse."[19] And finally, he agrees with charismatics that when we see the power of nothingness for example in bringing Jesus to the cross, here is a real enemy that we see "with fear and trembling as the adversary with whom God and God alone can cope." And he agrees that it is from the standpoint of Jesus and his birth, death, and resurrection "where our one real hope against it is grounded and established."[20] Thus, the evil powers are to be taken with the utmost seriousness, but when our hope is squarely on the cross and the resurrection of Jesus all fear can be taken away, something which was highly valued at St. George's.[21]

Other points of contact or agreement with charismatics could be noted.[22] However, despite agreeing much concerning the reality of the evil powers and the basis of their defeat, most charismatics would part company with Barth in foundational aspects of his ontology of evil, both its nature and its origin. For Barth, evil is the "necessary" (even if only potential, before creation) antithesis of God in his goodness, which arises "from below" as if out of nowhere once creation occurs, as a threat to its continued existence. Barth to some extent ties himself in knots as he seeks to define "nothingness" by a large number of negative statements, yet asserts that "nothingness is not nothing," and indeed can have virulent power. It is not surprising that

---

17. Barth, *CD*, III/3, 311.
18. Ibid., III/3, 310.
19. Ibid., III/3, 352.
20. Ibid., III/3, 305.
21. See chapter 4, especially 4.5 and 4.6.

22. Moderate Anglican charismatics generally agree with the distinction between pain and suffering that can be classed as "natural" in the shadow side of creation, over against those that are evil associated for Barth with the realm of *das Nichtige*. Thus, Harper was eager to preserve the category of the natural over against the demonic, avoiding a polarized dualism. Harper Interview 20.4.2004. Hick sees the distinction between the shadow side of creaturely existence, and evil as enmity against God, as one of Barth's greatest achievements. Hick, *Evil and the God of Love*, 150.

he has to admit that its reality is paradoxical, and indeed that it is inherent contradiction and "impossible possibility."[23]

The paradox may be partly resolved by understanding his version of the meontic Platonic concept of "non-being," as distinct from the absolute "nothing." He would agree with Plotinus for example, that "if evil exists at all, [it must] be situated in the realm of non-Being; . . . not something that simply does not exist, but something of an utterly different order from Authentic Being; . . . think of the ever-undefined, the never at rest . . . ."[24] Barth, alongside some later thinkers, sees this notion of "non-being" as a necessity of thought.[25] For him, this "non-being" is what God actively wills against in creating—and by the very act of rejecting it, gives it the status of an enemy that is hostile to the good creation and must be combated and eventually destroyed.[26]

Understanding exactly what this "non-being" refers to depends on the particular view of the origin of this "chaotic" evil force. In Platonic thought, creation is the imposition of form on an independently existing, formless "matter"; for Plotinus, "matter" is the last "something after which nothing more can be produced"; having no residue of good in it, it is Evil.[27] Christians rejected the idea of any pre-existing substance, formulating the doctrine of *creation ex nihilo* to refute it. Barth's answer, however, is that the evil power of *das Nichtige* arises from the nature of chaos described in Gen 1:2, which was "that which as Creator he passed over . . . not giving it existence or being." So whilst the *being* (ontology) of creation is a work of the divine *Logos*, the chaos (*tohuwabohu* in Hebrew) is the negative of the divine affirmative of creation.[28] On this he builds his doctrine of "nothingness"; adding something of the old English alternative term "naughtiness," implying a moral evil potential in this chaotic state that God opposes.[29] The menace here is "far more serious than mere non-being," from "an enemy

23. Barth, CD, III/3, 351.

24. Plotinus, *Enneads*, i.8, page 3., cited in Hick, *Evil and the God of Love*, 46.

25. Tillich sees contingent being created *ex nihilo* as necessarily a precarious mixture of being and non-being, the latter producing instability and defectability that is the evil that threatens to overwhelm being. Augustine developed this idea in his *privatio boni*, but rejected the Platonic view that evil is a metaphysical necessity, attributing evil to the free choices of rational beings. *Evil and the God of Love*, 65, 191–92; Augustine, *On Free Choice of the Will*, 3.17 (126).

26. Hick, *Evil and the God of Love*, 192.

27. Ibid., 47; Plotinus, *Enneads*, i.8, p. 7.

28. Barth, CD, III/3, 73–77.

29. Barth's translators told Hendry that they considered this as a possible translation for *das Nichtige*. Hendry, "Nothing," 277, 82–83; Barth, CD, III/3, 289.

which is superior to created being"—destructive in character because "it is not elected and willed by God the Creator, but rather rejected and excluded . . . that to which God said No when he said Yes to the creature." His account of the "origin of evil" is thus philosophical, not temporal; evil arises as a philosophical necessity from the act of giving a positive reality to the creature—from the negative power of creating light and darkness (Gen 1:3–5). This "chaos," this abyss of non-being God chose not to create, is "not an adversary to God, but only the shadow of his work which both arises and is at once dispelled by his wrath. But to the creature it is an adversary for which the creature as such is no match . . . it has supreme power in the face of the creature." He states this philosophically: "to that which He denied he allotted the being of non-being, the existence of that which does not exist."[30]

This is not only paradoxical linguistically, but has serious theological and philosophical problems as well. How can God say "No" to it and yet choose to permit it to come into being at the same time? If evil is a *necessary* concomitant of creation, this would seem to threaten the sovereignty that Barth is so keen to assert.[31] Even though Barth with his concept of *das Nichtige* seeks to logically defend the complete goodness of God, it raises new logical difficulties.[32] Wright himself agrees this is theologically inadequate, implying God was powerless to prevent it happening.[33] Barth within a few lines can talk of "what God has eternally denied" as yet having "its own ponderable reality" everywhere in the Bible as "the shadow which flees before God";[34] yet if he really denied it for all eternity, then it should not merely flee but never have come into existence in the first place. Wright also considers Barth's account of the origin of evil based on Gen 1:2 as speculative *eisegesis*.[35] Ultimately, Barth is concealing the problems of theodicy behind this account of the nature and origin of evil which he has imposed on the text from the speculations of his own fertile and fascinating mind.[36]

However, Wright still sees the concept of nothingness as well suited to a description of the essence of evil—particularly because of Barth's

---

30. *CD*, III/3, 76–77.

31. See Hick, *Evil and the God of Love*, 193.

32. God's action in creation would appear to cause the very opposite of his intention. If so some other "good reason" (e.g., to prepare for the redemption of Christ) would be needed to justify creation, in danger of losing its original value. See Lloyd, "The Cosmic Fall," 14.

33. Wright, *Theology of the Dark Side*, 42.

34. Barth, *CD*, III/3, 76.

35. Wright, *Theology of the Dark Side*, 40–41; "Deliverance in Theological Perspective," 210.

36. Hick, *Evil and the God of Love*, 149–50.

"non-ontological" stance with its emphasis on the nature of evil as falsehood, and his agreement that demons, whilst very real, should be treated with only the contempt of "a quick, sharp glance," as all that is necessary and legitimate in their case.[37] Barth did charismatics a service in reminding them of the tendency for evil to deceptively over-inflate itself;[38] many charismatics do indeed make too much of the devil's power, and come under fear—although I found the opposite at St. George's. The charismatics I studied would agree that a key characteristic of the evil realm is falsehood, Satan being the father of lies, but would disagree with both Wright and Barth concerning the nature and origin of evil. Those at St. George's did use "nothing" in relation to evil, but differently—to express a healthy disdain for the power of Satan and his demons, as being "nothing" in comparison with the power of almighty God. They were using it in a relativistic sense, as in comparing the power of an ant with that of a human being, not because they put evil and Satan into a special meontic metaphysical category of "nothingness"; because they were enamored with the greatness of God and "his incomparably great power towards us who believe," which can overcome sin and the devil. This high view of God's goodness does not (as it did for Barth) result in ontologically discounting demons from being autonomous spiritual beings with some level of (albeit mostly stolen) power. It recognizes that perhaps the *primary* characteristic of evil is *rebellion*, which cannot merely originate from the shadow side of God or his creative act, but is an exercise of the will in proud contradistinction to God, as indeed Augustine describes the fall of Satan. Barth maintains that the devil "was never an angel . . . he was a murderer from the beginning";[39] but it is difficult to see how a scheming, lying, and murdering entity can arise without having been endowed at some point by the Creator with the intelligence required for this. This is one of the chief weaknesses of Barth's argument. On one hand, he talks of the kingdom of nothingness as "very similar to the kingdom of heaven with its angels"—it is an invisible and incomprehensible kingdom, undoubtedly superior to man and the earthly creation, with a kind of throne and ruler, with powerful messengers; it tries to do what God does, playing at creation, dominion, grace, and judgment.[40] In so doing, like Wright, he credits the demonic kingdom with a high degree of reality. Yet, he maintains this is *all* a

---

37. Barth, *CD*, III/3, 519; Wright, *Theology of the Dark Side*, 42; "Deliverance in Theological Perspective," 210.

38. Barth warned that looking too closely at the devil (as perhaps Luther did) may cause us to become "just a little or more than a little demonic." Barth, *CD*, III/3, 519, 522.

39. Ibid., III/3, 531.

40. Ibid., III/3, 527.

mimicry, all falsehood—in its very essence. Evil for Barth is all form and no essence—"the existence of that which does not exist." This stretches credulity and is indeed an "incomprehensible kingdom"—incredibly complex in form, and somehow superior to creation, yet with no ontological substance or true existence, which cannot therefore have an organizing center—which would also seem to discount the concept in the Gospels (and Epistles) of Satan as being in charge of a kingdom (e.g., Matt 12:26).

Why is Barth so concerned to reject the possibility that Satan and his demons are fallen angels? He does allow for the theoretical possibility that an angel who did not fulfill his role as a mere messenger would become like a lying spirit or a demon.[41] But since Barth's foundational concept of nothingness is a category of "non-being" which inherently involves falsehood, lies, and all that is opposed to God, he sees the need to maintain that demons (from below) and angels (from above) "do not grow from a common root" and have "nothing in common." Even though passages such as Rev 12:7 mention them together in conflict, to him "this radical conflict ought to have been regarded as a radical and *essential* determination on both sides."[42]

Barth is inconsistent here. For him, the chief manifestation of nothingness is man's sin, "the most important of all its forms"; yet he does not argue that we also must in very essence have come from nothingness below. His denying ontological substance to demons (as does Wright) is more speculative than the scriptural hints that behind sin and evil there are malevolent spiritual beings which must have some created essence to be termed "real." Seeing Satan and his minions as fallen created beings may have its own problems, but granting them some positive ontological reality makes more sense than seeing them as arising out of a metaphysical vacuum which is itself a doubtful philosophical construct.

If he wished to maintain a negative ontology for evil, Barth would perhaps have done better to follow Augustine more closely. Augustine ascribes the origin of evil to the wrong choices of free rational beings, first angels and then mankind: "Therefore a wicked will is the cause of all evil."[43] Evil only enters in when some member of the universal hierarchy renounces its proper role in the divine scheme and ceases to be what it is meant to be—thus not a separate entity, but the absence of proper being in the creature, his well-known *privatio boni*: "Evil has no positive nature; but the loss of

---

41. Ibid., III/3, 481; Wright, *Theology of the Dark Side*, 64–65.

42. Barth, *CD*, III/3, 74, 520.

43. Augustine, *On Free Choice of the Will*, 3.17 (126). He later clarifies: "The cause of evil is the defection of the will of a being who is mutably good from the Good which is immutable. This happened first in the case of angels and, afterwards, that of man." Augustine, *Enchiridion* 8.23, quoted in Hick, *Evil and the God of Love*, 65.

good has received the name "evil" . . . there can be no evil where there is no good . . . unless [evils] are parasitic on something good, they are not anything at all."[44] This approach has the advantage of denying any simple metaphysical dualism, without relying on a mysterious speculative realm of "non-being" as the source of evil—it is a more clearly justifiable theological account rather than a speculative philosophical one.[45] It also restores the parallel between the root of evil as sinful rebellion in mankind, acknowledged by Barth and Wright, and the root of evil in the invisible heavenly realm as proud rebellion of spiritual beings with real ontological substance, rather than postulating such beings as all form but no substance; without losing their key parasitic quality, and nature as falsehood and lies.

5.4 Evil as "God-forsaken space"

Before leaving this debate with the meontic tradition concerning the origin of evil, we must consider briefly Wright's reference to Moltmann's account of creation.[46] In this, the omnipresent God, in order to first create an empty space or *nihil* outside of himself within which to create the world, withdrew his presence and restricted his power (Isaac Luria's concept of *zimzum*, meaning concentration and contraction[47]); this literally "God-forsaken space" calls forth a Nothingness identified with hell and absolute death, the negation of God, which is demonic and remains a constant threat of non-being to the creation that is "let-be" within the space. This annihilating Nothingness is only finally overcome when in Christ God enters the space and defeats the demonic onslaught of the *nihil* on the cross. For Wright, this helps him to argue that God's creative work *of necessity* gives rise to a "demonic" threat to that creation, without directly implicating God in its origin.[48]

---

44. Augustine, *City of God* 11.9 and *Enchiridion* 4:13–14, cited in *Evil and the God of Love*, 53–54.

45. The privative view of evil can be validly inferred from prior positions of Christian faith. Ibid., 186–87. Some of Augustine's other Platonic philosophical ideas are much more speculative, e.g., that "being" itself is good.

46. Found in Moltmann, *God in Creation*. Moltmann developed his theology very much under the influence of Karl Barth, whose concept of *das Nichtige* or "Nothingness" (capitalized by Moltmann) he further develops.

47. Moltmann notes that Luria developed this Kabbalistic idea of "a withdrawing of oneself into oneself" from the Jewish doctrine of the Shekinah, where the infinite God so contracted his presence as to be able to dwell in the temple. Ibid., xiii, 87.

48. Ibid., 87–91; Wright, *Theology of the Dark Side*, 48–51.

Moltmann introduces a new slant to the concept of "non-being," based on the contraction (*zimzum*) of God's presence being a necessary precondition of creation—a speculative but logical deduction from the notion of an eternal, omnipresent God. This new aspect is "the non-being of the Creator": "In a doctrine of Nothingness, a distinction has to be made between the non-being of a creature, the non-being of creation, and the non-being of the Creator. It is only in connection with the last of these that we can talk about Nothingness."[49]

The key issue is what imparts to the *nihil* its menacing or demonic character in this reasoning. On the one hand, Moltmann asserts that the original *nihil* "represents the partial negation of the divine Being, inasmuch as God is not yet Creator; . . . the *nihil* in which God creates his creation is God-forsakenness, hell, absolute death; and it is against the threat of this that he maintains his creation in life." On the other hand, he then admits that "as a self-limitation that makes creation possible, the *nihil* does not yet have this annihilating character." Instead "the *nihil* only acquires this menacing character through the self-isolation of created beings to which we give the name of sin and godlessness." As a result of this self-isolation:

> Creation is therefore threatened, not merely by its own non-being, but also by the non-being of God its Creator—that is to say, by Nothingness itself. The character of the negative that threatens it goes beyond creation itself. This is what constitutes its demonic power. Nothingness contradicts, not merely creation but God too, since he is creation's Creator. Its negations lead into that primordial space which God freed within himself before creation; . . . this implies the possibility of the annihilating Nothingness.[50]

This brief dense argument is all that Moltmann gives to explain the postulated "demonic" power of this form of non-being. He seems to be saying that because created beings rebel (or "isolate themselves") within the creation occupying the *nihil*, these rebellious creatures fall under the threat of entering back into the primordial space where even God is absent, and so being eternally annihilated.

Wright observes that Moltmann's "Christian poetics" often plays with ideas that cannot be easily tested for theological rigor, but argues that it supports the idea that creation necessarily gives rise to the threat of evil. We need to be cautious here, however. Firstly, Moltmann himself admits that the "threat" of evil only becomes reality through the free choice of created

---

49. Moltmann, *God in Creation*, 88.
50. Ibid., 87–88.

beings: "Admittedly the *nihil* only acquires this menacing character through the self-isolation of created beings to which we give the name of sin and godlessness." The original *nihil*, even if it is emotively described as "literally God-forsaken space," need have no power of its own.[51] And secondly, it is true that the rebellion of created beings introduces an alien, evil element into the creation, which we can if we wish call "annihilating Nothingness" because it opens up the threat of the extinction of life;[52] but it is by no means clear that its negations *necessarily* "lead into that primordial space which God freed within himself before creation."[53] Such a space might simply be "nothing"—as Hick points out, we do not have to assume that an entity corresponds to every noun, and both "nothing" and "non-being" could be prime examples of this.[54] The existential *angst*, the fearful threat of death experienced by sentient beings, should be recognized for what it is—in Christian terms, it reveals our sinful estrangement from God and need for salvation; but such feelings need not be imposed on the empty space in which we were created. And we must also deconstruct Moltmann's poetic language here, in describing this extended threat of non-being "going beyond creation itself" as constituting "its demonic power." He does not define "demonic," nor indicate how the self-isolation of sin and godlessness endows any additional "demonic" energy upon the primordial space. It is the arena of "the God-forsakenness of sin and death" which for Moltmann characterize the evil realm of Nothingness—which God enters and overcomes in Christ through yielding him up to death in God-forsakenness on the cross, "surrendering him to hell" as he enters the Nothingness out of which he created the world "and makes it part of his eternal life." Moltmann's account of redemption

---

51. Wright himself implies this by comparing evil and "death"; "death" can be personified in Scripture, and like evil is also a formidable negative power—but being the absence of life lacks ontological substance. Wright implies the "demonic" is reduced primarily to a fear of [eternal] death in Moltmann's "annihilating Nothingness"; a plausible argument, however such fear arises from sinful rebellion ("self-isolation"), not as a feature of the *nihil* itself.

52. Including apocalyptic anxiety and concrete historical manifestations such as the horrific mass annihilations of Auschwitz and Hiroshima. Moltmann, *God in Creation*, 91.

53. Ibid., 88. Wright himself does not fully accept Moltmann's argument; he sees it as an *example* of how evil can be a necessary consequence of creation, similar in structure to the "free will defense," where the possibility of sin and evil within creation is a *necessary* consequence of its freedom; in my view a much better ontological ground for the existence of evil. See Wright, *Theology of the Dark Side*, 50, 64, 83–86.

54. Hick, *Evil and the God of Love*, 192–93.

from sin, evil, and death thus proceeds without reference to any specific Satanic or demonic powers.[55]

For Moltmann, it is the sinful self-isolation of God's creatures that brings the prospect of Nothingness as the threat of eternal destruction. However, this is an inadequate basis for the malevolence of evil, and gives no support to Wright's assertion of the "reality" of the demonic powers themselves. In Moltmann's terms, this reality could not arise spontaneously from the *nihil*, but only from the "self-isolation of created beings"; either through the rebellion of spiritual beings such as angels, or secondarily from human sin and godlessness. The latter is Wright's preferred option, and he turns to Walter Wink for support.

5.5 The origin of evil: evil as arising from human sin

The nature of something is closely linked to its origin, and so it is necessary to examine alternative theories concerning the origin of evil. Robert Cook helpfully describes four possibilities. Firstly he introduces the traditional view of a fall of the angels, or some other created entity beyond our universe, though he does not support this view.[56] He alternatively describes evil as the "infernal noumenon" or "black noise" ("a Barthianesque *Nichtige* which is perceived phenomenologically in different ways according to culture and worldview") and offers three further possible explanations for its origin—it being the shadow side of God, who "created both good and evil" (Isa 45:7); as forces of primeval chaos arising in the created universe; or arising at the level of humankind in its collective displacement from God (which we call sin).[57]

Wink himself is quoted by Cook as also having sympathy with evil as the shadow side of God—following Jung who in Job saw God working through his shadow side. Cook suggests this is because Wink revealingly sees Satan more "as grey noise rather than black."[58] Wright however distances himself from Wink's view here, saying Wink has fallen captive to "the fair face of evil."[59] Cook himself favors forces of primeval chaos as the origin of evil (drawing on Old Testament imagery of Rahab and Leviathan,

---

55. Moltmann, *God in Creation*, 88–91.

56. He seems to wish to discredit this because of a lack of unanimity amongst its proponents and various questions he raises that he considers may suggest fanciful answers—Cook, "Devils and Manticores," 168–70.

57. Ibid., 180–82.

58. Ibid., 180; Wink, *Unmasking the Powers*, 40.

59. Wright, *Theology of the Dark Side*, 47.

or the sea-monster of chaos in Job 7:12, as possibly lying behind the image of "the great dragon" of Rev 12:9), identifying chaos as evil.[60] But Wright also disagrees here, seeing chaos more as the *occasion* for evil rather than as evil in itself—of itself "chaos" is a stage in God's creative work.[61] Wright follows Noble in favoring the fourth option, particularly by drawing on Walter Wink's analysis.[62]

Wink's views are persuasively presented on a massive scale.[63] In taking evil and the spiritual battle seriously, Wink's views have been welcomed by some charismatics.[64] Wink is a perfect ally for Wright's non-ontological realist stance: Wink denies being a simple reductionist, repeatedly asserting the spiritual reality of the powers; yet he denies them a separate, spiritual existence, seeing them as the innermost essence of material realities such as earthly institutions.[65] Wink's ideas foster a strong sense of human responsibility, and recognize that evil is essentially parasitic, drawing its strength by preying on the energy of sin found in humankind and human society.[66] Wink also helpfully reintroduces the corporate perspective; he describes Satan and demons as archetypal realities encountered deep in our personalities, but also transcending us as creatures of the collective unconscious—echoing the biblical perspective of the corporate unity of humanity, including our corporate fallenness "in Adam."[67] Wright emphasizes the inextricable link between human sin and the demonic realm, such that "purely spiritual" acts of binding and rebuking the devil "will not avail if the supply lines of sin that enable the power of darkness to replenish itself . . . are not also dealt with."[68]

How does all this sit with the charismatic view of evil and its origin? In St. George's, there was agreement that Satan largely gets his power from

60. Cook, "Devils and Manticores," 181.

61. Wright, *Theology of the Dark Side*, 68. I agree this makes more sense in relation to Gen 1:2; unless subscribing to the "gap theory" of creation, favored by Gregory Boyd—see footnotes in chapters 7:4 and 8:4.

62. Noble, "The Spirit World," 214–20.

63. Three large volumes—Wink, *Naming the Powers*; *Unmasking the Powers*; *Engaging the Powers*. We shall return to Wink's views in examining Amos Yong's pneumatology (chapter 6) and the biblical texts concerning authorities and powers (chapter 8).

64. In my interviews, David MacInnes was particularly appreciative of Walter Wink's insights.

65. Wink, *Naming the Powers*, 5, 103–5, 135, 140; Noble, "The Spirit World," 211–12.

66. Wright quotes C. S. Lewis (from *Mere Christianity*): "Badness is only spoiled goodness. And there must be something good before it can be spoiled . . . evil is a parasite, not an original thing." Wright, *Theology of the Dark Side*, 66.

67. Cook, "Devils and Manticores," 175; Noble, "The Spirit World," 213.

68. Wright, *Theology of the Dark Side*, 46–47.

human sin; and, alongside "resisting the devil," similarly emphasized the need to "cut the supply lines"—through repentance and then "replacing" the sinful belief, attitude or behavior with biblically-based opposing ideas and actions, once an area of evil influence had been identified. However, the idea that evil *only* arises in response to human sin and has no independent existence was unacceptable to them and all of the pioneers, and would indeed be considered reductionist. Their experience instead seemed to reinforce what they saw in Scripture, that there are independent forces of evil which are "prowling around like a roaring lion" (1 Pet 5:8) seeking to tempt and gain influence and a foothold (Eph 4:27) in their lives, with intentionality and scheming (e.g., Eph 6:11), pointing to an adversary or adversaries with some independence of will and action. Thus, Wink asserts that "a mob spirit does not hover in the sky waiting to leap down on an unruly crowd at a football match," but instead "*comes into existence* (my emphasis) . . . when the crowd reaches a certain critical flashpoint of excitement and frustration . . . then ceases to exist the moment the crowd disperses";[69] but this contradicts indications from Jesus's words and actions that evil spirits have an independent continuing existence.[70] So it is not enough for Wright and Noble, in explaining this view, to emphasize that Satan must be *more* than merely a mythical projection or personification, instead being "a real and objective supreme power of evil which draws its reality and strength from the perverted corporate unconscious of humanity."[71] To this we might answer "strength," yes, but "reality," no. The reality of which they speak is compared by Wright to that of a vacuum, intensely powerful, yet consisting of sheer emptiness; or a "black hole," unobservable apart from its impact upon other stars and its capacity to suck matter into itself.[72] Such empty "nothingness" might indeed be the final end of evil;[73] but it is hard to imagine how "nothingness" could project intelligent, malevolent scheming into the world of substance, and exert willful and rebellious opposition to all that comes from God, if it is in essence merely "godless emptiness." If evil powers were indeed "nothingness" in essence, they could in Barth's terms be easily dismissed with "a quick sharp glance."[74] However, the experience

69. Wink, *Naming the Powers*, 105.

70. Notably the apparently factual description of evil spirits roaming around in arid places seeking rest (Luke 11:24–26), and the curious case of the legion of spirits cast out of a man into a herd of pigs (Mark 5:6–13).

71. Noble, "The Spirit World," 215.

72. Wright, *Theology of the Dark Side*, 70.

73. Wright follows Moltmann in capitalizing Nothingness; I prefer "nothingness" so as not to accord it with a pseudo-ontological substance.

74. Noll, "Thinking about Angels," 23; Barth, *CD*, 519.

of charismatics seems to mirror that of Jesus—when the Holy Spirit fills a person, evil forces often manifest with a forcefulness of opposition that at least requires an authoritative command to counter their stubborn rebellion and dismiss them from the scene.[75] Praxis would seem to confirm that the "reality" is much more likely to be autonomous spirit beings which have willfully chosen to rebel against God, and tempt human beings to join them in their rebellion, rather than in Wink's terms being the innermost essence of an earthly reality "lacking a separate spiritual existence."[76]

5.6 Evil and the concept of "personhood"

Another plank in Wright's construction is that the devil is less than fully personal: "The devil possesses a much reduced and essentially malevolent way of being which to dignify as personhood would be to vastly overrate."[77] He again speaks favorably of Noble's assessment, in granting the devil an atomic individualistic personhood according to the minimalist definition of Boethius as "an individual substance of rational nature,"[78] which the devil might be able to fulfill in so far as he is "an agent able to think, to know, to will and to act"; but lacking true personhood as theologians are increasingly coming to understand it, as "persons-in-relation."[79]

Thus far, however, this is not particularly contentious, more about use of language. Whilst Ferdinando and others do argue convincingly that the New Testament writers "in their references to Satan, demons and powers [clearly] had in mind personal spirit beings";[80] but Green observes that "what most people mean [by a personal devil] is to claim that Satan is an organizing intellect, a single focus and fount of evil inspiration.... Scripture depicts him as a spirit . . . but not "personal" in any meaningful sense; . . .

---

75. "He even gives orders to evil spirits and they obey him" (Mark 1:27); cf. interviews with Harper, Green, Collins, and Walker.

76. Wink, *Naming the Powers*, 105.

77. Wright, *Theology of the Dark Side*, 73.

78. In "A Treatise against Eutyches and Nestorius," see Boethius, *The Theological Tractates and the Consolation of Philosophy*, 85. Boethius's definition is rarely used, because it fails to rise up to a Trinitarian personhood which clearly also requires relationality.

79. Wright, *Theology of the Dark Side*, 73; Noble, "The Spirit World," 217. This Trinitarian understanding of personhood has been seen as a model for all concepts of self, as having more to do with relationality than with substantiality—see Grenz, *The Social God and the Relational Self*, 4.

80. Ferdinando, "Screwtape Revisited," 108.

the great 'It' is in every way the pale imitation of the ultimate 'He.'"[81] The emphasis is on distinct spiritual beings, but which may be very different from human persons, or "person" as defined in relation to God as a Trinity of persons.

What is in dispute however is Wright's jump from this to asserting that the devil is not an individual but a power, a dynamic which *takes on* the character of agency and intelligence and chaotically wars against God—for him evil is not ordered rationality but chaos, masquerading as personhood. For him, just as in one sense "all human personhood is *constructed* . . . via the relationships that surround us, . . . is there a way in which out of the unconscious, fallen human collective psyche the devil and even the demons might be constructed as hypostases?" He also uses the analogy of "machine intelligence" as potentially connected with demonology.[82] Presumably, by sticking to his minimalist Boethian definition of personhood paraphrased as "as individual entity endowed with intellect," he speculates that the devil might somehow be "endowed with intellect" from the human collective psyche—yet still be "an *agent* able to think, know, will and act,"[83] it is very unclear how the independence implied by agency could be constructed from the fallen human collective psyche—any more than human agency is "constructed via the relationships that surround us," Wright's unhelpful analogy with human personhood that serves to obfuscate the issue.[84]

This then is clearly a reductionist argument and highly speculative. It is well known that the human psyche, particularly under pressure, can produce all kinds of images, evil and otherwise, from its unconscious, some of which may account for the voices not only heard in the minds of the mentally ill but possibly voiced at times in those claiming to be possessed by demons, as Jung proposed;[85] but this is a long way from endowing a previously non-existent spiritual being with intellect and will of the kind that Scripture recognizes as Satan.[86] Even Noble is not a strong ally here—Noble

---

81. Green, *I Believe in Satan's Downfall*, 30.

82. Wright, *Theology of the Dark Side*, 73.

83. Noble, "The Spirit World," 192.

84. Wright admits malevolent agency is real: "Paul proclaimed "we are not ignorant of his designs" and this sense of agency must count for something." Wright, *Theology of the Dark Side*, 65.

85. Robert Cook summarizes well Jung's perspective, with which he strongly sympathizes—for Jung, forces experienced as devilish resided deep within our minds, but he also hinted that some might have an existence beyond it. Cook, "Devils and Manticores," 172–75.

86. For example in Jesus's reference to asking to sift Peter (Luke 22:31), or Pauline references to the devil's schemes (e.g., Eph 6:10).

recognizes that personality is something we are born with, "but we will be damaged persons unless we develop into loving persons in a matrix of stable, loving relationships."[87] He provides an acceptable description of how we might describe the devil's "personhood," acknowledging agreement with Green's position: "perhaps the concerns of those who fear reductionism here will be satisfied if we conceive of him as a malevolent intelligence, willing, acting and knowing, but totally lacking in personal feeling or sympathy, and obsessed with self-aggrandizement." Noble suggests that Satan and his demons "may possibly be conceived of as damaged persons, or perhaps better as "anti-persons," parasitic on human wickedness."[88] Charismatics have little problem in conceiving of them as "anti-persons," as long as, unlike Wright, they are also seen as "damaged persons"—for just as human personality, however marred, is created and fallen, so it is difficult to imagine the devil and demons constructing themselves from the fallen human collective psyche, rather than being fallen created beings;[89] and "machine intelligence," which Wright suggests as a possible ally to compare with demonic intelligence, is purposefully created by human beings, even if it could in some sense become an independent center of "will" (which is doubtful).[90]

So could the devil and demons be "anti-persons," or "non-persons"? Wright finds support in Paul for the idea that the evil behind idolatry is nothingness, because, although on the one hand Paul identifies false gods with demons (1 Cor 10:20), he also affirmed that, whilst there was some kind of real existence for these "many gods," nevertheless "an idol is nothing at all" (8:4–5).[91] This may indeed suggest that demons exercise their power insofar as people believe in them,[92] but we can hardly conclude that Paul would see their very existence as arising from "nothingness."[93] In Eph 6:12, the language concerning the "powers" implies supernatural cosmic forces in

---

87. Noble only clearly affirms that their energy would derive from human wickedness, hesitantly bracketing "possibly indeed their very being?" Wright, *Theology of the Dark Side*, 71; Noble, "The Spirit World," 215.

88. Green, *I Believe in Satan's Downfall*, 30, 126; Noble, "The Spirit World," 217.

89. If not fallen angels, then (Derek Prince's view) possibly the offspring of fallen angels and men (Genesis 6). See chapter 7.

90. Wright, *Theology of the Dark Side*, 73.

91. Ibid., 71; Noble, "The Spirit World," 215–16.

92. "The Spirit World," 216; Arnold, *Powers of Darkness: A Thoughtful, Biblical Look at an Urgent Challenge Facing the Church*, 94–95.

93. Paul's use seems to parallel the descriptions of idols as "nothing" in the prophets, meaning "futility," being "profitable for nothing" and unable to do what people demand of them, e.g., interpret the course of history (Isa 41:21–24; 44:10). Hendry, "Nothing," 277.

a hierarchy of spiritual beings, which exist "ἐν τοῖς ἐπουρανίοις" ("in the heavenly realms"), a phrase considered highly significant at St. George's.[94]

Wright also complicates the debate by developing false antitheses. He frames his own analysis as turning on whether the powers are "personal, ontological, organized and purposeful," or (as he proposes) essentially "chaotic, non-relational, depersonalizing and non-ontological."[95] However, some of these are not mutually exclusive—if evil powers are "damaged persons," they could retain personal, organized, and purposeful characteristics, as well as acquiring chaotic and depersonalizing tendencies.[96] Furthermore, purposeful and chaotic are not necessarily opposites—the traditional view of the devil is that he makes it one of his purposes to bring chaos to the order of God's creation, particularly through his intention to "kill, steal, and destroy" (John 10:10).

5.7 Conclusion: towards a charismatic ontology of evil

Wright wisely advises charismatics to "reflect upon its experience with the help of wisdom which resides in the pastoral practice and theological tradition of the church." On this basis he considers it dangerous to conceive of the dominion of darkness existing as the counterpart to the divine kingdom in that "it assumes a kind of legitimacy within the created sphere." Because evil in essence is deception (John 8:44), the demonic realm may only be *masquerading* as ontological and structured. He supports this with a favorite quotation, that "the power against which faith is faith has its own reality, just as certainly as it does not have its own validity."[97]

There are right concerns here that evil's domain should not be legitimized as a necessary part of God's creation, and that it should not be credited with more power and structure than it actually has. However, the wisdom from pastoral practice and theological tradition that he advises charismatics to reflect on is long and varied, and it is questionable how much weight should be given to twentieth-century modernism, that may (through Wink in particular) have eventually begun to recognize a demonic reality, only to

---

94. See also Ferdinando, "Screwtape Revisited," 108.

95. Wright, "Charismatic Interpretations," 158.

96. One church leader from my pilot study hinted at evil being both purposeful and chaotic, using the illustration of the giants in "The Silver Chair" whose rock-throwing practice Lucy and Edmond stumbled into. Similarly, Wright's quotation of Screwtape inadvertently turning into a centipede from Lewis's *Screwtape Letters* actually supports this interpretation of a mixture of purpose and chaos. *Theology of the Dark Side*, 72.

97. "Charismatic Interpretations," 163. His quotation is from Otto Weber, *Foundations of Dogmatics* Volume 1 (Grand Rapids: Eerdmans, 1982) 489.

define it in psychological and socio-spiritual terms; or to Barthian theology which, in applying to the essence of evil his own concept of nothingness derived primarily from a Platonic category of "non-being," remains more speculative than biblically rooted. For example, it is interesting that some who entered the debate concerning evil moved in the Orthodox direction, and have remained much more open to a positive ontology of evil.[98] Whilst Wright accuses charismatics such as Green and Arnold as remythologizing in applying the biblical imagery concerning evil too literally,[99] he has done his own remythologizing by ascribing reality to the forms of evil, and allowing them to obtain a limited form of personhood, yet retaining a modernist denial of ontological substance—because in drawing on the Barthian "meontic" theological tradition, he follows Noble and Wink in suggesting they originate as a projection of the corporate spirit of fallen humanity.[100]

In synthesizing his own version of meontic ontology, where the devil is "not something or someone" but God is "Being Itself,"[101] Wright appears to confuse two different issues (ontology and legitimacy) which do not need to be conflated. He is concerned that the devil should have no "legitimacy," no "place assigned to him by God." But a theory of rebellion of good spiritual beings does not necessarily entail their having a legitimate God-given role—neither for Augustine or for more radical "free-will theists" such as Gregory Boyd (discussed in chapter 7). Wright in his description of demonic non-being says that "evil exists as chaos to order, as lie to truth, darkness to light or death to life"[102]—but if we add "as pride to humility, as rebellion to submission, as disobedience to obedience" it does not increase the devil's "legitimacy," rather clarify more vividly the nature of the enmity between the devil and his kingdom and God. In bringing "rebellion" to center stage as the nature of evil, strengthening the link between human sinful rebellion and the power of evil, charismatics may help ensure retaining a Barthian contempt for the demonic kingdom, without having an excuse to avoid discovering and using the necessary tools to follow Christ in

---

98. Both Michael Harper, and Andrew Walker—who despite concerns about "the paranoid universe," still sees the devil as an angelic being who freely rebelled and cast himself off from the creator's love, now drifting towards non-personhood. Walker, "The Devil You Think You Know," 102.

99. Wright, "Charismatic Interpretations," 158; Arnold, *Powers of Darkness*; Green, *I Believe in Satan's Downfall*.

100. Noble, "The Spirit World," 214, 217–18; Wright, *Theology of the Dark Side*, 70–71; Wink, *Unmasking the Powers*, 24–25; Cook, "Devils and Manticores," 182.

101. Wright borrows the term from Paul Tillich—Wright, *Theology of the Dark Side*, 31–33.

102. Ibid., 31.

exposing and destroying the works of the evil one. If evil is seen as having no substance and only masquerading in various forms, the danger instead is not to take its virulence seriously, and to try and defeat it by human attempts to disregard, disbelieve or disperse such vacuous "forms"; rather than through the only sure theological ground for the defeat of evil, the death of Christ upon the cross.

Wright correctly points out that the texts concerning a fall of angels are problematic and of uncertain interpretation.[103] However, there are more hints in Scripture of evil having arisen in this way than the even more speculative accounts of Cook, Wright, and Wink. Not only does the Gospel of Matthew ascribe to Jesus words of judgment on "the devil and his angels," but we find a similar phrase in Revelation.[104] And, whilst the timing of the events they refer to is difficult to interpret, both Jesus and Revelation record a "fall" of the devil (and his angels),[105] which for Jesus could be an allusion to one of the two "problematic" Old Testament texts, Isa 14:12.[106] There is certainly significant exegetical evidence here that the "devil and his angels" share a similar positive ontology as spirit beings to "Michael and his angels" (Rev 12:7), and that it was willful rebellion that led to their loss of status.[107]

And as to the origin of such destructive forces—borrowing Wright's analogy, even a black hole was a powerful star once, otherwise it would not exist at all.[108] Walker may be correct to follow C. S. Lewis in suggesting the devil is undergoing a depersonalizing metamorphosis towards non-personhood;[109] but it would accord with biblical data and pastoral experience that this is not because the devil has arisen from it, but in his fall has lost the goodness of full personhood possessed by the angels, and is fighting to steal back whatever he can from humans, who give it away through their individual and corporate sinful actions.[110]

---

103. Ibid., 63.

104. Matt 25:41, Rev 12:7 (where the dragon is identified as "the devil, or Satan").

105. "I saw Satan fall like lightning from heaven" (Luke 10:18); "he was hurled to the earth, and his angels with him" (Rev 12:9).

106. Green argues that "the king of Tyre" is a spiritual power behind the earthly "prince of Tyre" in the other text (Ezek 28:1–19), though it is not strong exegetically. But he rightly observes that Jude 6 and 1 Tim 3:6 point in the same direction. Green, *I Believe in Satan's Downfall*, 36–39.

107. Cf. the fivefold emphatic rebellious "I will . . ." in Isa 14:12–14. We will re-visit the fallen angels hypothesis in chapters 7 and 8.

108. As Wright himself points out—Wright, *Theology of the Dark Side*, 70.

109. Walker, "The Devil You Think You Know," 102.

110. As Wink acknowledges in relation to Luke 4:6—Wink, *Unmasking the Powers*, 24.

Wright has challenged charismatics for their "apparent reluctance to go beyond the mythological and narrative imagery of Scripture to ask more *theological* questions about the actual nature of evil." However, in the "ordinary theology" of members of St. George's there is indeed a clear theological answer as to the nature of evil, in characterizing its essence as "rebellion"; requiring either an Augustinian privative account of evil, or a more positive ontology.[111] Evil as "rebellion" arises from choosing to sever a relationship of willing submission to an all-loving God; this most naturally fits with an origin in the fall of angels that parallels, and then draws power and sustenance from, the fall of human beings. Characterizing evil as "rebellion" also points to the most effective way to overcome demonic influence, through continuous repentance from our own rebellion against God; so that, forgiven and filled with the Spirit of Christ, Christians can exercise the authority Jesus delegated to them over all the power of the enemy, discovering the vastly superior power and greatness of God, whose love carries us up in Christ into a position of spiritual authority even in the heavenly realms.[112] Far from necessarily resulting in an increase in paranoia, my studies reveal that a charismatic spiritual warfare praxis thus grounded can progressively release from fear, and bring growth in inner spiritual freedom and security in God.

---

111. Presented with some of Cook's alternatives concerning the origin and nature of evil, one interviewee commented succinctly: "The fallen angels would be more my understanding, obviously because of the nature of rebellion in sin, and the whole nature of Satan is rebellion." Gail Interview 6.12.07.

112. Luke 10:19; Eph 1:19–23, 2:6.

6

Amos Yong

A Triadic Metaphysics of the Demonic

6.1 Introduction

THE FOREGOING INDUCTIVE RESEARCH raised the central question—what is the nature of the evil powers that charismatics claim to be encountering and struggling against? Having begun a dialogue with Nigel Wright and others who have addressed this question, we now turn to Amos Yong's contribution. His work is particularly helpful in this reflective interpretive phase in engaging with the debate concerning evil in the wider tradition of the theological "system"—for, although Yong himself is from the Pentecostal/charismatic tradition, he draws widely on the work of scholars and wider philosophical thinking outside his own tradition, intending his work as a contribution to the wider Christian conversation on the work of the Spirit.[1]

Yong's theological writing is extensive; but apart from some later publications, which indirectly touch on specific aspects of the subject,[2] and a recent volume that includes consideration of "the powers" in relation to political theology,[3] his approach to evil and the demonic is mainly laid out

---

1. As stated in the introduction to his exposition of a theology of religions—Yong, *Discerning the Spirits*, 10. The background thinking of his metaphysics is further developed in *Spirit-Word-Community*.

2. "*Ruach*"; *Theology and Down Syndrome*. More recently he has further developed it in *The Spirit of Creation*.

3. *In the Days of Caesar*.

in *Discerning the Spirits*;[4] and then in summary form in a paper.[5] Thus it is here that I begin.

In a typically triadic approach, Yong summarizes his theology of discernment in three theses, metaphysical, biblical, and theological respectively.[6] It is primarily in the context of developing his metaphysical argument that he discusses the nature of the demonic, and so we need first to sketch out his approach to this which he terms "foundational pneumatology."

6.2 Yong's foundational pneumatology

Foundational pneumatology is "the effort to articulate a fully public account of spiritual reality," in particular of the Holy Spirit, through attempting to discern the presence and activity of God in the world (and by contrast, God's absence).[7] He aims to be "fully public" so as to engage any and all interested parties, believing that God's Spirit is present and active in the world as a whole.[8] He therefore looks for a common public language, and finds metaphysics to be most appropriate, being a philosophical discourse concerned with what the world is and how it functions. In this he follows on from theologian Donald Gelpi and Yong's teacher Robert Neville, both of whom were inspired by the metaphysics of American pragmatist philosopher C. S. Peirce.[9] Yong, like Gelpi, prefers Peirce's "contrite fallibilism" approach to epistemology where all knowledge is provisional, subject to the

---

4. I have simplified Yong's own title, *Discerning the Spirit(s)*, which brackets the "s" to show that the book is more concerned with discerning the Holy Spirit at work than with other "spirits."

5. Yong, "Spiritual Discernment," 84, 99. This paper is almost entirely a reprint of chapter 6 of *Beyond the Impasse*, 129–61.

6. His metaphysical thesis is that all things consist of both *logos* and *pneuma*, "forms of concretions and dynamic vectoral trajectories." Secondly, he argues that the biblical authors understood discernment as the development of senses that can pierce through the concrete forms of things to their inner spirits; and thirdly he proposes theologically that this spiritual discernment is a broad "hermeneutics of life" that is both divine gift (e.g., the gift of discerning of spirits) and also a human activity. "Spiritual Discernment," 84.

7. *Discerning the Spirits*, 122; "Spiritual Discernment," 84. Yong adapts Harvey Cox's three categories in developing his own, proposing *religious cosmology* as the third one, relating Cox's notion of "primal hope" to the notion of divine absence. *Discerning the Spirits*, 222; Cox, *Fire from Heaven*.

8. Yong, "Spiritual Discernment," 84–85.

9. He also acknowledges that biblical scholar Walter Wink figures in his own thinking. Ibid., 85–87; *Discerning the Spirits*, 105–17, 121–30.

ongoing process of conversation and discovery; rather than a strong Cartesian foundationalism that bases all beliefs on self-evident intuitions.[10]

Peirce's metaphysics takes a triadic view of reality. *Firstness* is "pure potentiality," that which makes a thing what it is in itself, and forces itself on our perception—we see greens as greens, chairs as chairs, etc. *Secondness* is the brute resistant fact by which a thing is related to others or struggling or distinct from them—greens are not whites, chairs support sitting, parents support children, etc. *Thirdness* is "both what mediates between firstness and secondness on the one hand, and between that and others on the other . . . the universals, laws, generalities, or habits that ensure the continuity of the process of reality . . . that shape the temporal modality and relationality of things." For example, parents are constituted by the many features relating them and their activities to children; chair is a generality, but a chair can take many shapes, sizes, and functions, but does not determine who sits on it.[11] Yong regularly returns to this triadic view, particularly in his work on hermeneutics, *Spirit-Word-Community*, where he succinctly summarizes respectively the three elemental modes of Firstness, Secondness, and Thirdness: "Things are what they are precisely as the togetherness of *qualities, facts*, and *laws*—the hows, whats, and habits or tendencies of experience" (my italics).[12] He argues that it is the coinherence of these qualities, facts, and laws that constitutes our experience of reality. Pierce saw that we never have a pure experience of the firstness (qualities) of things, but this is abstracted from our experience of their secondness (facts) and thirdness (laws). Gelpi helped Yong to see the correlation here between Piercean metaphysics and trinitarian theology, which affirms that the Father makes himself present to the world not directly, but through the two hands.[13]

Yong thus brings his Piercean metaphysics into the theological arena by suggesting that all things in their "firstness" (their simple felt qualities) consist of both Word (*logos*) as concrete form (secondness), and Spirit (*pneuma*) as their inner spirit (thirdness).[14] All things are encounterable pheonomenologically as a perceptible concrete form (secondness), but also

---

10. *Discerning the Spirits*, 100. This "contrite fallibilism" accords well with the "critical realist" epistemology I have adopted—see chapter 1.4, and Cartledge, *Practical Theology*, 44–45.

11. Yong, "Spiritual Discernment," 87; Raposa, *Peirce's Philosophy of Religion*, 124. Raposa references to Hartshorne, Weiss, and Burks, *Collected Papers of C. S. Pierce*, 6:455.

12. For Yong, Pierce's approach bypasses the drawbacks of other systems, such as pantheistic monism or Cartesian dualism. Yong, *Spirit-Word-Community*, 93.

13. Ibid., 91, 94. Yong discusses this model extensively—ibid., 50–60.

14. This is his first, metaphysical, thesis.. "Spiritual Discernment," 84.

have an inner spirit (thirdness) of "laws, habits, tendencies, and energetic force that shape its processive actuality and direct its temporal trajectory."[15] As a specific example of how this might apply to personhood, firstly in relation to the person of Christ, Yong uses primarily a Spirit-Christology model which describes the person of Jesus of Nazareth (firstness) as having essentially both a Christological dimension (*logos*, or concrete form—his secondness) of the "Word made flesh," and a pneumatological dimension of the inner dynamic of the Spirit (*pneuma*, or inner dynamic field of force—his thirdness). He sees this as generalizable to all persons—"each of us are who we are precisely as felt emotive qualities (firstness) and bodies (secondness) integrated by that inner spiritual aspect of our being (thirdness)." For Yong, the latter is manifested for example in "intentional vectors or fields of force" which both draw from our concrete structures (including our biological genes) as well as our social environments and experiences.

As another example, Yong also applies this triadic metaphysical analysis to corporate entities such as communities, organizations, social and political groups, and nations—sensing not only the parallels with German idealistic philosophers such as Hegel who spoke of *Geist* as the inner characteristic features of nations and civilizations, but also the biblical concept of the Spirit as the life force of the church (the body of Christ), and Paul's language about governments which is suggestive of both outward institutional structures and their inner dynamic as spiritual authorities (Rom 13:1-6).[16]

6.3 Foundational pneumatology, the demonic, and Walter Wink

We have seen that Yong wishes to investigate the categories of divine presence and activity in the world; but also divine absence, which particularly concerns us in relation to the demonic. Yong argues that ontologically speaking, divine absence does not necessarily imply the presence of evil spirits, for "non-being" of itself does not have evil or demonic power; nevertheless, our human experience is that the *nihil* is not simply something we feel to be threatening, but has a positive and horrific aspect to our encounter with it which cannot simply be wished away, but has to be wrestled against and overcome, which is rightly termed demonic.[17] This leads into his second

15. Ibid., 87; *Spirit-Word-Community*, 93-94.
16. "Spiritual Discernment," 88-89.
17. In particular see the footnote 39 in *Discerning the Spirits*, 127-28. This conception is clearly similar to that of Moltmann and Wright discussed in 5.4 above. Yong (footnote 40, 128) also notes that experience of the *reality* of the demonic can go way

level of categorization of the demonic, as also signifying the forces that actively resist the arrival of the divine kingdom. Yong sees this characterization as not only having a pervasive element over which there can be a fair degree of consensus (e.g., its manifestations in anti-Semitism, the Crusades, witch hunts, sexism, racism, classism, etc.), but also often shifting according to its religious context, as religious persons and communities usually demonize religious traditions other than their own, or other perceived threats.[18]

Yong applies again the triadic metaphysical model to the demonic. In its firstness or "essential suchness, the demonic is a destructive reality that opposes the goodness and providence of God. As such the demonic is manifest in concrete forms and particular actualities [secondness], and sustained as forces with destructive capacities [thirdness]." It is here that Yong's distinctive view emerges. He submits that we often think of the demonic in terms of the "thirdness" of demonic forces; but because of his triadic metaphysical approach, demons too must always include the concrete outer forms of secondness; he maintains that a demonic spirit is irrelevant if it is not manifest concretely in space and time—"we can therefore speak meaningfully of a spirit of lust, or the spirit of murder, or the spirit of alcoholism, for example, only because we see its effects in ruined relationships, tragic homicides, civil wars, non-functional kidneys, or successive generations of families inflicted by habitual patterns of drinking." Thus, whilst he claims not to be denying the idea of a personal devil and his demons, he is denying that "such realities can be conceived *only* in a spiritual sense apart from concrete forms"—for example, what is demonic about the Holocaust is not any host of demonic spirits in the abstract ("Casper-like spirits floating about in mid-heaven"), but the concrete events of the putrid gas chambers of Auschwitz, or for racism the actual discrimination of peoples based on skin color. Any spirits for Yong that do not manifest concretely "could not be said to exist in any meaningful sense"—they are "at least irrelevant to the human condition, and at worst a figment of our imagination."[19]

In emphasizing both the inner dynamic and outer forms of corporate entities, Yong openly notes the influence and similarity with Walter Wink's proposals. Wink argues that "the powers" have an inner and outer aspect—"as the inner aspect, they are the spirituality of institutions, the "within" of corporate structures and systems, the inner essence of outer organizations of power. As the outer aspect they are political systems, appointed officials,

---

beyond the biblical and theological texts that refer to it, citing the reflections of Helmut Thielicke on his experience of Nazi Germany.

18. *The Spirit Poured out on All Flesh*, 252–53.
19. "Spiritual Discernment," 90, 102–3.

the "chair" of an organization, laws—in short, all the tangible manifestations which power takes."[20] These two dimensions belong together—the powers are both heavenly and earthly, divine and human, spiritual and material, invisible and structural. But they are also good as well as evil. Wink maintains that the biblical accounts identify the powers as servants of God—even Satan himself at times being the "sifter" or "prosecuting attorney";[21] but then for Wink Satan's fall did not in fact take place in time, but in the human psyche, an "archetypal movement of momentous proportions," assuming the aspect of a suprapersonal spiritual agency, the sum total of the darkness and fear of the whole race. But he resists personifying Satan, as "personification is too rationalistic to deal with archetypal realities," and he is afraid of reintroducing the literal "person" of popular Christian fantasy.[22] He maintains though, that Satan continues to have both roles as Servant of God and the Evil One; but it is primarily our own choices that give Satan so much power over the world and determine which side Satan is on—even suggesting we can redeem Satan by our choices—"we made Satan evil, only we can restore him to his rightful role at God's right hand."[23] Likewise, there are clearly a range of "powers" at work in the world, some of which are demonic in character, but are potentially able to be redeemed by our choices.[24]

Wink's theology is clearly congruent with Yong's more philosophical approach—Wink emphasized the inner aspect of the powers, equivalent to Yong's "thirdness," and the outer tangible aspects equivalent to "secondness." One of Wink's central theses is that the Powers, whilst spiritual, are generally only encountered as corporealized in some form; this parallels Yong's argument above.[25] Satan has an "outer" reality in some sense—since "the social sedimentation of human choices for evil has formed a veritable layer of sludge that spans the world."[26] However, Yong notes that Wink's main purpose is to reinterpret the biblical cosmological language of the powers for our time, and so there is little discussion of metaphysical issues. Yong therefore wishes to add to Wink's dipolar demonology the missing category of the "firstness" of the demonic, which for him arises from the existential spontaneity of things, which can inexplicably decide to act against

20. Wink, *Naming the Powers*, 5.
21. *Unmasking the Powers*, 10–22.
22. Ibid., 24–5.
23. Ibid., 34.
24. *Naming the Powers*, 5.
25. Ibid.; Yong, "Spiritual Discernment," 90.
26. Wink, *Unmasking the Powers*, 25. However, Wink's "inner" and "outer" phraseology verges on panentheism, denying the existence of an independent, transcendent, supernatural realm. Osborn, "Angels: Barth and Beyond," 29–48, page 44.

its divinely ordained purpose of being and turn away from God, and so unleash force-fields of the demonic. Yong here is being quite Augustinian—indeed, he agrees in a footnote that this truth lies behind the theory of evil as privation and negation.[27] This also agrees with my own emerging thesis that the essential nature of the demonic is rebellion. However, Yong is primarily referring to the "spontaneous self" of human beings turning away from God, and does not apply it to angelic ones—although Augustine himself made that application.[28]

Yong is thus highly appreciative of Wink's analysis of the powers as having outer concrete and inner spiritual aspects, but he is critical in other respects. Firstly, Wink relies heavily on process theology, whose dipolar doctrine of God and the world as interdependent Yong explicitly rejects.[29] Whilst Yong commends this positive attempt to overcome "the disastrous dualisms" of Enlightenment rationality, he sees Wink's reliance on process metaphysics as holding him back from filling this out by adopting "a more explicitly triadic and truly relational metaphysic."[30]

Secondly, whereas Wink seems to reduce the demonic to social, institutional, and organizational realities, Yong wishes to emphasize the multidimensionality of the demonic at natural, personal, and social levels.[31] This reflects his Pentecostal roots, where traditionally the main encounter with the demonic is considered to be at the personal level; and Yong's multidimensional approach does become more accessible to charismatics in British Anglican context. Wink does briefly discuss the demonic at the personal level, remaining agnostic as to whether there are real evil spirits as actualizations of the corporate demonic that can possess people individually. Yong rightly criticizes Wink here as inconsistent when he tries to make a clear distinction between the "inner personal demonic," which arises from suppression of essential elements of a person's being that need to be accepted and loved to bring healing, and "outer personal possession . . . of an individual by something alien and extrinsic to itself," the personalized actualization of "the collective malady afflicting an entire society," where exorcism of the demonic spirit might be appropriate.[32] Yong argues that the demonic has *both* outer and inner aspects, and sees the latter as personal

---

27. Yong, *Discerning the Spirits*, 129.

28. For example, Augustine, *On Free Choice of the Will*, 3.11 (113–15). However, Yong discusses this more fully in Yong, *The Spirit of Creation*.

29. *Discerning the Spirits*, 93.

30. As both Gelpi and Yong have done. *Spirit-Word-Community*, 88–91, 94.

31. "Spiritual Discernment," 90.

32. Wink, *Unmasking the Powers*, 43, 50.

aspects contaminated and perverted by outer social and "other larger-than-life forces," resulting in some loss of personal rationality or integrity, as (in Morton Kelsey's words) "demonic psychic content tries to possess the human psyche"[33] (whereas the Holy Spirit brings the opposite effects). Thus, whilst agreeing with Wink that psychotherapy can be helpful, he then seems to support the Pentecostal/charismatic approach in suggesting that "complete deliverance can only come about as a gift of the Spirit enabling repentance and discipleship in truth and righteousness."[34] This balanced view may be helpful on the practical level; however, Yong's ontological language here is again, like Wink's, very cautious—instead of "evil spirits" he talks of "other larger-than-life forces," or is content to borrow the phrase "demonic psychic content" in letting Kelsey do his talking for him.

6.4 Personhood, the Holy Spirit, and demonic ontology

Yong follows Gelpi in emphasizing the thirdness of the Spirit, in terms of a "law" or dynamic life force.[35] Yong notes that other theologians, such as Pannenberg and Moltmann, have also begun to speak of the Spirit as a field of force.[36] Pannenberg, for example, considers the Spirit as a creative and life-giving dynamic, the force field of God's mighty presence (cf. Ps 139:7), in contrast to the Greek idea of the deity as *nous* in the traditional theological doctrine of God.[37] Moltmann also describes the Spirit as a source of energy and a field of force, noting how charismatics often feel the experience of the Spirit as *vitalizing energy*.[38] Such theologians help to bring the ancient concept of *pneuma* in the biblical world, where spiritual and material reality are not divorced in a dualistic sense, into conversation with modern physics, which argues that material reality is nothing less than energy arranged within and sustained by force fields of activity.[39]

The question thus arises, in what sense is the Spirit "personal"? Yong maintains that the personal pronoun is still appropriate, for example,

---

33. Morton Kelsey, *Encounter with God: A Theology of Christian Experience* (Minneapolis: Bethany, 1972) 157, quoted in Yong, *Discerning the Spirits*, 299.

34. Wink, *Unmasking the Powers*, 53; Yong, *Discerning the Spirits*, 298–99.

35. *Discerning the Spirits*, 117.

36. Ibid., 117–18; "Spiritual Discernment," 89.

37. Whilst admitting the difficulty that "as a field . . . the Spirit would be impersonal." Pannenberg, *Systematic Theology*, I, 382–84.

38. He also highlights the biblical image of Holy Spirit flow, from the well of life— "the origin of the torrent of energy." Moltmann, *The Spirit of Life*, 195–96.

39. Yong, *Spirit-Word-Community*, 90.

because the Spirit is primarily "relationality"; which suggests divinity as personality, and the Spirit engages us as personal beings.[40] Unlike Pannenberg, Yong does retain the link between the Holy Spirit and the *nous* or mind of God; he also identifies the Spirit with rationality, partly because of the role of the Holy Spirit in his key epistemological concept, the pneumatological imagination.[41] Yong nevertheless wishes to preserve some mystery in how we talk of God in personal terms, beyond the supremely personal revelation of God in the person of Jesus as our Savior; he feels Gelpi may go too far in pressing for acceptance of the idea of a tri-personal God.[42] Yong himself favors an anti-individualistic, relational emphasis on the Trinity as three subsistent relations, rather than a triad of persons who "have" relations.[43] Yong concludes in describing the constitutive features of pneumatology as relationality, rationality, and dynamic life. Though not made explicit, this seems to point to relationality as the essential firstness of the Spirit (even though within the Trinity, relationality is the "thirdness" of the Spirit), rationality as its secondness, and dynamic life expressed as a field of force as its thirdness.[44]

Yong, therefore, whilst clearly Trinitarian in his approach, and acknowledging the relationality (and rationality) of the Spirit, primarily emphasizes the thirdness of the Spirit as a field of force. This is relevant to his demonic ontology, because Yong defines the demonic as "the contrast term to the Holy Spirit";[45] so in emphasizing the thirdness of fields of force, he unsurprisingly brings the same, or even greater ambiguity to the

---

40. For Yong, the ontology of the Spirit is inherently relational—"he will not speak on his own; he will speak only what he hears" (John 16:13–14); as the Spirit *of* God, or the Spirit *of* Christ, never calling attention to herself. *Discerning the Spirits*, 123. Moltmann shares this emphasis on relationality; in the all-embracing presence of the outpoured Spirit, we experience the reciprocal perichoresis of God and ourselves, as the eternal God participates in our transitory life. Moltmann, *The Spirit of Life*, 195.

41. Yong recalls the OT personification of human wisdom (see Prov 8:22–31), and the Spirit as the mediator of the divine mind for Paul, embodied concretely in Jesus (1 Cor 2:10–16). He is also influenced by Gelpi's characterization of the Spirit as the mediating "divine Breath" upon us. See Yong, *Spirit-Word-Community*, 95; Gelpi, *The Divine Mother*, 56–66.

42. Yong sees our present experience of God as to some extent empirically revealing God's personhood, but in other aspects articulating this sense of personhood is a matter of faith. Yong, *Discerning the Spirits*, 123–24.

43. Yong sees this as overcoming the false duality between personal individuality and personal relationality. *Spirit-Word-Community*, 56–57.

44. Yong accepted this as a valid extrapolation from his work. Yong, "Response to Chapter 6."

45. Yong, *Discerning the Spirits*, 127, footnote 38.

demonic in terms of its personal nature, or independent subsistence.[46] The pneumatological imagination "envisions the world as a complex interplay of non-material powers and forces . . . [and] recognizes that the spiritual realm is ambiguous in that . . . one can be inspired just as easily by demonic rather than divine powers."[47] Thus the presence and activity of the divine and the demonic are similar in form—but contrasted by their concrete outcomes (secondness), through which we can discern their essential nature (firstness—constructive [divine] or destructive [demonic]), seeing beyond concrete effects into their driving dispositions and tendencies, or the "fields of force" behind them (thirdness).

By thus concentrating on the "thirdness" of demonic powers, they are characterized as energies or forces that compete with the power of the force-field of God's Spirit in this world, and their true nature eludes us.[48] For the Holy Spirit, the person of Christ is always in the background for Yong, preventing a total loss of personhood and collapse into the Spirit's thirdness of a life-giving field of force; and he maintains the personal concept of rationality and "mind" behind the positive divine force. However, for the demonic, Yong follows the ambivalence of Wink and others rather than the more positive ontologies of his Pentecostal roots; although he acknowledges that Pentecostals see demons as discrete spiritual beings "as real as rocks and persons," which usually best accounts for the uncanny and unpredictable aspects of human experience.[49] Where he touches on the nature of human "persons" elsewhere he again emphasizes relationality.[50]

Recently, in the context of his discussion of the powers in Pentecostalism and political theology, Yong has more explicitly proposed an apophatic theology of the demonic.[51] He mentions the "personification" of natural

---

46. In comparing the divine Spirit and other spirits, Yong again emphasizes relationality, "power" (*dunamis*) and "wind" or "breath" (*ruach* or *pneuma*). *Spirit-Word-Community*, 133–40.

47. Ibid., 140–41.

48. His earliest definition also emphasizes thirdness, but with a hint of "agency": "a law or nexus of laws that attempts to pervert the determinate forms of being and establish force fields of destruction" (the biblical "law of sin and death" [Rom 8:2]). *Discerning the Spirits*, 129.

49. Ibid., 235–36.

50. His notion of full human personhood as relating to ourselves (embodied), others, and God (transcending), militates against identifying Satan or demons as personal in the sense that they lack relationship with God. *Theology and Down Syndrome*, 180–81, 324n38. However, if they are "fallen angels" they would once have had this relationship, and could still be "transcending or spiritual" without it—with an ontology of "decayed persons." See chapter 8.2.

51. Apophatic theology seeks to describe God, or here the demonic, in terms of

human powers over human affairs as "members of the divine council" in Hebrew thought, being "understood by the early Christians as angels."[52] He is more concerned with the "powers" related to the public realm (political, economic, and social), which he describes as natural human and social realities created good by God, but fallen—and so now "susceptible to demonic manifestations." He continues:

> The demonic has no ontological reality of its own but is rather a perversion of the goodness of the orders of creation—or, put alternatively, since the demonic is not created by God, it does not possess its own being . . . the demonic is, nevertheless, objective as an emergent reality, parasitic and dependent upon certain configurations of the material, institutional, and organizational structures of the powers, yet irreducible to the sum of its constituent parts; . . . once emergent, the demonic is manifest as a force of destruction wielded in and through the fallen and disordered powers, appearing in ways that suggest the powers have become transcendental realities, bigger than what they are, certainly overreaching their authority, and *seemingly* personal and intentional in their destructive capacities.[53]

Here, on the one hand, by "embracing a re-enchanted cosmopolis," Yong is (like Griffin, Welker, and Wink) seeking a *via media* "between the materialisms, naturalisms, and reductionisms of modernity on the one side and the fantastic cosmological anarchism of premodern worldviews on the other side."[54] But he is also identifying himself with a "non-ontological realist" view of evil, similar to that of Wright discussed in chapter 5.

6.5 Discussion and critical analysis of Yong's demonic ontology

In his earlier work, Yong was at pains to say in relation to Pentecostal ideas of demons that he is "not here denying the idea of a personal devil and his

---

what it is not (as opposed to cataphatic theology). Yong pointed out that this is specifically in the context of political theology, where "we need an apophatic moment precisely because we Pentecostals are all too keen to demonize our political opponents." Yong, "Response to Chapter 6." He also seeks to dissuade Pentecostals from focusing on evil by over-confidently identifying ruling spirits as "Cartesian subjectivities" over regions or nations. *In the Days of Caesar*, 164–65.

52. Quoting Heb 1:14—"angels sent to serve for the sake of those who are to inherit salvation." Ibid., 162.

53. My italics. Ibid., 162–63.

54. Ibid., 147, 64.

demons"; but at the same time he denied that they can be conceived "only in a spiritual sense apart from concrete forms";[55] and more recently, he at least wishes to deny them as "centers of Cartesian subjectivity."[56]

I suggest five main reasons lie behind these "denials," some practical and some more philosophical. The first reason for this ontological ambivalence towards any "independent" existence of evil spirits may be his aspiration to contribute to the possibility of a global theological enterprise. Yong is ambitious in aiming not only to write for his own Pentecostal constituency, and for his academic context, but for a global theological audience.[57] In his discussion with Wolfgang Vondey, Yong admits the tension this brings—attempting to maintain Pentecostal distinctives whilst respectfully engaging with theological and ecumenical tradition; and ambivalent in how to handle some issues so as to open up conversations with other religions.[58]

Secondly, he aims to bring Pentecostal or charismatic diagnoses of the presence or activity of evil spirits in a person or a situation out of the realm of the purely spiritual, which he considers to be an abstraction—"I can make no sense of the claim that the discernment of spirit is a purely spiritual exercise." This seems to reveal a certain frustration with Pentecostals or charismatics who seek to exercise a gift of discernment of spirits on a purely spiritual basis of personal revelation from the Spirit, without recourse to the more "empirical processes that the biblical authors suggest in our discerning" how much the inner spirit of a thing is influenced by the Spirit or by the demonic.[59] Whilst accepting an intuitive dimension to discerning in the pneumatological imagination, Yong emphasizes the more rational aspects of the process, for example discerning observable effects of the demonic in concrete events, sensitive to the many levels of influences and different methods that can be used—"in short, to discern a thing is to be sensitive to its complexity."[60] No doubt his own close proximity and reflection on the

55. "Spiritual Discernment," 90.

56. Seminar, University of Birmingham, April 2009. See also *In the Days of Caesar*, 164.

57. *The Spirit Poured out on All Flesh*, 5.

58. "Performing Global Pentecostal Theology: A Response to Wolfgang Vondey," 315, 317, 319. Yong for example dialogues with Buddhism and its ambiguous concepts of the demonic—"The Demonic in Pentecostal-Charismatic Christianity and in the Religious Consciousness of Asia," 127.

59. "Spiritual Discernment," 103-4. The original context of this paper was in a chapter in his book on the pneumatology of *all* religions; thus seeking more "objective" criteria that could potentially be applied to other religions in discerning what is good or evil in them—over against the tendency of many Pentecostals to instinctively demonize everything in other religions—Yong, *Beyond the Impasse* 129-61.

60. Ibid., 102, 104-5. He applies his method to an imagined example and lists some

theology of disability, and the sometimes naïve or even harmful responses of some Pentecostals and charismatics to those with disabilities, has influenced him in this regard.[61] In some respects his caution here is similar to that of Wink.[62]

A third reason for his reluctance to characterize Satan and demons as independent spiritual beings is his philosophical objection to essentialism, nominalism, and Cartesian dualism of mind and matter. Yong, without buying fully into process theism, clearly prefers more dynamic categories of reality, such as fields of force. He is probably influenced by Peirce here[63]— both Peirce's synechism (seeing space, time, and law as continuous, which concords well with modern field theory and recent theological conceptions of "spirit"), and his concept of the individual. Peirce saw "personality" as "not something shut up in a skull" but "some kind of coordination and connection of ideas" that endures in time, but is not permanently fixed but evolving.[64]

This leads to the fourth reason—whilst claiming to keep philosophy and theology in balance, he is influenced by the limitations of Peircean metaphysics, which may inhibit him coming to metaphysical conclusions about non-material realities.[65] Thus, unless demons (or angels for that matter) were to regularly appear in concrete and measurable physical manifestations independent of human beings or human structures, they

---

biblical examples, e.g., Mark 5:2–5, Acts 13:6–11, 19:23–41).

61. Yong sees an etiology for the persistence of sickness and disability as necessarily due to demonic interference, sin, or lack of faith as "extremely problematic." *Theology and Down Syndrome*, 241–42.

62. Wink describes a father hearing inner voices urging suicide after losing his ten-year-old son to cancer; whether the voice was from a defeated or despairing part of this man, or an external malevolent power exploiting a father's grief, cannot and need not be settled for Wink, phenomenologically. Wink, *Unmasking the Powers*, 26. Pastorally I agree that caution should be exercised in discerning how much psychological disturbances can be directly attributed to demonic powers; phenomenologically it is also hard to interpret—although some practitioners believe there are symptoms which help in such discernment—see chapter 8.2.

63. And also Whitehead's Trinitarian cosmology of God, world, and "creativity" linking them. See Yong, *Spirit-Word-Community*, 88–93, 112.

64. See Raposa, *Peirce's Philosophy of Religion*, 39–40.

65. Whilst Pierce was open to transcendental realities (particularly of "mind"), he placed greater emphasis on what could be discovered by principles of scientific investigation, rather than revelation from theological sources (such as reflection on the Scriptures). See ibid., 10, 30–32, 35–41. Yong responded that he sees the primary value of Peircean metaphysics in developing a *scientific* cosmology and theology of nature; it may not be so helpful when thinking about the demonic in a non-scientific context— Yong, "Response to Chapter 6."

could not in Yong's scheme be properly described, as for him they cannot be conceived in a spiritual sense apart from concrete forms. Yet I would argue that, for example, the angel Michael and the "prince of Persia" that he had been fighting against (in Daniel 10) could have as their "secondness" very real spiritual "bodies" that are normally inaccessible to human sensory perception; but Yong does not seem to have a category for this, nor feel that he needs one ("non-manifesting spirits could not be said to exist in any meaningful sense")—he in fact sees the need to offer an element of ridicule to the notion of "Casper-like spirits floating about in mid-heaven"; if they are unevidenced in the concrete world in which we live, in his view they could not be truly demonic.[66]

Ambiguity concerning how "personal" the demonic is (in privileging its "thirdness," see above) may also betray a weakness in the triadic metaphysical scheme in relation to invisible spiritual beings. Whilst not denying the idea of a personal devil and demons, he fails to indicate if this "reality" of "fields of force" has any "personal" characteristics such as intelligence, or malevolent willpower associated with personal agency.[67] The firstness for the person of the Holy Spirit appears to be "relationality," and for human persons is described as "our felt qualities";[68] but the firstness/secondness of the demonic is less clear—the externally felt qualities of destructiveness and opposition to God, mediated parasitically through the secondness of various concrete realities such as people or organizations, and the thirdness of a field of force perverting the divine intention of things. But where is this perverting demonic "intention" located? Does the demonic have the quality of "mind" that Yong attributes to the Holy Spirit? It is very unclear where biblical concepts such as "the devil's schemes" can be located metaphysically in this scheme.

A fifth reason for being reluctant to accept "disembodied spirits" is his views on the origin of the demonic. He has begun to embrace emergence

---

66. "Spiritual Discernment," 103. Charismatics might respond that there is evidence, though often subtle, of Satan's malevolent intelligent scheming, manifested particularly against God's servants. Where Satan masquerades "as an angel of light," the concrete effects of his activity would be even more difficult to discern—though not impossible, Paul having just described some in the preceding verses (2 Cor 11:3–14).

67. Yong has since begun to allow some "personal" language but only in relation to an "emergent" reality of the demonic: "Minimally, my account recognizes the demonic as personal to the degree that its emergent 'face' is manifest in destructiveness that touches the lives of human persons." *In the Days of Caesar*, 163n44.

68. "Each of us are who we are precisely as felt emotive qualities (firstness) and bodies (secondness) integrated by that inner spiritual aspect of our being (thirdness)." "Spiritual Discernment," 88–89.

theory in relation to the emergence of the human mind in creation;[69] and in relation to the human soul.[70] And he has begun to apply this to the demonic, described as "objective as an emergent reality, parasitic and dependent upon . . . [the] structures of the powers, yet irreducible to the sum of its constituent parts."[71] Here he parallels Wink, who speculates that a mob spirit "comes into existence" when an unruly crowd reaches a "critical flashpoint of excitement and frustration."[72] A belief in the emergence of human "mind" need not necessarily lead to the same conclusion for the demonic.[73] However, a major reason for preferring an emergent account of demonic origins is Yong's philosophical problems with the traditional account of the fall of Satan as the origin of evil.[74]

In response, the charismatics I have studied would raise objections of at least three kinds. Firstly, whilst accepting the need to be open to insights from other disciplines into demonic realities, they would question the appropriateness of some of Yong's foundational philosophical metaphysics. Yong's attempts to bring Pentecostal and charismatic perspectives into "conversations with those within and beyond the borders of the church" is laudable, and non-negotiable for him in his foundational approach to hermeneutics;[75] but choosing to build the metaphysical and epistemological framework for his cosmology from the pragmatist philosophy of Pierce, even though adapted theologically, tilts the foundations into a bias against Pentecostal and charismatic cosmological understandings informed by

---

69. See "*Ruach*," 188–99.

70. He is strongly against any dualistic soul-body anthropology, as the body helps to contribute to the soul's identity; for him souls need to be embodied, just as his metaphysics frowns on disembodied spirits. see *Theology and Down Syndrome*, 170–72, 240–41.

71. *In the Days of Caesar*, 162–63. For Yong evil arises when a thing inexplicably decides "to act against its divinely ordained purpose of being and turn away from God"—he appears more ready to see this as emerging from human choice than in angelic beings. "Spiritual Discernment," 90; *Discerning the Spirits*, 129.

72. Wink, *Naming the Powers*, 105; Yong, *Discerning the Spirits*, 129. See section 5.5.

73. Wrestling with the scientific data pointing towards a theory of emergence of the mind and consciousness, Yong agrees that theology requires maintaining a causal openness of the world, such that man can only become a living being with the breath of God (whose Spirit is clearly not emergent), which is inaccessible to scientific investigation. See "*Ruach*," 188–89, 198–99. Demonic spirits may be very difficult to scientifically "measure," but I maintain this does not disqualify them from possessing rational features of "mind," or even some "consciousness"; nor suggest that their "personal face" must be emergent out of human evil and rebellion.

74. See chapter 8.3.

75. Yong, *Spirit-Word-Community*, 306.

Scripture and their own experience. Yong is to be commended for proposing a hermeneutics that interacts with the world and allows this some influence on the interpretive process, helping restore the importance of experience within Pentecostal hermeneutics;[76] but the emphasis on the embodiment of "secondness" in his metaphysics finds little space for the New Testament concept of ἐπουράνιοι or heavenly realms, envisaged as populated in some way by spiritual beings such as angels and "spiritual powers of wickedness in the heavenly realms." Yong rightly wishes to caution against a dualism that exaggerates the gulf between spiritual and material realms; or the "cosmological anarchism" of some premodern worldviews.[77] Yong prefers a more integrated (and Trinitarian) view of reality; but not everything has to come in threes, and there are some binary distinctions we cannot easily escape, such as that between what is visible and what is invisible (Col 1:16, in relation to "thrones, powers or rulers"); and a major contribution of Pentecostal and charismatic theology should be a restoration of taking the reality and power of what is invisible with the utmost seriousness.[78] In his own words, "acceptance of St. Paul's principalities and powers is one way to complicate an otherwise one-dimensional universe without having to assume that we need to assign a Cartesian subjectivity to each principality and power that we think we might have identified";[79] the charismatic ontology of evil I propose would not require such specifics, but would acknowledge the more restrained ontology of evil that Jesus and the New Testament writers exhibited, that the "personal and intentional" aspects of the demonic in their destructive capacities are not just "seemingly" so,[80] but a function of their independent existence, primarily in the unseen "heavenly realms" but with definite concrete manifestations in the physical earthly realm.[81]

76. Ibid., 8; Bradnick, "Demonology and Anthropology in Conversation," 14.

77. Yong, *In the Days of Caesar*, 164.

78. Archer has perceptively observed that "the essence of Pentecostalism is its persistent emphasis upon the supernatural within the community." This supernaturalistic horizon believes that the invisible is always capable of impacting the visible; though often seen as an anomaly to the dominant contemporary scientific worldview. Archer, "Pentecostal Hermeneutics," 63–81, esp. 64–65.

79. Yong, *In the Days of Caesar*, 164.

80. Thus, Yong in his description of the nature of *emergent* demonic forces—ibid., 163.

81. Here I mean transcendent in the sense of existing in dimensions of existence beyond what is directly observable in the physical world of our senses and measuring instruments. Yong's objection to this was that in his view, once we have "very definite concrete manifestations," we don't have "independent transcendent existence." ("Response to Chapter 6."). However, if God in any sense exists in a realm or realms beyond the physical created order, there is no logical reason why other beings such as angels or demons cannot also have a measure of existence in such realms.

Secondly, Yong urges us to "strive for the greater gifts" in continuous submission to the Spirit of God in terms of the theology and practice of discernment.[82] If a primary characteristic of the Holy Spirit is relationality and not just rationality, why should charismatics be discouraged from seeking the higher gifts of the prophetic, in the sense of an increased openness and ability to "hear God's voice" more directly in spiritual discernment, as long as it offered in humility and is open to be tested? Yong correctly asserts that reality is complex and often ambiguous, and the material world only permits partial glimpses of the spiritual world—all the more reason for a praxis of listening prayer that is open to God's revelation in discernment of the spirits. Whilst Yong rightly looks for a greater humility and reasoned reflection in dealing with complex issues (such as the nature of the relationship between the demonic and sickness, mental health and disability), not all charismatics are able to investigate every issue from multiple perspectives and modes of investigation, in seeking to discern the Spirit or spirits at work in a particular situation.

And finally, although the metaphor of force fields is very helpful for describing the pervasiveness of the demonic, both Wink and Yong seem averse to concluding that behind this lie "spiritual beings," whether "personal" or otherwise.[83] Wink, for example, senses a danger in seeing Satan as the personification of evil, in breeding a paranoid or neurotic view of reality, allowing us to demonize our opponents (a concern of Yong's also), whilst concealing our own ambivalence towards evil.[84] My case study suggests this need not be so; where there is a willingness for the Spirit to identify our own complicity with the demonic in a lifestyle of continuous repentance, an awareness of personal forces of evil found to be readily overcome in repentance and prayer can help set free from fear, and promote personal responsibility for spiritual growth.

However, his main recommendation for praxis in relation to "exorcising the demonic" (particularly in the political realm) should be more warmly received by charismatics. He sees Pentecostal worship as potentially carving

---

82. *Beyond the Impasse*, 160–61.

83. Yong commented that he believes this creates more difficulties than it resolves. But his concerns are not only the practical dangers such as that of paranoia or "demonizing opponents," but equally driven by philosophical concerns relating to the problem of evil and its origin in beings that were created wholly good; as well as his disagreement with a personal metaphysics. "Response to Chapter 6." These philosophical concerns, however, are in my view rarely shared by other charismatics.

84. Wink, *Unmasking the Powers*, 9–10. "The liturgical imagination worships God and refuses to demonize the powers, especially people, as enemies of God . . . removing any possibility of legitimating violence by utilizing the rhetoric of spiritual warfare." Yong, *In the Days of Caesar*, 165.

out political space as a public expression of an alternative community in Christ through the Spirit, not only engaging with God (and rehabilitating our cosmological imagination to be aware of "the presence of angels"), but also with the spiritual principalities and powers in taking authority over personal turmoil, economic devastation or forces of persecution.[85] Although cautious about "serving notice" to such principalities and powers directly,[86] he encourages "creating ritual space for exorcism in the church's liturgical life" in corporate rites of exorcism "to purify the wider public square."[87] Interestingly, the minimal liturgical elements he lists in such a ritual (following McClain) approximately parallel the various steps used in individual prayer ministry for deliverance in the "Jesus Ministry" model used at St. George's.[88] His constant desire to "tread carefully" reflects wider theological concerns over not giving demonic powers "more 'air time' than they deserve," and "the more radical practices advocated by Wagner and others in the "spiritual warfare" movement."[89] Adopting an apophatic ontology aligns him with Barth who, seeing the demonic powers as having no real substance, sees no need to give them more than "a quick, sharp glance."[90] However, my research demonstrates that such concerns can be exaggerated; at least on the individual and church level, granting the demonic a positive ontology, and learning to resist the demonic routinely within a context that focuses on God's greatness and pursues holiness as a lifestyle, can release

85. *In the Days of Caesar*, 155–56, 159.

86. He endorses the cautions of Clinton Arnold and others in terms of engaging directly with "territorial spirits." Arnold, *Three Crucial Questions About Spiritual Warfare*, 167; Yong, *In the Days of Caesar*, 160.

87. Taking his cue from the burning of occult books in Ephesus; and giving the example of social exorcisms such as one confronting the spirit(s) of Apartheid at the South African consulate in New York City, referencing George McClain—*In the Days of Caesar*, 160.

88. He lists invocation, the reading of Scripture, discerning of spirits/powers, confession of sins and their absolution, Holy Communion, words of deliverance, prayer for renewal of the institution's purpose, prayer for thanksgiving and exhortation and benediction—followed by a continuing witness for peace and justice. Ibid., 160–61. The charismatic "Jesus ministry" prayer model generally included invoking the Spirit's presence (and silencing the enemy), regular use of scriptural truth, listening prayer to discern the negative activity of spirits of fear/pride/control etc, confession and repentance followed by receiving forgiveness at the cross ("absolution"), words of deliverance resisting the devil and any spirits discerned, and after exhortation to "replace" the negative thought and behavior patterns, usually prayers of blessing and a renewal of God's intended purpose for the person—with a reminder that 95 percent of the change will come as the person continues to work at the replacement of wrong attitudes in his or her own life. See chapter 4, especially 4.5.

89. Ibid., 158, 60–61 and footnotes.

90. Barth, *CD*, III/3, 519.

a confidence to seek greater levels of personal freedom and see demonic influence increasingly marginalized.

6.6 Conclusion

Yong wishes to strongly assert the reality of the demonic as that which "regulates" the inexplicable and horrific features of human experience that go beyond what is explicable on the basis of divine absence alone. As a Pentecostal he at times uses the language of spirits, such as spirits of lust, murder or fear, to describe demonic manifestations. He is nevertheless reluctant to characterize Satan and demons as personal beings with agency and intelligence to govern their destructive opposition to the goodness of God, preferring the language of fields of force as to their mode of influence. Whilst such language is surely appropriate to the pervasive and often hidden influences of the demonic on individuals and corporate entities, it appears deficient from a charismatic perspective, in that rebellious opposition of the demonic to God seems to exhibit a willfulness that requires a "personal" center of action, at least in the Boethian minimalist definition as "the substance of rational nature." Yong may wish to counter some of the excesses of global Pentecostal communities in the area of deliverance;[91] but a metaphysic in danger of denying the existence of evil spirit beings is unlikely ever to be accepted by most Pentecostals and charismatics who consider them "as real as rocks and persons," and also see Jesus in the Gospels speaking of evil spirits and dealing with them in the same matter-of-fact way.

However, whilst Yong's demonic ontology would be questioned by many Pentecostals and charismatics, his emphasis on the need to discern the demonic by a careful examination of its concrete effects, with an openness to the insights of other disciplines, offers a welcome corrective to some charismatic praxis in deliverance.

---

91. Yong, "Response to Chapter 6."

— 7 —

Gregory Boyd

A Spiritual Warfare Worldview

GREGORY BOYD IS A former professor of theology at Bethel College, St. Paul, Minnesota; he originally comes from a Oneness Pentecostal background, though remains critical of some of their beliefs.[1] He does not like labels, such as "evangelical" (whilst holding to a high view of biblical inspiration); he is influenced by a wide range of theologians (he cites favorites such as Kierkegaard, Bonhoeffer, Barth, Ellul, Jonathan Edwards, Dallas Willard, and John Yoder); and no doubt developed a natural affinity with British charismatics, having ministered several times alongside Roger Forster of Ichthus Christian Fellowship and viewing him as a role model.[2] In his Princeton doctoral thesis he critically examines the dipolar theism of Hartshorne's process theology;[3] he has since attained theological prominence as one of the group espousing "open theism."[4] He has written a number of serious theological and philosophical books, but his most distinctive theological contribution is his comprehensively argued two-volume presentation of a spiritual warfare worldview—*God at War*, focusing on the Bible and spiritual conflict, and *Satan and the Problem of Evil*, presenting his own theodicy.[5] His main thesis is that whereas most Christian thinkers since Augustine have attempted to intellectually grapple with "the problem of evil," New Testament writers grappled much more with overcoming evil.[6] He nevertheless sees both Old and New Testaments as essentially adopting what he considers to be the simplest solution to the problem of evil in

1. Boyd, *Oneness Pentecostals and the Trinity*.

2. *Gregory Boyd Faqs*. At the time of writing he is the pastor of Woodland Hills Baptist Church.

3. *Trinity and Process*.

4. See *God of the Possible*.

5. *God at War*; *Satan and the Problem of Evil*.

6. In my own field of study, the approach of Anglican charismatics, the same priority given to practical spiritual warfare has tended to again come to the foreground.

protecting God's goodness (and he would also claim, God's sovereignty), that of ultimately accrediting all that appears to be evil (both in the natural and moral realm) to the free choices of created beings, crucially not just human but also angelic spiritual forces; rather than seeking to justify God as directly or indirectly responsible for them. I have chosen him as a dialogue partner because of this detailed espousal of a spiritual warfare worldview, but also because by my follow-up visit in November 2008, his books had been discovered and recommended by leaders of "St. George's."

Although Boyd is clearly situated in evangelical theology, he takes a scholarly academic approach and positively engages with a range of prominent writers in philosophy and theology. For example, in presenting his main thesis he dialogues with Walter Wink's comprehensive analysis of the biblical "powers." He affirms Wink's thesis that the powers refer to the corporate "interiority" of social wholes, and that the interdependence between spiritual and physical aspects means that combating the powers is not just by prayer but also through social activism; but he also notes Wink's admission that it is difficult for the modern mind to believe in real demonic angelic powers.[7] Boyd thus sees it as inevitable that many modern people, influenced by the increasingly materialistic presuppositions of a secularized Western culture, will object to any claim that angels might actually exist and interact with human affairs; or may reinterpret them, as Wink does, as the corporate interiority of social groups.[8] Whilst his reintroduction of a host of angelic and demonic powers to the theological arena is already a radical step, he also takes on arguing against what he calls "the blueprint worldview,"[9] as he just as radically adopts an "open theist" position—the view that because love requires self-determining freedom, and granting such freedom implies genuine risk, the future in part is open and not certainly known by God. However, he maintains that this is not his central thesis, which is his "trinitarian warfare worldview"; this not only supports the view shared by many modern and ancient cultures (including the ancient Near East and biblical writers) of the reality of a spiritual war surrounding us involving a host of supernatural beings, but also must reconcile this

---

7. He quotes Wink: "We moderns cannot bring ourselves . . . to believe in the real existence of these mythological entities . . . it is as impossible for most of us to believe in the real existence of demonic angelic powers as it is to believe in dragons or elves, or a flat world." Boyd, *God at War*, 59–60; Wink, *Naming the Powers*, 4; Boyd, *God at War*.

8. *God at War*, 59, 273–74, 300–301.

9. This is the belief in God's detailed foreknowledge (which he labels EDF, "exhaustive definite foreknowledge") and his sovereign control over all events, either directly or indirectly through his permissive will. See for example *Satan and the Problem of Evil*, 418.

with the belief in an all-powerful, all-good God who created the world as an expression of love—the Father who sent his Son to defeat the devil and rescue humans through the power of the Spirit.[10] He thus also espouses a trinitarian warfare theodicy, which he argues theologically and philosophically in *Satan and the Problem of Evil.*

On the scientific front, whilst proposing his own version of the "gap theory" of creation, he is helpfully respectful of modern science; he seeks compatibility of his ideas with at least three possible views on creation including a theistic evolutionary one, seeing some of the big holes in the kind of creationism that takes early Genesis (and the age of the earth) too literally.[11] Such issues are rarely of special concern to charismatics, though they have some bearing on the problem of natural evil.[12]

7.1 Boyd's contributions to a theology of spiritual warfare

In seeing how Boyd's approach can contribute to a charismatic theology of spiritual warfare, he brings three strong contributions. Firstly, his approach clearly presents a realist and pragmatic view of evil. Boyd argues that the New Testament authors expect bad things to happen even to good people; they see this as primarily an existential rather than an intellectual problem, to be resolved by spiritual activism, because they presuppose a conflict between God and evil spiritual forces into which believers are drawn (cf. Eph 6:12). Here he also makes an even wider appeal in the contemporary context, as he frames his argument around the concrete nightmares or radical evil exemplified in accounts of horrifying suffering of Jews under the Nazis, and the problem with "the problem of evil" that seeks to solve this in cold intellectual terms, and even worse suggest that somehow behind every detail of such "frowning providence hides a smiling face." Such romanticized abstractions may not just ring hollow but appear positively immoral, as famously suggested by Dostoyevsky's Ivan in *The Brothers Karamazov.*[13]

Secondly, however well the approach of Wink and others may fit with the contemporary mind in suggesting that powers of structural evil do not

---

10. Ibid., 86–87, 18.

11. He notes how this contradicts the nearly unanimous view of geologists that the earth is billions of years old, and of paleontologists that animals were devouring one another millions of years before humans arrived. Ibid., 313.

12. Not a focus of this study, but Boyd's views will be referred to briefly in chapter 8.5.

13. Boyd, *God at War*, 33–40.

have a separate spiritual existence, Boyd presents a strong case from the biblical material, supported with scholarly reference to extrabiblical sources, that the NT writers clearly had personal agents in mind; and he sees no reason to abandon this view of the nature of evil forces. Alongside this, he argues strongly for an angelic fall as the origin of evil forces.

Thirdly, he also helpfully highlights the classic theory of atonement of the early church and retrieved by Gustav Aulen, as a theological basis for the victory of Christ over the devil and the forces of evil.[14] This is perhaps more assumed than discussed by many Pentecostals and charismatics, who have often tended to uncritically adopt the evangelical view of the centrality of a penal substitutionary view of atonement; so Boyd helps to open up this debate of the nature of the atonement in a constructive way for charismatics, particularly in relation to spiritual warfare; so I will discuss this in chapter 8 in seeking to construct a charismatic biblical theology of spiritual warfare.[15]

I will here discuss his theses under four headings: the role of spiritual beings (particularly in relation to mythological monsters) in the Old Testament; the spiritual warfare worldviews of Jesus and Paul;[16] the "fall of angels" hypothesis; and objections in relation to the problem of evil and God's sovereignty.

7.2 Old Testament spiritual beings: mythological monsters and "sons of God"

Traditionally, evangelical theology has strongly resisted the expositions of more liberal theologians who seek to emphasize the mythological nature of certain Old Testament accounts. They saw a threat to their understanding of the inspiration of Scripture; a loss of belief in the historicity of key events in salvation history such as the fall or the exodus; and a tendency to compromise on the monotheistic belief of the Hebrews, in favor of an evolutionary account of their monotheism having arisen from the polytheistic beliefs of the surrounding nations of the Near East, with their richly mythological creation narratives. In this evangelical approach, the simplicity of the Genesis creation accounts, and differences from Near Eastern alternatives, are emphasized; and any references to strange creatures tend to be explained in purely naturalistic terms.[17]

---

14. Aulen, *Christus Victor*; Boyd, *God at War*, chapter 9, 238–68.

15. Boyd's own discussion with his opponents is presented in "Christus Victor View."

16. Mainly deferred to chapter 8.

17. For example, the footnotes in the NIV translation of Job seek to identify the

Surprisingly then we find Boyd re-mythologizing some of these accounts that evangelicals have sought to de-mythologize, drawing on the insights of a wider range of scholarly insight and extra-biblical accounts from the Near East. He rightly argues that such demythologizing was essentially the result of the influence of Enlightenment thinking on our Western materialistic worldview, whereas the biblical worldview was much closer to most other cultures in the world today, where a warfare worldview remains widespread.[18] Rather than dismiss such stories as ignorant, primitive superstition, he encourages us to see myth as anticipating reality approximating and anticipating the truth revealed in Scripture, where he believes a warfare worldview (whilst significantly different from those of most other cultures) is woven into the fabric—the ultimate example of myth becoming reality being in the person of Jesus Christ.[19]

Boyd spends four chapters on teasing out such hints of a warfare worldview in the Old Testament, claiming that its authors understood the world to be inhabited by demons and engulfed by hostile destructive forces. He illustrates this from the surrounding ancient Near Eastern cultures,[20] which generally illustrate the themes of a primordial rebellion of a hostile monster threatening creation, where order and good must war against chaos and evil as the explanation for the imperfect nature of the world; and some have even argued that the prevailing view (even for the Hebrews) was that all evil was the direct result of demonic activity.[21]

Mythological monsters

Even without looking at the exegesis of individual passages, the use of words such as *tehom* for "the deep/cosmic deep" (e.g., Gen 1:1), and *yamm* for "the sea," as well as more specific named monsters such as Leviathan and Rahab

---

vivid descriptions of strange monsters with known animals—"behemoth" as "possibly the hippopotamus or the elephant" (Job 40:15), or "leviathan" as "possibly the crocodile" (41:1), when the details clearly do not fit—crocodiles do not have seven heads!

18. He describes some contemporary examples in Boyd, *God at War*, 11–21.

19. Echoing here a phrase from C. S. Lewis. Ibid., 17–19. Longman and Reid similarly see references to conflict myths as illustrating and anticipating the reality of Yahweh's conflict with the forces of chaos. Longman III and Reid, *God Is a Warrior*, 74–78, 82.

20. Notably the well known *Enuma Elish*, *Epic of Gilgamesh* and other conflict-with-chaos (the German *Chaoskampf*) myths.

21. Boyd refers to Otto Bocher's *Damonenfurcht und Damonebabwehr* (Stuttgart: Kohlhammer, 1970) comprehensive work on demonology—whilst recognizing that some scholars see this as an overstatement. Boyd, *God at War*, 74–79, 314–15.

particularly in Job, Psalms, and Isaiah, bring in strong echoes of the surrounding cosmic battle mythologies, as recognized by a range of scholars, many of whom (e.g., B. W. Anderson, Day, Levenson, Driver, Lindstrom, etc.) Boyd has referenced.[22] The key question is, what precisely do they reveal concerning the cosmology of the Old Testament writers? Boyd does bring out some of the different emphases in the biblical texts, for example accepting that in Genesis 1 "the waters have been not only neutralized, but demythologized and even depersonalized."[23] Yet Boyd not surprisingly tends to privilege commentators that tend to support his point of view,[24] and boldly asserts:

> Given the general cultural context within which all this is being written, one cannot take these statements as mere metaphors; ... such expressions make sense only on the assumption that the biblical authors did believe in the existence of these anticreation cosmic forces, and did believe that Yahweh had to genuinely battle them.[25]

A group of distinguished Scandinavian scholars, who recognize similar dynamics in the texts, are however more cautious, concluding that "it is thoroughly typical of the OT that we find this tension between a mythological and a more reflectively theological view of things side by side."[26]

One weakness here is that Boyd fails to establish criteria as to how to interpret such mythological language in its context; elsewhere he criticizes Calvinists' inconsistencies in deciding which biblical texts are anthropomorphic, yet he himself simply asserts that "we cannot take these statements as mere metaphors." Yet some passages (as Boyd admits) where Rahab, the dragon and other mythological phrases are invoked refer to the parting of the Red Sea at the exodus (e.g., Pss 77:15-19; 74:10-17; Hab 3:8, 10, 15;

22. Ibid., 73-113, 320-25.

23. Quoting from Levenson—ibid., 33; Levenson, *Creation and the Persistence of Evil*, 122. Childs agrees that the writer has broken but not fully destroyed the myth by his affirmation in 1.1—but for him the vestige remaining is a Barthian nothingness, an active chaos opposing God and threatening his creation. Childs, *Myth and Reality in the Old Testament*, 41-42.

24. For example, Levenson, who like Boyd, strongly emphasizes some of the mythological elements in other texts "that the Torah tries to suppress"; whereas Kaufmann emphasizes the overriding mastery of Yahweh over all of creation. See Levenson, *Creation and the Persistence of Evil*, 1-5.

25. Boyd, *God at War*, 89.

26. The Israelite view is both that chaos is a real power that Yahweh is forced to do battle with and to repeatedly subjugate; yet also as Sovereign ruler Yahweh uses chaos as his willing tool, as in the Genesis flood narrative. Otzen, Gottlieb, and Jeppesen, *Myths in the Old Testament*, 38.

Isa 51:9–11), or Yahweh's defeat of the "surging waters" of the nations (Isa 17:12–13); so the use here seems primarily metaphorical in these essentially poetic contexts.[27] Whilst the biblical authors are here using some of "the language of Canaan," they are also putting it to new use in relation to their own faith in Yahweh.[28] It is natural to use figurative language when describing evil, particularly in relation to supersensible realities,[29] but more difficult to decide exactly how much this language is still used conceptually to refer to real spiritual beings.[30]

His case, therefore, seems to be overstated on exegetical grounds—despite the variety of these texts, the main emphasis of the Old Testament overall is that Yahweh sovereignly imposes order on his creation through his Word, and mythological elements are played down. However, he demonstrates that the elements of such a "warfare worldview" are present in the Old Testament; and reminds us that, unlike our compartmentalized Western materialistic worldview, there was no bifurcation between what occurs "in heaven" and "on earth" for the ancient Israelites, and need not be for us.[31] And he has highlighted an Old Testament theme of cosmic forces of chaos, often personified as monsters, which in one sense have been defeated or "slain" by Yahweh, and yet in another only "captured," thus representing a continuity of force underlying destructive and chaotic experiences.[32]

Rebellious angels: "sons of God," the council of the gods, and demons

He draws on this principle too in discussing another layer of more explicit references to spiritual beings in the Old Testament, that of the "sons of God,"

---

27. For his discussion of these texts, see Boyd, *God at War*, 88–89. One of his own criteria elsewhere for admitting that language could be anthropomorphic and thus metaphorical in relation to God (e.g., God's "protecting wings," Ps 17:8) is that the genre of the passage is poetic—*God of the Possible*, 118.

28. Wakeman, *God's Battle*, vii. Wakeman summarizes references to monsters in the Old Testament and what happens to them.

29. See Soskice, *Metaphor and Religious Language*, 152–53.

30. The language of creation myths sometimes mixes with the drama of the exodus (e.g., Pss 74:13–14; 77:16–19); this may signify that the enemy is no longer mythical primeval chaos but, rather, "undergoes a sort of reduction to the purely historical" (Anderson); as when Rahab has simply come to signify Egypt (Ps 87.4; Isa 30:7). Anderson, *Creation Versus Chaos*, 105–6; Wakeman, *God's Battle*, 62.

31. For example, Isa 51:9–11. Boyd, *God at War*, 88–90.

32. Leviathan is sometimes depicted as captured from the sea (Job 40:25–6; Ps 104:26), but he can still be roused (Job 3:8), to be finally slain eschatologically "in that day" (Isa 27:1). See Wakeman, *God's Battle*, 65–67, 137, 149.

or "gods." Along with N. T. Wright and others, he affirms that the biblical view is less one of pure "philosophical monotheism" as one of "creational monotheism," affirming that there are a multiplicity of gods, but only one is the eternal Creator and omnipotent Lord, all others having their power initially given by their Creator.[33] Apart from references to God as sitting with a heavenly council (e.g., Ps 82; Job 1; 1 Kgs 22; Jer 23:18), he discusses references to "sons of God" often understood as referring to angels, some rebellious.[34] The "prince of Persia" in Daniel 10 is also discussed as possibly being a divine or angelic figure who rebelled—as Wink also suggests, perhaps it refers to the guardian "god" assigned to this nation, who in continuing to contend for the best interests (narrowly defined) of the Persian Empire tries to censor a message that foretells of its destruction.[35] Boyd maintains that perhaps the main value of such passages is in revealing belief in a "society in between" us and God that may have free wills like us and influence the flow of history—parallel to Hiebert's "excluded middle" in Western thinking.[36]

7.3 Jesus, Paul, and spiritual conflict with Satan's kingdom

Whereas Nigel Wright and Amos Yong held back from affirming a positive ontology of evil spiritual beings, Boyd is a strong proponent of their real existence; and like many charismatics, his primary ground for this belief is his understanding of New Testament evidence. Whilst this will be a major part of my discussion in chapter 8, here I give a brief summary of Boyd's

---

33. Boyd, *God at War*, 118–20, 330–32; Wright, *The New Testament and the People of God*, 248–59.

34. He considers the "sons of God" in Genesis 6 which led to "the Watchers" myth, that saw these as rebellious angels. In some versions, the progeny of the intermarriage of their giant Nephilim offspring may have become the demons of the world; see Boyd, *God at War*, 131–38, 341, 143–67. This idea is taken up by some charismatic teachers, notably Derek Prince. See also chapter 8.3.

35. Boyd and Wink see the "sons of God" as "angels" appointed to represent each nation's interests in the heavenly council, following the LXX translation of Deut 32:8–9, "When the Most High gave to the nations their inheritance . . . he fixed the bounds of the peoples according to the number of the sons of God . . . ." Wink suggests that Daniel 10 "provides the fullest picture of these angels of the nations in action," revealing that each "has a will all of its own." Boyd however criticizes Wink's unwillingness to postulate a real existence of such angels beyond the invisible spirituality within the nations, as doing injustice to the biblical text and undermining its value in explaining the power of evil. Ibid., 136–38, 340–41; Wink, *Unmasking the Powers*, 88–91.

36. Where Westerners do believe in angels, Boyd suggests they are often seen as innocuous, volitionless messengers completely controlled by the will of their Creator. Boyd, *God at War*, chapter 4, particularly 136–40. For a helpful comparison of worldviews, see Hiebert, "Spiritual Warfare and Worldviews," 114–24.

approach, as he argues his primary thesis—that almost everything Jesus and the early church were about is colored by the central conviction that the world is caught in a crossfire of a cosmic battle between the Lord and his angelic army and Satan and his demonic army.[37]

Boyd argues that Jesus's teaching about the rule of Satan and his army was not just a marginal piece of first-century apocalyptic he happened to embrace, but the kingdom of God as a warfare concept is the driving force behind all his words and actions. New Testament scholarly consensus is that Jesus carried out his ministry against the background of the apocalyptic thought of the day—a "modified dualism" where the highest mediating agent of Yahweh had abused his God-given authority and taken the entire world hostage.[38] In the apocalyptic literature this highest mediating agent is variously named, but Satan (or Satanel) is prominent amongst them.[39] Jesus, according to John (12:31; 14:30; 16:11), directly takes up this idea of Satan as the "prince of demons," intensifying the concept that Satan heads up a unified kingdom of demons; Jesus had come to combat this by driving them out (cf. Mark 3:22–24), seeing demonic activity as the extension of that of Satan himself (e.g., Luke 13:11–16).[40] Boyd argues that the line between healing and exorcism in the gospels is a fine one, Acts 10:38 also supporting the idea that all disorders are at least the indirect result of the world having been taken hostage by the devil; and that the kingdom of God and the kingdom of Satan are correlative concepts—the former expands, primarily through Jesus's healings and exorcisms, and the latter diminishes.[41] The clustering of references to Satan, demons, and Jesus's conflict with them in the opening chapters of Mark, and the prominence of "casting out demons" in the summary statements of Jesus's ministry, would certainly seem to indicate that this warfare motif was highly significant in Jesus's ministry and the understanding of the Gospel writers.[42]

---

37. Boyd, *God at War*, 84.

38. Ibid., 180, 357.

39. Key sources here are 1 Enoch, Jubilees, 2 Enoch, Tobit, and Martyrdom of Isaiah. See notes in chapter 8.2 and section 7.4 below.

40. He also sees this as exemplified by the reference to "the devil and his angels" as if the latter belong to the devil, in Matt 25:31, 41. Boyd, *God at War*, 179–82, 357.

41. Ibid., 182–85, 360. He sees the violent reaction of persecution from the world that Jesus predicts (e.g., Matt 10:24–5) as evidence that "spreading the kingdom of God invites retaliation from the evil one," such that in the Lord's Prayer (which he sees also in an eschatological warfare context) they should ask protection from "the evil one." (Matt 6:13). Ibid., 222–23.

42. See further discussion in chapter 8.2.

Boyd also examines the wider New Testament's conception of the demonic realm. Like Jesus in the Gospels, but unlike contemporaneous apocalyptic literature, the Epistles consistently identify the chief evil ruler as Satan.[43] In other respects the references are much in keeping with the apocalyptic thought of his day;[44] and viewed against that background, it is difficult to deny that Paul had personal agents in mind, especially in references to Satan intentionally inspiring disobedience.[45] And whilst accepting some of Wink's premises that Paul also refers to some qualitatively different "powers" linked to human structures and institutions, Boyd disagrees that their volition has been reduced to that of the people under them—when, for example, carrying out "the wiles of the devil" (Eph 6:11 KJV). He also notes the clear distinction between powers "in heaven" and "on earth"; the former cannot be exhaustively reduced to the latter.[46]

Boyd highlights to the need for believers to carry on the battle Jesus began. Satan's continuing power over the world is not only referenced in the Johannine epistles, but also in Paul—if anyone was put out of the church as discipline, it is seen as turning them over to "the god of this world," Satan.[47] And of course there is the admonishment to stand against the devil and the spiritual heavenly powers (Eph 6:10–12)—portrayed as hierarchically structured, but unlike contemporary apocalyptic literature, Paul like Jesus shows no interest in its details.[48]

The relative lack of other Pauline references to the demonic realm is however a reminder that the warfare motif is not as central as Boyd maintains. Thus Guelich can conclude that spiritual warfare is only one of several biblical metaphors for the Christian life "that does not appear at all in the Gospels and in only one passage in the Pauline corpus with reference to Satan and the evil forces"; and that the primary source of evil is portrayed by Jesus as vices arising from the human heart (Mark 7:21–22), or in Paul as sins of the flesh that are opposed to the Spirit (Gal 5:19–21), not the demonic.[49]

---

43. Boyd, *God at War*, 270, 274.

44. Boyd lists many of the apocalyptic terms, which correspond with Paul's vocabulary, particularly from 1 Enoch and 2 Enoch. Ibid., 271.

45. Eph 2:2, 1 Cor 5:4–5, 2 Cor 2:11, 11:14; also the reference to demons, and a Satanic messenger (1 Cor 10:19–21; 2 Cor 12:7).

46. Boyd, *God at War*, 273–75, 283.

47. 1 John 5:13, 2 Cor 4:4, 1 Cor 5:1–5, 1 Tim 1:20. See ibid., 276–79.

48. Ibid., 270.

49. Guelich, "Spiritual Warfare: Jesus, Paul, and Peretti," 58–59. Thus E. Janet Warren has proposed elaborating additional metaphors from the Scripture to better portray the biblical approach to overcoming evil. Warren, "Spiritual Warfare: A Dead

7.4 The fall of angels hypothesis and intertestamental apocalyptic

Boyd presents strong New Testament evidence that Jesus (and Paul) saw real demonic opposition under Satan to the extension of God's kingdom. Whilst this provides evidence for the existence of real malevolent spiritual beings, their nature (e.g., "personal" or otherwise) depends on their origin, and specifically whether they originate from a fall of angels, as Boyd argues.[50] This complex issue will require us to range more widely than Boyd and his immediate sources.[51]

This matter is certainly not easily settled. For example, Ball rightly suggested in his criticism of Michael Green's book that the account in Ezekiel 28 (and Isaiah 14) in original context is open to other interpretations than describing the fall of Satan.[52] Whilst Boyd argues convincingly that there are not only elements here that point beyond Semitic hyperbole,[53] but also strong echoes of the language of Canaanite myths of rebellious gods,[54] he also admits that at least for Isaiah 14 "the traditional exegesis is certainly not required by the text as it stands."[55] I suggest our exegesis should instead begin with Jesus and the Gospels, take seriously other allusions to evil angels and their rebellion in the New Testament writings (with help from historical

---

Metaphor?"; *Cleansing the Cosmos*. The fact that sins of the flesh are as much the source of evil in the New Testament indicates the need for a broader, integrated understanding of the battle with evil —the world, the flesh, and the devil in interconnection. See chapter 8.6.

50. Boyd, *God at War*, 284-87.

51. Notably, two doctorate studies—the first concerning the role of fallen angels in a Free Will Defense in solving the problem of evil; the second a detailed study of the first part of 1 Enoch, the Book of the Watchers—Lloyd, "The Cosmic Fall."; Wright, *The Origin of Evil Spirits*. See also references in Stuckenbruck, "Evil in Jewish Apocalyptic Tradition," 87-118.

52. Whilst Green follows an interpretation that goes back at least to Origen, Ball suggests it parallels the king of Tyre's pretension to divine kingship with *Adam* and his expulsion from the garden of God, and not of Satan. Ball, "Review of I Believe in Satan's Downfall," 34; Green, *I Believe in Satan's Downfall*, 36-39; Page, *Powers of Evil*, 39-42; Boyd, *God at War*, 161.

53. For example, the language of a "guardian cherub walking among the fiery stones," on "the holy mount of God." Ezek 28:12-15, *God at War*, 161.

54. Athtar the Rebel was too small for the throne of Baal so was given rulership of the earth (or underworld)—Athtar means "Shining One, Son of Dawn," paralleling Hellel in Isa 14:12. See references in ibid., 159-62, 350.

55. Ibid., 158. For another interpretation, see Albani, "The Downfall of Hellel," 62-86.

studies of intertestamental apocalyptic), then where relevant interacting with Old Testament texts.[56]

Jesus clearly refers to Satan as a spiritual being with his own kingdom, and deals with demons as real spiritual entities.[57] Whilst much of Matthew 25:31–46 may be a Matthean redaction,[58] there is a clear reference to it in Matt 25:31, 41, where Satan's "angels," are contrasted with "the Son of Man and his angels"; the same antithesis involving the fall of the dragon's rebellious angels occurs in Revelation 12; and in Jude 6/ 2 Pet 2:4, angels who sinned or abandoned their positions of authority are kept for judgment. These three strands of New Testament tradition all agree with much contemporaneous apocalyptic literature that there are angels that have rebelled (though the timing is not explicit); and two of them ally such fallen angels with Satan. That Satan himself fell is described in Revelation 12 and clearly implied in 1 Tim 3:6 (where identifying the devil's sin as pride may be an allusion to Isaiah 14). With this New Testament witness, it is thus not surprising that some early Christians began to specifically interpret Isaiah 14 and Ezekiel 28 in terms of the fall of Satan.[59] Indeed, in view of striking parallels Isaiah 14 may be a prototype for later descriptions of the downfall of God's enemies, both human and demonic—notably the fall of Antiochus IV (2 Macc 9, cf. Dan 8:9–11, also Acts 12:23), and the fall of Satan in Rev 12:7–9 (e.g., 2 En. 29:4; Luke 10:18).[60]

Here we enter the complex world of apocryphal and intertestamental literature and its relation to traditions behind biblical texts; for some Jews and Christians probably inherited and passed on these documents as inspired.[61] Lloyd sets out to examine Mascall's assertion of "a doctrine of an angelic fall";[62] and Wright thoroughly examines the Watcher tradition

---

56. There are dangers in over-privileging intertestamental apocalyptic references to the demonic—see Thomas, *The Devil, Disease and Deliverance*, 14–16.

57. See chapter 8, section 8.2 for more detail.

58. Twelftree, *Jesus the Exorcist*, 221.

59. Notably Origen for Isaiah 14, and Tertullian for Ezek 28:11–19. See Albani, "The Downfall of Hellel," 62. If The Book of the Secrets of Enoch (which connects Satan with Lucifer in Isa 14) is first century, Paul himself may have known of this. Boyd, *God at War*, 395n49.

60. E.g., Satan also echoes Isa 14:13–14 in Life of Adam and Eve 15:2–3, "I will set my throne above the stars of heaven and will be like the Most High." See Lichtenberger, "The Down-Throw of the Dragon," 119–47.

61. Debates continued even beyond the main date AD 90 in Jamnia for fixing the OT canon; so the early pseudepigrapha were composed when for some people the limits of the canon remained fluid. Charlesworth, *Pseudepigrapha 1*, xxiii.

62. And the claim that "a firmly based tradition ascribes to the angels, among other occupations, the tending of the material world." Mascall, *Christian Theology and Natural Science*, 302–3; Lloyd, "The Cosmic Fall," 224–26.

in relation to the origin of evil spirits. He considers the Book of Watchers (1 Enoch 1–36) as an expansion of the enigmatic text of Gen 6:1–4, whose author was probably drawing on myths (Israelite or foreign) to help explain the Flood, particularly by elaborating on negative nuances behind the *bene elohim* story.[63] Wright suggests it provided a multifaceted explanation of the problem of evil; the *bene elohim* were interpreted as angels that fell (led by Shemihazah or Asa'el (Azazel) in the two traditions incorporated in chapters 6–11), bringing negative effects on humanity and creation, yet they were removed for punishment,[64] such that the spirits of the giants become the central characters of the story, their offspring seen as the origin of evil spirits that roam the earth but also seek to reoccupy human bodies.[65]

Whilst the original tradition of the Watchers may predate Genesis 6, it could not account for evil before the flood, which may be why it was gradually eclipsed by the fall-story of the expulsion of Satan.[66] After the Maccabean revolt, two other fall-stories, the Adam narrative in Genesis 3 and the development of a demonology focused upon Satan as the leader of the demonic band, were on the increase—Satan being the most commonly mentioned demon in the Jewish canon.[67] The clearest "expulsion from heaven" story linked to Isaiah 14 is in 2 Enoch, probably early enough to provide a plausible background to the NT allusions to the tradition.[68] In the possible allusion of Jesus's words (Luke 10:18), the verb ἐθεώρουν is

63. Evidence from later Targums suggests the *bene elohim* (and more ambiguously the *gibborim* ("mighty men") and *nephilim* (*gigantes* in LXX)) had been viewed negatively in earlier traditions that were picked up and elaborated in the Book of Watchers. See also "The Cosmic Fall," 227–38; Hendel, "The Nephilim Were on the Earth."

64. 1 En. 10:4–15; see Wright, *The Origin of Evil Spirits*, 145–46, 221. In 1 Enoch 21:6, 10, the rebellious fallen angels (or "stars") are bound in prison, so this legend is probably behind 1 Pet 3:18–20; and could be the one alluded to in Jude 6 and 2 Pet 2:4–7. See Boyd, *God at War*, 262, 285–86; Charlesworth, *Pseudepigrapha 1*, 24.

65. As clearly identified in the gospels, notably Mark 5:12, and Matt 12:43–5/Luke 11:24–26. Wright, *The Origin of Evil Spirits*, 138–65, 221–22; Stuckenbruck, "Evil in Jewish Apocalyptic Tradition," 117.

66. See Lloyd, "The Cosmic Fall," 238.

67. Although outside the Old Testament often referred to by other names, such as Azazel (e.g., Apocalypse of Abraham 23:12, 29:7, in the Edenic fall story), or Beliar (frequently in the Dead Sea Scrolls). Charlesworth, *Pseudepigrapha 1*, 700, 703; Wright, *The Origin of Evil Spirits*, 157–60; Lloyd, "The Cosmic Fall," 239–40.

68. On the second day of creation, after lightning and fire were created, and from them the ranks of angels: "But one [Satanail] from the order of the archangels deviated, together with the division that was under his authority. He thought up the impossible idea, that he might place his throne higher than the clouds which are above the earth, and that he might become equal to my power. And I hurled him from the height, together with his angels." 2 En. 29:4–6, in Charlesworth, *Pseudepigrapha 1*, 148. Andersen opts for a late first century AD Jewish origin for this (Slavonic) Enoch. Ibid., 91, 94–95, 97.

imperfect (usually meaning continuous and protracted), thus "I have been seeing Satan falling like lightning from heaven," thus most likely referring to the exorcistic ministry of the early Christians, rather than an earlier Satanic fall;[69] however, the shape of this comment could reveal knowledge of a fall from heaven tradition.[70]

In terms of the biblical material then, which largely accepts evil as a factual reality, there is not a singular unified tradition of a fall of angels, but this nevertheless appears the best "theory" for the origin of evil. Robert Cook's other possibilities, whilst possibly more intellectually satisfying, do not have as much biblical support as the traditional view he seeks to discredit, and fail to account for the existence of Satan and demons.[71] For those, like Boyd, who also see "evil" in the natural world as requiring a spiritual explanation, the fall of angels hypothesis also helps explain the presence of such evil before the fall of man.[72]

7.5 Evil spiritual beings, theodicy, and God's sovereignty

Boyd argues that the early post-apostolic church essentially saw the "problem of evil" as a pragmatic one—of how to combat the evil agent who is believed to have inflicted evil upon the earth;[73] the modern intellectual problem of evil was a later development.[74] Most charismatics are similarly more interested in the practical task of overcoming evil than of intellectually justifying its persistence. However, some theological reflection on

---

69. "Lightning" probably infers bright, spectacular and obvious in the context. Twelftree, *In the Name of Jesus*, 140. Alternatively, it might refer to Jesus's own defeat of Satan in the wilderness. Page, *Powers of Evil*, 109–10.

70. Lloyd, "The Cosmic Fall," 242.

71. See section 5.5, and Cook, "Devils and Manticores," 168–70, 180–82.

72. Boyd particularly sees the hand of evil at work in natural disasters and events, ascribing full responsibility for these at the hands of fallen angelic beings, favoring a "restoration theory" similar to the "gap theory" of Gen 1:2. Boyd, *God at War*, 102–13; *Satan and the Problem of Evil*, 309–18. See chapter 8.4.

73. Levenson also sees this as essentially the way the "problem of evil" (which is more "why do the evil prosper?") is dealt with in the Old Testament—but there the expected response is a renewal of activity from the God of justice—"drive them out like sheep to the slaughter." Jer 12:1–3; Levenson, *Creation and the Persistence of Evil*, xvii.

74. It was not until Augustine, Boethius, and others proposed that "providence is the unchangeable power that gives form to all things," and "the Creator of all nature . . . directs and disposes all things for good" that the modern intellectual problem of evil arose, in terms of how to reconcile God's goodness with his ordaining, or allowing, particular evils to occur. Boethius, *The Theological Tractates and the Consolation of Philosophy*, 4:91, 96; Boyd, *God at War*, 54.

how God's goodness and omnipotence operate in the world is relevant, and much of that debate remains linked to the whole problem of theodicy (literally, "justifying God"), which Boyd contributes to from a new angle.[75]

While it may be impossible to solve the problem of evil as classically formulated,[76] some form of "free will defense" has often seemed the most promising way out of its apparent contradictions, as for example clearly enunciated by Plantinga. Whilst Mackie argued that the presence of evil is not a *logically necessary* concomitant to free will,[77] Alvin Plantinga produced a detailed Free Will Defense.[78] Plantinga noted that Augustine was one of the first to propose free will as an account for the origin of evil, and including in it a concept of the rebellion of angels which particularly helped to account for natural evil.[79] However, in his later works, Augustine emphasized much more that the suffering caused by such use of free will should ultimately be attributed to the will of God the creator, actually contributing to the beauty of the whole which remained under God's meticulous control; [80] he encouraged a detached perspective, seeing even horrendous evils as "antitheses" within a poem that renders it more exquisite by "the opposition of contraries."[81] This may satisfy at an abstract level if evil is considered merely as "the absence of good," and may even practically bring some comfort in suffering for those who can exercise faith that God has some "higher purpose" or harmony, and all will come right in the end; but it fails to deal with the widespread existential protest in the face of cruel or needless suffering, as voiced by Ivan in the *Brothers Karamazov*, "I renounce the higher harmony altogether . . . it is not worth the tear of . . . one tortured child."[82]

Boyd's solution is a stronger free will argument. He accepts that his theodicy overlaps with most theodicies, even from the "blueprint" worldview, that affirm the reality of human and angelic free will, but argues differently that such agents are only genuinely free if they are the ultimate

---

75. Mainly in his second more philosophical volume—see *Satan and the Problem of Evil*, 18.

76. See *God at War*, 44, 303.

77. Mackie, "Evil and Omnipotence," 86.

78. Plantinga maintained that it may not have been within God's power to have created a world containing moral good but no moral evil, because "if he aims to produce moral good . . . then he must create significantly free creatures upon whose cooperation he must depend." Plantinga, "The Free Will Defense," 114–15.

79. Ibid., 117. This argument is taken up by Lloyd, "The Cosmic Fall," 224–38.

80. Augustine, *The City of God*, 5.10; Boyd, *God at War*, 45.

81. Augustine, *The City of God*, 11.18.

82. Dostoevsky, *The Brothers Karamazov*, 286–92; Augustine, *The City of God*; Boyd, *God at War*, 45–46.

explanations of their own free actions (see 1 below), rather than seeking an ultimate reason in their being ordained or allowed by God. Secondly, he agrees that *sometimes* God may allow, or even ordain, suffering as a way of punishing sin, building character or contributing to some "greater good"; but denies that Scripture, reason, or experience require that suffering must *always* serve a divine purpose. His six theses are:

1. Love must be freely chosen.
2. Love entails risk.
3. Love, and thus freedom, entails that we are to some extent morally responsible for one another, and can influence one another.
4. Our power to influence for the worse must be roughly proportionate to our power to influence for the better.
5. Freedom must be, within limits, irrevocable.
6. This limitation is not infinite, since our capacity to freely choose love is not endless—angels and human beings possess only a finite capacity to embrace or thwart God's purposes for our lives.

This final thesis explains why God must at present genuinely war against rebellious creatures, though he is certain to overcome them in the future.[83]

A thorough examination of this theodicy is beyond the scope of this thesis; but we must consider briefly how these arguments interact with his conclusions from the biblical material. Whilst he rightly argues that freedom must have an irrevocable element to be coherent, why did God set the limits on this where they are?[84] If God is able to rebuke the waters and "set a boundary that they cannot cross" (Ps 104:9), why did he not constrain spiritual beings even more in the extent to which they can cause evil in the world? Does he really value their freedom so much that he would delegate to them so much potential for evil?[85] If, as Boyd maintains, he is still omnipotent and so powerful that he can bring about whatever he promises, why does he not intervene in the midst of certain tragic evils, particularly in answer to the prayers of his people? His position is rendered more coher-

---

83. *Satan and the Problem of Evil*, 19, 22–25.

84. Unless God has entirely limited himself to working through the free obedience of loyal angels, reduced in number due to angelic rebellion; or to the extent to which people pray and so release his answers to prayer, a reasonable self-limitation if the government of the earth has essentially been given to human beings.

85. Whilst Balthazar and others have argued that one choice fixed their destiny, it may be more coherent (as Lloyd suggests) that even rebellious angels continue to have free choice, and could potentially be reconciled to God's love; otherwise it is difficult to see why he would he not judge them now. See chapter 5 in Lloyd, "The Cosmic Fall."

ent by his assertion that God does not exert micro-control over all events in creation, because he has irrevocably given areas of freedom to created beings to influence the course of events, but some questions remain unanswered.[86] Similarly, he argues that a God who is constrained to the one possibility he foreknows will happen, and requires this knowledge in order to act, is weaker and less free than a God who is "open" to the future.[87] But he struggles to convincingly explain a number of biblical texts that suggest a detailed foreknowledge of events.[88]

7.6 Conclusion

Boyd presents a strong argument for a belief in the real existence of evil spiritual beings pervading the Scriptures, in particular New Testament thought, in accord with the prevailing worldview of the time. The existence of demons, and of Satan in whose kingdom demons belong, is clearly stated and demonstrated by Jesus in the Gospel accounts as he resists them; and the same worldview underlies the Pauline writings and other references in the Epistles.

He shows that the reality of this warfare motif is crucial for Jesus, and present also for the other biblical writers, including oblique references to Yahweh's battle with cosmic spiritual forces, and he re-emphasizes the Scriptures that support a classical view of the cross as a victory over evil forces.[89]

---

86. For example, if God sets the limits to angelic and human freedom, he would appear to share some responsibility for what created beings do with this freedom. God must have had "higher purposes," such that an eschatological argument is still needed— "our present sufferings are not worth comparing with the glory that will be revealed in us . . . the creation was subjected . . . in hope that the creation itself will be liberated from its bondage to decay and brought into the glorious liberty of the children of God" (Rom 8:18–21). Scripture itself recognizes that God bears this responsibility: ultimately it was God who subjected creation to frustration, "not by its own choice." There remains a strong element of unfathomable mystery as to why God allowed angelic beings so much power and influence (as, similarly, why did he let Satan go quite so far with Job?).

87. God is like an infinitely intelligent chess master, who infinitely knows all future possibilities and is confident that he can still act to carry out his essential purposes. Boyd, *God of the Possible*, 126–28; *Satan and the Problem of Evil*, 117–30.

88. Such as the story of Saul and his donkeys in 1 Samuel 10, or Luke 22:10–13; or Peter's denial—Boyd maintains that God has sufficient *influence* over the future events to bring about these incidents. *Satan and the Problem of Evil*, 130–32. Boyd's problem with foreknowledge only arises because he is committed to the "process" view that God follows through time in parallel with his creation; if God inhabits additional dimensions beyond time, his knowledge is not necessarily prior to the actions, so the actions are not made necessary by God's knowing them.

89. See section 8.4.

However, whilst taking a scholarly approach, Boyd tends to overstate his argument and its conclusions—for example in seeing this "spiritual warfare worldview" as more important than the whole New Testament discourse on the sacrifice for sin, or the struggle between Spirit and flesh in Paul. And his suggestion that the Bible speaks of such spiritual beings as being involved in all the battles on earth involving both natural and moral evil is an overstatement—in reality specific references are decidedly sparse. Nevertheless, he does not go into detailed speculations as to the structure and operation of such evil spiritual beings, and so his version of a "demonized worldview" need not lead to a more fearful "paranoid worldview."[90]

Boyd rightly emphasizes that the biblical writers were much more concerned with the practical problem of evil than the philosophical one, as are most charismatics today. Despite its weaknesses, the strength of his free will argument lies in the assertion that it is sufficient to ascribe ultimate responsibility to free beings for their actions (such that God is not held responsible for specific evils). His more radical denial of God's foreknowledge of the future remains much more controversial.

Perhaps the greatest significance of his contribution is in bringing together a wide range of theological and historical evidence that a significant part of the biblical worldview is a realm of unseen spiritual realities affecting material reality in complex ways. This belief is shared by most non-Western cultures today, and also taken up by charismatics even in the Western world, as they seek to re-emphasize the concept of what Boyd calls "the world in between" (equivalent to part of "the heavenly realms," τοι ἐπουρανίοι, as described by the writer of Ephesians) and its inter-relation with the course of events in the material world—a concept which I shall revisit in seeking to construct a charismatic theology of spiritual warfare.

---

90. Boyd would argue that his proposals reduce the anxiety associated with trying to reconcile the suffering we see and experience with an all-loving Creator—though evil things may happen in the short term, the final victory is certain.

8

Constructing a Charismatic Theology of Spiritual Warfare

8.1 A charismatic hermeneutical approach: methodological considerations and the contribution of charismatic Anglican pioneers

THIS CHAPTER SEEKS TO construct a spiritual warfare theology—primarily from the biblical texts, as the key normative component of the "system" (together with insights from the reflection of chapters 5 to 7), but now bringing in more directly the results of my descriptive-empirical research in the "lifeworld."[1]

However, first we need to revisit the issue of hermeneutical method. Coming myself from the charismatic tradition I shall be primarily adopting a charismatic hermeneutical approach—though not surprisingly there is some disagreement as to exactly what that is. For example, there have been debates as to the right use of Luke-Acts as opposed to Paul as normative for understanding "baptism in the Spirit," and the relevance of authorial intention in relation to historical precedent (Dunn, Fee, Menzies, and others[2]); Archer's approach in seeing the community and its story as central in providing a framework for hermeneutics;[3] or the tendency to identify particular events or experiences as "this is that" which was prophesied in the Bible (Stibbe/Lyons).[4]

The general principles of "charismatic hermeneutics" Stibbe enumerates during this debate are of wider relevance—especially his "first characteristic of a charismatic hermeneutic" as to normally *begin* where

1. See Cartledge, *Practical Theology*, 28–29.
2. For a summary of this debate and its sources, see Noel, "Gordon Fee and the Challenge," 183.
3. See, for example, Archer, "Pentecostal Story"; *A Pentecostal Hermeneutic*.
4. Stibbe, "This Is That," 181–93; Lyons, "The Fourth Wave," 169–80.

biblical text and experience meet, being impressed with "a burning sense of the relevance of certain Scriptures for his situation."[5] Just as Pentecostal hermeneutics often focuses on early pioneers as setting paradigms for what follows,[6] I shall consider here the Anglican charismatic pioneers and how their charismatic experience affected their hermeneutics and theological conclusions.

Stibbe offers his model in response particularly to evangelical criticism that his approach is too subjective and influenced by post-modernism. His version of Anglican charismatic hermeneutics aims to be a mediating one, both objective in using the historical-critical approach of evangelicals, and subjective in its emphasis on charismatic "reader response" in the light of present (but also shared and communal) experience.[7] Stibbe considers such a reading to be experiential, analogical, communal, Christological, eschatological, emotional, and practical. In chapter 3 we described the development of a theology of spiritual warfare particularly for Harper, Watson, and Green, who all previously received evangelical theological training at Ridley Hall, Cambridge; here I shall also consider how much they moved from a traditional evangelical model towards Stibbe's newer charismatic dimensions.

First of all, their hermeneutic is clearly more *experiential*, which Stibbe considers deserves to come first—as charismatics normally *begin* "with a sense of rich harmony between biblical texts and present experience."[8] We have seen that our pioneer writers were primarily motivated by their experience to start publishing their interpretation of scriptural teaching on spiritual warfare. This was particularly personal experience in ministry, and experience of their social context particularly with the rise in forms of spiritism and occult—both mentioned by all three, and Green describes clearly how ministry experience confirmed a belief in Satan's existence and malevolent power.[9] However, the most novel systematic development is that all find that personal experience of spiritual conflict is heightened through experience of the Spirit. Green observes that "for me and almost everyone I know" acute awareness of the Holy Spirit and of "the unholy spirit" seem

---

5. Stibbe, "This Is That," 183.

6. Archer, "Pentecostal Hermeneutics," 75; "Early Pentecostal Biblical Interpretation," 32–70.

7. Stibbe, "This Is That," 181–82.

8. Ibid., 183.

9. "Anyone who has seen the astounding contrast between a person possessed by an occult force and that same person set free by Christ fully and completely—it may be only an hour later—will not need any persuading that man has a mighty, hateful enemy in Satan." Green, *I Believe in Satan's Downfall*, 23.

to come in "a double pack"; and Harper maintains that "nearly always Satan challenges us when we first begin to exercise this gift [of tongues]."[10] In ministry, the contexts where they most often experienced a sense of "power encounter" were in evangelism ("a titanic confrontation" [Green], "a powerful spiritual warfare . . . battling with unseen spiritual forces" [Watson]),[11] or in ministering the fullness of the Spirit (Harper).[12]

Secondly, certainly our pioneers were reading Scripture *analogically* in the sense that they believed their experiences of spiritual warfare were analogous to others in the Gospels (the exorcisms of Jesus), Acts (e.g., spiritual conflict with Elymas, or at Ephesus), and the Epistles (especially Paul in Ephesians 6, or 2 Corinthians 10). This follows New Testament practice in beginning with *"What is the Spirit doing right now in my life and community?"* and then seeking analogies between that and scriptural events, which is not "eisegesis."[13]

Thirdly, Stibbe and others (e.g., Archer, Pinnock) agree our reading should be a *communal* one, if we are to transcend the limitations of our interpretations.[14] Many charismatics (e.g., Green in Oxford[15]) found their experiences took them by surprise, but then discovered mutual confirmation through friendships (e.g., between Watson and Green) and conferences (e.g., Harper's Fountain Trust), and resonances with Scriptural experiences and teaching. Stibbe's other criteria are also relevant—particularly a *Christological* reading, for charismatics often find their experience brings the ministry of the historical Jesus alive for them (Jesus's exorcisms in Mark resonated strongly for Harper[16]); and we have also seen that it is intensely *practical,* concerned with how Christians should actively engage in spiritual warfare.

The evidence suggests that these early charismatic pioneers exemplify a "mediating hermeneutic"—they (and contemporary Anglican charismatics

10. Harper, *Walk in the Spirit*, 27. Boddy parallels this experience—see chapter 2.2.

11. Green, *I Believe in the Holy Spirit*, 70; Watson, *I Believe in Evangelism*.

12. In this context Harper discovered the need for deliverance ministry, "the reality of Satan's power, and the greater power of the name of Jesus." Harper, *None Can Guess*, 90, 139–40. See chapter 3.2.

13. Stibbe, "This Is That," 185. Jesus in Luke similarly cites Elijah and Elisha (4:24–27) and David (6:2–4) as historical precedent. See Noel, "Gordon Fee and the Challenge," 74, 77.

14. E.g., Pinnock, "Work of Holy Spirit in Hermeneutics," 10; Archer, *A Pentecostal Hermeneutic*; Stibbe, "This Is That," 185–87.

15. His logically-minded colleague, John Woolmer, also expressed continuing surprise at encounters with evil powers. Woolmer Interview, 16.3.06.

16. Interview 20.4.04. He writes: "More healings of Jesus are related to Satanic influence than any other single factor." Harper, *Jesus the Healer*, 29.

like Stibbe) are unlikely to depart altogether from historical critical exegetical methods, beloved by evangelicals.[17] Evangelicals like to clearly separate the Spirit's inspiration of the Scriptures, and his work of illumination in the readers as "the Spirit of wisdom and revelation" (Eph 1:17);[18] however, Pinnock rightly points out that both are "breathings" of the same Spirit, and both crucially important as part of the larger revelatory work of the Spirit always present to help interpret God's will in the community of faith.[19] One helpful insight of contextual theology, shared by charismatic practical theology, is that the Spirit always has to bring the biblical texts into dialogue with our own contextual experience—and one insight of new approaches to hermeneutics and textuality (such as reader-response criticism) is that they are "opened up" in the presence of new reader horizons.[20]

Many pioneers experienced expanding horizons, seeing familiar texts in new ways and with fresh relevance—through their experiences they went through a "paradigm shift" in their understanding of Scripture in relation to spiritual warfare that effectively brought it into being as a subject in itself.[21] David MacInnes described this in detail, recounting how his experiences brought to life what was already there in biblical revelation but not apprehended, concerning demonic reality.[22] Bob Dunnett developed a significant typological approach to reading motifs of physical warfare in the Old Testament (particularly in Nehemiah) out of his experience of the spiritual battle in council estate ministry; although not accepted by all pioneers (perhaps being more influenced by the historical-critical method), Barrington-Ward

---

17. Green, for example, has been widely respected as an evangelical scholar, by John Stott, Jim Packer, and others—Green, *Adventure of Faith*, ii–iii.

18. See Stott and others, *The Anglican Communion and Scripture*, especially 22, 40.

19. Pinnock quotes F. F. Bruce and Wesley as supporting this view. Pinnock, "Work of Holy Spirit in Hermeneutics," 4–5.

20. Ibid., 13; Thiselton, *New Horizons*, 44–46, 55–79.

21. Yong helpfully discusses as to how experience of God breaking into our lives by the Spirit can be valid for our interpretation of Scripture, as it was for Augustine (Rom 13:11), Luther (Rom 1:17), and Paul's use of Hab 2:4, apparently deviating from authorial intention. Yong, *Spirit-Word-Community*, 247–49.

22. After describing personal encounters with people or situations perceived to be influenced by demonic forces: "It seemed to me that in order to assess this properly one needs first of all revelation from which you've got your understanding that there is a separate demonic entity. You then need the encounter with it in order to recognize that this was something which wasn't just biblical understanding of a psychological condition, which is often how it is represented." He then reflects on how the "community of interpreters" helped him to assess this—first reading Nevius and Koch, later Green and his theology of the cross as central to Satan's downfall. David MacInnes Interview 6.4.06.

also argued in favor of it.²³ And this sense of "the illumination of Scripture" was mentioned as one of the key signs associated with receiving "baptism in the Spirit" by some pioneers, particularly Harper.²⁴

My own hermeneutical method

Whilst these pioneers often had to wrestle with Scripture on their own to interpret their experiences, they could also test their views with others in the emerging charismatic community.²⁵ As Archer puts it, the sequence is often experiential knowledge *revealed* by the Holy Spirit, *validated* by the Scriptures, and *confirmed* by the community.²⁶ Lyons raises the important question though of which community helps decide the correctness of an interpretation.²⁷ Different communities have different "templates" through which experiences are filtered; some can almost *a priori* filter out certain understandings concerning evil spirits and deliverance ministry.²⁸ As a charismatic theologian, my primary "community" will be the "community of interpreters" from the charismatic and Pentecostal tradition who wrestle to interpret the Scriptures in the light of our shared experiences of the working of the Spirit. However, in asking fundamental questions as to the nature of reality, the world (*kosmos*) as it really is, we are not just seeking to draw privatised conclusions for one Christian sector, but also to further the public understanding of reality. Like Yong, I value a wider range of input into "the pneumatological imagination," and the testing of interpretations with the breadth of the theological and scholarly community;²⁹ hence for example my willingness to engage with theologians such as Barth and Wink, pragmatist philosophy, and some phenomenological methods of sociology.

---

23. "It is [reasonable to allegories OT war passages] because it seems to me that that was what the New Testament was already doing. And indeed in the inter-testamental period the whole move from actual conflict with enemies to conflict with spiritual enemies became more and more apparent." Ward Interview 20.4.04. The New Testament's use of the Old in 1 Corinthians 10 and Hebrews supports this typological approach.

24. See chapter 3.2.

25. Through the Fountain Trust, or *Theological Renewal* (1975–83), which featured a heated debate following publication of Green's *I Believe in Satan's Downfall*.

26. Archer, *A Pentecostal Hermeneutic*, 106. See also Thomas, "Women, Pentecostals and the Bible," 41–56.

27. Lyons, "The Fourth Wave," 179–80.

28. See Theron, "The Ministry of Deliverance," 196–97. See also Archer's "hermeneutical filter"—Archer, "Pentecostal Story."

29. See for example Yong, *Spirit-Word-Community*, 19. Other Pentecostal theologians have also called for this dialogue—Theron, "The Ministry of Deliverance," 204.

And to be credible and coherent, we should consider the compatibility of our conclusions with the observations of modern science.[30]

However, in constructing here a theology of charismatic spiritual warfare, unlike Yong I shall be primarily drawing on scholars from the charismatic/Pentecostal tradition. Like many of my research subjects, I largely accept a canonical approach to biblical exposition—not denying differences between authors and books (and their sources), but preferring to let them speak in the context of the whole canon of Scripture.[31] However, I will also draw on the work of those who have used some tools of the historical-critical method (such as redaction criticism) to try and undercover the cosmology of the biblical writers and of Jesus himself, in seeking to contribute to wider debate in systematic theology and construct a cosmology that most accurately reflects reality.[32]

8.2 The nature of evil—ontology and cosmology

The Old Testament view

In chapter 7, I already discussed evidence for a belief in evil spiritual beings in the Old Testament cosmology. Boyd correctly picks up on the weight of scholarship demonstrating a belief in some kind of evil forces of chaos that God opposes, often represented as the monsters of the myths of the neighboring Canaanites and the ancient Near East. Yahweh seems to be portrayed as defeating such forces both in the process of creation and at least symbolically in interventions such as the exodus—though references to such monsters are often in poetic and prophetic discourse, making it difficult to decide what exactly they referred to conceptually for the writers. There are however clearer references to "demons" linked to the worship of other gods, and "sons of God" which appear to be angelic beings which can also rebel against God (Psalm 82, probably Genesis 6), and which may even have been delegated some kind of authority over nations (such as Persia or Greece, Daniel 10). Amongst these we find Satan appearing as an accuser,

---

30. I discuss briefly below phenomenological evidence for evil spirits; but further engagement with psychology in relation to the demonic, an important area for further research.

31. Following Brevard Childs—see Gooder, *Searching for Meaning*, 63.

32. For example the work of Graham Twelftree, well-trained (notably under George Caird and James Dunn) in critical study of the New Testament, but also active in the charismatic/Pentecostal community. See Twelftree, *Jesus the Exorcist*, v. J. C. Thomas commends a similar methodological approach. Thomas, *The Devil, Disease and Deliverance*, 15–16.

although only in Job and Zechariah (accusing Joshua the high priest), and as an *agent provocateur* in 1 Chr 21:1.[33]

Jesus, exorcism of demons, and the clash of kingdoms

In the New Testament, by contrast, Satan and demons are regularly mentioned especially in the Gospels, and were apparently seen as real spiritual beings. Seeing the reality of this clash between Jesus and demonic beings in Mark and the other Gospels particularly influenced some early Anglican charismatic pioneers.[34] However, some modern Anglican theologians later publicly opposed the very idea of exorcism of any kind;[35] revealing the importance of seeking to understand what Jesus was doing, and understood himself to be doing, in the gospel accounts—not least because systematic theology should be strongly Christocentric.

This aspect has rarely been a subject of research in trying to uncover the historical Jesus; partly because modernist biblical criticism was too influenced by Bultmann's "demythologizing" approach, which presupposed that miraculous or supernatural events did not occur.[36] Twelftree thus explores the practice of Jesus in exorcism,[37] against the background of material considered reliable for reconstructing first century understandings of spirits, demons, possessions, magic, and exorcisms, particularly in Galilee in northern Palestine.[38] There were enough stories to produce a general pattern for exorcistic practice to compare with that of Jesus. There was strong evidence of widespread belief of a need for protection from hostile spiritual beings infecting the world, and few but enough contemporary stories concerning exorcists with which to compare the gospel accounts of Jesus, which stand out as unusual. He concluded that on one hand he was a man of his time in using recognizable formulae in commands to demons (and also in the disturbed initial reactions, and violence of the exorcisms, whether in convulsions or the drowning of the pigs); yet where other exorcists often had difficulty in getting demons to speak, Jesus uniquely charged them to be

---

33. Wink, *Unmasking the Powers*, 11–12.
34. Especially Harper—see 8.1, footnote 16.
35. See section 2.3, and Cupitt, *Explorations in Theology 6*, 50–53.
36. See Twelftree, *Jesus the Exorcist*, 2–7.
37. He defines exorcism as a form of healing used when demons or evil spirits were thought to have entered a person by attempting to expel them. Ibid., 13.
38. His wide range of sources, encompass both the Jewish but also the Hellenistic milieu of Jesus and earliest Christianity. Ibid., 12–21.

silent.[39] Also, unlike contemporary exorcists he never adjured (ὁρκίζω) the demons in the name of a higher authority, instead simply ordering the demon "I," seeming to operate out of his own resources; yet he believed it was God operating in his activity.[40] In general, Twelftree's conclusion that Jesus was a particularly successful and powerful exorcist, appears well-founded.[41]

The evidence is strong therefore that Jesus treated many conditions as if they were caused by δαιμόνια (or τα πνεύματα τα ἀκάθαρτα, "unclean (evil) spirits") thus appearing to view these as real spiritual beings. Key objections raised here are that, in exorcising demons and talking about Satan, either Jesus was a man of his time and so operated within that worldview, whereas modern scientific evidence has tended to discount the existence of demons; or, that he knew demons were not real spiritual beings, but he was accommodating to the superstitious beliefs of his time in using exorcistic techniques. For example Edward Ball, whilst willing to accept that "Jesus fully believed in the reality of Satan and demonic powers," did not find Michael Green's arguments concerning these questions convincing.[42]

However, Twelftree's analysis strengthens the case that Jesus's exorcisms and associated teaching provides compelling reasons for believing in the reality of Satan and demons. One of the strongest arguments is that, rather than distance himself from contemporary beliefs concerning the real existence of these demons and the afflictions they could cause, Jesus raised them to a new level of coherence by linking his exorcisms with eschatology.[43] He linked an ordinary exorcism with the notion of a cosmic, supernatural battle against the kingdom of Satan in the eschaton, in which his (and his disciples') exorcisms were the first stage of Satan's defeat. This conclusion comes particularly from a careful examination of the Beelzebul controversy;[44] in particular, from the saying (probably Q material) "but if I

---

39. Ibid., 148–56.

40. Thus, "by the Spirit/finger of God" (Matt 12:28/Luke 11:20); both revealing God's activity. Dunn, *Jesus and the Spirit*, 44–45.

41. The charge that Jesus was a magician is only evidenced post-second century—the only contemporary accusation recognized, and refuted, is the more horrific criticism that Jesus was operating in Satan's power rather than God's. Twelftree, *Jesus the Exorcist*, 225–27; Williams, *The Case for Angels*, 157–63; Yamauchi, "Magic or Miracle?," 140–42.

42. Partly reacting against Green's characteristic polemical style—Ball, "Review of I Believe in Satan's Downfall," 34–35; Green, *I Believe in Satan's Downfall*, 26–29.

43. Yamauchi and others makes a similar argument—that Jesus brought a radically new conception in seeing all demons as belonging to the kingdom of Satan, thus deepening the concepts of the day regarding demons, rather than accommodating himself to contemporary thought. Yamauchi, "Magic or Miracle?" 142.

44. Matt 9:32–34; 12:22–30; Mark 3:22–7; Luke 11:14–23. All three include the accusation (whether from the scribes (Mark), Pharisees (Matthew) or the crowd (Luke));

drive out demons by the Spirit of God, then the kingdom of God has come upon you" (Matt 12:28).⁴⁵ The evidence is weak that there was an expectation at the time that exorcisms signified the coming of the messianic Son of David, as references to this are all in material either written or redacted by Christians.⁴⁶ However, this suggests that the connection between exorcism and eschatology may have been made for the first time in the authentic words of Jesus. Thus, Jesus ascribes the efficacy of his authoritative commands to the demons as a sign that he is operating by the eschatological Spirit (Matt 12:28/Luke 11:20, where ἐγω is emphatic); where the Spirit was operating in Jesus (here, casting out demons) there was the focus of the coming of the kingdom.⁴⁷ Like others of his time, though, he still saw the final defeat of Satan as yet to come at the eschaton.⁴⁸

Thus, it was Jesus himself who seemed to introduce the concept that his exorcisms were part of a clash between the kingdom of God and Satan's kingdom.⁴⁹ Warrington largely agrees with this analysis; adding that the

---

the affirmation that Satan could not be divided against Satan; and the "stronger one" first binding the strong man. See Twelftree, *Jesus the Exorcist*, 98–104. The similar accusation of being demon-possessed is also recorded in John 7:20; 8:48–49, 52; 10:20–21, meeting the criterion of multiple source attestation; Williams notes how this contributes to a very high chance of the authenticity of this material, which also satisfies the criterion of admission by antagonistic witnesses (that Jesus was actually casting out demons), the criterion of dissimilarity (much here of Jesus's teaching differs from first century Judaism). Williams, *The Case for Angels*, 157–63.

45. This saying is widely accepted to go back to Jesus. See Twelftree, *Jesus the Exorcist*, 106–10.

46. The scholarly consensus may well be misled here—for example, the foundational Matt 12:23 "Can this be the Son of David?" is probably a later redaction of Matthew. Ibid., 101–2, 219–20, 227.

47. Ibid., 216–20, 28. Warrington, and Dunn to a lesser extent, similarly observe that Jesus is emphasizing his own uniqueness, as the exorcisms are not just in God's power, but performed by himself. Dunn, *Jesus and the Spirit*, 48; Warrington, *Jesus the Healer*, 78–79.

48. Twelftree argues that whilst Matthew's explanation of the Parable of the Wheat and Tares is probably from his own hand, the parable itself (Matt 13:24–30) is likely to go back to Jesus, with its explicit reference to "an enemy did this" but the tares being left to the time of the harvest. Twelftree, *Jesus the Exorcist*, 221–24.

49. In Matt 12:24, 26–27, he equates Satan with Beelzebul, probably hinting that he is "the master of the house" i.e., leader of the heathen gods who were seen by that time (e.g., Pss 96:5; 106:37 cf. 1 Cor 10:20) in Judaism as demons—see ibid., 105. In the apocalyptic speculation of the time, however, their leader of the fallen angels is variously identified, even within texts—in 1 Enoch 69, Azazel (often identified with Satan) is only number ten in a list of over twenty chiefs; but earlier (1 Enoch 6 to 9) Azazel, a key deceiver of the earth, is singled out with Semyaz for special judgment; and in 1 Enoch 53/54, judgment falls on Satan alone. Charlesworth, *Pseudepigrapha 1*, 15–19, 37–38, 47. See also Boyd, *God at War*, 180, 357n33.

violence often shown by demons on exit reveals something of their personality, that contrary to popular Jewish belief "the demonic realm is not inhabited by mischievous imps but malevolent savages."[50] Certainly the Matt 12:22–30 discourse reveals Jesus's belief that Satan and demons are strongly inter-connected in a way that is at least analogous to a kingdom. Secondly, his action represents the power breaking in of a superior kingdom "coming upon you."[51] The term ἐκβάλλω is used for exorcism for the first time here in "Q" and Mark.[52]

Given the common occurrence of exorcisms at the time, and that Jews were not habitually seeing such miracles as eschatological signs, his claim that his exorcisms were not only the vanguard of his battle with Satan, but the coming of the kingdom of God itself, are audacious and astounding.[53] Even without other evidence from the Gospels,[54] these assertions of Jesus's self-understanding that his actions in exorcism are part of plundering Satan's "house,"[55] and an expulsion of demonic emissaries of Satan's "kingdom," would seem to merit Green's comment that if "Jesus did not mean what he said in this matter . . . it is hard to see how we can trust him on any other."[56] There are indications too in the ethical realm that Jesus clearly saw ὁ πονερος as a personal force of evil.[57] Cupitt suggests that "the church has never expected that her members must necessarily share all Jesus's beliefs—in the field of eschatology for example"; Dow responds that even if

---

50. Warrington, *Jesus the Healer*, 104. Warrington also notes that Jesus's response "How can Satan cast out Satan?" may imply that "Satan is so integrally involved with his demonic minions that to cast them out is to cast out him." Ibid., 77.

51. Matt 12:28/Luke 11:20—Twelftree, *Jesus the Exorcist*, 108–9. Wink also supports these conclusions: "Jesus regards his healings and exorcisms as an assault on the kingdom of Satan and an indication that the kingdom of God is breaking in. The gospel is very much a cosmic battle in which Jesus rescues humanity from the dominion of evil powers." Wink, *Naming the Powers*, 26.

52. Other Jewish writings often use the language of fleeing (φεύγω) for demons departing; whereas in the LXX, ἐκβάλλω is often used for casting out an enemy blocking God's purposes for Israel. Twelftree, *Jesus the Exorcist*, 109–10.

53. *In the Name of Jesus*, 48–49.

54. Satan is also Jesus's adversary in the temptation narratives, in Mark 4:15, and Luke 10:18.

55. This saying of Jesus is also most probably authentic. It is not only in different gospel sources, but also the Gospel of Thomas; and the comparison of a possessed person to a "house" is still common in the East. Twelftree, *Jesus the Exorcist*, 111.

56. Green, *I Believe in Satan's Downfall*, 27–28.

57. "Anything else comes from the evil one" is by far the most likely translation of Matt 5:37, and therefore by implication in Matt 6:13 in the Lord's prayer ("deliver us from the evil one"). 1 Enoch 69:15 also brings together the activity of "the evil one" with oath-taking. Boyd, *God at War*, 221, 373; Charlesworth, *Pseudepigrapha 1*, 47.

criteria could be established to decide which beliefs of Jesus were culturally conditioned, in view of the evidence that Jesus saw his mission as a struggle with Satan, and clearly understood Satan and demons to be linked, it would be difficult to accept Jesus's claim to divine authority in his mission and yet discard these parallel beliefs.[58] Yamauchi, in his analysis, agrees that to safeguard Jesus's honesty, it is easier to accept the existence of demons as independent entities, than to suggest he simulated exorcism to accord with common belief, or was immersed in the mistaken views of his time.[59]

The demonic and deliverance amongst early Christians

Whilst Jesus emphasizes a certain uniqueness in what God was doing through and around him at in his healings and exorcisms,[60] there is also good evidence that he commissioned his followers to drive out demons, and that they actually did so during his lifetime. Most prominent is the tradition of the sending out of the twelve and the seventy(-two).[61] The reference in the commissioning charge to performing exorcisms may reflect Mark's own interest (it is not in the Q source); but there is independent evidence that Jesus's followers were involved in exorcism in the story of "the unknown exorcist" (Mark 9:38), and the report of the seventy-two (Luke 10:19), both generally considered historically reliable, and of their doing so "in the name of Jesus."[62]

Concerning the extent of deliverance ministry amongst Christians post-Easter, the New Testament witness is more mixed. Twelftree sees no strong evidence that Mark's emphasis on exorcism represents a battle with the Romans, rather being a genuine battle against Satan at the personal, spiritual, and cosmic level. And in the context of Mark's main theme of discipleship, it seems that he views exorcism in the name of Jesus (imitating Jesus methods in "prayer" (Mark 9:28–29), seen as faith-filled statements to the demons in dependence on the Holy Spirit) as of primary importance in his readers' ministry, because through it their compassionate God is

---

58. Dow, "Case for Existence of Demons," 204–5.

59. Yamauchi, "Magic or Miracle?," 142–49.

60. Note also his reply to John the Baptist (Matt 11:2–6). Twelftree, *Jesus the Exorcist*, 118–21; Dunn, *Jesus and the Spirit*, 60–61.

61. These may have arisen from Mark 6:7–13. Palestinian elements, and the charge to proclaim "the kingdom of God" not Jesus, give evidence that they are not post-Easter. Twelftree, *In the Name of Jesus*, 49.

62. Ibid., 51–52.

eschatologically active in saving people from a mighty enemy.[63] Although Matthew makes only minor changes in the tradition, his Great Commission is significant.[64] Luke-Acts broadens the scope of the demonic. In his statement of Jesus's ministry "doing good and healing all who were under the power of the devil" (Acts 10:38), he suggests that all sickness has an evil, demonic dimension, even though it may not be caused by demons;[65] and in all healing, God's adversary is being subdued.[66] In Acts, Luke continues to signal that exorcism was part of the early Christians' regular activities (Acts 5:12–16; 8:4–8), for Peter (5:16), Paul (16:16–18; 19:11–12), and particularly for Philip in the context of evangelism (8:7), as the continuing activity of Jesus himself through the power of the same eschatological Spirit (Acts 1:1, 4; 2:4) upon his followers (and even their clothing, 19:12).[67]

John's Gospel further widens the scope of the demonic to bring a very different perspective. Demon-possession is recognized, but curiously only as a charge brought against Jesus on a number of occasions. Yet Satan still has a major role to play, in fact a much bigger role which helps to explain this anomaly. Whilst the Synoptics see occasional exorcisms as pre-figuring the defeat of Satan (but say little connecting this to the cross), for John the whole of Jesus's ministry is a battle with Satan and the realm of darkness, focused on its climax, his victory on the cross.[68] This is a grand cosmic exorcism involving the heavenly realm—looking to the cross (12:23–24, 33), Jesus says, "Now is the time for judgment on this world; now the prince of this world will be driven out" (12:31); John wants nothing to distract from this, or for relatively commonplace and ambiguous exorcisms to take away from his unambiguously divine and stupendous miracles, which point to his identity.[69] Instead, the irony of the Pharisees' charge of demon possession, and associated unbelievable lies (7:20; 10:20–21), is that it is they, as children of the devil the father of lies, who are blinded with error and "demon

---

63. Ibid., 127–28.

64. Matthew widens the scope with Jesus's open-ended charge to the disciples in 10:18–19, implying it is to be fulfilled after he has gone through his Great Commission to them—"all authority has been given to me.... Therefore *in going* (πορευθέντες, aorist participle, still to be fulfilled and open-ended) make disciples... teaching them to obey everything I have commanded you" (28:19–20). Ibid., 164–67.

65. Whilst some sickness is specifically ascribed to evil spirits (Luke 13:10–17), other accounts have no mention of demons (e.g., the lepers in 5:12–16).

66. Twelftree, *In the Name of Jesus*, 133–34; *Christ Triumphant*, 104.

67. *In the Name of Jesus*, 142–54.

68. Note the use of "darkness" and "night," reaching a climax after Satan enters into Judas. John 9:4; 11:10; 13:27–30.

69. Twelftree, *In the Name of Jesus*, 194–97.

possessed," not him (8:40–52). The continuous battle is primarily between truth and lies—Jesus is "full of grace and truth" (1:14, cf. 14:6), and it is Jesus statement, "You will know the truth, and the truth will set you free" (8:32) that prompts the discussion centering on demon possession.[70]

The other epistles have some discourse relating to the devil, spirits, and rebellious angels;[71] but only indirect references to deliverance or exorcism. Anointing with oil "in the name of the Lord" (Jas 5:14) and reference to demons shuddering at the truth that "God is one" (2:19), may reflect knowledge of exorcistic practice;[72] however, there is also a general interest in the devil, who is to be resisted (3:15; 4:7), and evil is personified (1:13–14) in relation to sin. The fact that, compared to other apocalyptic writings, the epistles and Revelation consistently focus on the devil, regularly identified as Satan,[73] as the head of the wider range of demonic beings, is significant; it is further evidence that Jesus himself identified Satan as the "prince of demons" (Mark 3:22–23), bringing a sharper focus to the description of evil ruling powers that was otherwise only in the background of contemporary apocalyptic thought.

Other specific issues for debate arise in the Pauline epistles, and that is where we now turn.

Paul, principalities and powers, and "the heavenly realms"

Some scholars (e.g., Nicholaus Walter) assert that Paul did not know the narrative tradition of Jesus. There are only enough clear references to show that he knew the bare bones of Jesus lineage, family, and the meal on the night he was betrayed.[74] However, there are strong indications that he not only shared Jesus belief in the existence of demons and Satan,[75] but also

70. The scale of the battle is also cosmic in the Johannine letters (e.g., "the whole world is under the control of the evil one."(5:19), and in different language in Revelation (e.g., 12:7–12, Satan being thrown to the earth possibly alluding to the victory of the cross (John 12:31), before Satan's final defeat (20:7–8)). Ibid., 200–205.

71. For example, 1 Pet 3:18–19, 22, see 8.3 below; Heb 2:14, see 8.4.

72. "Shudder" was used in some exorcistic texts to describe the reaction of demons to them; and creedal statements such as this one (εἰς ἐσιν ὁ θεος, cf. Deut 6:4), often found their way into the vocabulary of exorcists, e.g., using "the God of Abraham, Isaac, and Jacob" as a source of power-authority. Twelftree, *In the Name of Jesus*, 179–80.

73. At least in the Pauline corpus (see footnote 75) and in Revelation—2:9, 13, 24; 3:9; 12:9; 20:2, 7.

74. E.g., Gal 4.4, Rom 1:3; 9:5; 1 Cor 9:5; Gal 1:19; 1 Cor 11:23–25. See Twelftree, *In the Name of Jesus*, 60.

75. Specific references to Satan in undisputed Pauline letters are Rom 16:20, 1 Cor 5:5; 7:5; 2 Cor 2:10–11; 11:14–15; 1 Thess 2:18 (cf. 2 Thess 2:9; also 1 Tim 1:20; 5:15).

Jesus's ministry of exorcism. The strongest clue is Rom 15:18–19, when he summarizes his ministry as "what Christ has accomplished through me . . . by what I have said and done—by the power of signs and miracles, through the power of the Spirit . . . from Jerusalem to Illyricum." It is reasonable to infer Paul considered himself to have conducted miracles with Jesus as his model;[76] as Luke also portrayed him in Acts, including powerful exorcisms such as 16:16–18. Whilst some consider Luke's accounts to be exaggerated, there is good intratextual evidence this is historical.[77]

However, the most important language that implies a demonic dimension to Paul's cosmology is that of "principalities and powers," which has been variously interpreted. We began to discuss these in relation to Nigel Wright, Wink, and Yong.[78] Berkhof brought the language of principalities and powers to the fore, linking this with the political and economic spheres; he re-affirmed these powers were created by God as primordial structures of earthly existence, but sees them as fallen, maintaining some role in preserving the world, dethroned rather than destroyed by Christ's triumph on the cross, still awaiting their full redemption at the end of the age.[79] Yoder developed this in advocating non-violent resistance to the powers, and Ellul saw the "new demons" of the modern world as the various "isms" that need to be exposed, critiqued and confronted.[80]

Demons are only mentioned once in these—"but the sacrifices of pagans are offered to demons, not to God" (1 Cor 10:20–21).

76. Paul's phrases "signs and wonders" (2 Cor 12.12), and "word and power" (1 Cor 4:20), also support this. Twelftree, *In the Name of Jesus*, 61–71.

77. Evidence of eyewitness details in this "we" passage (e.g., Paul's annoyance, "servants of the Most High God," rarely used in the early church), outweigh Haenchen's weak arguments against its historicity. The sons of Sceva exorcising "by the Jesus whom Paul preaches" (Acts 19:13–16) also implies Paul was himself an exorcist. Ibid., 71–73.

78. See chapters 5 and 6. Both Arnold and Yong have reviewed the history of interpretation of these Pauline powers, Yong begins from Tillich, who in the 1930s saw all of political history as a battlefield of the divine and the demonic. Yong, *In the Days of Caesar*, 135–48; Arnold, *Ephesians: Power and Magic*, 42–51.

79. Yong, *In the Days of Caesar*, 139–40; Berkhof, *Christ and the Powers*, 23, 42. Instead of seeing the powers as either good angels or fallen angels, Berkhof links them with *stoicheia*, ("the elements . . . the framework of creation . . . such as the Jewish law, the powers of politics and philosophy . . ."). The believer is not to strive *against* the Orders, but to battle for God's redemptive intention for them, for "they have become gods" (Gal 4:8). Berkhof describes how while studying in Berlin (1937) "I myself experienced almost literally how such Powers may be 'in the air'" (cf. Eph 6:10, 2:2). Ibid., 16–19, 23, 25.

80. Both of these influenced Wink in his advocacy of non-violent resistance to the Domination System. See Yong, *In the Days of Caesar*, 142–43; Yoder, *The Politics of Jesus*; Ellul, *The Subversion of Christianity*; Wink, *The Powers That Be: Theology for a New Millennium*, 37–62, 112–27.

In the debate concerning what the powers actually refer to, Wesley Carr was the first to recover a spiritual interpretation over against the demythologizing of Bultmann, by radically proposing them to be essentially positive angelic powers in their regulatory functions, "led in triumphal procession" rather than "disarmed" in Col 2:15 (seeing the dualistic evil aspect as a second-century gnostic interpolation, including Eph 6:12). Several have however exposed weaknesses in his exposition, notably Arnold.[81]

The cosmological backdrop to Paul's thought has long been recognized.[82] Arnold has forcefully defended the traditional view that the powers are personalized cosmic forces of evil (evil spirits and hostile angels), noting that the majority of first century readers of Paul's letters would be immersed in a milieu of magical beliefs, and he would expect the terms to be understood as the demonic powers they feared.[83] Beker had argued that Paul restricted contemporary apocalyptic terminology to apocalyptic sections (mainly 1 Cor 15:24–28, Rom 8:38–9 where ἄγγελοι are clearly hostile powers), as evidence that he has anthropologically reinterpreted them—becoming death, sin, the law and the flesh personified in ethical contexts. However, whilst agreeing that Paul prefers such terms especially in Romans, Arnold responds by listing ethical contexts where the language of personalized evil forces is also used.[84]

Wink follows from Beker in arguing that Ephesians has travelled further down this road of demythologization.[85] However, Beker's own criterion would argue against this, there being few references to sin (1), law (1), death (0) or the flesh (ten approximately, but mostly "in the flesh" and only one (2:3) in any sense personified); but multiple references to the "personal" or "mythical" powers, such that if anything Ephesians has been

---

81. Arnold argues for the integrity of Eph 6:12, and produces evidence that belief in the demonic realm is substantially verifiable in the first century AD. Arnold, "Critique of Wesley Carr," 71–87; Carr, *Angels and Principalites*; Arnold, *Ephesians: Power and Magic*, 47–48.

82. MacGregor, "Principalities and Powers"; Yong, *In the Days of Caesar*, 146. Cullmann argues strongly that the plural ἐξουσίαι in Paul always refers to *heavenly* powers—though in Romans 13 (and some other places) agreeing it double references also to the human aspect of "the powers." Cullmann, *Christ and Time*.

83. Arnold, *Ephesians: Power and Magic*, 50–51.

84. For example, Satan can destroy the flesh (1 Cor 5:4–5), tempt (1 Cor 7:5), scheme to use people (2 Cor 2:11) and deceive by appearing as an angel of light (2 Cor 11:14); and partnering with demons by participating in pagan sacrifice is ethically abhorrent to Paul (1 Cor 10:19–21). These contexts, and others where Beker himself accepts (e.g., blinding (2 Cor 4:4), deceiving (Rom 7:10), and hindering (1 Thess 2:18)), evidence Paul's concern to respond to them where relevant to the Christian life, rather than give detailed apocalyptic descriptions. Ibid., 130–32.

85. Wink, *Naming the Powers*, 61.

"remythologized."[86] More significantly, Eph 2:2-3 shows clearly how in Pauline anthropology the internal power of "the flesh" within man is coordinated under the external "ruler of the authority of the air" (τον ἀρχοντα τῆς ἐξουσίας του ἀέρος), together intent on exerting dominion over man in this present age.[87]

Ephesians displays a higher degree of realized eschatology than earlier Pauline writings, probably reflecting the author's desire to address particular spiritual needs in the readers.[88] We can notice three key interlinked concepts in this eschatology. Firstly, the emphasis on the resurrection and exaltation of Christ, shared by believers who are "co-seated" with Christ (2:6), and thus in Christ in a position of power and authority far superior to the hostile cosmic "powers." Whilst similar to Col 3:1, this concept is not found in undisputed Paulines; however, the governing phrase "in Christ Jesus" co-ordinates with Paul's strong emphasis on ἐν Χριστῷ and participation in the death and resurrection of Christ (e.g., Rom 6; Gal 2:20), as well as the idea of a present experience of heaven (e.g., Phil 3:20).[89] Secondly, the "once/now" (ποτε/νῦν) schema throughout 2:1-22 and in 5:8 ("once" darkness, "now" light in the Lord) is central to the epistle's thought. This emphasizes both the absolute transfer of dominions experienced by the believer, a decisive break with the past (cf. Col 1:12-13); and the shift to a vertical spatial emphasis rather than a time antithesis emphasizes that they are no longer "under" the power of the hostile supernatural "powers" (2:1-6). Thirdly, the expression ἐν τοῖς ἐπουρανίοις ("in the heavenlies") is regularly used in close connection with both divine power and evil "powers" in Ephesians. It is generally agreed this is used with a consistent meaning, and had some local significance for the readers. While some argue for an existential interpretation (Schlier) or a Platonic eternal timeless reality, Lincoln has demonstrated its use in a variety of Jewish contexts (e.g., six times in Hebrews), as well as the adjectival form in Paul, which make its

---

86. Wink's case is primarily based on other considerations, as discussed in chapters 5 and 6, and further below. See also Arnold, *Ephesians: Power and Magic*, 47-51.

87. Wink's claim that the author of Ephesians "has taken a radical step away from the mythicization of evil in personified demonic spirits" lacks evidence—there is no basis for interpreting ἐξουσία in this context as abstract rather than personified. Ibid., 132-33, 207; Wink, *Naming the Powers*, 83.

88. For example the disorientation of many in the Hellenistic world as they came under Rome's power, perceived as a destabilizing threat of evil demonic powers in the once-ordered cosmos. Rather than the escapism of mystical cults (e.g., the Ephesian Artemis cult), against these threats the Ephesian author emphasizes the *present* experience of salvation. Arnold, *Ephesians: Power and Magic*, 146-47.

89. Also Gal 4:26, 1 Cor 15:47-49, 2 Cor 12:2-3. Ibid., 148.

similarity to οὐρανοὶ much more likely.[90] It is also used as a possible location for a demon in a Jewish exorcistic script of the Solomonic magical tradition (which has links with Ephesus). Its use in Ephesians seems to connect with Paul's eschatology which saw in the Christ-event an overlap between the age to come and the present age; the writer thus uses primarily spatial (ἐν τοῖς ἐπουρανίοις) but also temporal terms (the two age structure). The passage on spiritual warfare (6:10–20) clearly reveals that the eschatology is not fully realized, with the devil and a host of evil "powers" still set on assailing believers, who can nevertheless resist them on the basis not of magical techniques, but of strength arising from their union with Christ as children of the new age.[91] Thus, as Lincoln puts it, "He is under no illusion that sharing in Christ's victory brings removal from the sphere of conflict. Those who have been *seated* with Christ in the heavenly realms are at the same time those who must *walk* in the world (cf. 2:10; 4:1, 17; 5:2, 8, 15) and who must *stand* in the midst of the continuing battle with the powers (cf. 6:11–16)."[92]

Having thus reviewed the biblical material relating to Satan, demons, and the principalities and "the heavenly realms," we can now revisit the ontological and cosmological debate concerning the true nature of evil powers.

The ontology of evil: rebellious spiritual beings

Post-modernism has again opened up the realm of spiritual beings, whether angelic or demonic, to renewed theological discussion, taking experiences in this realm seriously. However, we should not stop there—as Fackre observes, "the upper cosmos is not a fictive realm. Biblical ontology, while modest, is not missing."[93]

As we have seen, Boyd and others take the New Testament cosmology almost at face value; but many other theologians, including our other two dialogue partners (both influenced by Wink), are reluctant to do so. Wright seeks to be a non-ontological realist, with an essentially Barthian view of evil, and Yong in his triadic metaphysical scheme seems reluctant to speculate much concerning the nature of any invisible spiritual beings behind "the demonic" manifestations that he sees in the concrete material world. We therefore need to briefly reconsider the grounds for their objections.

Wink like most "moderns" finds it difficult to conceive of the real existence of angels, Satan and demons. But he also fears limiting or distorting

---

90. Lincoln, "The Heavenlies," 478–79. See also Gooder, *Only the Third Heaven?*
91. Arnold, *Ephesians: Power and Magic*, 150–57.
92. Section on "Eschatology," Lincoln, *Ephesians*, 20.
93. Fackre, "Angels Heard and Demons Seen," 356.

our understanding of evil through popular misconceptions associated with the images of Satan "that are served up in actual encounters with primordial evil":

> "Belief" in Satan serves only to provide a grid that one can superimpose on the actual experiential phenomenon in order to comprehend it, and even then the wrong kind of belief in Satan may do more harm than good, since it is usually so one-sided. But the phenomena itself is there, named or unnamed.[94]

Wright is more affected by the dangers of charismatic belief in "a paranoid universe," the deception that evil is more powerful than it is; and Yong seems frustrated by the "revelations" of Pentecostals of the names of multitudes of spirit beings in the unseen realm which may be of little value if fighting them is only "beating the air" and not connected with identifying, praying, and acting against the concrete manifestations of evil in individuals and communities.[95] He is also concerned with the dangers of harmful and insensitive deliverance ministry, and of "demonizing our opponents" in political contexts.[96] However, such problems could be addressed primarily by seeking a more accurate description of the nature of evil and its manifestations, and appropriate accompanying theological praxis—rather than attempting to "deconstruct" its nature, or to reduce it to a description of its observable phenomena.

So far we have focused on the biblical New Testament evidence for a positive ontology for Satan and demons. Like many charismatic thinkers, I do not wish to accept the worldview of early Christians uncritically.[97] A proposed positive ontology for demonic powers must be credible in relation to empirical evidence, and coherent both theologically and with insights from other disciplines.[98] Does present-day experience, and phenomenological investigation, confirm the biblical picture or call for radical reinterpretation? Has psychology produced better explanations for phenomena

---

94. Wink, *Unmasking the Powers*, 25.

95. See, for example, Yong, "Spiritual Discernment," 102–3.

96. See section 6.5.

97. Modern hermeneutical methods can help us, but we need not accept untenable presuppositions of many Western philosophical systems concerning supernatural reality. Theron, "A Critical Overview," 83.

98. The case for the existence of evil spiritual entities must also consider data from present experience, and undergo scrutiny from our society's "plausibility structures." Berger, *A Rumour of Angels*, 50–52; Dow, "Case for Existence of Demons," 199. However, whilst seeking coherence with other scholars, our faithful Christological focus means that aspects of our discernment "will be rejected by the world" (cf. John 15:26–27). Cartledge, *Practical Theology*, 61.

CONSTRUCTING A CHARISMATIC THEOLOGY OF SPIRITUAL WARFARE   201

labeled "demonic"? And does a sound philosophical metaphysics call for a non-personal ontology of evil, or even a "non-ontological" approach, or an appropriate personal ontology? So let us briefly examine the nature of evil forces from phenomenological and psychological viewpoints, before returning to metaphysics.

Many in the Western world are unlikely to interpret events as the action of demonic spiritual beings, primarily because it does not fit with their frame of reference or worldview.[99] Therefore an implausible metaphysical assertion needs to be examined with as little prejudice as possible in the light of the facts. We can try and explain the phenomena of exorcism only in categories of psychological science or "religious experience"; but we cannot disprove the existence of demons unless we assert that only what is empirically verifiable through our five senses truly exists (in which case God does not exist either).[100] However, with an open mind there is phenomenological evidence that can build a case for the existence of demons. Wiebe, for example, based on an analysis of Jesus's exorcism of the Gadarene demoniac and its evidence of transference behavior (destructive behavior in the man ceasing, suddenly replaced by the self-destructive actions of the pigs), postulates a case for finite spirits as theoretical entities.[101]

If similar effects were recorded on a number of occasions it would strengthen the case for their existence.[102] As evidenced earlier with many of the interviewed pioneers, "many of those with the greatest observational experience of this area of knowledge cannot but persist with explanations in

---

99. "We can easily accept that men and children froth at the mouth and that women go into cataleptic states . . . but what we may accept as facts has to be fitted to a theory, or more broadly a view of the universe." Smart, *The Phenomenon of Religion*, 147. The prevalence of "scientific method" makes "proving" the existence of spirits almost impossible—Karl Popper's maxim that any "rational" claim must be subject to falsification is still widely respected, even though it limits what can be counted as "science."

100. Dow, "Case for Existence of Demons," 203.

101. Using the logic of abduction, a form of inference from a series of data to the most probable cause, as proposed by C. S. Peirce. Wiebe, "Finite Spirits as Theoretical Entities"; "Deliverance in Philosophical Perspective."

102. Woolmer's logical mind was impressed by such transferences—the physical effect of an "evil presence" leaving a stable and almost knocking over a staff member, and an account of evil spirits leaving a village in Papua New Guinea and moving to the next—see section 3.5 and Woolmer, *Healing and Deliverance*, 344–45. On two of the few occasions I have been involved in deliverance ministry with someone previously involved in occult activities (one with Michael Green in 1980; another in 1986), I experienced an unseen, stifling force coming upon me after being commanded to leave another person—the first making me virtually unable to talk, until it was commanded to leave; the second nearly knocking me over, and temporarily stifling my ability to vocalize.

terms of demonic realities."[103] In addition, some professional psychiatrists and therapists have recorded changing their views on this issue towards a belief in the existence of demons.[104] In particular, Betty has listed the evidence from a health perspective, arguing that the experience of the victims, the universality of phenomena (including bizarre unnatural and superhuman aspects) across the world and different religions, and the relative success of religious exorcism compared to psychiatric treatment provides very strong evidence for the existence of "evil spirits."[105] It is reductionist to use a psychological theory such as MPD (which can explain the split personalities of many psychiatric patients), to explain all "evil spirits" as "*alter*" personalities, as clear differences have been observed between the two.[106]

Similarly, though the modern mind is often skeptical of such accounts, the reports of those claiming to have seen demons in one form or another, for example during charismatic prayer ministry, should not be dismissed as necessarily hallucinatory or auto-suggestive; some I interviewed admitted to regularly having such experiences of seeing what was going on in the spiritual realm when they were praying, though often reluctant to speak

---

103. Dow, "Case for Existence of Demons," 203–4. See also Appendix 2, table 1, and analysis in chapter 3.

104. Matt Lin describes how through anthropology and psychology he tried to explain away all manifestations of demonic activity, until experiencing how simple deliverance prayer worked where nothing else did. He later discovered hundreds of professional therapists (the Association of Christian Therapists) who combined healing and deliverance prayer with their professional practice. Linn, *Deliverance Prayer*, 5–7; Theron, "A Critical Overview," 83, 86. Scott Peck underwent a similar change of mind after much investigation—see Peck, *People of the Lie*.

105. Betty particularly cites Martin's five carefully documented cases, and two of Scott Peck, who concluded "Difficult and dangerous though they were, the exorcisms I witnessed were successful. I cannot imagine how otherwise the two patients could have been healed. They are both alive and very well today. I have every reason to believe that had they not had their exorcisms they would each be dead by now." *People of the Lie*, 189; Martin, *Hostage to the Devil*. Quoted in Betty, "Growing Evidence for "Demonic Possession," 22. Betty's arguments are particularly significant as he has no particular religious standpoint; charismatics would undoubtedly interpret differently his evidence from spiritualists talking with spirits. For an earlier contrary argument, see Cortes and Gatti, *The Case against Possessions and Exorcisms*.

106. Whilst patients are usually unaware of "alter" personalities in Multiple Personality Disorder (MPD) until near the end of treatment, they are usually very aware of "evil spirits" which they discern as an *alien* personality (Peck); and whilst it is impossible to "cast out" an "*alter*," being mostly fragments of a person's personality, casting out an oppressive spirit is not only possible but likely, when the necessary expertise is available, causing it to disappear completely (Betty/MacNutt). See Peck, *People of the Lie*, 192–93; Betty, "Growing Evidence for 'Demonic Possession,'" 23; MacNutt, *Deliverance from Evil Spirits*, 231.

of it openly for fear of ridicule.[107] Such aspects of the phenomenology of charismatic experience of the Holy Spirit, and of the demonic, whilst highly resistant to verification or falsification, would be fruitful areas for further phenomenological research.[108]

This does not mean that inexplicable phenomena in people's lives should uncritically be accepted as evidence of demonic presence; some practitioners noted that those presenting as demonized were often the least likely to be so.[109] And whilst some charismatic pioneers maintained that all poltergeist phenomena are caused by evil spirits,[110] many psychologists view them as best explained as "psychokinetic activity" linked to psychological stress, usually in a younger person living in the house.[111] More respectful interdisciplinary dialogue amongst practitioners, particularly in relation to people with psychiatric problems, would be very helpful here.[112]

Metaphysics and personhood

I believe we should be cautious in using a metaphysics which, for whatever laudable reasons, privileges the physical over the spiritual. Yong's Peircean metaphysics is helpful, and may be appropriate in relating to the arena of scientific enquiry;[113] but it has limitations in investigating the metaphysics of "the heavenly realms." Yong's view is that "because the material world

---

107. Sometimes "seeing" or "sensing" demons is witnessed by more than one person—e.g., Ian and his wife, see chapter 4. MacNutt describes how trusted helpers who could sense the presence of demons (in this case, through sensitivity to air pressure), independently located a demon in a particular spot in his church. As at St. George's, he also describes people in his ministry team having a gift of discernment, whom he regularly asks "has that one gone? What's surfacing now?" in a matter-of-fact way. *Deliverance from Evil Spirits*, 175, 265.

108. Those who have documented a large number of cases provide useful data here, e.g., Richards, *But Deliver Us from Evil*; Koch, *Between Christ and Satan*.

109. Pytches Interview 1.4.04, Walker Interview 28.3.04.

110. For example, see Dow, *Explaining Deliverance*, 38–39.

111. See Perry, *Deliverance*; Richards, *But Deliver Us from Evil*, 200–206. As with mental illness, psychological and spiritual (demonic) explanations and treatments are not necessarily mutually exclusive. MacNutt, *Deliverance from Evil Spirits*, 75.

112. Linn presents the report from one such symposium in 1980 convened by US Catholic bishops. Linn, *Deliverance Prayer*, 13–14. See also the Church of England healing and deliverance consultation report: Perry, Gunstone, and others, "A Time to Heal."

113. Its triadic structure helpfully gives a fuller, more integrated account of reality than binary schemes which can become dipolar dualisms (such as "God"/"the world" in process theology, or "inner"/"outer" in Wink's more limited "panentheistic" approach). It is also well-suited to the scientific-theological interface, and evolutionary theories of emergence of human self-consciousness. See section 6.5.

only permits partial glimpses of the spiritual world, discerning the spirits will always be inherently ambiguous."[114] However, there is little ambiguity in the direct, straightforward way Jesus talks about, and confronts, Satan and demonic spirits. It is thus hermeneutically appropriate to begin from what Scripture clearly reveals here, and bring this into a critical dialogue with relevant insights from science and philosophical thinking.

First we need to discuss what kind of ontology Scripture and experience reveals for Satan and his demons, in particular the controversial use of the term "personal." Wright's attempt to label Satan and the evil realm as "non-personal" reflects a current theological trend to discuss the "persons" of the Trinity, and particularly the Spirit, in relational terms.[115] In Trinitarian terms this relationality is a positive one of reciprocal love, thus an inappropriate category to use in assessing the personhood of evil spiritual beings.[116] This is also one reason for Yong's objection to a personalist ontology for demonic beings, seeing it as a philosophical category mistake.[117]

However, I believe the use of the term "personal" is still appropriate. Firstly there is the scriptural evidence for such beings having a degree of autonomous action—Scripture credits Satan (and sometimes evil spirits) consistently with a level of independent action or agency (the devil tempts, prowls, speaks, etc.). And if the observable phenomena, and the biblical accounts, suggest that the Satanic possesses characteristics such as malignance, willfulness, and intelligent scheming, as well as agency with a degree of rational thought that can speak through humans, then it is natural to characterize them as in some sense personal forces.[118] And secondly, the very nature of evil is not just something "destructive," but is rebellion against God. Yong recognizes this in describing the "firstness" of the demonic as "a destructive

---

114. Yong, "Spiritual Discernment," 106.

115. Yong also emphasizes this relationality of the Spirit, who is thus for him truly personal. See section 6.4 and 6.5.

116. Though not necessarily completely so—Jesus points out that even tax-collectors and sinners love those who love them (Matt 5:46–47), and affirms that even Satan's kingdom has to cooperate in a united way if it is to stand (Mark 3:24–26/Matt 12:24–26); and there is indirect evidence that demons communicate with one another and appoint a spokesman—"have you come to destroy *us?*" (Matt 8:29–31, Mark 1:24).

117. He argues: "Only God is truly personal, . . . we are all distorted persons/personalities. . . . Evil can only be the opposite, the destruction of personhood/personality. . . . Yes, evil, the satan, and demons can be said to 'intend' the destruction of human beings, but only insofar as such destructiveness concerns & relates to human beings, not just in the abstract." Yong, "Response to Chapter 6."

118. Boyd (who like Wink sees "the powers" as having had a role as God's servants before turning rebellious) emphasizes this particularly in wishing to re-characterize angels as free agents who choose to serve God or to rebel against him.

reality opposing the goodness of God,"[119] but later he emphasizes "destructiveness" (as arising "inexplicably") more than opposition to God.[120] The evidence of Scripture, however, and the existential experience of Anglican charismatics, is that the essence of evil is not just destruction or suffering, but a willful rebellion against God.[121] Its origin may be "inexplicable";[122] but once there, its rebellious force possesses a strength and malignancy that requires a "personal" center of volition, which cannot be reduced (as Yong is in danger of doing) to a nebulous force-field.[123] This is also a weakness in Wright's characterization of evil as real but non-ontological, and only possessing a reduced Boethian personhood with a rationality that might only be on the level of "machine intelligence."

The solution firstly as we have seen has been posited by Noble and Green, that we see Satan and demons as damaged persons and "anti-persons," parasitic on human wickedness.[124] Just as we in our sinful rebellion are all to a degree distorted persons contaminated by evil, then if Satan and demons are fallen angels they can also be distorted or decaying "persons"—much more radically so, but still experienced as malevolent "personal" spirit beings; and Luke 22:31 suggests that even in their rebellion there remains some possibility of interaction with God (cf. Job 1). The fact that only God is *fully* personal and relational, does not stop fallen personal beings from willfully attacking aspects of the gift of personhood (Noble's "anti-persons"), particularly relationship with God which they have themselves rejected.[125]

---

119. Yong, *Discerning the Spirits*, 129.

120. "Spiritual Discernment," 90. His caution here reflects the philosophical difficulty of what God created as good turning to evil; but this can be overcome is by a "necessary condition theodicy" based on the free will defense. See section 8.3.

121. Early charismatics especially experienced evil as "the god of this age" (2 Cor 4) opposing reconciling people with God in evangelism—see section 8.5. The oblique New Testament references to angels that fell include rebellion language ("sinned" 2 Pet 2:4, "did not keep their positions of authority" Jude 6, "war in heaven" Rev 12:7); paralleling "a strong theme of rebellion" in the Second Temple period stories of the *bene elohim* (Genesis 6). Wright, *The Origin of Evil Spirits*, 221.

122. Augustine calls it a "mystery of finite freedom," that the free, originally good creature originated an evil act. Augustine, *The City of God*, 12.7 (203).

123. See sections 6.3 and 6.4.

124. See section 5.6 (also for Noble's quotation from Green). Noble recognizes that personality is something we are born with, "but we will be damaged persons unless we develop into loving persons in a matrix of stable, loving relationships." Green, *I Believe in Satan's Downfall*, 30, 126; Noble, "The Spirit World," 217.

125. The Lutheran/Reformed debate as to whether the image of God is still present in humankind after the fall parallels this discussion—see Horton, "Post-Reformation Reformed Anthropology," 45–69.

We have seen that Barth's *das Nicthige* lies behind Wright's non-ontological stance.[126] However, Barth goes too far in characterizing *das Nichtige* as a demonic power without ascribing it any material substance or center of rebellious volition. The destructive disorder of primal chaos can be experienced as an evil threat, as the OT images of primal monsters vividly convey;[127] but this can only be experienced as "evil" by self-conscious beings in whom the prospect of return to the *nihil* fills us with fear, essentially the fear of death and eternal destruction (Luke 12:4-5). In Scripture this fear is associated both with loss of security in relationship to God (Rom 8:15), arising from human rebellion; and with the action of the devil who seeks to enslave humans into his rebellious opposition to God (Heb 2:14-15). A key characteristic of evil is therefore volitional; only through the rebellion of created free agents does *das Nichtige* truly develop the menacing character of evil.[128] Augustine's instinct here is more accurate than Barth's, for he recognizes rebellion as the root of evil;[129] and whilst his speculation concerning free will mostly relates to mankind's sinful rebellion, he hints at the same rebellious potential in the angelic realm.[130]

Yong, by characterizing the demonic as "destructive opposition" but in defining "the powers" as essentially corrupted human structures, tends towards locating the evil of rebellion purely in the will of human beings, which has its dangers.[131] Both Wink and Yong display a reluctance to go beyond the location of the demonic in the spiritual interiority of corporate structures.[132] Yong considers Wink's characterization of these spiritual reali-

---

126. See section 5.3. Yong similarly characterizes evil ontologically as the absence of God—see section 6.3.

127. Barth thus grounds *das Nichtige* biblically in Gen 1:2.

128. Boyd, *Satan and the Problem of Evil*, 339-45. Boyd proposes that by their free choice, angels can freely choose what God negates, and so *das Nichtige* becomes actualized.

129. "A wicked will is the cause of all evil." Augustine, *On Free Choice of the Will*, 3.17 (126).

130. He sees pride (*superbia*) as "the root of all sin" as causing the devil's fall. Ibid. 3.25, 146-48. See also Augustine, *The City of God*, 11.13.

131. If the choice and responsibility for evil is purely a human one, the temptation is to demonize individuals and "wrestle against flesh and blood" rather than evil "in the heavenly realms."

132. Yong commends Wink's view that the Powers in their "invisible, intangible interiority" are not "mere" symbols, but point to something real. However, both appear unwilling to accept the biblical picture of rebellious *spiritual beings* as more than symbolic. Thus Wink, in his otherwise insightful characterization of the "prince of Persia" (Daniel 10), considers such beings as symbols for the national spirit—Wink, *Unmasking the Powers*, 88-94; Boyd, *God at War*, 340-41. Although Yong goes further than Wink's dipolar metaphysic (an inner, potentially demonic spiritual reality in outer

ties as "fields of force" as appropriate for the "thirdness" of the demonic, but despite adding the qualities of the demonic as its true "firstness," he does not give demonic powers any "secondness" of their own (perhaps seeing them as "parasitic"), only seeing the "concrete" secondness of the demonic as embodied in sinful human actions or corporate structures—which for him are essentially human, blurring any distinction between human and spiritual evil powers.[133] Boyd and Arnold expose this weakness by arguing that despite some ambiguity in places in Paul's terms,[134] there is a clear Pauline distinction between "earthly" and "heavenly" powers, particularly in admonishing the Ephesians not to struggle against flesh and blood but against "spiritual forces of wickedness *in the heavenly realms*" (Eph 6:12).

Yong aims to avoid naturalistic reductionism in relation to the powers, but also both "rigid dualism on the one hand and polytheism on the other."[135] But some dualism is unavoidable—N. T. Wright lists ten types of duality, some being normal Judaistic thought, notably a theological/ontological duality, that there are heavenly beings other than the one God.[136] Boyd agrees, that the biblical worldview was never one of a monotheistic God in glorious isolation, but a "henotheism"; if such "gods" are exposed as rebellious angelic beings parasitic on human societal structures and the sinfulness of human beings, but now disempowered at the cross, the glory of the one true God is restored with no danger of "polytheism"; instead we can be rightly empowered to enforce the defeat of such spiritual powers.[137]

---

corporate structures) he only accepts that "the powers over the human realm *were understood* among the ancient Hebrews as members of the divine council, and by the early Christians as angels," instead defining such biblical powers as "prelapsarian natural, human and social realities . . . good as created by God." Yong, *In the Days of Caesar*, 162.

133. MacInnes agreed with Wink, over against Wagner, that "the mistake has been to try and produce a structure of demonic principalities apart from the human structure of principalities . . . your best understanding of the spiritual hierarchy is in terms of human hierarchy"; but is less reductionist, recognizing how "the demonic starts to manipulate that." MacInnes Interview 6.4.06.

134. For example in his use of ἀρχαί or δυνάμις; such as we also find, for example, in his use of words such as σάρξ or σῶμα.

135. Yong, *In the Days of Caesar*, 164.

136. The "normal" ones also include a moral duality between good and evil; but the three to avoid that posit a radical split in the whole of reality are: a theological/moral Zoroastrian duality between two ultimate sources of all that is; a cosmological duality seeing the physical world as a shadow of the "real world" (Plato); and an epistemological duality between what can be known by merely human means and that which can be known by divine revelation alone. N. T. Wright, *The New Testament and the People of God*, 253–56.

137. Boyd, *God at War*, 119–21. See also Wink's description (cf. Dan 10:13, 20–21) of "a complex antagonistic henotheism in which, under the sole sovereignty and

And there is no danger of "rigid dualism" if both theology and "the liturgical imagination is focused on the lordship of Christ and the majesty of God, not on the principalities and powers per se."[138]

Wink postulates a range of "powers" at work in the world, some of which are demonic in character, but potentially able to be redeemed by our choices.[139] Yong's construction however attempts to further simplify "the powers," as essentially natural and human structures that are fallen, and so demonically influenced to various degrees, but thus capable of redemption. This rightly reminds us that evil is essentially parasitic; that on earth it is us humans who have the responsibility for our wrong choices, and to seek the redemption of human institutions and structures through Christ; and that evil powers often masquerade as having more power than they do, to terrify. It also helpfully highlights "the unholy trinity," that evil is located not just in the *devil* and his cohorts, but in the human structures of this *world*, and the sinful choices we make in our own *flesh*, which will profoundly affect our theological praxis.[140] However, it is in danger of minimizing aspects of the reality and virulence of evil powers that are attested by Jesus and throughout the Scriptures; including the reality that ultimately our adversary is the devil (1 Pet 5:8), a spiritual force in the heavenly realms behind all our struggles with evil (Eph 6:12), who needs to be resisted directly (1 Pet 5:9; Jas 4.4).

8.3 The origin of evil—the case for fallen angels

In charismatic Anglican context, unlike the question of the reality of evil spiritual beings, that of their origin is relatively insignificant, being primarily theoretical rather than practical. It does however relate indirectly to our theoretical discussion as to why evil is there at all, with implications for the ontology of evil. If the theological case for Satan and demons being fallen angels is a strong one, the non-ontological view of evil becomes less tenable. Yong, for example, sees answering the question concerning the origin of evil as also deciding where the perverting evil intention is located, and thus how "personal" the demonic is. In chapter 7 we concluded that, whilst the biblical case for a fall of angels as the origin of evil is not strong on purely

---

permission of God, vying forces are able to prevail against one another to determine the unfolding of history." Wink, *Naming the Powers*, 27–28.

138. Yong, *In the Days of Caesar*, 165. Yong advocates this in liturgical praxis (see section 6.4), and many charismatics have experienced it—e.g., at St. George's, see chapter 4.

139. Wink, *Naming the Powers*, 5.

140. N. T. Wright's analysis of evil similarly reflects its three main dimensions—see 8.5 below, and Wright, *Evil and the Justice of God*, 48–50.

CONSTRUCTING A CHARISMATIC THEOLOGY OF SPIRITUAL WARFARE

exegetical grounds, it is stronger than the other alternatives proposed by Cook, especially taking into account evidence from intertestamental apocalyptic.[141] Here we consider briefly the more philosophical questions.

The key philosophical objection is how something God created good could become evil. For Karl Barth, Nigel Wright, and Amos Yong, it is an offence to God's goodness that some of his angels, created good and full of his light and glory, could choose to rebel and become the personification of evil. Wright thus suggests that evil emerged from the fall of man, who, faced with the frailty of his contingent existence chose to take his destiny in his own hands and lost connection with God's presence. He sees all evil as arising this way, abandoning the concept of "fallen angels," seeing the biblical evidence for an angelic fall as too slender.[142] Yong agrees that evil gains its power from human sinful rebellion, then becoming an "emergent reality," dispensing with the need for a positive ontology for evil spiritual beings.[143]

Yong's specific objection is that if Lucifer was created good, rebellion could not have arisen out of his personality; and he could not still be "personal," as God alone is truly personal.[144] However, Yong here seems too constrained by philosophical and linguistic considerations. If human beings are still personal after rebelling against our creator (though "distorted persons" because of the fall), then there is no inherent contradiction in postulating "personal" angelic beings that have inexplicably rebelled, as Augustine asserted. Kreeft demonstrates simply this logical possibility: "If angels are persons (selves) they have intellects and wills. If they have wills, they can choose between good and evil. . . . If they choose evil, they become evil. So if there are good spirits, there can be evil spirits."[145] And in biblical thought, there is no sense of contradiction, simply a few statements concerning angels that have rebelled.[146] This accords with Boyd's stronger "free will argument"; we don't have to look further than free will itself as the explanation for choices that have evil consequences, rather than tie ourselves in philosophical knots.[147] So whilst Yong argues "we can't say God created a creature with the capacity to do evil (for this would locate the origins in

141. See section 7.4.
142. See section 5.5, and *Theology of the Dark Side*, 67–73.
143. See sections 6.3 and 6.4, and Yong, *In the Days of Caesar*, 162–63. For his recent thesis of the emergence of demonic (and angelic) realities, see *The Spirit of Creation*, 217–21.
144. "Response to Chapter 6."
145. Kreeft, *Angels (and Demons)*, 111.
146. Primarily 2 Pet 2:4, Jude 6, and Rev 12:7–9; and 1 Tim 3:6 concerning Satan. See section 7.4.
147. See section 7.5.

God as creator)," Boyd would say God did just that—in Barthian terms "nothingness" was a necessary but non-ontological concomitant of creation, but with the potential to be actualized if self-determining agents can freely choose that which God negates; thus "nothing" has become "something," as the character of an angel chooses to take on the nature of evil.[148] Williams discusses the objection that if angels were living in God's immediate presence they could not fall; but following Aquinas argues that only those who freely chose to serve God were transformed into the wholly good beings angels are today. Whilst God is responsible for creating the possibility of a fall resulting in demons, this was intrinsic to creating creatures with significant free will (a good thing), and a necessary condition of the existence of angels (who are wholly good things). He sees no reason why God could not gift angels with significant free will.[149]

It is not surprising that St. George's liked Boyd's essentially "black and white" view of good and evil, where free agents are ultimately responsible for all evil and not God, whilst acknowledging the complexity of individual situations. However, not all will be convinced by some of his more controversial views (e.g., concerning "open theism").[150] But in seeking to make room for Hiebert's excluded middle,[151] Boyd's argument of complexity takes us a long way;[152] but concerning free will and sovereignty I suggest there remains a strong element of mystery concerning God's unfathomable wisdom. In Scripture, God's ultimate control over demonic activity is not only witnessed in Job, but also in Jesus's remark concerning Satan's asking permission (Luke 22:31–32).[153] Cullman's illustration, quoted by Woolmer, may come nearest to describing the sovereignty of God in relation to demonic freedom—God has the devil on the end of a long leash, but at times seeming to be able to escape from it, and to be fought against.[154]

---

148. "We have to think of evil as nothingness and the incarnation of that evil as a something (Someone)." Cunningham, "Satan: A Theological Meditation," 360.

149. Williams, *The Case for Angels*, 70–72. Williams refers to Swinburne's "*necessary condition theodicy*"—Swinburne, *Providence and the Problem of Evil*, 108. To explain why rebellious angels are still tolerated, Lloyd suggests they may still have the possibility of reconciliation. Lloyd, "The Cosmic Fall," chapter 5.

150. See section 7.5.

151. See section 7.2.

152. That positing a realm of free angelic beings influencing creation contributes to a complex causation behind events; disallowing simplistic explanations for particular manifestations of evil. Boyd, *Satan and the Problem of Evil*, 308–10.

153. See Ferdinando, "Screwtape Revisited," 123.

154. Cullman's illustration suggests that . . . evil cannot ultimately prevail; but we can choose evil and greatly hinder God's purpose." John Woolmer Interview 16.3.06; Cullmann, *Prayer in the New Testament*, 141.

In conclusion, Scripture reveals little directly concerning the origin of Satan, demons, or evil powers; and though Scripture and pastoral practice points to evil spirits as ontologically real entities, rebelliously opposed to God, there is some mystery as to how such rebellion arose among spirit beings that were created good.[155] But the explicit references to "angels" allied with Satan, and to rebellious angels being punished, including the devil himself (1 Tim 3:6), echoing intertestamental legends of such a fall, suggest that an angelic fall remains the best available theory for the origin of evil.[156]

Humans, however, cannot avoid responsibility in the spread of evil, as we shall now consider.

8.4 The extent of evil—sin, spiritual blindness, social oppression, and sickness

It is one thing to conclude that evil powers are ontologically real, another to determine where and how they influence affairs in this world, with implications as to how the spiritual battle is to be fought. Whilst my theological reflection has focused primarily on the fundamental ontology of evil powers, here I explore some implications concerning the extent of their influence, with particular reference to my descriptive-empirical findings from the Anglican charismatic "lifeworld."

Yong rightly observes that disembodied spirits that do not manifest concretely are in danger of being rendered meaningless.[157] He is therefore not averse to the Pentecostal language of "spirits of lust, murder or alcoholism," manifested in concrete patterns of sin and ill health, such as ruined relationships, homicides, dysfunctional kidneys, and habitual drinking passing down generations. But are these merely the effects of human rebellion; how are Satan and evil forces involved?

The New Testament Scriptures are cautious here, and different writers betray different emphases, but in relation to sin there are hints of such an interaction.[158] The clearest is the Ephesians reference to anger giving the devil a foothold (*topos*, 4:26-27); but there are indications in earlier Paulines of

---

155. Also concerning demonic ontology—but then, "why would Scripture give us a clear ontology of the demonic if Satan had already fallen (Luke 10:18)?" Fackre, "Angels Heard and Demons Seen," 357.

156. See section 7.4.

157. See section 6.3, and Yong, "Spiritual Discernment," 90, 102-3.

158. Ooi reflects on this interaction between sin and the demonic in relation to "spirits of rage, lust," etc.; though noting that in Romans slavery is to sin and death, not directly to demonic powers. Ooi, "A Study of Strategic Level Spiritual Warfare from a Chinese Perspective," 143-61.

such a link, notably to Satan's scheming to exploit unforgiveness (2 Cor 2:11). And in relation to the personification of the powers such as sin, the flesh, and death, we have noted the clear link between the devil and the "cravings of our flesh" (Eph 2:2–3).[159] The association of Satan with temptation is most evident in the synoptics, notably in the wilderness temptation narratives, the Lord's prayer, and the Satanic inspiration for Peter's impassioned opposition to Jesus (Mark 8:33; cf. "sift like wheat," Luke 22:31).

Two other related areas of personal sin or disobedience deserve specific comment. Firstly, hints that fear itself can have a demonic inspiration; notably demonic slavery to "the fear of death" described in Hebrews (2:14–15).[160] At St. George's an increasing freedom from fear was seen as a benefit of their spiritual warfare approach.[161] Secondly, there is a demonic inspiration for lies and falsehood, particularly in relation to deceptive religious arguments. Whilst most obvious in the pastoral epistles,[162] it probably underlies the polemic in Galatians (and Colossians);[163] and especially the portrayal of Satan in John's Gospel, as "the father of lies" who uses the Pharisees as "children of the devil" in their opposition to the truth that sets free, such that they are "slaves to sin."[164] Both these areas were highlighted at St. George's.[165]

Linked to this is another key area of Satanic activity, the blindness of unbelief, and a resistance to its removal. Whereas John prefers the

---

159. See section 8.2, especially note 84, and Arnold, *Ephesians: Power and Magic*, 130–32. This "ethical dualism" of "flesh and spirit" is reflected in some Dead Sea Scrolls; see references in Wright, *The Origin of Evil Spirits*, 176–77.

160. Also Rom 8:15, where the Holy Spirit is contrasted with "a spirit that makes you a slave again to fear," and the similar contrast for a "spirit of timidity" in 2 Tim 1:7—a significant verse for some interviewees at St. George's.

161. See sections 4.9 and 4.10. Not all fear was considered to be sinful, but only inasmuch as it represented unbelief in the Father's loving care for us (as in Rom 8:15).

162. Notably "deceiving spirits and things taught by demons" (1 Tim 4:1), and 2 Tim 2:26. See also 2 Cor 11:3–4.

163. Gal 4:3, 8–9 (cf 1 Cor 8:5/10:19–20), Col 2:8. (Cf. 2 Cor 10:2–5). See Arnold, "Stoicheia as Evil Spirits," 60. However, the meaning of τὰ στοιχεῖα τοῦ κόσμου is hotly debated, partly as the usage of στοιχεῖα in Heb 5:12 and 2 Pet 3:10 may be different. Page, *Powers of Evil*, 263–65; Wink, *Naming the Powers*, 67–77. The evidence from the Testament of Solomon (where it is used for demonic powers) is ambiguous. See Angel, *Angels*, chapter 11; Charlesworth, *Pseudepigrapha 1*, 940–43.

164. John 8:31–34, 42–45; to Pilate —"everyone on the side of truth listens to me," 18:37–38, and the "cosmic exorcism" of the cross 12:31. See section 8.2, and Twelftree, *In the Name of Jesus*, 194–201. Whilst Satan by nature uses falsehood to deceive and remain hidden, there is no evidence that Satan is non-ontological evil falsely masquerading as ontological, as Wright suggests. See section 5.3.

165. See chapter 4, and section 8.6 below.

CONSTRUCTING A CHARISMATIC THEOLOGY OF SPIRITUAL WARFARE

metaphor of spiritual deafness for those who refuse to believe and are "of the devil,"[166] Paul refers to "the god of this age" blinding the minds of unbelievers (2 Cor 4.4).[167] Whilst this is the only direct Pauline reference, the one specific prayer request in the Ephesians 6 spiritual warfare context is to be able to proclaim the gospel fearlessly;[168] and experiences of a "titanic confrontation" when coming against such spiritual blindness in evangelism and mission was significant in highlighting the reality of spiritual warfare for several charismatic Anglican pioneers (especially Green, Watson, MacInnes, and Collins).[169] Pioneers with overseas experience confirmed this even more strongly.[170] The experiences of what James Collins calls Evangelical Fundamentalists, particularly those with experience in mission in the global South, considerably influenced the developing theological praxis of Anglican charismatics,[171] both amongst early pioneers and in St. George's.[172] The observed charismatic response was essentially on three levels—"setting forth the truth plainly" (2 Cor 4.2, the fundamental "truth encounter"); prayer ("prayer is spiritual warfare" (Diana Collins)); and "the power of the Spirit" (e.g., Rom 15:18–19), which in itself can heighten the intensity of spiritual conflict.[173]

What of the wider social evils in the world? Wink and other biblical commentators have sought to shift the whole focus of spiritual conflict to the sociopolitical arena. There is a danger of overstatement here. For

166. John 8:43, 47; 18:37–38.

167. Walker, Pytches, and others noted that much of the battle is hidden, because Satan's chief strategy is to blind the minds of people to the truth—of the gospel, to Satan's existence, and to God's glory. See section 3.5.

168. Eph 6:19–20; see also Col 4:2–4.

169. See sections 3.4 and 3.5, and Appendix 2, table 4. "Titanic confrontation" was Green's description—Green, *I Believe in the Holy Spirit*, 70. In the pilot study, such experiences taught them the effectiveness of prayer in "binding the strongman," especially in advance before outreach. One interviewee learned to see "spiritual opposition" as a positive sign that they were doing the right things—as did MacInnes (MacInnes Interview 6.4.06).

170. Notably, John Woolmer had made several trips to Zambia; and Collins to Kenya.

171. James Collins, "Deliverance Ministry in the Twentieth Century." Collins mentions Merill Unger and Kurt Koch, both strongly influential on the early pioneers (e.g., Harper, Walker, Green, Dunnett, Pytches); and James Fraser's intense spiritual battle experiences amongst the Lisu were highly influential for Bob Dunnett in his council estate ministry—see Taylor, *Behind the Ranges*.

172. Leaders at St. George's were impressed by the theological reflection on "binding & loosing" by CMA missionaries, and their own experiences in Kenya and South Africa—see Foster and King, *Binding and Loosing*, 266–67, 79.

173. See section 8.1, and 8.5 below.

example, some have interpreted Mark's use of the exorcism motif as symbolic for political liberation from Roman oppression. But Twelftree demonstrates that the opposite is true; Jesus's battle with Satan is clearly linked to otherworldly concerns of his identity as God's Son, and his exorcisms take place in the spiritual or cosmic arena expressed in the personal liberation of the demonized, not in the sociopolitical sphere.[174] Nevertheless, not only Wright, Yong, and Boyd but also several pioneers appreciated Wink's contribution in highlighting the pervasive nature of the demonic "interpenetrating the power structures of society."[175] Warren, for example, cited drug trafficking and corruption as key manifestations of Satanic activity.[176] Both pioneers and members of St. George's recognized that Satan only had as much authority as we give him (cf. Luke 4:5–6);[177] such that at least in the human, social and moral sphere Wink and others are right to place the responsibility almost entirely on the shoulders of human beings for choosing and allowing evil to flourish. In this study, Wink's contribution has thus helped to highlight the validity of the traditional formula for Christians' spiritual enemies—not only "the devil," and "the flesh" or sinful nature, but also "the world" and its fallen structures—all of which interpenetrate, such that a focus purely on Satan and demons is too simplistic.

Charismatics have been regularly criticized for an overdeveloped dualism between God and Satan that leaves little place for natural causes.[178] Thus far we have focused on the extent of evil in relation to human sin and rebellion, but now consider briefly issues relating to "natural evil," ranging from large scale natural disasters such as earthquakes and tsunamis, through suffering in the animal world, to specific debates around sickness, healing, and the demonic.

The relationship of evil powers to the suffering arising from the natural realm is complex and controversial, yet not easily accessible to investigation. Boyd particularly sees the hand of evil at work in natural disasters, ascribing full responsibility for these at the hands of fallen angelic beings.[179] There is

---

174. Twelftree, *Jesus the Exorcist*, 105–11.

175. Walker, "The Devil You Think You Know," 99–100. Wink and Yong's language of "force fields and vectors" is appropriate to describe this diffuse interpenetration.

176. See section 3.5.

177. See Appendix 4, table 1.

178. For example, Walker, "The Devil You Think You Know," 88–89.

179. Boyd's own favored "restoration theory" is a revival of the "gap theory" of Gen 1:2; this suggests the ensuing account in Genesis 1 actually describes God's re-creation of the world out of a battle-torn chaotic abyss, creating human beings in His image (Gen 1:26) to re-establish God's good plan for his creation, over which we have been given the command to "subdue" (*kabas*, suggesting the suppression of hostile forces, cf.

also a philosophical argument for this—if we consider natural catastrophes as truly "evil," then fallen angels could seem to present the best explanation for this aspect of evil—especially if we see it as predating the fall of man, which is otherwise credited in more evangelical circles as the source of the fallenness of creation itself.[180] From this study, some Anglican charismatics would welcome Boyd's approach in ascribing responsibility for these at the hands of fallen angelic beings;[181] but not all would agree with Boyd here.[182] Woolmer, for example, whilst agreeing that physical places with troubled history can be in need of deliverance, saw accidents and natural disasters more as a necessary concomitant of the natural world that we live in.[183] However, Tom Walker's discovery from several pastoral cases that accident black spots or places visited on holiday could become a source of demonic oppression (or even loss of life at black spots) caused him moral outrage that evil powers could exploit such apparently neutral or random occurrences.[184]

Num 32:22, 29; Josh 18:1). But God's intended vice-regents surrendered their authority over the earth to the enemy (cf. Luke 4:6) and joined the satanic rebellion from within the pre-existing angelic heavenly court—which "let *us* make man" (Gen 1:26) may indeed refer to. Boyd, *God at War*, 102–13; *Satan and the Problem of Evil*, 309–18; Wenham, *Genesis 1–15*, 1, 27–28.) This depends on Gen 1:2, which does have "some form of mythological content," but Levenson concludes this translation controversy is probably impossible to resolve. See Otzen, Gottlieb, and Jeppesen, *Myths in the Old Testament*, 33, 36; Levenson, *Creation and the Persistence of Evil*, 157–58.

180. See Boyd, *Satan and the Problem of Evil*, 309. There is a strong eschatological argument, according with Rom 8:22, a scripture Boyd never discusses. Lloyd develops Mascall's suggestion that if angels have a role in caring for creation, a "fall" would also affect the natural world; he argues that if fallen angels are still bound up with the maintenance of this fallen world, this could help explain why God did not destroy them immediately when they rebelled. See Lloyd, "The Cosmic Fall," chapter 5; Mascall, *Christian Theology and Natural Science*, 302–3.

181. At least one of the leaders at St. George's, whilst happy to talk of natural causation on other levels (for tiredness, lack of fitness, etc.), saw such disasters as primarily the devil's work.

182. Harper illustrates well the argument of "complexity" in causation—he sees disasters as part of the fallen side of the natural world, but recognizes that both God and Satan can use them (including causing car punctures!). Harper Interview 20.4.04.

183. Whereas Boyd, Warrington, and some pioneers see evidence of demonic involvement in the storm on Lake Galilee that Jesus had to "rebuke" (a word used for personal beings normally), Woolmer (who had been struck by lightning before a mission) in interview did not agree the devil had that much power; although he believed in "lay lines" and local demonic holds on localities through past sins. See Woolmer, *Healing and Deliverance*, 69–72, 100–103, 348–50.

184. Walker Interview 28.3.04. For a detailed consideration of causes of "strain" on places, from the more neutral "place memories" to the more clearly demonic effects of occult activities often centered on pagan sites, see Richards, *But Deliver Us from Evil*, 192–211. Walker shares one of Richards's sources here, *The Experiences of a Present Day Exorcist* by Father Donald Omand.

But on the larger scale, if earthquakes and tsunamis from a geological perspective are caused by the slow movement of tectonic plates over millennia, it is difficult to imagine (though not impossible) how fallen angels could in any way be responsible for causing such natural disasters.[185] Part of the whole difficulty here is the one expressed well by Barth—trying to separate the positive but imperfect "shadow side" of creation which "belongs to the essence of creaturely nature," from that which is evil (Barth's *das Nichtige*).[186] But one conclusion seems well-founded—there is a category of natural causation of suffering and pain with an element of randomness, as Jesus clearly taught (Luke 13:4, the tower of Siloam), which is neither attributed directly to God's judgment (potentially tarnishing his goodness), nor directly to the devil, avoiding an exaggerated dualism.[187]

Making this often subtle distinction in practice is beyond the scope of this thesis, except for a brief discussion concerning the important relationship between the demonic and sickness. Many of the pioneers expressed their views on this. On the one hand, some believed that "sickness came in through the demonic," thus being seen as an indirect causation for all sickness.[188] On the other, it was more often recognized as only one possible direct cause for sickness. Harper characterized negative spiritual causes as evil spirits, general Satanic attack,[189] or personal sin.[190] Tom Walker pointed out that anything non-recognizable medically might often have a spiritual source.[191]

Broadly this agrees with the careful analysis of J. C. Thomas. Thomas recognizes that in the NT a malady can be caused by demon possession

---

185. Whilst MacInnes was agnostic concerning possible demonic causation for storms and lightning, he definitely could not see this behind movement of tectonic plates. MacInnes Interview 6.4.06.

186. For Barth creation is of three sorts—that from God's positive will (right hand), for his positive will but imperfect (the "shadow side," from his left hand), including such things as darkness (Gen 1:3), decay, failure, tears and physical death; and the evil *das Nichtige*, the product of God's non-willing. Barth asserts the shadow side is a necessary limitation and imperfection—but when seen as evil, we allow the real adversary a participation in the creation. Barth, *CD*, III/3, 296.

187. As pointed out by Harper and other pioneers, thus agreeing with Andrew Walker of the dangers of an overdeveloped dualism. Walker, "The Devil You Think You Know," 88–89.

188. Pytches and Woolmer respectively—see Table 3 in Appendix 2.

189. Collins gave the example of a fever he had when on an African mission, or attacks on the family. Collins Interview 30.4.04.

190. Cf. Pytches: "Not all disease is due to my personal sin." Pytches Interview 1.4.04.

191. Walker Interview 28.3.04.

requiring exorcism; can in two or three cases be a demonic affliction (Luke 13:10–16; 4:38–39, and probably Paul's thorn in the flesh); or could occasionally be a sinister attack against God's servants (the snake on Malta, Acts 28:1–6). It could also be the result of sin requiring confession (James 5), or occasionally caused by God himself for specific reasons; but otherwise appears due to neutral or natural causes.[192] He does not see evidence in the texts to support attributing all infirmities to the devil, despite its popularity. This would concur with the warning of Harper and others against a dualism that does not have a place for the natural. However, Thomas does notice that Luke-Acts blurs the distinction between healing and exorcism, and Twelftree gives this more weight.[193] There is thus biblical support for those charismatics who, like the leaders at St. George's, emphasize God's opposition to all sickness and believe that Jesus truly "healed all who were oppressed by the devil" (Acts 10.38);[194] and certainly for their recognition that there may be an "energizing" of the demonic on both natural and sinful causes of sickness.[195]

8.5 The defeat of evil—the goodness of God, the role of the cross, and the power of the Spirit

Charismatics and Pentecostals have often emphasized how the power of the Spirit overcomes the demonic, often using John Wimber's characterization, a "power encounter." Percy has however critiqued this approach which he feels can be dangerous if Wimber or others somehow appropriate power to themselves such that they may not be operating in God's power.[196] Pytches and others considered this an inappropriate criticism, especially in relation

---

192. Thomas, *The Devil, Disease and Deliverance*, 297–305, 313.

193. "Luke . . . has blurred the distinction between demon possession and other kinds of sickness so that in effect all sickness (and healing) is given a demonic and cosmic dimension." Twelftree, *In the Name of Jesus*, 154. Woolmer reflects insightfully on this unclear line between healing and deliverance (e.g., in Luke 13:10–13), including his theological discomfort with the healings of Fred Smith in Oxford who prayed against all cancers as evil spirits; which yet produced an instant healing from cancer he had personally verified months later. Woolmer, *Healing and Deliverance*, 93–94, 287–89, 368.

194. Unlike Page and several others, Thomas interprets this phrase as only referring to demon possession and the demonically-induced sickness; seeing "doing good" as including healing from natural causes. Thomas, *The Devil, Disease and Deliverance*, 260–61; Page, *Powers of Evil*, 119–20.

195. Watson also believed that the physical, psychological, sin and demonic can all interplay. Watson, *Discipleship*, 174.

196. Percy, *Words, Wonders and Power*.

to Wimber himself.[197] There are clear New Testament examples which illustrate how the power of the Holy Spirit, operating through believers, overwhelms and subjugates evil and occult power; and the power of the Spirit must surely play its part in any charismatic theology of the defeat of evil.[198] Nevertheless, there are dangers if the defeat of evil is primarily seen as a "power encounter," which Percy and others, including the leaders of St. George's, have pointed out. Whilst Wimber rightly suggests that Jesus's hearers were impressed with the power of Jesus's exorcisms, strictly speaking they were impressed with the authority of his teaching (Mark 1:21–28).[199] This was clearly linked to the truth of who Jesus was;[200] and arguably the concept of "truth encounter" adopted at St. George's is a more satisfactory theological basis for understanding the defeat of evil for charismatic believers, who not only seek to apprehend the authoritative power of the Spirit and of "the name of Jesus," but also the power of the objective truth—of the goodness of God,[201] and of what Jesus accomplished in overcoming the devil and all his works, particularly through the cross.[202] There is a danger particularly in the West in viewing the "clash of kingdoms" as primarily a

---

197. MacInnes commented: "If you knew John Wimber it was very clear that he's an extremely humble man who was constantly astonished by the power of God. And also very willing to revise his ideas." MacInnes Interview 6.4.06. Pytches similarly observed that sometimes Wimber would walk out of the room during ministry time and allow the Holy Spirit to continue working without him. Pytches did agree that charismata such as healing and deliverance were powerful in removing spiritual blindness and revealing God as the "great power," but not as Percy's narrow view of "power circuitry"; he emphasizes that blindness is only really removed when people see that God's Kingdom is good, pure, loving, holy—and real. Pytches Interview 1.4.04.

198. Not only in the NT exorcisms, but also the classic "power encounters" of 1 Kings 18 (Mount Carmel) and Acts 13 (Elymas). Wimber and Springer, *Power Evangelism*, 29–30, 41. An example from the pioneers was Walker's discovery of the surprising power of praying in tongues in deliverance ministry. See sections 3.5, 3.6.

199. "If Jesus's teaching lifts him to the status of full rabbinic authority in the view of the people, the exorcism exalts him to the sphere of supreme authority." Warrington, *Jesus the Healer*, 75.

200. Here for example, as Mark (1:24) has it in the mouth of the evil spirit crying out, "I know who you are—the Holy One of God."

201. In Christian "spiritual warfare," we are admonished to "overcome evil with good" (Rom 12:21); and human goodness is derived from God who alone is good (Jas 1:13–21; 2 Pet 1:3–5), as Jesus himself emphasizes (Mark 10:18). The goodness of God is thus foundational in the theological model presented below (section 8.6).

202. Cf. Heb 2:14, 1 John 3:8. At St. George's, when asked how much power Satan has, Peter replied: "Compared to God, nothing. [But] we do teach as well that spiritual warfare is a truth encounter not a power encounter."

power struggle, rather than as one of legitimacy of authority, which is much more the biblical worldview.[203]

Whilst the goodness of God is the ground of evil's defeat, and the power of the Spirit makes it effective, our focus here is primarily on how the Son of God brings about the defeat of evil.[204] Several pioneers emphasized the centrality of the cross in spiritual warfare;[205] and any theology of spiritual warfare needs to consider how the death of Jesus enables the defeat of evil in any objective sense, and how we receive its benefits. So we now turn to the soteriological debate concerning the atonement—which Boyd entered vigorously in defense of Aulen's *Christus Victor* or classic theory of atonement.[206]

This has recently been enlivened since so-called "new perspectives" on Paul in relation to his Jewish context have opened up fresh debates on key Pauline themes such as law, justification, and soteriology.[207] Sanders argued that much scholarship on Rabbinic Judaism had been based on a mistaken conclusion, that Judaism became almost uniformly a legalistic religion in which one must earn salvation by compiling more good works than transgressions.[208] Sanders concludes from a re-examination of Rabbinic material and Paul that both essentially agree on the premise that salvation is by grace, but judgment is by works; salvation is the condition of remaining "in," but

---

203. Through Jesus's death on the cross, the devil's authority has been undermined and superseded by a higher authority, reverting to the rightful ruler of creation. See Hiebert, "Spiritual Warfare and Worldviews." Holloway described a well-balanced understanding of power and authority: "We have the Holy Spirit in us which is the same Spirit that raised Christ from the dead; you couldn't get more powerful than that. But how we use that will be how the Holy Spirit trusts us . . . God sometimes gives little people an awful lot of authority at any one moment, and sometimes those people don't have any authority . . . it's all dependent on him, [and] our cooperation with him; to be the channels He might want to use." Holloway Interview 17.8.06.

204. Another valid approach to evil's defeat would be considering the eschatological "clash of kingdoms" (Matt 12:28), as begun in 8.2.2 above—see Twelftree, *Jesus the Exorcist*, 106–10. However, my concern is with the underlying dynamics of how spiritual evil is defeated by good.

205. Notably Green, Pytches, Barrington-Ward, and MacInnes; both from practical experience in spiritual warfare situations (e.g., when preaching on the cross), and theologically (Green's emphasis on the power of the cross in defeating evil was influential for MacInnes).

206. E.g., Boyd, *God at War*, 238–68.

207. As opposed to the "older" Lutheran and Calvinist perspectives; especially after publication of Sanders, *Paul and Palestinian Judaism*. See also Wright, *Paul: Fresh Perspectives*.

208. Sanders, *Paul and Palestinian Judaism*, 38, 59.

"works" do not earn salvation.[209] He also proposes that Paul does not develop this into a new "covenantal nomism," with Christians as the new Israel having been set free in parallel to the exodus; instead, Christians are set free by participation in a new aeon of new creation, through change of lordship from serving sin to serving Christ, through participation in Christ our representative as the second Adam (not the second Moses), in parallel to being "in the Spirit" as opposed to being "in the flesh."[210] This participatory transfer language, unlike a "new covenant," is alone able to explain Paul's key soteriological concepts of dying with Christ and thus to the power of sin, and of obtaining new life and initial transformation leading to resurrection as a member of the body of Christ, united in Spirit with him.[211]

Not all scholars have been convinced by the "new perspective" approach.[212] The main debate is not directly relevant here, but it has opened up new exploration of soteriological theories of atonement, as to the centrality or otherwise of the substitutionary theory of atonement,[213] the resurgence of mystical and participatory theories (see Sanders above), and also appropriation of the victory motif in relation to Christ's work.[214]

In his classic work on the atonement, Vincent Taylor's careful study of early preaching across the New Testament points to Christ's death being widely understood both as a vicarious act, and also in some sense representative; and that these two fundamental themes, together with the sacrificial character of Christ's death (particularly in Hebrews), underlie the New Testament doctrine of atonement.[215] He thus gives strong exegetical grounds for

---

209. Ibid., 517, 543. Sanders develops this further in *Paul, the Law, and the Jewish People*.

210. Sanders does not deny that for Paul Christianity functions as a new covenant, once established, such that remaining in it requires obedience, and repentance is the required remedy for disobedience (2 Cor 12:21). However, his primary appeal against immorality, for example, is that it is mutually exclusive with the union with Christ (1 Cor 10:1-5; 2 Cor 6:13-18). *Paul and Palestinian Judaism*, 454-6, 511-15.

211. Ibid., 513-14.

212. Schreiner lists several critics of Sanders's views; Schreiner, "Penal Substitution Response," 51.

213. Precipitated in Britain by Steve Chalke's views on the atonement, influenced by such new perspectives. See Cartledge, "Why Did Christ Die?."

214. See N. T. Wright, *Jesus and the Victory of God*, 609-11; *Evil and the Justice of God*.

215. Representative, in that Christ accomplishes a supreme work for men they are unable to do for themselves (though he sees no sign of a substitutory work done "in our stead"); and vicarious in that he had entered into, and endured, the consequences of sin (cf. ransom language, bore/died for our sins, Gethsemane, and the cry of Mark 15:34). Taylor himself opts for a doctrine of atonement centered on God's work of reconciliation between God and men (see 2 Corinthians 5). Taylor, *The Atonement*, 74-75, 245, 54-61.

an objective atonement, as opposed to the then popular subjective "moral example" theory of Abelard. In relation to sacrifice he sees the NT as almost, but not quite, substitutionary.[216] This is not the place to debate the inherent validity of substitutionary atonement theory (although traditionally widely accepted in charismatic evangelical Anglicanism, and central to deliverance praxis at St. George's).[217] However, I wish to consider whether other theories should be allowed greater prominence, or even dominance, in relation to it.

In many works the *Christus Victor* theory is hardly mentioned; thus Taylor only refers to it in relation to the "obscure verse" of Col 2:15. Different theories are often privileged by the controlling narrative Paul (or Jesus) is considered to adopt to answer the basic questions framing the scholar's worldview;[218] and such theologizing is highly contextual, conducted "with at least half an eye on the results . . . expected in the scholar's own world."[219] Thus, in Taylor's day the notion of "victory over evil powers" was indeed obscure (and penal substitution extremely unfashionable), but the postmodern turn has rendered it more acceptable.[220] Amongst the "new perspective" writers, N. T. Wright has adopted a theology of victory based on Jesus's defeat of evil on the cross. Conscious of the dangers of an unhealthy interest in the demonic, his focus is on *human* evil in all its forms (personal, political, and religious); yet he also urges us to recognize the supra-personal dimension of evil, for which the language of the demonic is still "the least inadequate," particularly recognizing these "deeper, darker forces" opposing Jesus in the Gospels.[221] For Wright (similarly to Anglican charismatics), the Gospel accounts do not give a philosophical explanation of evil,

216. He acknowledges that Paul uses legal categories, but sees vicarious and representative themes, as well as "expiatory" sacrifice, as best explaining this. Ibid., 124–25, 270–78, 288–90.

217. For example, in prayer ministry forgiveness of sins following repentance was seen as a legal transaction; and visualizing coming before the cross of Christ and receiving cleansing from the blood of Jesus was often used to bring assurance of forgiveness of sins.

218. Key questions such as the relation of God and the world, evil and its solution, and how to become more fully human. Wright, *Paul: Fresh Perspectives*, 7–14.

219. Ibid., 15.

220. Because of a re-acceptance of the problem of evil as real and powerful, and a new openness to spiritual dimensions and supernaturalism. *Evil and the Justice of God*, 13–15, 18. See also Lederle, "Life in the Spirit and Worldview," 24–26; Theron, "A Critical Overview," 84.

221. Wright helpfully emphasizes the interrelatedness of the dimensions of evil working together in a downward spiral to kill Jesus—effectively the "world" (the political powers (Rome and Herod), corruption within Israel), the "flesh" (Judas's betrayal, Peter's denial), and "the devil" (the Satan, the accuser, the shrieking demons, the power of darkness (Luke 22.53), death itself). Wright, *Evil and the Justice of God*, 18–19, 48–50.

or suggestions for behavioral change so that it may mysteriously disappear, but primarily describe the story of an *event* in which the living God, the world's creator, meets cosmic and global evil and deals with it by exhausting it, making space for new creation, new covenant, forgiveness, and hope. He therefore sees the atonement theme of *Christus Victor* as central in taking us to the heart of the matter—that on the cross Jesus has won the victory over all evil dark powers, with other theories playing their part under this.[222]

We thus return to Boyd's vigorous defense of a spiritual warfare worldview, seeing Christ's death as the locus of the defeat of evil forces as the controlling New Testament narrative, particularly in Paul. This argues against the scholarly consensus of centuries; at least since Anselm in the eleventh century, and reinforced in the Reformation, the Western church has tended to focus on the anthropomorphic (rather than cosmic) dimension, primarily in accomplishing reconciliation to God.[223] Whilst Gustav Aulen (*Christus Victor*, 1931) argued that Christ as the victor over death and Satan was the "classic" theory of the patristic period, this has been shown to be an oversimplification.[224] Nevertheless, this major strand in early New Testament thought has often been overlooked, and has a foundational quality in at least three writings, even if they also describe the effects of Christ's sacrifice in bringing forgiveness of sins. Thus, the reason Christ appeared was "to destroy the works of the devil" (1 John 3:8, cf. John 12:31; 16:11); he shared in our humanity "so that by his death he might destroy him who holds the power of death—that is, the devil" (Heb 2:14); and he "disarmed the power and authorities . . . triumphing over them by the cross" (Col 2:15)—such that "he has rescued us from the dominion of darkness and brought us into the kingdom of the Son he loves, in whom we have redemption . . ." (Col 1:13).[225] The understanding that Christ's resurrection and ascension to God's right hand was linked to a subjugation of his enemies is clearly part of the earliest appropriation of the frequently quoted messianic psalm 110:1 (and Ps 8:6), notably in Peter's first sermon (Acts 2:32–35), Hebrews (1:13), and Paul's key passage on the victory of the resurrection (1 Cor 15:24–6—"he must reign until he has put all his enemies under his feet").[226] John also links Jesus's death and glorification with condemnation

---

222. *Jesus and the Victory of God*, 57–60, 73.

223. Boyd, *God at War*, 240. Some later theories focused on its subjective dimension, for example Abelard's theory of the cross as a moral example. MacGrath, *Christian Theology*, 355–60.

224. *Christian Theology*, 348.

225. Boyd adds less well-known Pauline references —2 Tim 2:26, Gal 1:4; and Acts 26:17–18. Boyd, *God at War*, 240–41, 260.

226. One of the frequent citations of Ps 110:1 evidencing the centrality in early

and judgment on "the prince of this world" who "will be driven out."[227] The language of "redemption," "ransom" and "setting free" points to the cross freeing us from slavery to sin (e.g., Rom 6:7, 18–20; Heb 9:15; Rev 1:5), accusation (Col 1:22) and the fear of death (Heb 2:14); but, as Heb 2:14 describes, Boyd maintains that "the most fundamental reality we are set free from is the devil."[228]

Whilst this aspect of the atonement in NT thinking is now more widely accepted, the *primary* meaning of the atonement has been hotly debated, especially amongst evangelicals wary of yielding any ground on the centrality of penal substitution.[229] Boyd concedes there is much common ground between the penal substitution view and *Christus Victor*, notably in accepting that Christ's blood was shed as a ransom for us, and his substitutionary death, offered as an unblemished sacrifice, bore our punishment and the curse of the law, setting aside the just requirement of the law that would have us slain.[230] Boyd even agrees that the wrath of God burns against sin; but maintains that it is not God (in whom wrath and love are equally "deep") who demands a "kill," but instead "the cosmic accuser who preys on all who have forfeited their lives and put themselves under his authority by their treason"—unaware that there is a "deeper magic" still, that of self-sacrificial love, which overturned the "deep magic" of the "written code" (Col 2:14). Boyd maintains that this passage teaches clearly that the cross disarmed Satan and his minions in this way, but did not disarm God.[231]

Schreiter accepts the importance of the *Christus Victor* theme and its cosmic dimension, but argues that it is not fundamental and sidelines the main narrative of Scripture, which is about human sin and the need for forgiveness. He is also concerned that Boyd's depiction of sin as primarily a satanically inspired power that enslaves may downplay personal responsibility. Boyd's view, that the way in which Christ's death erased the condemnation of the law and dismantled the principalities and powers is

---

Christian thought of Christ's victory over angelic powers. Cullmann, *Christ and Time*, 382; Boyd, *God at War*, 243–45.

227. John 12:28–32; 16:11. See also *God at War*, 245.

228. Also Col 2:15; John 12:31; 16:11; 2 Cor 4:4. Ibid., 266.

229. E.g., Cartledge, "Why Did Christ Die?," 214, 219.

230. E.g., Matt 26:26–29; 1 Cor 11:23–26; Mark 10:45; Heb 9:14; Isa 53:4–6, 10–12; 2 Cor 5:21; Gal 3:13; Rom 3:25; Col 2:14–15. Boyd however points out that substitutionary understandings of Old Testament sacrifice that are not penal may present fewer problems. Boyd, "Christus Victor Response," 102–4.

231. Ibid., 102–3. Boyd consciously uses language paralleling C. S. Lewis in *The Lion, the Witch and the Wardrobe*, as clearly representing both his and Lewis's *Christus Victor* view.

not explained and so must be taken on faith, he considers inadequate if it is to be truly "foundational." Instead, he proposes that the apocalyptic and anthropological are woven together—the devil and demons rule over us because we are sinners and not for any other mysterious reason, and so the devil's hold is broken when our sins were forgiven on the cross, by virtue of Christ taking our place and suffering our punishment.[232]

This debate will not be easily resolved, and we might be tempted to simply conclude that the New Testament gives a "kaleidoscopic view" of the atonement, including also strong hints of its healing power.[233] However, I believe three aspects rightly deserve prominence in a charismatic theology of spiritual warfare. Firstly, N. T. Wright and Greg Boyd rightly point out that the *Christus Victor* interpretation, in seeing the cross as defeating evil on every level and in every manifestation, has a comprehensiveness that takes it beyond an individualistic focus on "my sin problem" to the political and cosmic scale of Christ's work.[234] In this, Wright's approach in emphasizing the cosmo-political dimension, helps to counterbalance the tendency of Boyd to over-emphasize the demonic nature of the powers.[235] This comprehensiveness is true even if exactly how Christ's death extends beyond human beings to reconcile "all things" on earth or in heaven (Col 1:20), and enables the whole creation to eventually be released from its bondage to decay (Rom 8:19–21), is a mystery only hinted at in Scripture.[236] Secondly, whilst penal substitution theory may have its difficulties, the primary way God deals with the evil of human sin and rebellion is clearly through the power of Jesus's sacrifice in shedding his blood to bring forgiveness and cleansing from our sins;[237] and there is clearly a strong legal basis to this es-

---

232. Schreiner, "Penal Substitution Response," 50–53.

233. Green, "Kaleidoscopic View," 155, 157–85.

234. John and the Johannine school reflect this, lifting the primary arena for the spiritual battle from the Synoptic focus on Jesus's exorcisms to the cosmic level (cf. 1 John 5: 19), seeing the whole of Jesus ministry as a battle against Satan, reaching its climax in "the grand cosmic exorcism" of the cross event (John 12:31–32). See Twelftree, *In the Name of Jesus*, 196.

235. Just as Yong and Wink emphasize the cosmo-political dimension, for similar reasons; and this danger was also pointed out by Joel Green. Green, "Kaleidoscopic Response to Christus Victor View," 63; Wright, *Evil and the Justice of God*, 18–19, 59–63.

236. This key passage in Romans is often glossed over in relation to atonement theory, missing out its cosmic, eschatological dimension.

237. Both Hebrews (at considerably length) and 1 John primarily use the language of sacrifice to explain how the devil's power is destroyed (Heb 2:14; 1 John 3:8). In relation to the mechanism that liberates us (rather than the cosmic scale of atonement), the sacrificial category (broader than the forensic penal substitution category), is thus arguably the metaphor that has the most basic conceptual framework and holds the central position. Taylor, *The Atonement*, 271; Cartledge, "Why Did Christ Die?" 216,

pecially in much of Paul's terminology (e.g., Rom 3:25–26; 5:15–19; 8:3–4), which can be interpreted in penal substitutionary terms.[238] Integrating these two key aspects accords not only with Michael Green's re-emphasis of the victory of the cross, which as the culmination of Christ's sinless obedience dealt with the sin of the world, defeated death and conquered Satan;[239] but also with teaching and praxis at St. George's, where the devil was seen as a legalist, such that repentance and receiving forgiveness through the blood Jesus shed for us is viewed as objectively removing his right of access (Eph 4:26; Rev 7:13–14)—now "the guilt of sin has been atoned for, Satan no longer has any power over those who put their trust in Christ."[240]

However, this brings us to the third strand, the participatory view, which is implicit in the *Christus Victor* model[241] but I believe requires a new emphasis. Wright, like Sanders, emphasizes the representative language in explaining that "Christ died for our sins" (1 Cor 15:3)—seeing Christ as ultimately a representative of the whole human race and indeed the cosmos.[242] But for Paul, it is participation "in Christ" that enables us to benefit from Christ's work; whilst representation illuminates its objective side, participation highlights its subjective side (i.e., how the cross transforms humans). The "discoverers" of Paul's soteriological emphasis on participatory union (notably Deissmann and Schweitzer) over-emphasized this "mystical" view of the atonement, and it was too closely allied with participation in the eucharist, such that Bultmann and others de-emphasized it.[243] Nevertheless, Schweitzer argued persuasively that the key theme of being "in Christ," represented in a variety of phrases such as being "members of the body of

---

18. See also Green, "Kaleidoscopic View," 172–77.

238. I agree with Boyd that John Stott gives the best exposition of this "self-substitution of God"—Stott, *The Cross of Christ*, 133–63; Boyd, *God at War*, 380.

239. Green, *I Believe in Satan's Downfall*, 209–19.

240. Schreiner, "Penal Substitution Response," 53.

241. Boyd sees one advantage of this model as being that in it "what Christ does *for* us cannot be separated, even theoretically, from what Christ does *in* us and *through* us." One way this is effected is through our participation in baptism, which not only connects us with the death and resurrection of Christ, but in acceptance of Jesus as Lord enables us to participate in Christ's cosmic victory, as he is exalted to the right hand of God (cf. 1 Pet 3:21–22; Eph 1:22—2:8). Boyd, "Christus Victor View," 47; *God at War*, 245, 251, 382–83.

242. "To be released from sin is to be released from death; and, since Jesus died in a representative capacity for Israel, and hence for the whole human race, and hence for the cosmos (that is how the chain of representation works), his death under the weight of sin results immediately in release for all those held captive by its guilt and power." Wright, *Evil and the Justice of God*, 56.

243. Sanders, *Paul and Palestinian Judaism*, 453; Schweitzer, *The Mysticism of Paul*.

Christ," "one in Christ Jesus," is central to Paul's thought, and occurs in both polemical and paraenetical passages.[244] This rightly reasserts the corporate implications of our identity (both "in Adam," but more importantly "in Christ");[245] equally, the "new perspective" re-connects with the importance of personal relationship with Christ as the basis of salvation, for Paul's key phrase "in Christ" must be interpreted in the light of passages about "dying with Christ."[246] Such participatory union is not a figure of speech, but real for Paul.[247] It connects us with the new reality Christ's death brings into being. For as N. T. Wright observes, one of Paul's key narrative ideas is creation and "new creation"—such that "if anyone is in Christ, new creation!"[248]

The particular relevance here is threefold. Firstly, this emphasis on participation in Christ who died as our representative, and rose again, helps overcome weaknesses in the substitutionary view. The objective emphasis on "legal transaction" (for example in prayer ministry at St. George's), and subsequent to repentance receiving the cleansing of forgiveness through Jesus's blood, is limited in its "subjective" dimension. It can fail to open up the full power of Christ's redemption from sin and evil, which is only released when the believer discovers not just that he is forgiven and can try again, but when he knows he has "died to sin," having been "crucified with Christ," and so can now participate in Christ's risen life within.[249] Secondly, it underscores a key aspect of charismatic spiritual warfare theology, that experiencing freedom and victory over evil is based on being united with Christ in his resurrection and ascension, so that believers are now "seated in Christ in the heavenly realms," "far above all rule and authority"—thus potentially able to exercise spiritual authority in Christ over "all the power of the enemy," but foolish to attempt this in their own strength rather than

---

244. Key passages are 1 Cor 12; Gal 3:25-29; 2 Cor 5:17-21; Phil 3:8-9; Rom 8:1, also Rom 8:10 ("Christ in you"), and 1 Cor 6:17; "justification by faith" being mainly in polemical contexts. Sanders, *Paul and Palestinian Judaism*, 455-59; Schweitzer, *The Mysticism of Paul*, 122-27.

245. Seyoon Kim reaffirms the Jewish concept of the *Stammvater* (patriarch/ancestor) as incorporating his whole descendants in himself (Rom 5:12-19; 1 Cor 15:22-24). Kim, *Paul and the New Perspective*, 194, 211-12.

246. Sanders, *Paul and Palestinian Judaism*, 453n19.

247. Schweitzer, *The Mysticism of Paul*, 128.

248. I am indebted to Paula Gooder for pointing out this literal translation of ὥστε εἰ τις ἐν Χριστῷ καινὴ κτίσις (lecture, June 2009); thus not just an individualistic experience, but a new cosmic reality. See also Wright's emphasis on new covenant and new creation in the Pauline solution to evil, and the personal participatory dimension of the cross. Wright, *Paul: Fresh Perspectives*, 37-39; *Evil and the Justice of God*, 60-61.

249. Hence my recommendation for prayer ministry praxis at St. George's—see section 9.3.

out of their participatory union with Christ.[250] This again connects with the power of truth (John 8:32), particularly of our identity in Christ.

Thirdly, it reinforces the essential unity between the power of Christ's death and resurrection which liberates us from sin, and the power of the Holy Spirit in whom Christ baptizes and fill us. And it takes us back to the very inception of charismatic renewal in Anglican context—a fresh understanding of these participatory passages in Romans, which preceded or accompanied a release of the baptism of the Holy Spirit in some key pioneers.[251] Indeed, this threefold understanding of the atonement (deliverance from evil, substitution, and participation in Christ's death) takes us even further back, to the first "Pentecostal Anglican," Alexander Boddy, who concludes his 1911 Good Friday meditation on the cross's victory with this prayer, emphasizing especially the participatory theme:

> Lord Jesus, ere my thoughts are turned from this story of Thy victory, may Thy Holy Spirit make a living reality these blessed truths:
>
> 1. Thou hast lovingly paid the full price for my eternal redemption. I am redeemed by Thy precious Blood-shedding. Thou HAST delivered me from Hell, and from the guilt of my many sins. Hallelujah!
>
> 2. In Thee I died. At Thy cross old things passed away. Because of Thy work at Calvary I reckon myself dead indeed to sin. For Thou didst become sin for me—Thou, who knew no sin—that I in Thee might have the Righteousness of God. Oh, worthy is the Lamb that was slain!
>
> 3. My old man was indeed crucified on that first Good Friday, crucified with Thee, Lord Jesus. The old "I" was crucified with Thee when the nails were driven into Thy Hands and Feet. It shall be no longer I, but Thou, Blessed, Crucified, Risen Savior, alone living in my heart. Glory be to Jesus![252]

---

250. Hence this study has highlighted the positive value of "repentance" as a "weapon," as well as prayerfully "putting on the armor of God," as important components of charismatic warfare praxis enabling "praying from a place of authority"—whether resisting the devil in temptation, breaking bondages to habitual sin, or facing demonic manifestations in deliverance ministry.

251. Notably, Collins, and Watson—Collins Interview 30.4.04, and Hocken, *Streams of Renewal*, 96. Watson devotes a chapter in his spiritual warfare book to Romans 6, influenced by Nee and Lloyd Jones—Nee, *The Normal Christian Life*; Lloyd-Jones, *The Christian Warfare*; Watson, *God's Freedom Fighters*, 44.

252. Alexander Boddy, *Confidence 4 no 3*, 58. See also section 2.2.

8.6 Charismatic spiritual warfare: renewing theological praxis

The language of spiritual warfare

Having thus discussed the nature of evil and the basis for its defeat at the level of academic theological discourse, I here present a theological model and its implications for charismatic praxis that mediates with the ecclesial level of discourse of Anglican charismatic leadership.[253] However, we must first consider whether the metaphor of "spiritual warfare" is a helpful one at all. We have seen how this was a novel spiritual delineation appropriated by Harper and others in the early stages of British charismatic renewal; yet in a context where pacifism was already increasing; such that now, for example, "hymns with militaristic imagery are out of favor," as "devotion has moved into phase with theology," and thus a worldview of warfare may no longer be credible (except for certain personality types).[254] From another perspective, the spiritual warfare metaphor in recent Pentecostal and particularly Third Wave theology may have become loaded with specific theological ideas such that it has become a "dead metaphor" inextricably bound to certain concepts (e.g., "strategic-level spiritual warfare against territorial spirits"), making it difficult to invest it with other meanings.[255]

Here are thus two main objections to its use: is it credible, and is it intelligible (or too easily misunderstood). I would contend that the more important question is the one we have been focusing on—is the notion of a battle against ontologically real evil powers coherent, and does it correspond to reality. Concerning intelligibility, even "dead metaphors" are still metaphors that can come to life and surprise us in new ways, unlike "dead" metonymies;[256] the key question is how accurately they represent reality.

The older pioneers were emphatic on this, because of the reality of the battle they experienced and saw in Scripture. MacInnes puts it clearly:

---

253. Thus, particularly in the praxis section (8.6.3), moving from Cartledge's "level 3" discourse towards "level 2." See Cartledge, *Testimony in the Spirit*, 19–20.

254. Strange, "Dispensing with the Devil," 33–35. Kay found a link amongst Pentecostal pastors between psychotic traits and a worldview of a daily battle with demons—Kay, "A Demonised Worldview," 25–26.

255. See Soskice, *Metaphor and Religious Language*, 71–5. This is E. Janet Warren's contention, though more within a North American context. Warren, "Spiritual Warfare: A Dead Metaphor?"; *Cleansing the Cosmos*.

256. Such as "shoe horn," from when these were made of horn. Soskice, *Metaphor and Religious Language*, 74.

> You can't escape from the fact that there's a conflict. Conflict is fundamental to life anyway, so trying to avoid terms which express conflict is to live in cloud cuckoo land. There's a kind of Christianity which is sentimental and so is the peace; and there is no peace. I don't know whether the term spiritual warfare is necessarily the best but it does express something that goes on. "Spiritual conflict" . . . may be more comfortable for some people but it's the same thing. There's a violent confrontation between two opposing forces.[257]

Similarly, Walker adopted the term "spiritual warfare" because he saw it as a neutral description of the fact that the Christian life is a battle in all kinds of ways.[258] Walker agrees that the language of some charismatic choruses can appear confusingly aggressive for new Christians unaware of the seriousness of *spiritual* warfare; but his answer is the need for clear accompanying teaching about the continuing conflict between Christ and Satan, and instead of "triumphalistic flag-waving and sabre-rattling," adopting a genuine attitude of sustained praise and adoration "which is immensely effective in the spiritual battle."[259]

Holloway was more wary of using "spiritual warfare" and "spiritual battle," being aware (like Janet Warren) of how they had become loaded metaphors for North American charismatics. But she also recognized that it had often been neglected recently in the British Anglican context, only just beginning to come back in a more balanced way through courses such as "Freedom in Christ." Although she preferred not to highlight "spiritual warfare," she was willing to teach on the area when asked to.[260]

Yong raises another serious objection in relation to Pentecostal political theology, wishing "to remove any possibility of legitimating violence by using the rhetoric of spiritual warfare."[261] Robert Warren and Green also highlighted the dangers of the "war on terror" language; however, Warren quoted Wink concerning the importance of military metaphors even in the work of pacifism, as the only metaphors strong enough to represent the virulence of this spiritual conflict.[262] Janet Warren, wishing to marginalize the

---

257. MacInnes Interview 6.4.06. Similarly John and Diana Collins are forthright: "(John) I like to think of Jesus Christ, he fasted 40 days, well that is a *battle*, it's a long time . . . (Diana) I can't see how you can live in the world and not see a spiritual battle." Collins Interview 30.4.04.

258. Walker Interview, 28.3.04.

259. Walker, *The Occult Web*, 45.

260. Jane Holloway Interview 17.8.06.

261. Yong, *In the Days of Caesar*, 165.

262. Robert Warren Interview 23.7.08, Green Interview 18.3.04.

spiritual warfare metaphor, proposes broadening the range of metaphors (for example, cultic and spatial metaphors) used to describe the battle with, and defeat of evil.[263] Such a development is to be cautiously welcomed; Guelich notes that references to the spiritual warfare metaphor are relatively few overall, even in Pauline writings.[264] However, like MacInnes above, I support the conclusion that no other metaphor does justice to the reality of the "violent confrontation between two opposing forces" that the Bible, and spiritual experience, bears witness to; such that, despite its drawbacks, "spiritual warfare" needs to be taught and understood to equip the church to take seriously and be victorious in a conflict which by nature is invisible to the human eye, but nevertheless real.

Theological foundations for spiritual warfare

From this study, building on the explorations of the pioneers, generalizing to theory from the case study,[265] and our dialogue with key theologians and the Scriptures, I here propose a theological model of "charismatic spiritual warfare." There is no single valid approach to spiritual warfare and deliverance ministry. Twelftree and Cartledge have rightly highlighted some differences in the scriptural models; thus, John Wimber adopts a Marcan paradigm of a "power encounter" exorcistic ministry, whereas this model is based more on the Pauline approach (specifically the thought behind the letter to Ephesians).[266] It however also has strong resonances with other Scriptures, especially the book of James.[267]

Firstly, any Christian pneumatological model of spiritual warfare should have a soundly Trinitarian foundation, as Yong has reminded us, and I believe one emerges from this study.[268] Firstly (Yong's "*firstness*"), it

263. Warren, "Spiritual Warfare: A Dead Metaphor?."

264. Guelich overemphasizes this point, however. Arnold lists twenty-two occasions when images of warfare and struggle are used in the New Testament, some with multiple references. More significantly, conflict with Satan and the power of evil is a major theme in the Bible, and therefore an integral part of Christian experience that cannot be ignored. Arnold, *Three Crucial Questions About Spiritual Warfare*, 19–25.

265. I believe that this theology emerging from the fieldwork meets Schreiter's criteria (e.g., cohesiveness with broader Christian tradition, the praxis test of "bearing good fruit," openness to testing and willingness to share its benefits) and so has "normative value" in influencing broader Christian theology and praxis. Schreiter, *Constructing Local Theologies*, 117–21.

266. See Twelftree "Deliverance and Exorcism in the New Testament"; Cartledge, "Demonology and Deliverance."

267. Notably Jas 4:1–10 (cf. 1 Pet 5:6–9), also 1:13–18.

268. Whilst Piercean metaphysics has limitations in dealing with spiritual realities,

is grounded on *the goodness of God the Father*. If God is good, we can be confident that he does not directly cause the evils that we see around us in this world, which are essentially the direct or indirect results of the actions of free spiritual beings, whether angelic or human, that have chosen to rebel against God their creator, to whom God is implacably opposed inasmuch as they are in rebellion. Such a view does not commit to a particular philosophical or theological solution to the problem of evil (e.g., the more Augustinian *privatio boni*, or those who, like Boyd, put greater emphasis on creaturely freedom as the explanation for the horrors of evil); nor does it entail over-simplistic judgments concerning specific causes of particular evils.[269] It does, however, imply a call to become co-workers with God in the struggle against evil.

Secondly (*secondness*), the *victory of Christ the Son* in defeating evil, is the central "brute fact" which orients all spiritual warfare praxis.[270] Christ defeated the cosmic powers of evil that were opposed to him, through his life of obedience and resistance to temptation, his death upon the cross which dealt with sin, his resurrection that defeated death, and his ascension that exalted him far above all other spiritual and earthly powers.[271] Those who are "in Christ" (and they alone), having been set free from the law of sin and death and through faith and baptism incorporated into the new creation in Christ, are now seated in Christ in the heavenly realms; and can truly participate in this victory and take their stand in it, as they resist evil in its various manifestations.[272] It is primarily these "truths" that are the basis of victory over evil (hence the phrase "truth encounter").

Thirdly (*thirdness*), the *power and leading of the Holy Spirit* is the force and vector that applies this victory, particularly in its invisible spiritual dynamics.[273] Jesus says "my sheep listen to my voice," but it is the Holy Spirit who "takes from what is mine and makes it known to you."[274] It is those who

---

nevertheless I believe these three dimensions correspond well to the Piercean metaphysical scheme of firstness, secondness, and thirdness particularly as interpreted by Yong, so I have included these terms in brackets.

269. Boyd has demonstrated that belief in another layer of spiritual beings potentially adds to the complexity of specific causes. Boyd, *Satan and the Problem of Evil*, 308–10. See section 8.4.

270. Boddy's pithy phrase emphasizes this: "A great Christ means a very small devil." See section 2.2, and Boddy, *Confidence 1 no 2*, 3–4.

271. Eph 6:12; Col 2:15; Phil 2; Eph 1:20.

272. Rom 6:1–12; 1 Cor 12:12; 2 Cor 5:17; Eph 2:6; 6:10–12.

273. Again, Boddy summarizes this succinctly—the truth ("the Blood") releasing the power ("the Spirit"): "The pleading of the Blood in the power of the Holy Spirit will put to flight all the powers of darkness." Boddy, *Confidence 1 no 2*, 3–4.

274. John 10:16, 27; 16:14; 2 Tim 1:7;

are filled with the Holy Spirit who will most often provoke and encounter resistance and attack from Satan; those who are led by the Spirit of God as sons of God who will "pray in the Spirit" with all kinds of requests and be most effective both in resisting evil and fearlessly proclaiming the gospel, which will often involve us in a "titanic confrontation."[275] This confrontation will not only be with the "god of this age who has blinded the mind of unbelievers," but in seeking to bring justice and social transformation will also confront the "rulers of this age" that "crucified the Lord of glory," the powers of evil in their embodiment in political, economic, and social structures that seek to orient the world away from its created purpose.[276] "Spiritual discernment" therefore plays a key role in guiding spiritual warfare praxis. [277]

A spirituality of repentance, renewal, and resistance

In terms of spiritual praxis, the Anglican pioneers and the case study research revealed a wide range of "weapons" employed in the spiritual battle.[278] However, I believe that a spirituality of *repentance, renewal, and resistance* highlights three key steps in a holistic approach to spiritual warfare. These could be applied not only in charismatic prayer ministry, but in daily personal spirituality as well as at a more corporate level.

A charismatic spirituality of spiritual warfare at its best will be one that takes holiness or sanctification very seriously.[279] The interconnection of "the world, the flesh, and the devil" implies a strong link between powerlessness in overcoming evil and the extent to which a person needs to be set free from "sins of the flesh" that can "give the devil a foothold," or from strongholds of false worldly thought patterns.[280] This is through *repentance*, humbly

---

275. Luke 4:1, cf. Acts 7:55–57; Rom 8:14–15; Eph 6:18–20; Green, *I Believe in the Holy Spirit*, 70.

276. 2 Cor 4.4; 1 Cor 2:8. Whilst not this study's main focus, the perspectives of Yong and Wink have much to contribute here.

277. Thus, at St. George's "recognition" of particular issues (e.g., "strongholds") the Holy Spirit was drawing attention to at a prayer ministry session was considered a key initial step. Yong (see section 6.4) recommends a process of spiritual discernment at a more cautious, reflective, and rationalistic level—Yong, *Beyond the Impasse*, 158–59; "Spiritual Discernment," 104–5.

278. See particularly the analysis in table 3, Appendix 2.

279. One observer of the "Jesus ministry" approach adopted at St. George's called it "a new holiness movement." Ward, "Freedom Prayer."

280. "Foothold" (τοπος) in Eph 4:27; the strongholds of "arguments" and "pretensions" in 2 Cor 10:2–5.

turning back in submission to God the Father in his goodness,[281] whenever such compromise is recognized with the help of the Spirit's discernment; and a renouncing of ways of thinking that are based on "the principles of this world."[282] This should become part of a spiritual lifestyle of "continuous repentance" and not just on rare occasions.[283] Secondly, a *renewal* through faith in the life of Christ indwelling by the Spirit (Eph 3:16–17). This participatory union with Christ begins with an appropriation of death with Christ (not just "externally" receiving forgiveness and cleansing) that breaks the power of sin in the flesh, as well as rising with Christ which releases the life and power of new creation, and exaltation in Christ to a position of spiritual authority over evil.[284] Appropriating this truth of Christ's victory enables effective *resistance* in the power of the Spirit towards the devil and evil spirits that may be afflicting or oppressing a person (or a group), and energizing habitual sin patterns.[285]

In this way, in simplified terms, repentance, renunciation, and return to God as Father breaks the hold of "the world"; participating in the atoning death of Christ and his resurrection breaks the power of "the flesh"; and resistance appropriates the spiritual authority and the power of the Spirit that causes "the devil" to flee. This is not a "quick fix"; particularly where negative thought patterns and behaviors have become "a stronghold." These need replacing through "a renewing of the mind" (Rom 12:1–2) and filling with

---

281. Whilst μετάνοια is most often used in relation to initial conversion in the New Testament, other language such as confession (e.g., 1 John 1:9), submission to God (e.g., Jas 4:7–10; Eph 3:16), or "putting off"/"getting rid of" (e.g., Eph 4:25, 31) conveys a similar meaning.

282. Col 2:8; see also Gal 4:3, 8–9; 2 Cor 10:2–5. These texts hint at a battle with evil spiritual powers that can build up fleshly "strongholds" (through habitual thought patterns), lying behind the principles and pretensions of this world—especially if στοιχεῖα refer to demonic spirits—see section 8.4.

283. Pioneers had similar insights, for example: "So strongholds are dealt with first of all by *discernment* so that you identify them and experience them, and then by *repentance* because nearly always it means unlearning or *renouncing* attitudes that you see to be perfectly legitimate." David MacInnes Interview 6.4.06. Barrington-Ward also recommended a lifestyle of continuous repentance. Ward Interview 20.4.04. This lifestyle becomes easier once repentance is seen as a gracious turning back to God in his goodness—and so valued as a special gift (as emphasized at St. George's—cf. Acts 5:31).

284. Rom 6:1–7; Gal 2:20; 2 Cor 5:14; Eph 2:5–6; 2 Cor 5:15–17; Eph 2:6; Luke 10:18–19. Boddy is very practical: "Let us magnify Jesus until he is so great as to completely shut out the Devil from our thoughts." Alexander Boddy, *Confidence 1 no 2*, 3–4.

285. Jas 4:7; 1 Pet 5:9; Eph 4:26–7. This praxis can also be used corporately, for example in a church seeking to humbly discern and be released from its habitual negative thought patterns.

the Spirit, grounded on the truth of the goodness of God.[286] Thus praise will be an essential part of any spirituality that seeks to consistently appropriate in Christ the gift of victory over sin, death and the powers behind them (1 Cor 15:57, 24), as emphasized by the early pioneers;[287] as will some form of the traditional charismatic discipline of "putting on the armor of God" (Eph 6:10–19), which rightly comes after appropriating both the theological truths we have highlighted and the ethical exhortations of Ephesians 1 to 5.

Such an integrated charismatic spirituality can I believe recover a balanced approach to "spiritual warfare" which is not demon-centered, but Trinitarian and Christ-centered. It helps to recover ancient Catholic emphases on the world, the flesh, and the devil, and the dynamics of the baptismal promises (see below). It also emphasizes personal responsibility—central to the prayer ministry model at St. George's where the recipient rather than the prayer team was expected to pray the prayer of resistance towards the enemy and his attacks through fear, pride, or accusation. Whilst loss of personal responsibility is one of the key accusations brought against "the paranoid worldview,"[288] this had not been generally witnessed by the pioneers.[289] As a clear practical, biblical, and effective approach to resisting evil this approach should release from fear rather than engender it.[290] Evil is often overcome in this model primarily by an undramatic "truth encounter" rather than a "demonic exorcism" with dramatic manifestations. It thus further develops Twelftree's application of his analysis of early Christian exorcism to the contemporary situation, concluding that the New Testament canon presents a range of options such that the church may confront the demonic in the form of an exorcism *or* in the form of Truth.[291] This model integrates truth and deliverance from the demonic as part of regular charismatic praxis—a repentance that aligns the believer with the truth, and a resistance to the devil that confronts and seeks freedom from the demonic.

286. Cf. Phil 4:8. This theological foundation undergirding any warfare spirituality needs to be emphasized to avoid an exaggerated dualism focusing too much on evil forces.

287. Especially Watson, MacInnes, and Dunnett (cf. Eph 5:18–20).

288. For example producing the unacceptable excuse, "the devil made me do it." Scotland, "The Charismatic Devil," 105.

289. John Collins commented "people say it does, but pastorally I've never found that . . . they are far more likely to ignore what the devil is doing and not to take it seriously"; although Diana recognized that inadequate Christians sometimes hid behind blaming the devil. Collins Interview 30.4.04. MacInnes summarizes: "The truth is that wherever the devil holds sway it's because man is at fault." David MacInnes Interview 6.4.06.

290. This was overwhelmingly the experience at St. George's—see chapter 4.

291. Twelftree, *In the Name of Jesus*, 293–94.

This model is also a challenge to praxis that has become over-dependent on the pre-packaging of popular courses (such as Alpha, or "Freedom in Christ"). Embracing the humility and risk required to learn to minister to one another, and a more radical openness to the voice of the Spirit, can lead individuals and churches into a freedom from fear and a confidence in the authority given to believers in Christ to overcome all the works of the enemy.[292]

Proposing this as a helpful constructive model does not however mean that the dangers of charismatic spiritual warfare praxis are minimal; there remains plenty of scope for distortion and pastoral abuse. Some of the most worrying cases occur when there is an "institutional abuse" of power by church leaders and misuse of confidentiality and secrecy, as described by Parsons (who himself believes in the phenomenon of demon possession).[293] It was nevertheless encouraging to see that in St. George's where there was a considerable volume of deliverance prayer ministry, with many in the congregation and from outside (at conferences) involved in prayer teams, there was a constant emphasis on the recipient's freedom to accept or reject what was offered during the sessions, and an encouragement to pass back to the leaders anything they were unhappy with, especially so that it could influence further training. Another danger is when this model is applied in a too formulaic manner, or its emphasis on "dismantling strongholds" is used to try and dismantle (or worse, "exorcise") emotionally broken areas that instead indicate a gentle integrative healing approach.[294] I would suggest that often both dynamics are needed, but ministering in the compassion and love of Christ should be the overriding dynamic.[295]

---

292. John 10:3–4; 14:14; Jas 4:7; 1 Pet 5:9; Eph 4:26–27. The radical faith and associated praxis, in believing that all Christians can regularly hear God's voice, was developed first in a non-charismatic evangelical church naturally against the idea; which is a strong argument from "dissimilarity" that such praxis should be taken seriously. See Riches, *Hearing God's Voice*.

293. See Parsons, *Ungodly Fear*, 10. Hollenweger summarizes this as "that fear with which ministers manipulate their congregations and clients for their own egoistic ends." Hollenweger, "Review of 'Ungodly Fear,'" 135; Thomas, *The Devil, Disease and Deliverance*, 302–3.

294. Wink describes this dilemma from his own dreams, commenting "everything depends on whether the spirit is inner or outer . . . a matter of healing one's own soul or being freed from an alien power." Wink, *Unmasking the Powers*, 56–57. Yong however criticizes Wink here, arguing that the demonic has both outer ("larger than life forces") and inner (here in the human psyche) aspects. Yong, *Discerning the Spirits*, 299.

295. Whilst it is right to emphasize taking responsibility for fleshly sinful reactions (even to injustice done to that person) through repentance, and resisting the devil's attempts to manipulate these (Jas 4:6–10), there is invariably a need for healing of associated hurts through receiving the forgiveness and love of Christ, often mediated by

Not being a prominent feature in the main case study church, corporate spiritual warfare praxis in relation to wider social transformation did not become a main focus here, although it was discussed particularly in the pioneer interviews.[296] Theologically there have often been two polarized views. On the one hand, liberal Christianity has advocated vigorous social action in communities, and often the power of non-violence.[297] On the other, charismatics have often emphasized the power of prayer and praise (e.g., in the "*March for Jesus*" movement[298]) and "strategic level spiritual warfare" against "territorial spirits,"[299] potentially leading to social transformation.[300] The Anglicans I interviewed had varied but generally cautious reactions to Wagner's theology, aware of its dangers;[301] but some were supportive of the practical value of united prayer across cities as part of spiritual warfare,[302] and the need for "healing wounded history."[303] Many were realistic as to how far such transformation could go.[304] Some theological observers have also expressed serious concerns over "territorial spirits."[305]

---

prayer for filling with the Holy Spirit (Rom 5:5). Where there has been deep hurt or psychological stress, however, healing is rarely instant, and needs ongoing "self-care" in regularly seeking encounters with God's love (cf. Eph 3:16–20).

296. See section 3.5, and Appendix 2, tables 2 and 3.

297. As, for example, Wink has emphasized following Yoder—see Wink, *The Powers That Be: Theology for a New Millennium*, 114–27.

298. See for example Ediger, "Proto-Genesis of March for Jesus."

299. See Wagner, *Territorial Spirits*; Wagner and Pennoyer, *Wrestling with Dark Angels*; Wagner, *Warfare Prayer*.

300. For example, the book and videos produced by Otis—Otis Jr, *Informed Intercession*; "Transformations."

301. Woolmer seemed more open to Wagner's theology, most others were much more cautious. Generally, some of the methods were considered useful (e.g., "spiritual mapping," "identificational repentance"), as long as they didn't take the focus away from God in a "How to . . ." approach. See Appendix 2, table 3.

302. Holloway believed some real transformation had begun in some cities mainly through prayer, discernment, and worship (e.g., linked with youth social action in Manchester). She seemed to prefer "[going] in, wise to what's there, seeking God in prayer, praising him, and allowing him to remove stuff," to Wagner and Cindy Jacobs's approach of "confront everything with all your canons out there." Holloway Interview 17.8.06. One charismatic Anglican has written supportively, but with critical awareness—Leach, *Community Transformation*.

303. For two Anglican approaches to "healing wounded history," see Petrie, *Releasing Heaven on Earth*; Parker, *Healing Wounded History*.

304. For example: "If you talk about social transformation, unless you have an entire neighborhood converted you're not going to have social transformation in the sense of the Kingdom of God on earth . . . [but] what is important is that society is being affected by the ministry." MacInnes Interview 6.4.06.

305. Andrew Walker for example is concerned over ideas of "ruling demonic spirits"

Wink's work has helped to bridge the gap between these polarized approaches of social action and prayer; and more charismatics, as well as Pentecostal scholars such as Yong and Boyd, are now urging a conjoined approach of challenging the powers through both prayer and social action.[306]

Pneumatology and Spiritual warfare in the Anglican context

Most of this study would be relevant for Christians from any churches influenced by, or open to, the charismatic tradition. Let us consider briefly its specific relevance in the Anglican context.

The report of the Church of England on the charismatic movement suggested that, paradoxically, the impoverished pneumatology in the Church of England, as well as the partial intellectual vacuum in the area of the doctrine of the Holy Spirit in the church and in the West generally, had actually permitted new growth here. It nevertheless suggests a need for "a more defined Anglican stance in spirituality, faith, and in pastoral theology . . . to be Anglican these would have to be more than partisan, and yet without loss of sight of the particularities within the Church of England."[307] That has not really happened, at least not in relation to the pneumatology of evil. Even in charismatic Anglican churches, one pioneer noted that there had been very little teaching directly on spiritual warfare for several years.[308]

There has indeed been almost no exploration of pneumatology in the last century among non-charismatic Anglicans, apart from one by Taylor,[309] and some writings by G. W. H. Lampe.[310] However, partly as a result of the controversies relating to exorcism in charismatic renewal, appointing diocesan exorcists is standard practice in most Anglican dioceses; and there

---

(e.g., based on Daniel 10). Walker, "The Devil You Think You Know," 100. Another concern is an over-accommodation of Christianity to the "pre-modern" worldview of many other cultures and religions. See for example Ooi, "A Study of Strategic Level Spiritual Warfare from a Chinese Perspective," 160–61; Theron, "A Critical Overview"; Lowe, *Territorial Spirits and World Evangelisation?*

306. More charismatic Anglicans, for example in the New Wine movement, have been giving an increasing emphasis on social action. MacNutt also recommends a "both/and" approach—MacNutt, *Deliverance from Evil Spirits*, 253–64.

307. Buchanan et al., "The Charismatic Movement in the Church of England," 42, 48.

308. Holloway Interview 17.8.06.

309. Taylor, *The Go-between God*.

310. See Lampe, *God as Spirit*. In 1975 Lampe opposed the reintroduction of exorcistic practice in the church. See Cupitt, *Explorations in Theology 6*.

is an increasing openness to discuss the psychological and pastoral issues amongst clergy.[311] In so doing, one pioneer noted that this whole area "got buried in its memory, but often it's forgotten that it is there in the attic."[312] It can have a significant impact on the Anglican church in its parish-based mission, as local priests are still often called out into the community where there is a sense of an evil presence, "ghosts," or poltergeist activity, which benefits from awareness of the real possibility of the involvement of evil spirits as well as discernment as to other common causes.[313] The need Harper and Watson saw for discernment and an understanding of spiritual warfare in the 1960s is as real today in an era of spiritual experimentation, where experiences of an "evil presence" are common.[314]

The whole theology of spiritual warfare thus does "go with the grain" in the Anglican church,[315] giving plenty of space for a renewed theology of the nature of evil and how it is overcome.[316] I would highlight here three specific areas in which my proposed general model can re-invigorate Anglican spirituality, linked to aspects of its liturgical tradition. Firstly, there is the liturgy of baptism. To actively "reject the devil and all rebellion against God," "renounce the deceit and corruption of evil," repent and also commit to "fight valiantly . . . against sin, the world and the devil . . . to the end of your life" brings the baptismal promises alive and re-connects with the standard practice of the church for much of the first millennium.[317] Thus, new believers or confirmation candidates, as well as existing members, could be helped to find deliverance from the effects of past sin or injustices com-

---

311. I have attended such training days in the dioceses of Birmingham and Lichfield, the latter being heavily over-subscribed.

312. MacInnes also highlighted the value placed on reflection and reason amongst Anglicans: "I think Anglicanism has a way of giving a bit of sanity to some of these things. It's very heady stuff to suddenly find you're dealing with witches and so on . . ." David MacInnes Interview 6.4.06.

313. See, for example, one official handbook in this area, Michael Perry, *Deliverance*. Also practical guidelines in John Perry, Gunstone, and others, "A Time to Heal," 167–81.

314. Morgan, *Renewal: What Is It and What Is It For?* 16.

315. Collins Interview 30.4.04.

316. Barrington-Ward comments: "I believe it fits in with the old liturgy where lighten our darkness, defend us this day and against things that can attack us . . . are very much present in the Collects and the liturgy itself. The whole sense of warfare is there . . . I think it's in the great tradition of Christus Victor, not only Anglican but patristic." Ward Interview 20.4.04.

317. Hippolytus (*Apostolic Tradition* 21:7–10, early third century) records that explicit renunciation of the devil, and sometimes elaborate rituals of exorcism, were part of the liturgy for initiation into the body of Christ—see also Yong, *In the Days of Caesar*, 158.

mitted against them, being open also to the possibility of "healing the family tree."[318] As we have seen, submitting to God in continuous repentance, and resisting the devil is a valuable part of a lifestyle charismatic spirituality (based particularly on James 4). Secondly, the charismatic approach espoused brings alive the Lord's prayer, said at the majority of Anglican services, in all its dimensions—moving from the emphasis on focusing on worshipping God in the heavenly realms, and praying for his kingdom rule to be released here on earth, to an awareness of the centrality of confession and repentance, forgiveness towards others, resisting temptation, and praying for deliverance from the evil one as all vital aspects of a spirituality of "spiritual warfare."[319] And finally, the emphasis on the victory of Christ's death on the cross, through Jesus's substitutionary death ("my body broken for you") and cleansing from sin ("my blood shed for you"), is at the heart of the Eucharist, preserving a strong Christological focus; and bringing a new depth of victory to every member who renews his *participation* in the death and resurrection of Christ both at the Eucharist, and carried forward into daily spirituality.[320]

Finally, the Anglican church has always been a fruitful place for cross-fertilization of different spiritual traditions. A number of charismatics have already enriched this process;[321] and the findings here have similar potential—there are surprising resonances between the contemporary understanding at St. George's of the interaction of the earthly and heavenly realms and the Celtic roots of Anglican spirituality;[322] just as Mitton similarly discovered in the 1990s in helping to bring excesses of charismatic spiritual warfare into balance.[323]

318. Dr McAll's work highlights the value of this, which connects with the surprising frequency with which freedom prayer ministry at St. George's seemed to reveal issues of "generational sin." McAll, *Healing the Family Tree*.

319. The Litany in the Book of Common Prayer was essentially an elaboration of the petition "deliver us from evil"—see section 2.1. The Lord's Prayer and Anglican confession are often read out in church services, providing space for repentance but usually with little reflection on the deep underlying sin patterns at play. May-Ward, "A Critical Examination of Freedom Prayer."

320. In the context of warfare or mission, Ian, the vicar at St. George's, often took communion every day.

321. For example, Barrington-Ward cross-fertilised with the Orthodox in his rediscovery of the Jesus Prayer (see section 3.5). Finney notes that many Anglican charismatics move on to explore other forms of spirituality, such as Celtic or Ignatian. Finney, *Renewal as a Laboratory for Change*, 17.

322. See section 2.1. "Jesus Ministry," in seeking to set people free from the bondage of evil forces so that God's original design in creation for them may be restored, has Celtic resonances.

323. See Mitton, *Restoring the Woven Cord*.

9

Conclusion and Recommendations for Praxis

9.1 Conclusions

INDEPENDENT, INTELLIGENT, MALEVOLENT EVIL forces are ontologically real and need to be taken seriously. Jesus treated Satan and demons as real spiritual beings, linked together in opposition to the coming of God's kingdom. The nature of evil is "rebellion"; concepts of "nothingness" and "negation" whilst helpful are inadequate in describing the essence of evil, which is centered around a willful opposition to God's rule. This can only come from created beings exercising their God-given freedom of choice, whether human beings or fallen spiritual beings. Whilst this may appear to give philosophical difficulties in relation to the goodness of God, it is consistent with the testimony of the Scriptures that angelic beings as well as human ones are capable of rebellion. Despite the weak biblical evidence, the fall of angels hypothesis appears to have been assumed by the New Testament authors and remains the best available concerning the origin of evil. The nature of such powers has a "personal" dimension in the sense of agency, will and malevolent intelligence; but equally in the negative sense of being both "damaged or decaying persons" and also "anti-personal," because in their opposition to God they are focused on destroying the positive relational aspects of personhood in human beings.

Just because it is normally inaccessible to our five senses, this does not preclude the existence of a dimension of reality that the writer to the Ephesians calls "the heavenly realms." Nevertheless, the warning not to treat this too dualistically as a realm disconnected with the earthly should be heeded; Yong's emphasis on the need to discern concrete effects, and on the operation of the powers as force-fields and vectors, are a helpful counterbalance to an over-transcendentalist emphasis. Although difficult to investigate phenomenologically, the effects of the actions of such spiritual powers (as indeed, the effects of the Holy Spirit's actions) can be observed; charismatic Christians have a sound hermeneutical basis for interpreting these as confirmatory evidence for Scripture's testimony to the reality of such powers.

Focusing on the goodness, greatness, and love of God, the victory of Christ and the power of the Spirit is the key foundation for spiritual warfare, not focusing on evil. Although Christians should not "be ignorant of Satan's schemes," and learn more often to "resist the devil,"[1] it is more fundamental to rejoice in our identity as children of God and the freedom and authority that brings, and our participation in the life and death of Jesus that sets us free from sin, than to focus on demons and their activities.[2] This can help Christians to live in the "real" spiritual world, and avoid some of the excesses of "the paranoid universe," and in particular to be increasingly free of any fear associated with encountering evil.[3]

It is debatable how much inherent power "the devil and his angels"[4] have if they are indeed fallen angels; however, Satan's present power is primarily dependent on how much is given to him by human beings individually and corporately, through our own sinful rebellion against God. The only real solution for sin is the cross, where evil is disarmed and defeated;[5] therefore any "spiritual warfare" that does not through humility and repentance focus on the atoning power of the cross to forgive sin will be unbalanced and unhealthy. Nevertheless, the diffuse and inter-connected nature of evil as "the world, the flesh, and the devil" means that sin opens a door for increase in the devil's influence.[6] It is thus appropriate that the New Testament sees not only submission to God (the antidote to our own rebellion) but also resisting the devil as a normal part of Christian spirituality (e.g., James 4; 1 Peter 5), which some charismatics are helping to recover in an undramatic way. Therefore besides a renewal of faith in God's goodness and the believer's participation in the death, resurrection and victory of Christ, a spirituality based on repentance and resistance is recommended. Nevertheless, such activity needs to be integrated into a continuous sense of humble dependence upon the Spirit's leading and power, and Christ's love and compassion, not dependence on a formula.

"Prayer is spiritual warfare." This was the instinct of many of the pioneers studied, that the battle is real and pervasive on a spiritual level— not against flesh and blood, but against a range of spiritual forces "in the

1. 2 Cor 2:11; 1 Pet 5:9.
2. Luke 10:18–19.
3. Cf. 1 John 4:18, "perfect love drives out all fear."
4. Matt 25:41.
5. Col 2:15; Rev 12:11.
6. Cf. Eph 4:26–27.

heavenly realms," waged on a broad front in "all kinds of prayers."[7] This is a dimension of spirituality that Anglican and many other churches need to keep rediscovering, particularly in Britain, where (unlike much of the rest of the world) the rationalistic mindset tends to focus on methods in mission rather than the less tangible spiritual dynamics that Scripture exhorts Christians to put first.[8]

The awareness of this spiritual conflict is invariably heightened when the church takes the spiritual initiative, particularly in evangelism; but also in seeking social transformation. For charismatics, this heightened awareness (particularly for the early pioneers) especially came upon receiving the baptism or fullness of the Spirit, or seeking to impart it to others. Since it is the Spirit who often seems to bring us into the realm of conflict, engaging in the battle should similarly entail "praying in the Spirit at all times."[9]

9.2 Recommendations for further research

Several areas beyond the scope of this thesis are suggested for further research. Firstly, the pioneers clearly found that their experiences of the Spirit, and of spiritual warfare, brought a paradigm shift into new horizons in their interpreting of Scripture; whilst there has been a fair degree of theoretical discussion concerning Pentecostal and charismatic hermeneutics,[10] such "charismatic exegesis" in relation to experience merits further research.[11]

In the case study church, the credibility of their charismatic approach to discernment in prayer ministry relied considerably on the accuracy of the prophetic revelation received in listening prayer. A questionnaire survey of recipients agreed with the estimate that around 80% of the prophetic revelation was considered accurate.[12] This surprisingly high figure suggests it would be worthy of further investigation, not only quantitatively but qualitatively from a sympathetic observer, talking to prayer ministry recipients and their verification or otherwise of the prophetic information.[13] Also,

---

7. Eph 6:12, 18.

8. E.g., Matt 6:33; Col 3:1. See also Green, *I Believe in Satan's Downfall*, 248.

9. See Matt 4:1; Eph 6:18. Some pioneers highlighted "praying in the Spirit" specifically in relation to the use of tongues in the spiritual battle, but this phrase points generally to the "charismatic dimension" that should inspire all prayer (cf. Rom 8:26).

10. See section 8.1.

11. Such research would do well to dialogue with philosophical analysis of the evidential force of religious experience. Cartledge, *Testimony in the Spirit*, 89–90.

12. See section 4.5, and May-Ward, "A Critical Examination of Freedom Prayer."

13. Where verification is possible this would be of particular interest in view of

whilst observed "outcomes" from prayer ministry were generally positive, further study would be helpful particularly in following up cases where results were not immediately obvious, or benefits appeared short-lived; and in relation to people with more serious emotional, mental, and physical health issues, where there has been criticism of the dangers of formulaic deliverance approaches that may too readily try and "split off" areas of the psyche that may instead need to be reintegrated.[14] Clearly the interface between theology and psychology is important in relation to experiences of the demonic, and there is much scope here for further interdisciplinary research—for example as to how significant or effective is the emphasis not only on repentance but also resisting and rebuking the demonic energizing of sin patterns;[15] or investigation of the experiences of those who claim to regularly "see" demons.[16] More study of the phenomenology of other aspects of apparent demonic activity would continue to be of value.[17]

A variety of approaches to healing in relation to the demonic persist amongst Pentecostals and charismatics (and Anglicans[18]), partly reflecting different emphases within Scripture; and despite Thomas's thorough work, this remains fertile ground for further research.[19] Finally, the whole area of the influence of evil powers on geographical areas or local communities, and the effectiveness of various forms of prayer in "healing the land" and hastening spiritual and social transformation, remains poorly understood and yet is a vital issue for the church's mission.[20]

---

the high incidence of "generational issues" in such prophetic prayer ministry—rarely investigated apart from several well-documented cases in McAll, *Healing the Family Tree*, 5–21.

14. This constructive criticism was offered by a local church leader who had benefitted from "Jesus Ministry" himself, but had also seen some of its potential dangers in cases he related to in his counseling ministry. (Private phone conversation, 11.7.11).

15. This is highly rated as "absolutely strategic" in the practice of "Jesus Ministry," but is controversial in potentially giving too much focus on demonic powers. See Riches, *Strongholds*, 70–73.

16. See section 8.2.5.

17. Specifically, further study and phenomenological inquiry into poltergeist activity and other paranormal phenomena (both in houses and linked to individuals), involving well-documented case studies, would shed further light on this difficult area in terms of involvement or otherwise of demonic spirits (or possibly spirits of "the unquiet dead"). See section 8.2.

18. See in particular Perry, Gunstone, and others, "A Time to Heal," 167–81.

19. Thomas, *The Devil, Disease and Deliverance*. See also Twelftree, "Deliverance and Exorcism in the New Testament."

20. See pilot study (chapter 4.1). Two Anglicans taking a serious but popular approach here are Petrie, *Releasing Heaven on Earth*; Brown, *Angels on the Walls*.

9.3 Recommendations for praxis

I would make the following recommendations for praxis at St. George's:

Within their own healing praxis (e.g., in visualization during Freedom Prayer), I would encourage a discovery of the potency of the more dominant understanding of the atonement in Paul as representative as well as substitutionary (e.g., Gal 2:20; Romans 6).[21] Sin is dealt with not only by cleansing from the sinful act at the cross giving the "legal" right to rebuke the devil in that area, but going deeper in taking hold of our identity in Christ, participating in his death and resurrection, which takes the old self down into death with Christ so that he might then live his risen life through us.[22]

The praxis in ministry times of asking God questions in simple faith and expecting God to answer proved highly affirming and faith-building for prayer recipients. However, there is a danger here, not only of relying on the "tools" and expected answers rather than the Spirit's leading; but there needs to be a greater openness for God to *not* speak directly in answer to the questions if they are the wrong ones to ask; or for him to say "wait" and "trust," because now is not the time, accepting the mystery of the sovereign God who sometimes withholds himself.

Greater maturity in self-care needs to be encouraged, to prevent dependency on "prayer ministry" or "Freedom Prayer appointments," or on the revelation of others rather than discerning God's voice for oneself; a danger in our consumerist society.

The church emphasizes relentless pursuit of the supernatural, which does help correct current imbalance in Western theology and practice. However, this can lead to over-emphasis on causality in the heavenly realm—where sometimes practical actions to change circumstances might be just as much indicated. A more explicit theology of how God's Spirit works in and through the natural world[23] and physical causality within it would help correct an over-focused dualism, and would enable an easier partnership with those who are committed to compassionate social ministry as well as to the

---

21. In addition to visualizing being forgiven at the foot of the cross, and then coming before the risen Jesus, (before being asked to "resist the devil"), a powerful meditation might be seeing oneself united with Christ's death in the waters of baptism, and rising to new life with Christ's life within.

22. This theory of atonement is already explicit within some of the older literature that was recommended at St. George's, notably Watchman Nee's *The Normal Christian Life*.

23. See the conclusion to Nigel Wright, "The Theology and Methodology of Signs and Wonders," in Smail, Walker, and Wright, *Charismatic Renewal*, 84.

ecological renewal of creation; and also enable more support to those who are not always experiencing high doses of God's supernatural intervention.

Whilst the spirituality displays aspects of "yearning" as well as "blessing,"[24] developing "yearning" would help counterbalance the strongly realized eschatology. This might be through learning from other strands of spirituality, such as "the Jesus Prayer," in releasing the "groaning" of the Spirit;[25] rediscovering the Pentecostal power of waiting on God or "tarrying";[26] or making more space for the compassionate Jesus who weeps over Jerusalem, and over Lazarus' death. Such compassion would also bring greater motivation to again move out as a church to address more of the social needs in the area, building on the good foundations that have begun in outreach to disillusioned youth.

As people are rightly encouraged to seek their own personal freedom, there is the danger of developing an introspective "hospital mentality," the self-focus of always seeking more prayer, which can distract from the vital task of mission in the world.

---

24. See Lord, *Spirit-Shaped Mission: A Holistic Charismatic Missiology*, 9–12.

25. We have already seen how Barrington-Ward found this even more effective than tongues in mediating a sense of the Spirit's intercession (see chapter 3), as Lord also discovered in quoting Barrington-Ward—ibid., 131–32.

26. Or even the honesty of the Psalms in the spirituality of "lament," particularly in situations where prayers do not appear to be answered—see Ellington, "The Costly Loss of Testimony"; Lord, *Spirit-Shaped Mission: A Holistic Charismatic Missiology*, 128–30; Torr, *A Dramatic Pentecostal/Charismatic Anti-Theodicy*.

Appendix 1

Interview Questions for Pioneer Leaders in Anglican Charismatic Renewal

A. GENERAL: CHARISMATIC RENEWAL & MISSION

1. What do you understand as the primary purposes of the church's mission?
2. How would you assess success or effectiveness in mission? What has CR (*charismatic renewal*) contributed to the church's mission?
3. What are some of the most important factors that have led to the growth of charismatic churches in Britain (& worldwide)?
4. How significant is awareness of the spiritual battle in prayer in this growth?
5. Has the CR brought much social impact & transformation? Has SW (*spiritual warfare*) prayer played any role in this?

B. ORIGINS AND INFLUENCES

1. Before your involvement in charismatic renewal, what was your understanding of "spiritual warfare" or "the spiritual battle," and where did it come from?
2. How did your understanding of it change after experiencing char. renewal?
3. How much did your experiences shape your understanding and practice?
   (What kind of experiences?)
4. Were there any particular people whose writings, thinking or practical experience especially influenced you *(particularly in the early days)*?

5. Were there any biblical passages that gained new meaning & depth with respect to SW?
6. Do you think your views on SW have changed significantly since your early experiences of char renewal? *If so, how and why?*

C. BASIC BELIEFS

1. Are the terms SW or "the spiritual battle" helpful? If so, what do you understand by them?
2. What is the nature of the enemy, and what are the most important ways he influences people and the world? *(Can you give some specific examples?)*
3. How much power does Satan and his demons have, and where does it come from, both originally and in the world today? *(Has God limited his omnipotence?)(Does Satan regularly work through natural events?)*
4. How does SW fit in with your understanding of the kingdom of God & eschatology? *Does a right understanding of SW depend on holding particular eschatological views?*
5. What are the most effective ways for reducing the enemy's influence in the world?
6. In what circumstances or situations do you think the spiritual battle tends to be most acute? *Can you give some examples?*
7. What is the special contribution of CR to the theology and practice of SW? *How does a charismatic understanding of SW differ from a traditional or evangelical one?*

D. SPECIFIC ISSUES

1. Could evil powers be just the product of psychological and socio-spiritual forces?
2. *Is it important to believe that these forces are independent & intelligent? If so, why?*
3. How important is understanding and practice of SW in evangelism & the mission of the church? *Can you describe any instances where it was central?*

4. Is it reasonable to call the char renewal worldview dualistic? *(In what sense?)*
5. How true do you believe it is that: *(If so, can you illustrate from experience?)*
   a. evil spirits attach themselves to objects, buildings, or larger pieces of territory?
   b. there are different levels of SW? *(e.g., Strategic Level Spiritual Warfare, & Occult Level)*
   c. this can be approached methodically, e.g., through spiritual mapping, identificational repentance?
   d. SW plays a vital part in intercession for evangelism & mission?
   e. SW can play an important part in seeing social transformation?
6. Is a focus on SW likely to decrease a sense of personal responsibility?
7. Is SW primarily defensive, offensive, or both?
8. How much authority and power is given to Christians as God's agents in SW?

   What is God's part, and what is our part in the battle, and how do they relate?
9. What spiritual gifts are most important for SW, and why?

   How much is SW prayer for all Christians, & how much for those specially gifted?
10. What do you say to those who find the whole language of spiritual warfare unhelpful and dangerous, when we are trying to minimize wars, conflicts, and displays of power?
11. How relevant is SW in our current post-modern context?

E. OTHER HERMENEUTICAL ISSUES

1. Are OT themes of war and conflict relevant to our understanding of SW? If so, on what hermeneutical basis?
2. How much does the Bible tell us about the nature of the principalities & powers in Eph 6:12?
3. What does Paul mean by "strongholds" in 2 Cor 10, and how can they be torn down? What are the spiritual weapons he refers to here? *What are some key strongholds in Britain today?*

4. 2 Cor 4:4 talks of a spiritual blindness of unbelievers. How can this best be removed?

F. ANGLICAN RENEWAL

1. Do you know of any examples of Anglican CR where you believe SW has played a very significant part in the effectiveness of the church's mission in terms of a) evangelism & church growth, b) social transformation?

2. Compared to other key features of CR, e.g., worship, baptism/filling with the Spirit, tongues, etc., how significant is the SW dimension as a contribution to the renewal and mission of the Anglican Church?

3. How adequate is the grasp of SW issues in Anglican churches in this country, whether charismatic or non-charismatic?

4. How well do you feel the CR's approach to SW fits in with the tradition and spirituality of Anglican churches?

5. Is an emphasis on SW less relevant to Anglican churches in Britain than in other parts of the world because of the different religious, cultural, and economic environment here?

6. How important would a greater appreciation of SW be to help Anglican churches be more effective in mission rather than just maintenance? (*Why?*)

Appendix 2

Analysis of Pioneers' Warfare Theology and Praxis

(unless specifically referenced, information is from interviews, or referenced in chapter 3)

Table 1: ontology, nature, and origin of evil powers

	1. Ontology	2. Nature & character	3. Origin and explanation (theodicy)
Harper	Satan and evil spirits, which are personalities like angels, not impersonal influences; also carnal powers at another level	Clearly possess intelligence; Satan's great design is to "deceive the nations"[1]	Fallen angels (cf. Isa 14); a rebellion that parallels the human. Only have the power we allow them; God chose to exercise his omnipotence through man's free will
Watson	Flesh, world, and devil; "Satan and his angels . . . now disembodied spirits"[2]	Adversary of God: Angel of light, father of lies, enticing serpent, roaring lion[3]	Fallen angel (Isa 14) thrown out because of pride. *Suffering is evil but can be used by God*
Green	The devil, operating primarily undercover through the world and the flesh[4]	A violent, intelligent, liar, but bound; persistent, but fearful of the name of Jesus[5]	Fallen angelic spirit. Still God's devil: under His ultimate control, but has a lot of freedom and power[6]

APPENDIX 2: ANALYSIS OF PIONEERS' WARFARE THEOLOGY AND PRAXIS

	1. Ontology	2. Nature & character	3. Origin and explanation (theodicy)
Woolmer	Satan (the prince of this world) and evil spirits Must be more than psychological forces, argues against Wink's ontology	Scripture suggests some organization (Matt 10:25; 25:41); a subtle serpent, angel of light[7]	Origin/power unclear; now gets power when people open up to him. Devil can at times even loose himself from the line he is bound to
Collins	Independent and intelligent powers ("you see them doing things, then they stop!")	Spirits who become attached to things, e.g., a spirit of fear	It seems Satan was a fallen angel, but [Bible] has very little on that
MacInnes	A spiritual entity, beyond scientific observation, but effects can be recognized	Intimidates (roaring lion); deceiver (angel of light); cross illuminates nature of evil	Only hints in OT, so not clear; only Jesus really brings things of darkness to light
Walker	A real, personal spiritual being, Beelzebub the prince of demons	God's adversary, the rival for the throne; dragon/serpent/lion, power/malice/deceit; "god of this world"	"the originator of evil in us" but defeated at the cross and through believers (D-day analogy)[8]
Dunnett	A fallen angel—wholly wrong to think evil is impersonal	Powerful cognitive thinking; able to find your weaknesses; father of lies, prince of this world	We don't know how or why Satan did what he did, but evil is not eternal (see C. S. Lewis)
Holloway	Independent, intelligent evil forces taught from page 2 of Bible to the end	The complete opposite of who God is—death not life; and mimics (e.g., angel of light)	Has as much power as I give him—we have freedom of choice
Pytches	Satan and fallen angels	Deceiver, deludes, the tempter; seeking to devour & bring death	Satan fell from heaven with a third of the angels; we give him power. God allowed evil, misuse of the good
Warren	Forces often have psychol./socio-spiritual roots, but stand behind them. Bible tells us little but all we need to know	A malicious, secretive, hidden personal intelligence	From Job (cf. Wink) Satan is one of God's agents—but Darfur etc is profound evil

APPENDIX 2: ANALYSIS OF PIONEERS' WARFARE THEOLOGY AND PRAXIS

	1. Ontology	2. Nature & character	3. Origin and explanation (theodicy)
Barrington-Ward	He is a cunning and insidious, distorting and disintegrating power (but exact portrayal can become a caricature)	The Destroyer—fundamentally disintegration, alienation, dividing up, and breaking down	Augustinian: evil is absence of good, parasitic; Satan gets his power from a lie, loss of our true center

1. Harper, *Spiritual Warfare*, 32, 98.
2. Watson, *God's Freedom Fighters*, 52; *I Believe in the Church*, 142–49.
3. *God's Freedom Fighters*, 53–57.
4. Green, *I Believe in Satan's Downfall*, 53–57.
5. Ibid., 49–53.
6. Green Interview, and ibid., 33–41, 49–50.
7. Woolmer, *Healing and Deliverance*, 100–105.
8. Interview and Walker, *The Occult Web*, 38–39.

(Tables 2(a), (b), (c), and 3 can be found in the original thesis on the University of Birmingham website, etheses.com)

Appendix 3

Case Study Protocol: Interview Questions

PERSONAL DETAILS:

Date _____ Time started _____

Name _____ Pseudonym _____

Sex _____ Age group: -19/20-29/30-39/40-49/50-59/60-69/70-79/80+

Marital status _____ (children?) _____

Occupation _____

Original church background _____

How long at St. G _____

Would you personally identify with the charismatic renewal? *(i.e., have you had identifiable experiences of being filled with the Holy Spirit and/or operating in spiritual gifts such as tongues, prophecy, healing etc?)* How did it begin for you and when?

(NARRATIVE)

1. Tell me something about your church—why do you go there? What do people like about it? What has really helped it to grow?
2. Are the terms "spiritual warfare" (SW) and "spiritual battle" helpful? What do you mean by them?
3. In what way is spiritual warfare a significant part of the story of the church?
4. At what times have you personally been most aware of being in a spiritual battle?

(PRAXIS)

5. How do you tell whether a situation requires a spiritual warfare approach?
6. Is SW primarily defensive, offensive, or both?
7. What are the main weapons that you use in spiritual warfare?
8. When engaging with the enemy, what forms of prayer do you most often use?

    (e.g., praise, tongues, asking God for protection or deliverance, confession/repentance (personal or representative), speaking to the devil in rebuke or resistance, praying using the Word of God, fasting)

9. What charismatic spiritual gifts have you found most useful in the area of spiritual warfare? Describe briefly how they are used in this context.

    (e.g., discernment of spirits, word of knowledge, prophecy, tongues, gift of faith, etc)

10. What motivates you when you engage in spiritual warfare?
11. Is there a "strategy" in fighting the enemy in this parish—if so, how would you describe it?
12. How often:
    a. does SW form a conscious part of your own personal prayers
    b. is some form of SW prayer used in prayer meetings you have taken part in
    c. is SW taught about in the church?
13. How important is spiritual warfare in a) evangelism, b) seeking social transformation? *Can you give any examples?*
14. Do you think there are different levels of spiritual warfare, e.g., individual, "strategic-level spiritual warfare"?
15. How far can SW be approached methodically e.g., through "spiritual mapping," or "identificational repentance," or other models or techniques *(e.g., the 4 "R"s)*?

(ORIGINS AND INFLUENCES on interpretation and praxis)

16. When and how did you become aware that we are involved in a real spiritual battle?

17. What influences have most strongly formed your ideas and practice of SW?
18. How much have you been influenced by: *(be specific where relevant)*
    a. your experiences
    b. the Bible (any especially significant scriptures?)
    c. your leaders and other teachers and speakers
    d. books you have read
    e. conferences
19. Do you find OT themes of physical conflict relevant to your understanding of spiritual battle? If so, why?

(ONTOLOGY/THEOLOGY)

20. What is the nature of the evil spiritual forces we struggle against as Christians?

    How true for you are these possible descriptions of the powers of evil:

    personal *or* impersonal

    intelligent & purposeful *or* chaotic

    independent forces *or* the by-product of human evil

21. Which explanation(s) best fit for you as a description of the nature and origin of evil, and why?
    a. fallen angels
    b. forces of primal chaos (cf. Gen 1:1, Leviathan, etc.)
    c. an empty shadow, like a black hole
    d. psychological and socio-spiritual forces
22. How much power do evil forces have, as opposed to God? Where does their power come from?
23. How much can supernatural evil forces influence natural events?
24. What is the relationship between sickness, healing, and the demonic?
25. Where do you believe they locate or attach themselves—a) people, b) physical buildings, and places c) wider geographical areas?
26. How would you say these forces most often attack a) Christians b) the wider society in your area?

27. When would you say that the spiritual battle is most acute or intense?
28. What do you think is actually going on when you come against evil in prayer?
29. What benefits or effects of spiritual warfare prayer have you experienced or seen?
30. How important is it for Christians to believe that they are in a real spiritual battle?

Time Finished: _____

Appendix 4

Case Study Category Analysis

These diagrams were constructed primarily from content analysis of the interview scripts, supplemented by other data from participant observation.
  a) Sub-categories which were more widely emphasized are put higher in a list
  b) Categories where uncertainty was expressed or were weakly supported, I have written as:
  Questioned or uncertain?
  Weakly supported?

THEOLOGY - Validation:

Scripture — 'the plumb line'
- Eph 2.6, 4.27, 6.10-18; 2 Cor 10:3-5; Gal 4:8-9 *(stoicheia)*; 2 Tim 1:7; Rom 8:37-9
- 1Pet 5:8-9, Jas 4:7 *(resist the devil)*
- Jesus in the gospels, John 14:14; the Lord's prayer
- Rev 13:1 *(dragon on the shore of the sea)*
- 2 Kings 6:16-17 *(seeing heaven's armies)*, 2 Sam 5:24

Experience
- Encounters with the demonic
- Power of repentance
- Reaction against bad practice
- Good fruit from integrating SW into a lifestyle

Tradition
- early charismatic *(deliverance ministry)*
- 'Third Wave' *(Wimber, e.g. value of repentance)*
- Teaching
  - Leaders *(esp. St George's, Tacoma)*
  - Conferences
  - Writers/books *(see text)*

APPENDIX 4: CASE STUDY CATEGORY ANALYSIS

THEOLOGY – Ontology/cosmology:

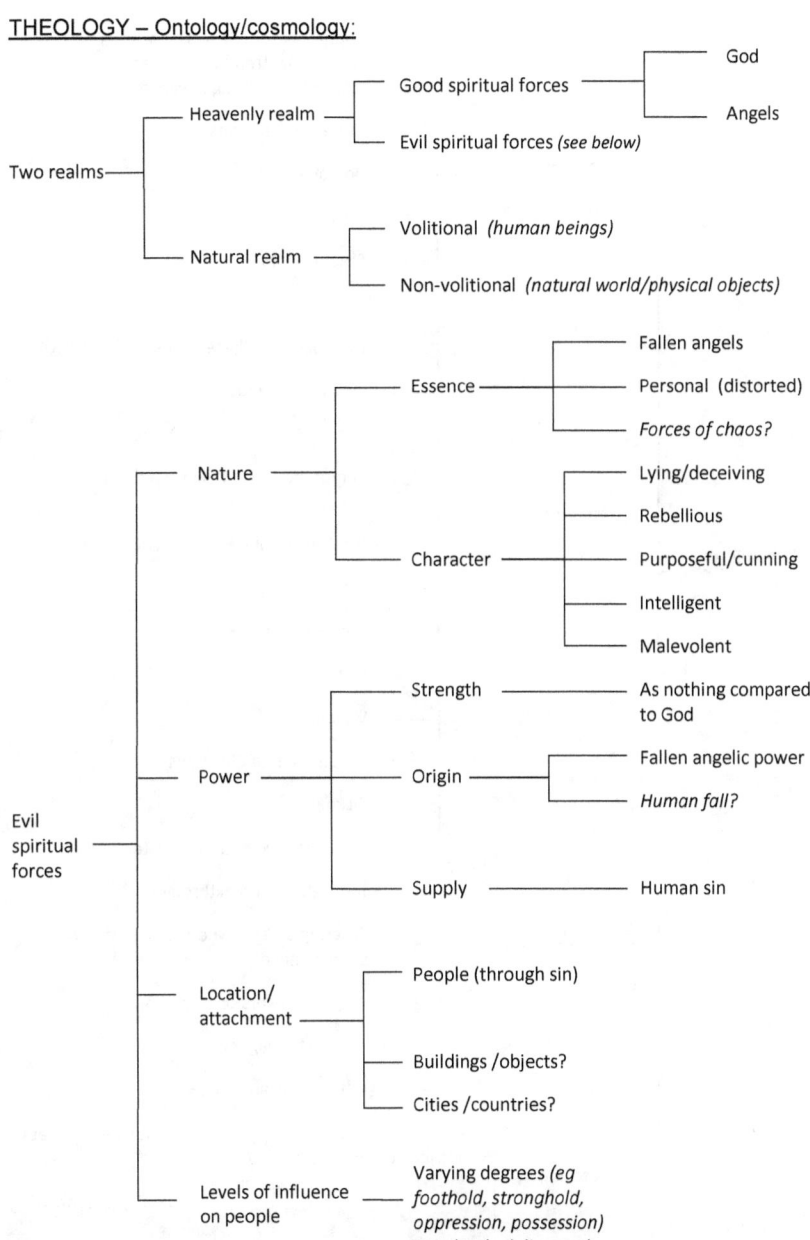

APPENDIX 4: CASE STUDY CATEGORY ANALYSIS

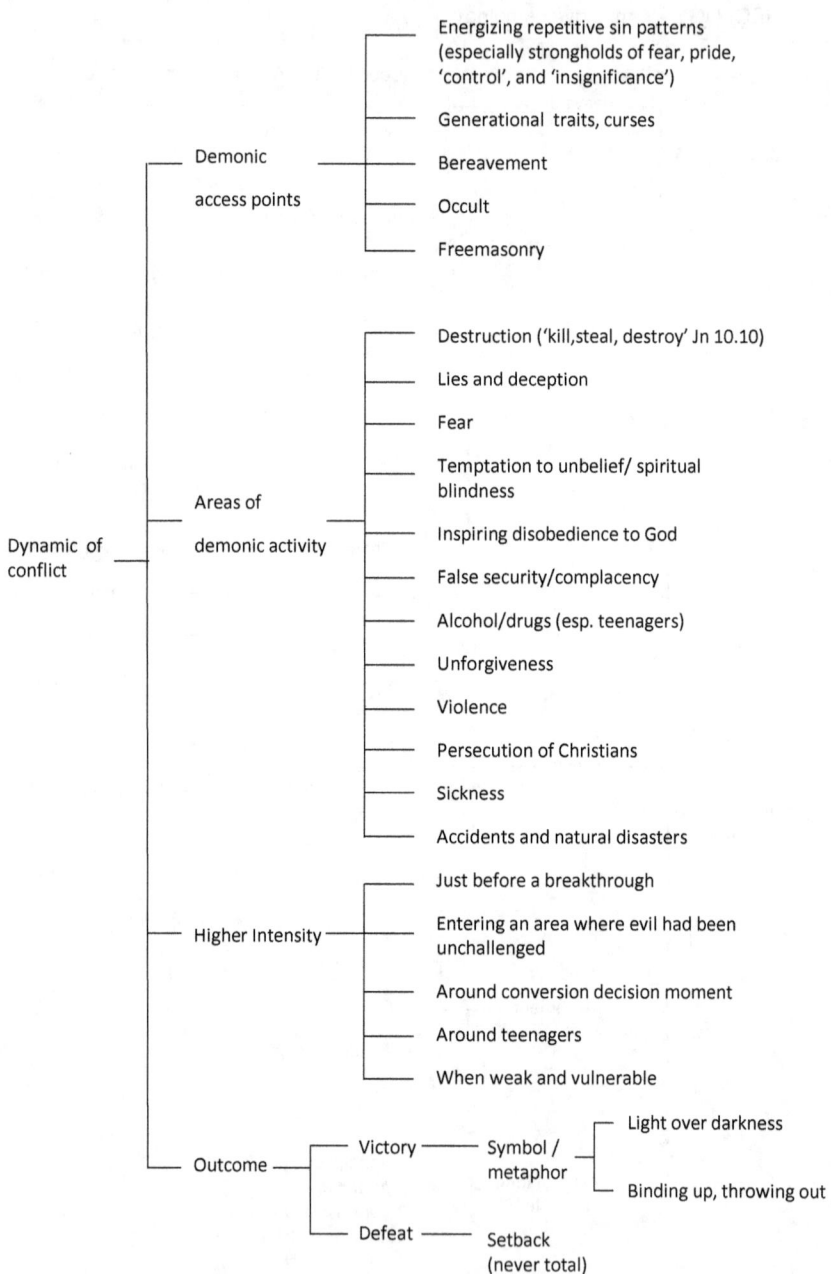

APPENDIX 4: CASE STUDY CATEGORY ANALYSIS   261

PRAXIS – 'spiritual weapons':

[There is considerable overlap between some categories below – for example 'authority' was given as a main weapon by some interviewees, but it is naturally also included as a mode of prayer.]

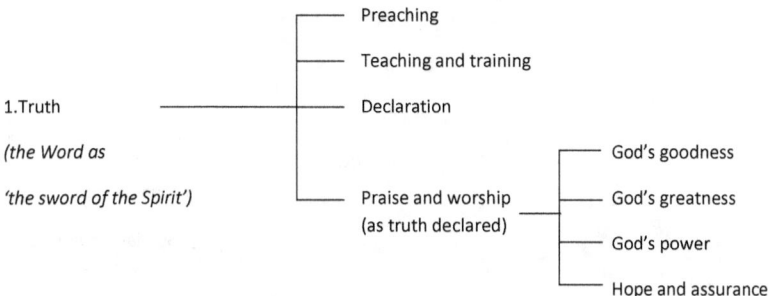

1. Truth
   (the Word as
   'the sword of the Spirit')
   - Preaching
   - Teaching and training
   - Declaration
   - Praise and worship (as truth declared)
     - God's goodness
     - God's greatness
     - God's power
     - Hope and assurance

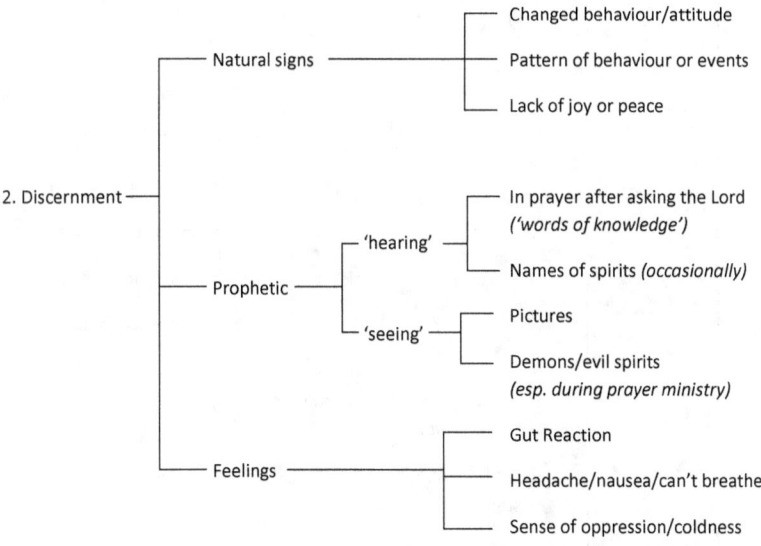

2. Discernment
   - Natural signs
     - Changed behaviour/attitude
     - Pattern of behaviour or events
     - Lack of joy or peace
   - Prophetic
     - 'hearing'
       - In prayer after asking the Lord ('words of knowledge')
       - Names of spirits *(occasionally)*
     - 'seeing'
       - Pictures
       - Demons/evil spirits *(esp. during prayer ministry)*
   - Feelings
     - Gut Reaction
     - Headache/nausea/can't breathe
     - Sense of oppression/coldness

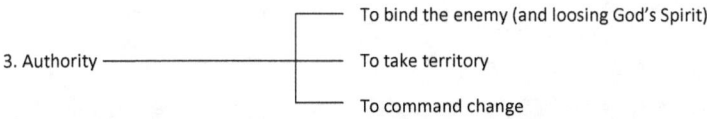

3. Authority
   - To bind the enemy (and loosing God's Spirit)
   - To take territory
   - To command change

APPENDIX 4: CASE STUDY CATEGORY ANALYSIS

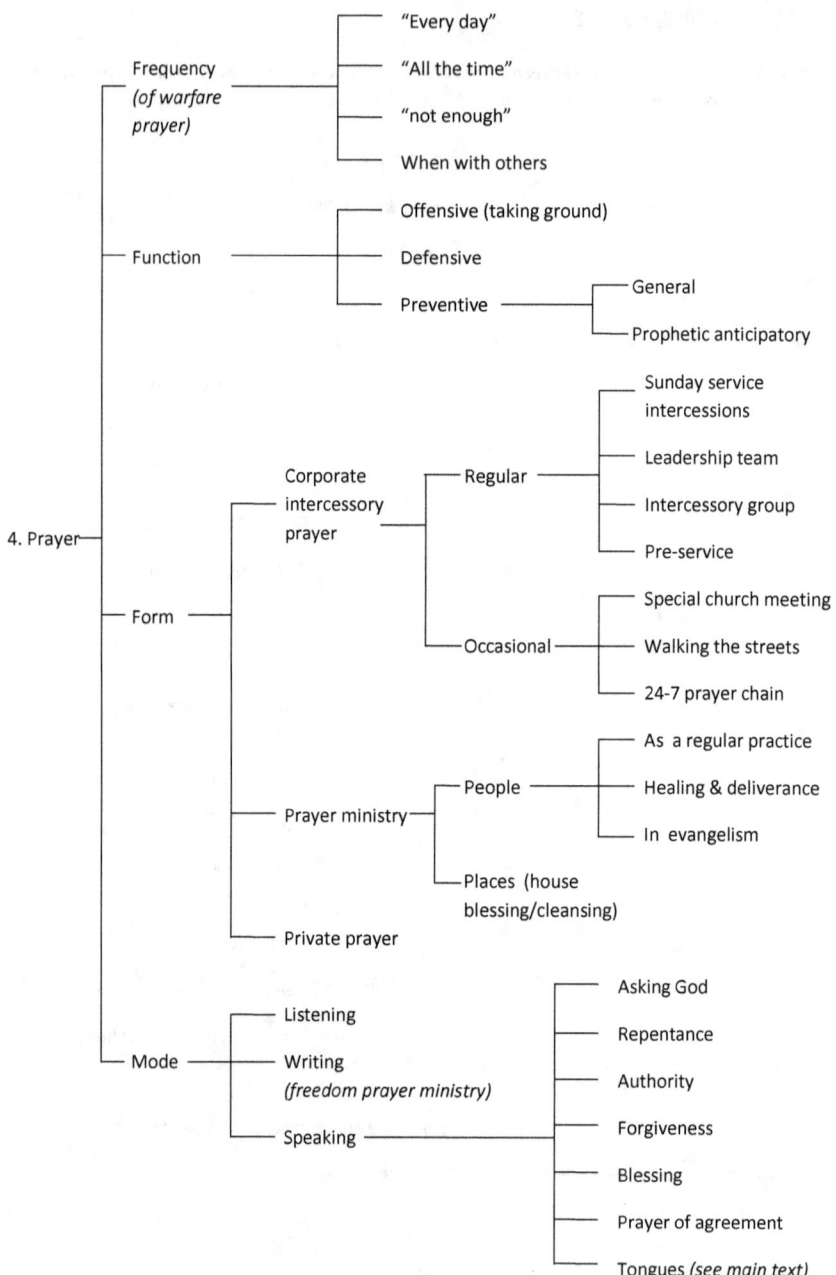

APPENDIX 4: CASE STUDY CATEGORY ANALYSIS 263

PRAXIS (continued) – Motivating Affections and Outcomes:

Motivating affections
- Anger and Indignation
- Compassion
- Desire to set people free
- Desire for God
  - To meet/engage (even 'play') with God
  - To walk closely with Him
  - To be effective for Him
- Prospect of
  - Greater joy and encouragement
  - Hopes realised
  - Discovering the power of the cross
- Courage and determination

Outcomes
- 'Good fruit'
  - Personal spiritual transformation (eg 'lightness of spirit', 'becoming the person I'm meant to be')
  - Transformed relationships (eg marriage, with children, in church)
  - Physical Healing (e.g. from infertility)
  - Increased Commitment to church life (esp. men)
  - Prophetic encouragement ('God has spoken to me')
  - Increased love for Christ and others
  - Sense of empowerment
  - Increased expectation God can use me to help others outside church
- Possible dangers
  - Demon focus bringing fear
  - Reliance on techniques
  - Doing it alone (not in community)
  - Arrogance
  - Superspirituality

Bibliography

Adam, David. *The Rhythm of Life: Celtic Daily Prayer*. London: SPCK, 1996.
Albani, Matthias. "The Downfall of Hellel, the Son of Dawn: Aspects of Royal Ideology in Isa 14:12-13." In *Fall of the Angels: Themes of the Biblical Narrative*, edited by Christopher Auffarth and Loren T. Stuckenbruck, 62-86. Brill: Leiden, 2004.
Albrecht, Daniel E. *Rites in the Spirit*. Sheffield, UK: Sheffield Academic Press, 1999.
Anderson, Allan. *Origin & Development of Global Pentecostalism*. University of Birmingham Lecture notes, 2004.
Anderson, Bernard W. *Creation Versus Chaos*. New York: Association Press, 1967.
Anderson, Neil T. "Finding Freedom in Christ." In *Wrestling with Dark Angels*, edited by C. Peter Wagner and F. Douglas Pennoyer, 126-59. Ventura, CA: Regal, 1990.
Angel, Andy. *Angels: Ancient Whispers of an Ancient World*. Eugene, OR: Cascade, 2012.
Archer, Kenneth J. "Early Pentecostal Biblical Interpretation." *Journal of Pentecostal Theology* 18 (2001) 32-70.
———. *A Pentecostal Hermeneutic for the Twenty-First Century: Spirit, Scripture and Community*. JPT Supplement 28. London: T. & T. Clark, 2004.
———. "Pentecostal Hermeneutics: Retrospect and Prospect." *Journal of Pentecostal Theology* 8 (1996) 63-81.
———. "Pentecostal Story: The Hermeneutical Filter for the Making of Meaning." *Pneuma* 26, no. 1 (2004) 36-59.
Arnold, Clinton. "A Critique of Wesley Carr's View of the Role of Evil Powers in First-Century AD Belief." *Journal for the Study of New Testament* 30 (1987) 71-87.
———. *Ephesians: Power and Magic: The Concept of Power in Ephesians in Light of Its Historical Setting*. Cambridge: Cambridge University Press, 1989.
———. *Powers of Darkness: A Thoughtful, Biblical Look at an Urgent Challenge Facing the Church*. Leicester, UK: IVP, 1992.
———. "Returning to the Domain of the Powers: *Stoicheia* as Evil Spirits in Galatians 4:3, 9." *Novum Testamentum* 38, no. 1 (1996) 55-76.
———. *Three Crucial Questions about Spiritual Warfare*. Grand Rapids: Baker, 1997.
Astley, Jeff. *Ordinary Theology*. Aldershot, UK: Ashgate, 2002.
Au, Connie. "Grassroots Unity and the Fountain Trust International Conferences: A Study of Ecumenism in the Charismatic Renewal." Ph.D., University of Birmingham, 2008.
Auffarth, Christopher, and Loren T. Stuckenbruck, eds. *Fall of Angels: Themes of the Biblical Narrative*. Brill: Leiden, 2005.
Augustine, Saint. *The City of God*. Translated by J. W. C. Wand. London: Oxford University Press, 1963.

———. *On Free Choice of the Will*. Translated by Anna S. Benjamin and L. H. Hackstaff. New York: Bobbs-Merrill, 1964.

Aulen, Gustaf. *Christus Victor: An Historical Survey of the Three Main Types of the Idea of the Atonement*. 1930. ET. London: SPCK, 1970.

Ball, Edward. "Review of *I Believe in Satan's Downfall*." *Theological Renewal*, no. 19 (Oct 81) 33–35.

Ballard, Paul, and John Pritchard. *Practical Theology in Action*. London: SPCK, 1996.

Barrington-Ward, Simon. "My Pilgrimage in Mission." *International Bulletin of Missionary Research* 23.2 (1999). Online: http://www.martynmission.cam.ac.uk/pages/published-papers.php. Accessed 31.8.10.

Barth, Karl. *Church Dogmatics: Authorised English Translation*. Translated by G. W. Bromiley and T. F. Torrance. Edinburgh: T. & T. Clark, 1960.

Beckley, Pedr. *Mission in a Conspiracy Culture*. Ev 60. Cambridge: Grove, 2002.

Berger, Peter. *A Rumour of Angels: Modern Society and the Rediscovery of the Supernatural*. Harmondsworth, UK: Penguin, 1970.

Berkhof, H. *Christ and the Powers*. Translated by J. H. Yoder. Scottdale, PA: Herald, 1962.

Betty, Stafford. "The Growing Evidence for 'Demonic Possession': What Should Psychiatry's Response Be?" *Journal of Religion and Health* 44, no. 1 (2005) 13–30.

Bevans, Stephen B. *Models of Contextual Theology*. Maryknoll, NY: Orbis, 1992.

Boddy, Alexander. *Confidence* 1, no. 2 (May 1908).

———. *Confidence* 3, no. 8 (Aug 1910).

———. *Confidence* 4, no. 3 (March 1911).

———. *Confidence* 129 (Apr–Jun 1922).

———. "Faith Healing in Scripture and Experience." *Confidence* 6, no. 12 (Dec 1913).

Boddy, Mary. *Confidence* 1, no. 1 (April 1908).

Boethius. *The Theological Tractates and the Consolation of Philosophy*. Translated by H. F. Stewart and E. K. Rand. London: Heinemann, 1918.

Bonhoeffer, Dietrich. *Cost of Discipleship*. London: SCM, 1959.

Bowsher, Andii. *Demolishing Strongholds: Evangelism & Strategic-Level Spiritual Warfare*. Ev 21. Cambridge: Grove Books, 1993.

Boyd, Gregory A. "Christus Victor Response." In *The Nature of the Atonement—Four Views*, edited by Paul R. Eddy and James Beilby, 99–105. Downers Grove, IL: IVP, 2006.

———. "Christus Victor View." In *The Nature of the Atonement—Four Views*, edited by Paul R Eddy and James Beilby, 25–49. Downers Grove, IL: IVP, 2006.

———. *God at War: The Bible and Spiritual Conflict*. Downers Grove, IL: IVP, 1996.

———. *God of the Possible: A Biblical Introduction to the Open View of God*. Grand Rapids: Baker, 2000.

———. *Gregory Boyd Faqs*. Online: http://www.gregboyd.org/about/greg-boyd/faq/. Accessed 5.8.08.

———. *Oneness Pentecostals and the Trinity*. Grand Rapids: Baker, 1992.

———. *Satan and the Problem of Evil: Constructing a Trinitarian Warfare Theodicy*. Downer's Grove, IL: IVP, 2001.

———. *Trinity and Process: A Critical Evaluation and Reconstruction of Hartshorne's Di-Polar Theism towards a Trinitarian Metaphysics*. New York: Lang, 1992.

Bradley, Ian. *Celtic Christianity: Making Myths and Chasing Dreams*. Edinburgh: Edinburgh University Press, 1999.

Bradnick, David. "Demonology and Anthropology in Conversation: Applying the Theological Method of Amos Yong towards a Demonology for the Twenty-First Century." Paper presented at the 38th Annual Meeting of the Society for Pentecostal Studies, 2009.

Brown, Wallace, and Mary Brown. *Angels on the Walls*. Eastbourne, UK: Kingsway, 2000.

Bryman. *Sociological Research Methods*. Oxford: Oxford University Press.

Buchanan, Colin, Colin Craston, and others. "The Charismatic Movement in the Church of England." London: The General Synod of the Church of England, 1981.

Burgess, R. G. *In the Field: An Introduction to Field Research*. London: Allen & Unwin, 1984.

Burgess, S. M., and F. van der Maas, eds. *New International Dictionary of Pentecostal and Charismatic Movements*. Grand Rapids: Zondervan, 2003.

Cameron, Helen, Philip Richter, Douglas Davies, and Frances Ward. *Studying Local Churches—A Handbook*. London: SCM, 2005.

Carr, Wesley. *Angels and Principalities*. Society for New Testament Studies Monograph Series 42. Cambridge: Cambridge University Press, 1981.

Cartledge, Mark. *Practical Theology: Charismatic and Empirical Perspectives*. Carlisle, UK: Paternoster, 2003.

———. "Demonology and Deliverance: A Practical-Theological Case Study". In *Exorcism and Deliverance: Multidisciplinary Studies*, edited by William K. Kay and Robin A. Parry, 243–63. Milton Keynes, UK: Paternoster, 2009.

———. *Testimony in the Spirit: Rescripting Ordinary Pentecostal Theology*. Farnham, UK: Ashgate, 2010.

———. "Tongues of the Spirit: An Empirical-Theological Study of Charismatic Glossolalia." Ph.D., University of Wales, 1999.

———. "Why Did Christ Die? A Symposium on the Theology of Atonement." *Anvil* 22, no. 3 (2005) 213–20.

Charlesworth, James H., ed. *The Old Testament Pseudepigrapha* Vol. 1. New York: Doubleday, 1983.

Childs, Brevard S. *Myth and Reality in the Old Testament*. London: SCM, 1960.

The Church of England. *The Shorter Prayer Book: Being an Abbreviated Form of the Book of Common Prayer*. London: Oxford University Press, 1946.

Church of England Doctrine Commission. "We Believe in the Holy Spirit." London: Church House Publishing, 1991.

Collins, James. "Deliverance Ministry in the Twentieth Century." In *Exorcism and Deliverance: Multidisciplinary Studies*, edited by William K. Kay and Robin Parry, 86–100. Milton Keynes, UK: Paternoster, 2009.

Coleman, Simon. *The Globalisation of Charismatic Christianity*. Cambridge: Cambridge University Press, 2000.

Cook, Robert. "Devils and Manticores: Plundering Jung for a Plausible Demonology." In *The Unseen World*, edited by Anthony N. S. Lane, 165–84. Carlisle, UK: Paternoster, 1996.

Cortes, Juan B., and Florence M. Gatti. *The Case against Possessions and Exorcisms*. New York: Vantage, 1975.

Cox, Harvey. *Fire from Heaven: The Rise of Pentecostal Spirituality and the Reshaping of Religion in the Twenty-First Century*. London: Cassell, 1996.

C. S. Lewis Centenary Group. "Centenary Programme Reports." Online: http://dnausers.d-n-a.net/cslewis/prog_reports.html. Accessed 14.4.16.

Cullmann, Oscar. *Christ and Time*. Translated by F. V. Wilson. Rev. ed. London: SCM, 1962.

———. *Prayer in the New Testament*. London: SCM, 1995.

Cunningham, Lawrence S. "Satan: A Theological Meditation." *Theology Today* 51, no. 3 (1994) 359–66.

Cupitt, Don. *Explorations in Theology 6*. London: SCM, 1979.

Daniel, Evan. *The Prayer-Book: Its History, Language and Contents*. London: Wells Gardner, Darton & Co., 1909.

Dempster, M. A., B. D. Klaus, and D. Petersen, D., eds. *The Globalisation of Pentecostalism*. Oxford: Regnum, 1999.

Denzin, N. K. *Interpretive Ethnography*. Thousand Oaks, CA: Sage, 1997.

Dey, Ian. *Qualitative Data Analysis*. London: Routledge, 1993.

Dixon, Patrick. *Signs of Revival*. Eastbourne, UK: Kingsway, 1994.

Dostoevsky, Fyodor. *The Brothers Karamazov*. Translated by Constance Garnett. New York: Norton, 1976.

Dow, Graham. "The Case for the Existence of Demons." *Churchman* 94, no. 3 (1980) 199–207.

———. *Explaining Deliverance*. Tonbridge, UK: Sovereign World, 2003.

Droogers, Andre. "Globalisation and Pentecostal Success." In *Between Babel and Pentecost: Transnational Pentecostalism in Africa and Latin America*, edited by Andre Corten and Ruth Marshall-Fratani, 41–61. Bloomington, IN: Indiana University Press, 2001.

Droogers, Andre, and Peter Versteeg. "A Schema Repertoire Approach to Exorcism: Two Case Studies of Spiritual Warfare." In *Coping with Evil in Religion and Culture*, edited by Nelly van Doorn-Harder and Lourens Minnema, 105–24. Amsterdam: Editions Rodopi, 2008.

Duffy, Eamon. *The Stripping of the Altars: Traditional Religion in England 1400–1580*. New Haven: Yale University Press, 1992.

Dunn, James D. G. *Baptism in the Spirit*. London: SCM, 1970.

———. *Jesus and the Spirit*. London: SCM, 1975.

Ediger, Charles C. "The Proto-Genesis of the March for Jesus Movement, 1970–87." *Journal of Pentecostal Theology* 12, no. 2 (2004) 247–75.

Ellington, Scott A. "The Costly Loss of Testimony." *Journal of Pentecostal Theology* 16 (2000) 48–59.

Ellul, Jacques. *The Subversion of Christianity*. Translated by Geoffrey W. Bromiley. Grand Rapids: Eerdmans, 1987.

ESRC (Economic and Social Research Council). *Framework for Research Ethics*, 2010. Online: http://www.esrc.ac.uk/files/funding/guidance-for-applicants/esrc-framework-for-research-ethics-2010/. Accessed 14.4.16.

Fackre, Gabriel. "Angels Heard and Demons Seen." *Theology Today* 51, no. 3 (1994) 345–58.

Ferdinando, Keith. "Biblical Concepts of Redemption and African Perspectives of the Demonic." PhD, London Bible College, 1992.

———. "Screwtape Revisited: Demonology Western, African and Biblical." In *The Unseen World*, edited by Anthony N. S. Lane, 103–32. Carlisle, UK: Paternoster, 1996.

Finney, John. *Renewal as a Laboratory for Change*. Cambridge: Grove Books, 2006.
Flick, U. *An Introduction to Qualitative Research*. 2nd ed. London: Sage, 2002.
Foster, K. Neill, and Paul L. King. *Binding and Loosing: Exercising Authority over the Dark Powers*. Camp Hill, PA: Christian, 1998.
Gelpi, Donald. *The Divine Mother: A Trinitarian Theology of the Holy Spirit*. Lanham, MD: University Press of America, 1984.
Gooder, Paula. *Only the Third Heaven? 2 Corinthians 12:1-10 and Heavenly Ascent*. London: T. & T. Clark, 2006.
———. *Searching for Meaning: An Introduction to Interpreting the New Testament*. London: SPCK, 2008.
Green, Joel B. "Kaleidoscopic Response to Christus Victor View." In *The Nature of the Atonement—Four Views*, edited by Paul R. Eddy and James Beilby, 61-65. Downers Grove, IL: IVP, 2006.
———. "Kaleidoscopic View." In *The Nature of the Atonement—Four Views*, edited by Paul R. Eddy and James Beilby, 157-85. Downers Grove, IL: IVP, 2006.
Green, Laurie. *Let's Do Theology*. London: Mowbray, 2000.
Green, Michael. *Adventure of Faith*. Grand Rapids: Zondervan, 2001.
———. *Asian Tigers for Christ*. London: SPCK, 2001.
———. *Evangelism in the Early Church*. London: Hodder & Stoughton, 1970.
———. *I Believe in Satan's Downfall*. London: Hodder & Stoughton, 1980.
———. *I Believe in the Holy Spirit*. London: Hodder & Stoughton, 1975.
Green, Michael, and Jane Holloway. *Evangelism through the Local Church*. London: Hodder & Stoughton, 1990.
Grenz, Stanley J. *The Social God and the Relational Self*. Louisville, KY: Westminster John Knox, 2001.
Guelich, Robert A. "Spiritual Warfare: Jesus, Paul, and Peretti." *The Journal of the Society for Pentecostal Studies* 2, no. 1 (1991) 33-64.
Gumbel, Nicky. *Questions of Life*. Eastbourne, UK: Kingsway, 1993.
Gunstone, John. *A People for His Praise*. London: Hodder, 1978.
———. *Signs and Wonders: The Wimber Phenomenon*. London: DLT, 1989.
Hammond, Frank, and Ida Mae. *Pigs in the Parlour*. Kirkwood, MO: Impact, 1973.
Harper, Michael. *As at the Beginning*. London: The Fountain Trust, Hodder, 1965.
———. "Deliver Us from Gullibility." *Renewal* 45, Jun/July 1973, 128.
———. *The Healings of Jesus*. London: Hodder 1986.
———. *Jesus the Healer*. Guildford, UK: Highland Books, 1992.
———. "Ministry in Spiritual Warfare: Two Dutch Evangelists Visit Britain." *Renewal* 3, May/June 1966, 18-19.
———. *None Can Guess*. London: Hodder & Stoughton, 1971.
———. *Spiritual Warfare*. London: Hodder & Stoughton, 1970.
———. *Walk in the Spirit*. London: Hodder & Stoughton, 1968.
Hartshorne, C., P. Weiss, and A. Burks, eds. *Collected Papers of Charles Sanders Peirce*. 1935. Reprint. Cambridge: Harvard University Press, 1958.
Hendel, Ronald. "The Nephilim Were on the Earth: Genesis 6:1-4 and Its Ancient Near Eastern Context." In *Fall of the Angels: Themes of the Biblical Narrative*, edited by Christopher Auffarth and Loren T. Stuckenbruck, 11-34. Leiden: Brill, 2004.
Hendry, George S. "Nothing." *Theology Today* 39, no. 2 (1982) 274-89.
Hick, John. *Evil and the God of Love*. 2nd ed. Basingstoke, UK: Macmillan, 1985.
Hiebert, Paul G. "Spiritual Warfare and Worldviews." *Direction* 29, no. 2 (2000) 114-24.

Hocken, Peter. *Streams of Renewal: The Origins and Early Development of the Charismatic Movement in Great Britain*. Carlisle, UK: Paternoster, 1997.
Hollenweger, Walter J. "Biblically 'Justified' Abuse: A Review of Stephen Parsons, Ungodly Fear: Fundamentalist Christianity and the Abuse of Power." *Journal of Pentecostal Theology* 10, no. 2 (2002) 129–35.
———. *Pentecostalism: Origins and Developments Worldwide*. Peabody, UK: Hendrickson, 1997.
———. *The Pentecostals*. London: SCM, 1972.
Holloway, Jane. "Understanding Intercession." *Anglicans for Renewal* 82 (Winter 2000) 9–11.
Horton, Michael S. "Post-Reformation Reformed Anthropology." In *Personal Identity in Theological Perspective*, edited by Richard Lints, Michael S. Horton and Mark R. Talbot, 45–69. Grand Rapids: Eerdmans, 2006.
Hughes, Philip. *The Churchman* 76, no. 3 (1962) 131–35.
Hunt, Stephen. "The Anglican Wimberites." *Pneuma* 17, no. 1 (1995) 105–18.
———. "Deliverance: The Evolution of a Doctrine." *Themelios* 21, no. 1 (1995) 10–16.
Jones, Cheslyn, Geoffrey Wainwright, and Edward Yarnold, eds. *The Study of Spirituality*. London: SPCK, 1992.
Jorgensen, Danny L. *Participant Observation: A Methodology for Human Studies*. London: Sage, 1989.
Kay, William K. "A Demonised Worldview: Dangers, Benefits and Explanations." *Journal of Empirical Theology* 11 (1998) 17–30.
Kay, William K, and Robin A. Parry, eds. *Exorcism and Deliverance: Multidisciplinary Studies*. Milton Keynes, UK: Paternoster, 2009.
Kim, Seyoon. *Paul and the New Perspective: Second Thoughts on the Origin of Paul's Gospel*. Grand Rapids: Eerdmans, 2002.
Koch, Kurt. *Between Christ and Satan*. Berghausen, Germany: Evangelization Publishers, 1961.
———. *Occult Bondage and Deliverance*. Berghausen, Germany: Evangelization Publishers, 1970.
Kreeft, Peter. *Angels (and Demons)*. San Francisco: Ignatius, 1995.
Lalive d'Epinay, Christian. *Haven to the Masses: A Study of the Pentecostal Movement in Chile*. London: Lutterworth, 1969.
Lampe, G. W. H. *God as Spirit*. Oxford: Clarendon, 1977.
Land, Steven J. *Pentecostal Spirituality: A Passion for the Kingdom*. Sheffield, UK: Sheffield Academic Press, 1993.
Lane, Anthony N. S., ed. *The Unseen World*. Carlisle, UK: Paternoster, 1996.
Lawrence, Peter. *The Hot Line*. Eastbourne, UK: Kingsway, 1990.
Leach, John. *Community Transformation*. Cambridge: Grove Books, 2001.
Lederle, Henry I. "Life in the Spirit and Worldview: Some Preliminary Thoughts on Understanding Reality, Faith and Providence from a Charismatic Perspective." In *Spirit and Renewal: Essays in Honour of J. Rodman Williams*, edited by Mark W. Wilson, 22–33. Sheffield, UK: Sheffield Academic Press, 1994.
Levenson, Jon D. *Creation and the Persistence of Evil: The Jewish Drama of Divine Omnipotence*. Princeton, NJ: Princeton University Press, 1988.
Lewis, C. S. *Four Broadcast Talks*. London: Bles, 1942.
———. *The Screwtape Letters*. London: Bles, 1942.

Lichtenberger, Hermann. "The Down-Throw of the Dragon in Revelation 12 and the Down-Fall of God's Enemy." In *Fall of Angels: Themes of the Biblical Narrative*, edited by Christopher Auffarth and Loren T. Stuckenbruck, 119–47. Leiden: Brill, 2004.

Lincoln, Andrew T. *Ephesians*. Word Biblical Commentary 20. Dallas: Word, 1990.

———. "A Re-Examination of 'the Heavenlies' in Ephesians." *New Testament Studies* 19 (1972) 468–83.

Linn, Matt. *Deliverance Prayer: Experiential, Psychological and Theological Approaches*. New York: Paulist, 1981.

Lloyd-Jones, D. Martyn. *The Christian Warfare: An Exposition of Ephesians 6:10 to 13*. Edinburgh: Banner of Truth Trust, 1976.

Lloyd, Michael. "The Cosmic Fall and the Free Will Defence." DPhil, Worcester College, Oxford University, 1996.

Longman III, Tremper, and Daniel G. Reid. *God Is a Warrior*. Studies in Old Testament Biblical Theology. Grand Rapids: Zondervan, 1995.

Lord, Andrew. *Spirit-Shaped Mission: A Holistic Charismatic Missiology*. Milton Keynes, UK: Paternoster, 2005.

Lowe, Chuck. *Territorial Spirits and World Evangelisation?* Borough Green, UK: OMF, 1998.

Lyons, J. "The Fourth Wave and the Approaching Millennium: Some Problems with Charismatic Hermeneutics." *Anvil* 15, no. 3 (1998) 169–80.

Ma, Bonsuk. "A 'First Waver' Looks at the 'Third Wave'—Charles Kraft's Power Encounter Terminology." *Pneuma* 19, no. 2 (1997) 189–206.

MacGrath, Alistair. *Christian Theology*. Oxford: Blackwell, 1994.

MacGregor, G. H. C. "Principalities and Powers: The Cosmic Background of Paul's Thought." *New Testament Studies* 1 (1954) 17–28.

MacInnes, David. *Conflict with the Devil*. Nottingham, UK: St. John's Nottingham Library: Fountain Trust Tapes F79.3, 1977. F79.3.

Mackey, James P. *An Introduction to Celtic Christianity*. Edinburgh: T. & T. Clark, 1989.

Mackie, J. L. "Evil and Omnipotence." In *God and the Problem of Evil*, edited by William Rowe, 77–90. 1955. Reprint. Oxford: Blackwell, 2001.

MacNutt, Francis, O.P. *Deliverance from Evil Spirits*. London: Hodder & Stoughton, 1995.

———. *Healing*. Notre Dame, IN: Ave Maria, 1974.

Martin, David. *Pentecostalism: The World Their Parish*. Oxford: Blackwell, 2002.

Martin, M. *Hostage to the Devil: The Possession and Exorcism of Five Americans*. San Francisco: Harper, 1992.

Mascall, E. L. *Christian Theology and Natural Science: Some Questions on Their Relations*. London: Longmans, Green and Co, 1956.

Mason, J. *Qualitative Researching*. 2nd ed. London: Sage, 2002.

Mather, Ann. "The Theology of the Charismatic Movement 1964 to the Present Day." PhD, University of Wales, 1983.

May-Ward, Perry. "A Critical Examination of Freedom Prayer and Why It Is a Helpful Corrective for the Praxis of Ministry in Charismatic, Anglican Churches." M.A. diss., Heythrop College, University of London, 2007.

McAll, Kenneth. *Healing the Family Tree*. London: Sheldon (SPCK), 1986.

McBain, Douglas. *Fire over the Waters: Renewal among Baptists and Others from the 1960s to the 1990s*. London: DLT, 1997.

McClung, L. Grant Jr., ed. *Azusa Street and Beyond: Pentecostal Missions and Church Growth in the Twentieth Century*. South Plainfield, NJ: Logos, 1986.
McIntosh, Mark. *Mystical Theology*. Oxford: Blackwell, 1998.
Meyer, Birgit. *Translating the Devil: Religion and Modernity among the Ewe in Ghana*. International African Library. Edinburgh: Edinburgh University Press, 1999.
Mitton, Michael. "Editorial." *Anglicans for Renewal*, no. 45 (Summer 1991).
———. *Restoring the Woven Cord: Strands of Celtic Christianity for the Church Today*. London: DLT, 1995.
Moltmann, Jürgen. *God in Creation*. London: SCM, 1985.
———. *The Spirit of Life: A Universal Affirmation*. Translated by M. Kohl. London: SCM, 1992.
Morgan, Alison. *Renewal: What Is It and What Is It For?* Cambridge: Grove Books, 2006.
Moustakas, Clark. *Phenomenological Research Methods*. London: Sage, 1994.
Mursell, Gordon. *English Spirituality:1700 to the Present Day*. London: SPCK, 2001.
Nee, Watchman. *The Normal Christian Life*. 3rd ed. Eastbourne, UK: Kingsway, 1961.
Noble, Thomas A. "The Spirit World: A Theological Approach." In *The Unseen World*, edited by Anthony N. S. Lane, 185–223. Carlisle, UK: Paternoster, 1996.
Noel, Bradley Truman. "Gordon Fee and the Challenge to Pentecostal Hermeneutics: Thirty Years Later." *Pneuma* 26, no. 1 (Spring 2004) 60–80.
Noll, Stephen F. "Thinking about Angels." In *The Unseen World*, edited by Anthony N. S. Lane, 1–27. Carlisle, UK: Paternoster, 1996.
O'Sullivan, Anthony. "Roger Forster and the Ichthus Fellowship: The Development of a Charismatic Missiology." *Pneuma* 16, no. 2 (1994) 247–63.
Oliver, Paul. *The Student's Guide to Research Ethics*. 2nd ed. Maidenhead, UK: Open University Press, 2010.
Onyinah, Opuku. "Akan Witchcraft and the Concept of Exorcism in the Church of Pentecost." PhD, University of Birmingham, 2002.
Ooi, Samuel Hio-Kee. "A Study of Strategic Level Spiritual Warfare from a Chinese Perspective." *Asian Journal of Pentecostal Studies* 9, no. 1 (2006) 143–61.
Osborn, Lawrence. "Angels: Barth and Beyond." In *The Unseen World*, edited by Anthony N. S. Lane, 29–48. Carlisle, UK: Paternoster, 1996.
Osmer, Richard. *Practical Theology: An Introduction*. Grand Rapids: Eerdmans, 2008.
Otis, George Jr. *Informed Intercession: Transforming Your Community through Spiritual Mapping and Strategic Prayer*. Ventura, CA: Renew, 1999.
———. *Transformations: A Documentary*. 58 min. Lynnwood, WA: The Sentinel Group, 1999.
Otzen, Benedict, Hans Gottlieb, and Knud Jeppesen. *Myths in the Old Testament*. Translated by Frederick Cryer. London: SCM, 1980.
Page, Sidney H. T. *Powers of Evil: A Biblical Study of Satan & Demons*. Grand Rapids: Baker, 1995.
Pannenberg, Wolfhart. *Systematic Theology*. Vol. I, Grand Rapids: Eerdmans, 1991.
Parker, Russ. *Healing Wounded History: Reconciling Peoples and Healing Places*. London: DLT, 2001.
Parsons, Stephen. *Ungodly Fear*. Oxford: Lion, 2001.
Pattison, Stephen. "Some Straw for the Bricks: A Basic Introduction to Theological Reflection." *Contact* 99, no. 2 (1989) 2–9.
Peck, M. Scott. *People of the Lie*. New York: Simon and Schuster, 1983.

Penn-Lewis, Jessie, and Evan Roberts. *War on the Saints*. 9th ed. 1913. Reprint. New York: Lowe, 1973.
Percy, Martyn. *Words, Wonders and Power: Understanding Contemporary Christian Fundamentalism and Revivalism*. London: SPCK, 1996.
Perry, John, John Gunstone, and others. "A Time to Heal: A Report for the House of Bishops on the Healing Ministry." London: The Archbishops Council, 2000.
Perry, Michael, ed. *Deliverance: Psychic Disturbances and Occult Involvement*. London: SPCK, 1987.
Petitpierre, Dom Robert, ed. *Exorcism: The Findings of a Committee Convened by the Bishop of Exeter*. London: SPCK, 1972.
Petrie, Alistair. *Releasing Heaven on Earth*. Grand Rapids: Chosen Books (Baker), 2000.
Pinnock, Clark H. "The Work of the Holy Spirit in Hermeneutics." *Journal of Pentecostal Theology* 2 (1993) 3–23.
Plantinga, Alvin. "The Free Will Defense." 1971. In *God and the Problem of Evil*, edited by William Rowe, 91–120. Oxford: Blackwell, 2001.
Plotinus. *Enneads*. Translated by Stephen MacKenna. 3rd ed. London: Faber & Faber, 1962.
Pomerville, Paul. *The Third Force in Mission*. Peabody, MA: Hendrickson, 1985.
Pratt, Thomas D. "A Review of the Debate on Signs, Wonders, Miracles and Spiritual Warfare in the Literature of the Third Wave Movement." *Pneuma* 13, no. 1 (1991) 7–32.
Purcell, William. *Anglican Spirituality: A Continuing Tradition*. Oxford: Mowbray, 1988.
Pytches, David. *And Some Said It Thundered*. London: Hodder & Stoughton, 1990.
———. *Come, Holy Spirit*. London: Hodder & Stoughton, 1985.
———. *Does God Speak Today?* London: Hodder & Stoughton, 1989.
———. *Leadership for New Life*. London: Hodder & Stoughton, 1998.
———. *Living at the Edge*. Bath: Arcadia, 2002.
———. *Prophecy in the Local Church*. London: Hodder & Stoughton, 1993.
Pytches, David, and Nigel Scotland, eds. *Recovering the Ground: Towards Radical Church Planting for the Church of England*. Chorleywood, UK: Kingdom Power Trust, 1995.
Raposa, Michael L. *Peirce's Philosophy of Religion*. Bloomington, IN: Indiana University Press, 1989.
Reason, Peter, ed. *Participation in Human Enquiry*. London: Sage, 1994.
Reid, Michael S. B. *Strategic Level Spiritual Warfare: A Modern Mythology?* Fairfax, VA: Xulon, 2002.
Richards, John. *But Deliver Us from Evil*. London: DLT, 1974.
Riches, Mike. *Hearing God's Voice*. London: Jesus Ministry International, 2007.
———. *One World—Two Realms: Operating in Christ's Authority*. Tacoma, WA: Jesus Ministry International, 2004.
———. *Strongholds: Understanding and Destroying Satan's Schemes*. Tacoma, WA: Jesus Ministry International, 2004.
———. "When God Invades His People." *Radiate*, July/Aug 2004, 14–16.
Riddell, Peter G., and Beverley Smith Riddell, eds. *Angels and Demons*. Nottingham, UK: IVP, 2007.
Robinson, Martin. "The Charismatic Anglican—Historical and Contemporary: A Comparison of the Life and Work of Alexander Boddy (1854–1930) and Michael C. Harper." MLitt, University of Birmingham, 1976.

Sanders, E. P. *Paul and Palestinian Judaism*. London: SCM, 1977.
———. *Paul, the Law, and the Jewish People*. London: SCM, 1985.
Saunders, Teddy, and Hugh Sansom. *David Watson: A Biography*. London: Hodder, 1992.
Schreiner, Thomas R. "Penal Substitution Response." In *The Nature of the Atonement—Four Views*, edited by Paul R. Eddy and James Beilby. Downers Grove IL: IVP, 2006.
Schreiter, Robert J. *Constructing Local Theologies*. London: SCM, 1985.
Schwarz, Hans. *Evil: A Historical and Theological Perspective*. Minneapolis: Augsburg Fortress, 1995.
Schweitzer, A. *The Mysticism of Paul the Apostle*. Translated by W. Montgomery. London: A. & C. Black, 1931.
Scotland, Nigel. "The Charismatic Devil: Demonology in Charismatic Christianity." In *Angels and Demons: Perspectives and Practice in Diverse Religious Traditions*, edited by Peter G. Riddell and Beverley Smith Riddell, 84–105. Nottingham, UK: Apollos, 2007.
———. *Charismatics and the New Millennium*. Guildford, UK: Eagle, 2000.
Sheets, Dutch. *Intercessory Prayer*. Ventura, CA: Regal, 1996.
Silvoso, Ed. *Prayer Evangelism*. Ventura, CA: Regal, 2000.
———. *That None Should Perish*. Ventura, CA: Regal, 1994.
Smail, T., A. G. Walker, and N. G. Wright. *Charismatic Renewal*. London: SPCK, 1995.
Smart, Ninian. *The Phenomenon of Religion*. London: Macmillan, 1973.
Soskice, Janet M. *Metaphor and Religious Language*. Oxford: Clarendon, 1985.
Spradley, James P. *Participant Observation*. New York: Holt, Rinehart & Winston, 1980.
Springer, Kevin, ed. *Riding the Third Wave*. Basingstoke, UK: Marshall Pickering, 1987.
Stake, Robert E. *The Art of Case Study Research*. London: Sage, 1995.
Steven, James H. S. "Praise Marches." *News of Liturgy* 179 (Nov 1989).
———. *Worship in the Spirit: Charismatic Worship in the Church of England*. Studies in Evangelical History and Thought. Carlisle, UK: Paternoster, 2002.
Stibbe, Mark. "This Is That: Some Thoughts Concerning Charismatic Hermeneutics." *Anvil* 15, no. 3 (1998) 181–93.
Stott, John, and others. *The Anglican Communion and Scripture*. Oxford: Regnum/EFAC, 1996.
Stott, John R. W. *The Cross of Christ*. Leicester, UK: IVP, 1986.
Strange, William. "Dispensing with the Devil: Reflection on Kay." *Journal of Empirical Theology* 11 (1998) 30–36.
Stuckenbruck, Loren T. "The Origins of Evil in Jewish Apocalyptic Tradition: The Interpretation of Genesis 6:1–4 in the Second and Third Centuries B.C.E." In *Fall of Angels: Themes of the Biblical Narrative*, edited by Christopher Auffarth and Loren T. Stuckenbruck, 87–118. Brill: Leiden, 2005.
Subritzky, Bill. *Demons Defeated*. Chichester, UK: Sovereign World International, 1986.
Swinburne, Richard. *Providence and the Problem of Evil*. Oxford: Clarendon, 1998.
Swinton, John, and Harriet Mowat. *Practical Theology and Qualitative Research*. London: SCM, 2006.
Synan, Vinson. *The Holiness-Pentecostal Tradition: Charismatic Movements in the Twentieth Century*. 2nd ed. Grand Rapids: Eerdmans, 1997.
Taylor, John V. *The Go-between God: The Holy Spirit and the Christian Mission*. London: SCM, 1972.

Taylor, Mrs. Howard. *Behind the Ranges: Fraser of Lisuland South-west China*. London: China Inland Mission (OMF)/Lutterworth, 1944.
Taylor, Vincent. *The Atonement in New Testament Teaching*. London: Epworth, 1940.
Theron, Jacques. "A Critical Overview of the Church's Ministry of Deliverance from Evil Spirits." *Pneuma* 18, no. 1 (1996) 79–92.
———. "The Ministry of Deliverance from Evil Forces: The Need for Academic Reflections in Pentecostal Churches in Africa." *Practical Theology in South Africa* 21, no. 3 (2006) 191–206.
Thiselton, Anthony. *New Horizons in Hermeneutics: The Theory and Practice of Transforming Bible Reading*. London: Harper Collins, 1992.
Thomas, J. C. "Women, Pentecostals and the Bible: An Experiment in Pentecostal Hermeneutics." *Journal of Pentecostal Theology* 5 (1994) 41–56.
———. *The Devil, Disease and Deliverance*. Sheffield, UK: Sheffield Academic Press, 1997.
Torr, Stephen. *A Dramatic Pentecostal/Charismatic Anti-Theodicy: Improvising on a Divine Performance of Lament*. Eugene, OR: Pickwick, 2012.
Turner, Max. *The Holy Spirit and Spiritual Gifts*. Carlisle, UK: Paternoster, 1996.
Twelftree, Graham H. *Christ Triumphant: Exorcism Then and Now*. London: Hodder & Stoughton, 1985.
———. "Deliverance and Exorcism in the New Testament." In *Exorcism and Deliverance: Multidisciplinary Studies*, edited by William K. Kay and Robin A. Parry, 45–68. Milton Keynes, UK: Paternoster, 2009.
———. *In the Name of Jesus*. Grand Rapids: Baker Academic, 2007.
———. *Jesus the Exorcist: A Contribution to the Study of the Historical Jesus*. Peabody, MA: Hendrickson, 1993.
Ukpong, Justin. "What Is Contextualisation?". In *Readings in World Mission*, edited by Norman Thomas. London: SPCK, 1995.
Unger, Merrill F. *Biblical Demonology*. Wheaton, IL: Scripture Press Foundation, 1952.
———. *Demons in the World Today*. Wheaton, IL: Tyndale House, 1972.
Urquhart, Colin. *Faith for the Future*. London: Hodder and Stoughton, 1982.
———. *When the Spirit Comes*. London: Hodder and Stoughton, 1974.
van der Ven, J. A., and F. Schweitzer. *Practical Theology—International Perspectives*. Frankfurt am Main: Lang, 1999.
van Doorn-Harder, Nelly, and Lourens Minnema, eds. *Coping with Evil in Religion and Culture*. Amsterdam: Editions Rodopi, 2008.
Wagner, C. Peter, ed. *Territorial Spirits: Insights on Strategic-Level Spiritual Warfare from Nineteen Christian Leaders*. Chichester, UK: Sovereign World, 1991.
———. *Warfare Prayer: Strategies for Combating the Rulers of Darkness*. Tunbridge Wells, UK: Monarch, 1992.
Wagner, C. Peter, and F. Douglas Pennoyer, eds. *Wrestling with Dark Angels*. Ventura, CA: Regal, 1990.
Wakefield, Gavin. *Alexander Boddy: Pentecostal Anglican Pioneer*. Carlisle, UK: Paternoster, 2007.
Wakeman, Mary K. *God's Battle with the Monster*. Leiden: Brill, 1973.
Walker, Andrew G. "The Devil You Think You Know: Demonology and the Charismatic Movement." In *Charismatic Renewal: The Search for a Theology*, edited by T. Smail, A. G. Walker and N. G. Wright, 86–105. London: SPCK, 1995.
———. *Enemy Territory*. London: Hodder & Stoughton, 1987.

———. *Restoring the Kingdom: The Radical Christianity of the House Church Movement.* London: Hodder & Stoughton, 1985.

Walker, Tom. *The Occult Web.* Leicester, UK: UCCF Booklets, 1987.

———. *Open to God—a Parish in Renewal.* Bramcote, UK: Grove, 1975.

———. *Renew Us by Your Spirit.* London: Hodder & Stoughton, 1982.

Ward, Kevin. *A History of Global Anglicanism.* Cambridge: Cambridge University Press, 2006.

Warren, E. Janet. "Spiritual Warfare: A Dead Metaphor?" *Journal of Pentecostal Theology* 21, no. 2 (2012) 278–97.

———. *Cleansing the Cosmos: A Biblical Model for Conceptualizing and Counteracting Evil.* Eugene, OR: Pickwick, 2012.

Warren, Robert. *Being Human, Being Church.* London: Marshall Pickering, 1995.

———. *Building Missionary Congregations.* General Synod Board of Mission Occasional Paper No 4. London: Church House, 1995.

———. *In the Crucible: The Testing and Growth of a Local Church.* Crowborough, UK: Highland, 1989.

———. *On the Anvil: The Art of Learning Leadership from Experience.* Crowborough, UK: Highland, 1990.

Warrington, Keith. *Jesus the Healer: Paradigm or Unique Phenomenon?* Carlisle, UK: Paternoster, 2000.

———, ed. *Pentecostal Perspectives.* Carlisle, UK: Paternoster, 1998.

———. *Pentecostal Theology: A Theology of Encounter.* London: T. & T. Clark, 2008.

Watson, David. *Discipleship.* London: Hodder & Stoughton, 1981..

———. *Fear No Evil.* London: Hodder & Stoughton, 1984.

———. *God's Freedom Fighters.* Croydon: New Mildmay, 1972.

———. *Hidden Warfare.* Carlisle, UK: STL, 1980.

———. *I Believe in Evangelism.* London: Hodder & Stoughton, 1976.

———. *I Believe in the Church.* London: Hodder & Stoughton, 1978.

———. *You Are My God.* London: Hodder & Stoughton, 1983.

Wenham, Gordon. *Genesis 1–15.* Word Biblical Commentary 1. Waco, TX: Word, 1987.

Wiebe, Philip H. "Finite Spirits as Theoretical Entities." *Religious Studies* 40 (2004) 341–50.

———. "Deliverance and Exorcism in Philosophical Perspective." In *Exorcism and Deliverance: Multidisciplinary Studies*, edited by William K. Kay and Robin A. Parry, 156–80. Milton Keynes, UK: Paternoster, 2009.

Williams, C. G. *Tongues of the Spirit: A Study of Pentecostal Glossolalia and Related Phenomena.* Cardiff: University of Wales Press, 1981.

Williams, Peter S. *The Case for Angels.* Carlisle, UK: Paternoster, 2002.

Wimber, John, and Kevin Springer. *Power Evangelism.* London: Hodder & Stoughton, 1985.

———. *Power Healing.* London: Hodder & Stoughton, 1987.

Wink, Walter. *Engaging the Powers: Discernment and Resistance in a World of Domination.* Minneapolis: Fortress, 1992.

———. *Naming the Powers: The Language of Power in the New Testament.* Minneapolis: Fortress, 1984.

———. *The Powers That Be: Theology for a New Millenium.* New York: Doubleday, 1998.

———. *Unmasking the Powers: The Invisible Forces That Determine Human Existence.* Minneapolis: Fortress, 1986.
Woolmer, John. *Angels.* Mill Hill, London: Monarch, 2003.
———. *Healing and Deliverance.* Mill Hill, London: Monarch, 1999.
———. *Thinking Clearly about Prayer.* Mill Hill, London: Monarch, 1997.
Wright, Archie. *The Origin of Evil Spirits: The Reception of Genesis 6.1-4 in Early Jewish Literature.* Tübingen: Mohr Siebeck, 2005.
Wright, N. T. *Evil and the Justice of God.* London: SPCK, 2006.
———. *Jesus and the Victory of God.* London: SPCK, 1996.
———. *The New Testament and the People of God.* London: SPCK, 1992.
———. *Paul: Fresh Perspectives.* London: SPCK, 2005.
Wright, Nigel G. "Charismatic Interpretations of the Demonic." In *The Unseen World*, edited by Anthony N. S. Lane, 149-63. Carlisle, UK: Paternoster, 1996.
———. "Deliverance and Exorcism in Theological Perspective 1: Is There Any Substance to Evil?" In *Exorcism and Deliverance: Multidisciplinary Studies*, edited by William K. Kay and Robin A. Parry, 203-21. Milton Keynes, UK: Paternoster, 2009.
———. *A Theology of the Dark Side: Putting the Power of Evil in Its Place.* Carlisle, UK: Paternoster, 2003.
Yamauchi, Edwin. "Magic or Miracle? Diseases, Demons and Exorcisms." In *Gospel Perspectives: The Miracles of Jesus*, edited by David Wenham and Craig Blomberg, 89-184. Sheffield, UK: Journal for the Study of the Old Testament Press, 1986.
Yin, Robert K. *Case Study Research: Design and Methods.* London: Sage, 1989.
Yoder, John Howard. *The Politics of Jesus.* Grand Rapids: Eerdmans, 1972.
Yong, Amos. *Beyond the Impasse: Toward a Pneumatological Theology of Religions.* Grand Rapids: Baker Academic, 2003.
———. "The Demonic in Pentecostal-Charismatic Christianity and in the Religious Consciousness of Asia." In *Asian and Pentecostal: The Charismatic Face of Christianity in Asia*, edited by Allan Anderson and Edmond Tang, 93-127. London: Regnum International, 2005.
———. *Discerning the Spirits: A Pentecostal-Charismatic Contribution to Christian Theology of Religions.* Sheffield, UK: Sheffield Academic Press, 2000.
———. *In the Days of Caesar: Pentecostalism and Political Theology.* Grand Rapids: Eerdmans, 2010.
———. "Performing Global Pentecostal Theology: A Response to Wolfgang Vondey." *Pneuma* 28, no. 2 (2006) 313-21.
———. "Response to Chapter 6." Personal email 16.12.10.
———. "*Ruach,* the Primordial Chaos, and the Breath of Life: Emergence Theory and the Creation Narratives in Pneumatological Perspective." In *The Work of the Spirit: Pneumatology and Pentecostalism*, edited by Michael Welker, 183-204. Grand Rapids: Eerdmans, 2006.
———. *Spirit-Word-Community: Theological Hermeneutics in Trinitarian Perspective.* Burlington VT: Ashgate, 2002.
———. *The Spirit of Creation: Modern Science & Divine Action in the Pentecostal-Charismatic Imagination.* Grand Rapids: Eerdmans, 2011.
———. *The Spirit Poured out on All Flesh: Pentecostalism and the Possibility of Global Theology.* Grand Rapids: Baker Academic, 2005.

———. "Spiritual Discernment: A Biblical-Theological Reconsideration." In *The Spirit and Spirituality*, edited by Bonsuk Ma and Robert P. Menzies. 83–107. Journal of Pentecostal Theology Supplement Series. London: T. & T. Clark, 2004.

———. *Theology and Down Syndrome: Reimagining Disability in Late Modernity*. Waco, TX: Baylor University Press, 2007.

www.ingramcontent.com/pod-product-compliance
Lightning Source LLC
Chambersburg PA
CBHW071240230426

43668CB00011B/1525